The Economy as a System of Power

A trilogy of books based on articles from the *Journal of Economic Issues*, edited by Marc R. Tool and Warren J. Samuels and published by Transaction Publishers.

The Methodology of Economic Thought

The Economy as a System of Power

State, Society, and Corporate Power

The Economy as a System of Power

Edited by
Marc R. Tool
and
Warren J. Samuels

Second edition completely revised

LONDON AND NEW YORK

Originally published in 1980 by Transaction Publishers

Published 1989 by Transaction Publishers

Published 2017 by Routledge
2 Park Square, Milton Park, Abingdon, Oxon OX14 4RN
711 Third Avenue, New York, NY 10017, USA

Routledge is an imprint of the Taylor & Francis Group, an informa business

Library of Congress Catalog Number: 88-20078

Library of Congress Cataloging in Publication Data

Samuels, Warren J., 1933-
The economy as a system of power / edited by Warren J. Samuels and Marc R. Tool. — 2nd rev. ed.
p. cm. — (Institutional economics ; v. 1)
Bibliography: p.
ISBN 0-88738-758-6
1. Institutional economics. 2. Power (Social sciences) 3. Corporations. 4. Industry—Social aspects. 5. International economic relations. I. Tool, Marc R. II. Title. III. Series.
HB99.5.S26 1988 88-20078
330.1—dc19 CIP

ISBN 13: 978-0-88738-758-6 (pbk)

Contents

Introduction vii

Part I: The Economy as a System of Power: Introduction 3

1. Economics: Allocation or Valuation? 9
   Philip A. Klein [December 1974, 8:4; 785–811]
   (Ed. I, Vol. I, 7–33)
2. Power and Illusion in the Marketplace: Institutions and Technology 37
   Thomas R. De Gregori [Dec. 1974, 8:4; 759–770]
   (Ed. I, Vol. I, 53–65)
3. The Impact of Economics on Technology 49
   Seymour Melman [March 1975, 9:1; 59–72]
   (Ed. I, Vol. I, 83–96)
4. Confronting Power in Economics: A Pragmatic Evaluation 63
   Philip A. Klein [December 1980, 14:4; 871–896]
5. Power and Economic Performance 89
   Wallace C. Peterson [December 1980, 14:4; 827–869]
6. Power: An Institutional Framework of Analysis 133
   William M. Dugger [December 1980, 14:4; 897–907]

Part II: The Corporate System: Introduction 147

7. The Problems and Prospects of Collective Capitalism 157
   Gardiner C. Means [March 1969, 3:1; 18–31]
   (Ed. I, Vol. I, 124–138)
8. The Rise of the Corporate State in America 171
   Daniel R. Fusfeld [March 1972, 6:1: 1–22]
   (Ed. I, Vol. I, 139–160)
9. Organizational Structure, Technological Advance, and the New Tasks of Government 193
   Robert A. Solo [December 1972, 6:4; 131–148]
   (Ed. I, Vol. I, 183–195)
10. An Institutional Analysis of Corporate Power 211
    William M. Dugger [March 1988, 22:1, 79–111]

11. Social Value Theory, Corporate Power, and Political Elites: Appraisals of Lindblom's *Politics and Markets* 245
Rick Tilman [March 1983, 17:1; 115–131]

12. Transfer of Control in Large Corporations: 1905–19
David Bunting and Mark S. Mizruchi 263
[December 1982, 16:4; 985–1003]

13. Centralized Private Sector Planning: An Institutionalist's Perspective on the Contemporary U. S. Economy
John R. Munkirs [December 1983, 17:4; 931–967] 283

14. Political and Policy Implications of Centralized Private Sector Planning 321
John R. Munkirs and Michael Ayres
[December 1983, 17:4; 969–984]

15. Oligopolistic Cooperation: Conceptual and Empirical Evidence of Market Structure Evolution 337
John R. Munkirs and James I. Sturgeon
[December 1985, 19:4; 899–921]

16. Idealism and Realism: An Institutionalist View of Corporate Power in the Regulated Utilities 361
David S. Schwartz [June 1985, 19:2; 311–331]

17. Corporate Power and Economic Sabotage 383
Walter Adams and James W. Brock
[December 1986, 20:4, 919–940]

18. Corporate Size and the Bailout Factor 405
Walter Adams and James W. Brock [March 1987, 21:1; 61–85]

Introduction

This volume of selected papers from the *Journal of Economic Issues* on the economy as a system of power is a second and heavily revised edition, with the same title, of an earlier publication by Transaction Publishers.[1] The recognition that economists must address the fact and use of economic power was omnipresent in the first edition, and is reaffirmed vigorously in this volume as well. This anthology adds new theoretical insights, philosophic depth, analytical refinement, and extensive recent evidential materials to the institutionalist literature concerning analyses of power-reflective judgments and their consequences.

From the beginning, institutional economists have seen power as inherent and essential to any social order. Where power is perceived as the capacity and opportunity to exercise discretion over the rules that organize social life, it is obvious that judgments reflecting use of power organize the social process and determine how the institutional structure of that social order is determined, modified, and replaced. Power-reflective judgments determine the level, character, and distribution of real and money income; they specify how the determination and administration of public policy will be accomplished in any culture. Prior power-reflective judgments have defined the extant institutional fabric of the economy, the polity, and the social order generally. Institutions are *prescribed* or *proscribed* patterns of correlated behavior and attitudes. The prescribing and proscribing are done by discretionary agents—people with power. In sum, power means discretion over the behavior of others. Prescribing and proscribing judgments delimit behavior in ways that reflect the agents' priorities and purposes; they may or may not reflect recourse to democratic criteria of choice.

In all cultures, power was used, and is used, to define what is "proper" conduct. While much behavior is conformist, not necessarily all of it is. People routinely obey laws, observe customary behavior forms, follow traffic codes, respect property rights, accept the rules of the game, and live ordered lives. But where they have continuing and effectual opportunity to share in the discretionary determination of the laws, behavioral forms, codes, rights, and rules under which they live, they hold some measure of economic and political power; they can become nonconformist. Institutions of democratic government are established to facilitate the exercise of that nonconformist discretion. Thus, when discretion over policy is provided to all adult members of the community—that is, when the rules that prescribe and proscribe correlated behavior are effectually and continuously self-imposed—the power to exercise choice is democratically constituted and controlled. When such rules are determined by individuals or minority fragments of a community (dictators, oligarchies, plutocrats, elites), power is held and is used undemocratically.

Therefore, the object of inquiry in this anthology is the locus and use of the power to determine economic institutions and their operations and outcomes. The economy is a system of power. The argument of these papers illustrates that it is possible through inquiry to determine who holds economic power; to explain how that power is used; to observe and assess the consequences of its use; and to determine the extent to which such power is, or can be, held accountable. To what extent do those who receive the incidence of the exercise of economic power have the right and capacity to hold the power-wielders responsible? Can they act in a manner to require that the rules be revised? Ralph Nader has remarked that if exercised power is, in fact, to be held accountable, it must be insecure. The opportunity to change decision makers and/or decisions must be continuously available if democratic controls on power are to be realized. Therefore, the issue is not the presence or absence of power as such; the presence and exercise of power is essential in all political economies. At issue are questions of, Who has power materially to affect the economy? On what does that power rest? In whose interests is it exercised? Are the consequences of its use normatively acceptable? Can achieved power be exercised responsibly? Can power be relocated and/or reconstituted, as necessary, to serve the public interest or to realize "the collective ought," as noted by Philip Klein? It is to questions of this kind that contributors to this volume address their inquiries.

In contrast, for traditional, neoclassical economists, the study of power is an inquiry into pathology; the presence of economic power, per se, constitutes an economic disease. Its observed presence is to be decried; its threat is to be removed. Since orthodox economists continue to hold to the normative use of the competitive model, in which unfettered markets seek equilibrium in a power-free context, the simple presence of economic power (in the hands of corporations, or labor, or government) provides for contra- or extra-market determination and, on that account alone, is systemically unnatural, abnormal, even parasitic. In brief, orthodoxy is devoid of a credible theory of economic power. Even neoclassical inquiries into antitrust, monopoly, and oligopoly are pursued in a context in which the ought is a power-free market. Their theory dictates that, wherever possible, policy should transform existing pathologically defined power structure into the closest possible approximation of a competitive power-free model. (In a competitive market, no participant can affect price by his/her own efforts.) That model's institutional givens include, of course, free private enterprise, unfettered markets, price competition, profit maximization, and a passive government.

After nearly a century, neoclassicists have not yet come to terms with the corporate revolution. Neither the followers of Edward Chamberlin's monopolistic competition and Joan Robinson's imperfect competition early in this century nor the present neoclassical institutionalists in their analysis of transaction cost implications within corporate firms are willing or able adequately to confront the fact and use of corporate power in a social context. The latter research program generates de facto apologia for the existing corporate power system. The contributions of this anthology, in comparison with orthodoxy, substantially extend the theoretical analysis of, and provide evidential grounding for, a large and critically significant inquiry into economic power well beyond what most past and present neoclassical analysts permit or encourage.

Moreover, as the papers herein demonstrate, inquiry concerning the economy as a system of power must necessarily be multidisciplinary. Economic aspects are reflected in the quest to understand who determines the character of production; how property rights confer discretion and entitlement; how price administration is accomplished; who sets the goals for economic institutions; and who decides, and on what grounds, what the distribution of real income shares shall be. Political aspects are reflected in the quest to understand the political deliberative processes through which economic institutions are designed and introduced; how private economic power can politically be held accountable; how political forces bear on economic processes (political business cycles?); how it is possible to keep economic regulatory efforts from being co-opted and corrupted, in consequence of which the regulators become the regulated; and how the normative concerns of "the collective ought" can be politically identified and implemented.

Sociological aspects are reflected in the quest to understand, for example, the emergence and retention of power relations within organizations;

how bureaucracies are created, sustained, and replaced; how the aculturation of various conceptions of power occurs and is modified; what models of social control of the economy are endemic in cultures and what constraints on evolving new models exist; and the extent to which the quest for corporate hegemony in the culture has penetrated and subverted educational, familial, and political institutions to serve corporate goals. Psychological aspects are reflected in the quest to understand the psychology of ego involvement and the relationship of power acquisition thereto; how the quest for self-identity comes to be identified with control of the behavior of others; how the position of power becomes itself a primary conditioner of subsequent behavior dedicated to the vigorous retention of such power; how "being well thought of" is given a power-acquisition and retention content in an economy; and the extent to which "profit motivation" is a significant acquired goal to economic power acquisition. Finally, philosophical aspects are also reflected in the quest to understand such topics as the emergence of power acquisition as a normative criterion of personal and social behavior; how democratically constrained power can facilitate the achievement of "the collective ought"; the hazards and limitations of using power acquisition and retention as a criterion of social value; the limitations and/or irrelevance of neoclassical criteria of Paretian optima or pecuniary benefit–cost analysis in assessing adequacy of use of power; the significance of recourse to instrumental value theory in appraising the use and abuse of economic power. Accordingly, the inquiry agenda for an institutionalist analysis of economic power is both extensive and complex. Institutionalists are quite willing, in these papers and elsewhere, to cross disciplinary boundaries in quest of more inclusive and more credible understanding of power and conduct.

There is no contention here that all questions posed and concerns expressed in the foregoing are responded to in the papers included in this anthology; however, a surprisingly large number are addressed. The volume is comprised of two main sections: Part I, entitled "The Economy as a System of Power," consists of six articles that address central and inclusive concerns with economic power. These papers include critiques of orthodox positions and, more importantly, set the institutionalist concern with economic power in an appropriate, if general, analytical context. Attention is given to matters of allocation versus valuation; to power and illusion in the marketplace, to power implications of technology in the economy; to the institutionalist view of economic power; to power and economic performance; and to an institutionalist analytic framework for analysis of power.

Part II, entitled "The Corporate System," includes twelve papers which address the character and particulars of the corporate system as it has evolved, especially in the United States. Individual articles describe the corporate revolution and its overall implications; consider the loci of control of such institutions; explain the recent emergence of "centralized private sector planning" and its political and policy implications; provide evidence of oligopolistic cooperation; review efforts to constrain economic power in the regulated industries; and consider and assess the use of economic power to generate "economic sabotage" in recent decades.

In this volume the primary concern of the coeditors is to present papers that will set inquiry in motion and sustain it. No final synthetic statement of position or conclusions to "chisel in stone" are provided. However, we do think that this anthology will provide, for those unfamiliar with this literature, a quantum leap in understanding about where the economic power centers are and how the actual economy in the United States operates, given the presence of achieved power. In addition, relevant and defensible ways of assessing the use of economic power in this economy and others are offered. Introductions to the individual papers will be found at the beginning of each of the two sections.

The *Journal of Economic Issues* will continue to publish material on the persistent and important questions and issues of economic power raised in these papers. The reader is cordially invited to continue the dialogue begun with these papers through recourse to future issues of the *JEI*.

Marc R. Tool
Warren J. Samuels

Note

1. Warren J. Samuels, ed., *The Economy as a System of Power* (New Brunswick, NJ: Transaction, 1979.

PART I

THE ECONOMY AS A SYSTEM OF POWER

Introduction to Part I: The Economy as a System of Power

The opening paper, by Philip A. Klein, argues that political economy is not yet, but must more fully become, an analysis of valuation instead of an analysis of allocation. Effectual consideration of the nature and use of economic power must rest on a clear recognition of the importance of this shift. Through an extensive critique of neoclassical microtheory, Klein demonstrates that the traditional contention that unfettered market operations reflect individual choices and that these can be aggregated to generate a social choice giving direction to the economy, simply cannot be sustained. Allocation through the price system is but a "small corner" of economic analysis. Traditional neoclassical analysis has tried to ignore the fact that nonmarket choices are continuously being made and that they are important. Indeed, choices that would appear initially to be simple market choices often reflect recourse to market influence or power. For example, corporate decision makers have considerable value-reflective control over the formation and character of consumer demand. In the public sector, value-based judgments determine economic and social priorities, and set military budgets. In all these areas where the nature of consumer demand, externalities, and social priorities relating to health, welfare, and progress intrude on the orthodox research program and psyche, choices reflecting valuation are, and must be, made. Power is held by corporations; power is held by other private bodies; power is held by the government. Concerning public sector allocation, Klein observes that "although the resources so allocated have prices attached to them, they are not fundamentally allocated by prices, but by fiat. The fiat comes from the political economy in the form of decisions to tax and to spend which are made by various officials."[1] In such cases, those with discretion and power make choices reflecting value positions and generate consequences for the economy. In sum, "only when economic theory concentrates on the meaning of the political economy—the problem of value—will we be able to assess the adequacy of our curent allocation . . . to accomplish the evolving ends which the participants in the economy currently set for it. . . . The frontier of the political economy, therefore, is to be found in developing criteria by which economies can be judged in terms of their ability successfully to express the emergent values of society."

Philip A. Klein builds on and extends his analysis of the treatment of economic power in political economy in the article that follows. Whereas Anthony Downs originally, and public choice theorists more recently, have "tried to use [neoclassical] economic logic and economic methodology to dissect the operation of the political system," Klein inverts the inquiry relationship and applies elements of political science to the study of economic power. "Power," for Klein, "can most simply be defined as disproportionate control over the decision-making process." "The distribution of both concentrated power and powerlessness . . . conditions the way in which the economy functions." Accordingly, economists would gain substantial realism and relevance if they confronted the fact of economic power directly, as political scientists do. The latter see the function of governments as that of making "binding (authoritative) allocation of values." "The political system both influences and is influenced or shaped by the values (priorities) of its participants and has the authority to force all participants in their roles in the system to abide by the commonly held emergent values." A demonstration device used effectively by Klein is the presentation of detailed characterizations of three paradigms—mainstream, institutionalist, and political science perspectives. He finds, "many striking parallels between the assumptions, perspective, attitudes, and presumed results emerging from the latter two." They see "the deployment of power in the economy and the polity as it is—not as one might wish it to be." And that deployment indicates that "virtually all economic decisions are affected by concentrations of wealth and power, either indirectly, directly, or both." But institutionalists, in Klein's view, "do not argue for a system of imposing values from normative Big Brothers on the rest of the community. They argue for developing a system in which information flows are open, discussion is free and candid, alternatives are presented and known, and decision-making channels can reflect the outcome of all these deliberations. That would produce the economic equivalent of representative democracy."

Arguments introduced by Klein are reinforced and extended in the paper by Thomas R. De Gregori. "It is the contention of this article," he writes, "that the normative interpretaion of market behavior is a major element in our current ideological confusion that frustrates effective government economic and social policy." The inability in recent years to resolve successfully major economic problems may be laid, in large measure, at the door of conventional economists who have an "obsession with the market" and insist that markets have the ability to generate "unhindered price signals to channel resources to problem areas"—energy, poverty, and development—and, therefore, that deference to market judgments is the best policy posture whatever the problem. Such economists impute "causal or creative attributes to markets," presume that price measures value and that market judgments are therefore moral, and therewith justify "grossly unequal distribution of income." But "those who would have us rely almost exclusively on market decisions neglect the role of power in shaping market behavior." Economic power derives not only from differential income receipt but from "position, prestige, and prejudice" as well. Therefore, the alleged "neutrality" of price theory is a sham. Private power is used to define human "needs," and to shape the public agenda. "We tend not to notice . . . public decisions if they tend to further the economic interests of the powerful." De Gregori draws on the work of Clarence Ayres, to establish an alternate institutionalist perception of how to get beyond the infinite wants–scarce means dictum of orthodoxy and the derivitive deference to market judgments that follows therefrom. It is Ayres's "theory of technological change as an explanation of the process of growth" that De Gregori finds most promising. With it, De Gregori can redefine the technological and cultural sources of economic progress, the nature of human needs, the promise of abundance, and the threat of "conspicuous waste." He concludes that "the power of vested interests and its corollary, the neglect of power by economists, is slowing . . . progress on economic problems that we face." The needed rethinking of "basic issues" should begin with the work of Ayres.

In the next paper, Seymour Melman objects both to the belief that technology "has an autonomous momentum and direction," and, by implication, to the assumption that technology can be taken as given, as in conventional economics. He sees the introduction of technology as an exercise of economic power by discernable people. He shows "how the specific design and selection from among technological alternatives is controlled decisively by the industrial managers, private and governmental, on whose behalf technologies are researched, developed, and produced." Defining *technology* as "the application of science and invention in the service of some social requirement," Melman contends that it is "economic decision makers who determined which technology . . . was most serviceable to their business advantage." He illustrates his analysis of technological determination by analyzing the ways in which the automobile industry has organized production. For example, he denies "that dehumanized and alienating conditions of work are intrinsic to the use of mass-production machinery" in automobile production. These conditions are not inevitable; they reflect "choices of economic decision makers and hence [are] subject to alteration given changed criteria and ways of decision making." Industrial managers "are confronted with the problem of choosing from among many alternative tools, devices, and machines available for accomplishing the given task." The usual decision criterion employed is cost-minimizing. As the wage level tends to grow faster than the price of machinery, the use of this criterion leds to displacement of workers with machines. Thus, "capitalist economic criteria" dominate such decision making. Even the division of labor reflects choices concerning the organization and integration of workers in the production process. Negative attitudes of alienation among workers derive, argues Melman, from the "absence of workers' decision power over their work." In conclusion, man and society have not "become the creatures of the machine." If one wants to alter technologies, "the place to look is . . . to the social structure . . . especially the economic rules of who decides on technology."

With the paper by Wallace C. Peterson, the focus shifts from concern with industrial managers' power of decision over technology to questions of corporate power and its bearing on the quest for stability and adequate performance in the economy. It is Peterson's opening contention that "power exists, that it is widespread, and that it is a phenomenon as "natural" to our economic order as is competition." His inquiry object is to explain "how power enters into the economic process and how it affects that process." His special contribution is to show how "the critical interplay among economic growth, income distribution, and power as it operates in the market side of the economy . . . has been the major source of the economy's unsatisfactory performance." Through an extensive analysis of the extent and character of economic growth in the U. S. since World War II, in part based on Keynesian theory, Peterson traces the emergence of a growth myopia in which mass production, in a high-intensity market society, is thought sufficient to resolve all other economic concerns. Emulation of a high-consumption lifestyle is urged; the "product becomes the determinant of the need, not . . . the other way around"; "wants accelerate more rapidly than output" generating a contrived and continuing scarcity. Corollary is an evidential demonstration that patterns of income distribution, since World War II, have remained heavily skewed toward inequality. In consequence, an "aspiration gap" appears where people perceive their relative income to be insufficiently high to share fairly in this expanded growth, especially of invidious display goods. This, in turn, generates pressure for people to gain increasing control over their income levels in order to enlarge their share. The quest for power is largely a quest "whereby people and business firms gain control over their own incomes." Peterson then turns to an extensive analysis of how economic power is attained. Drawing on the work of Adolph Berle, Gardiner Means, and John Kenneth Galbraith, he shows how corporate enterprise has, through administered pricing, target return pricing and other techniques gained substantial control over its own income flow. Consideration of the implications of this power reality, in the pursuit of noninflationary growth, concludes this paper.

The final paper in this section, by William M. Dugger, serves well both as a capstone for the preceeding papers and as an introduction to the concluding section of this volume. He offers "a holistic (institutional) framework for analyzing power." "Power," he contends, "shall refer to the ability to tell other people what to do with some degree of certainty that they will do it. When power wielders must coerce others, power is tenuous and obvious. When coercion is unnecessary, power is secure and unnoticed. In twentieth-century United States, coercion is minimal." People have the illusion of "individual choices and autonomy" of judgment. The reality is that economic institutions dominate the culture, patterning roles, imposing positive and negative sanctions, and conditioning people to accept such dominion. Of economic institutions operating, the modern corporation has nearly unrivaled hegemony. "The corporation ... uses other institutions as means for its own ends." It penetrates educational, military, family, political, and religious institutions in quest of its own values and goals. The hegemony of the modern corporation rests, not on conspiracy, but on four "social mechanisms" through which it gains and retains domination: "subreption, contamination, emulation, and mystification." "Subreption ties all institutions together so that noncorporate institutions are used as means to corporate ends. Contamination puts corporate role motives into noncorporate roles. Emulation allows corporate leaders to gain acceptance, even respect, in noncorporate leadership roles. And mystification covers the corporate hegemony with a protective ... cloak of the most-valued American symbols." Thus the source of power for the corporation is "institutional position," not "individual strength, will, or cunning." "Powerful individuals" do not "acquire their ends independently of the institutional roles they performed on their way to the top." Indeed, "both the ends and the means of their power are institutionally determined." In brief, the "processes and the structure of power they support (corporate institutional hegemony) are laid bare through an institutional not an individual framework of analysis." If that achieved power is to be democratized, it must be accomplished through change in "the institutions and processes that create and support it."

Note

1. All quotations in these introductory comments throughout the volume are from the respective author's paper being discussed.

1

Economics: Allocation or Valuation?

Philip A. Klein

"Whether or not it continues to be a science of price, economics must be a science of value."

Clarence E. Ayres
Theory of Economic Progress

Among the social sciences, economics long has suffered from a superiority complex. The economist's view of his field has been of a discipline that was rigorous and precise, with an advanced and pragmatic methodology leading to a highly developed theoretical structure. All this left far behind the imprecise and murky theoretical strivings of political scientists, sociologists, anthropologists, and historians.

The promised land which economic analysis made possible was known as equilibrium.[1] What sociologist or political scientist or anthropologist could offer any piece of analytical apparatus which for sheer beauty, precision, and logic could equal it? True, psychologists kept insisting that the behavioral assumptions of conventional economic theory—maximizing behavior, hedonism, rationality—all the characteristics of "Economic Man" which economics always has relied on for convenience, were fatally oversimplified. But economists mostly have ignored the complaints of psychologists (who after all had problems of their own). Moreover, the psychologists were only too willing to follow the economist down the quantitative primrose path. Both disciplines once worried about their ancient roots in philosophy and could never quite rid themselves of the nagging suspicion that questions of subjective valuation could not be eliminated entirely so as to render each a 100 percent pure science. Both embraced mathematics as the true methodological Messiah come at last.[2] Together economists and psychologists measured all visibly quantifiable variables, developed models for all problems, and achieved intellectual orgasm through the contemplation of the possibilities of the electronic computer. By enshrining quantification, they believed they had set a standard of scientific excellence sufficiently ahead of their laggardly sister social sciences to enable them to continue virtually indefinitely to play the role of superego to the lowly id of sociology or history.

Without in any way demeaning the very real accomplishments of quantitative procedures in advancing knowledge in critical areas, I should like to suggest that at least in the case of economics, schizophrenia always has been latent in the discipline and has been kept that way only by sweeping under the rug important problems which increasingly have crept out to disturb the neat world of economist and econometrician alike. We can cope with any number of variables in ever more elaborate models, but we cannot cope with underlying questions of direction and meaning, of goals and objectives for the system. The excessive preoccupation with tools with which to cope with problems at best comprising a small corner of economics, and the obsessive need to believe these tools coped with the heart of economics, long has characterized the discipline. Facing up to this obsession involves the fundamental question of whether economics is a science of allocation or a science of valuation. For most of its existence economics has managed to equate the two, and there is a long and bloody literary road devoted to establishing that economics as a "science of price" thereby was coping with all the value problems with which it need legitimately concern itself.

Economics as a Science of Allocation

The central core of economic theory—at least microeconomic theory—was spelled out by Adam Smith and elaborated upon by the well-known nineteenth-century mainstream economists. The culmination was its restatement by Alfred Marshall, who not insignificantly changed the name of the descipline from political economy to economics. The profound changes of the past eighty years have left remarkably untouched much of the field which Marshall defined as "a study of mankind in the ordinary business of life; it examines that part of individual and social action which is most closely connected with the attainment and with the use of the material requisites of wellbeing."[3] Marshall added that economics "concerns itself chiefly with those motives which affect most powerfully and most steadily man's conduct in the business part of his life."[4] The latter is a far narrower perspective and considerably closer to what in fact Marshall's *Principles* dealt with. It was a critical reinforcement to the continued confusion between economics as allocation and economics as valuation.

Marshall's emphasis on materialism subsequently was questioned, for example, by Lionel Robbins, who wondered how a science concerned exclusively with the material could determine the wage rates for opera stars or orchestra conductors whose productivity is not quite so easily viewed as the more concretely material output of ditchdiggers, carpenters, and others among the myriad toilers in the economic vineyards. Robbins concluded that Marshall's materialism was a "pseudo-materialism"[5] and that what was really at the heart of economics was not materialism but allocation. Robbins then defined the field in the way which is customarily utilized to this day: "Economics is the science which studies human behaviour as a relationship between ends and scarce means which have alternative uses."[6] Such a formulation extricated economists from the materialism quagmire; by adding to this the deceptively simple assumption that the allocation process as carried out through the use of prices in the market disposed of all the ends and scarce means that the proper study of economics need embrace, economists thought they were home free.[7] The pricing process was assumed to be the vehicle by which the economic system expressed *all* the allocating priorities of concern to the economist. Thus price became, if it had not always been, the *only* measure of value with which economics had to concern itself.

Robbins himself reached this conclusion unequivocably by saying that the significance of economic science lay in the fact that "when we are faced with a choice between ultimates, it enables us to choose with a full awareness of the implications of what we are choosing." But he was very careful to add that "it is incapable of deciding between the desirability of different ends. It is fundamentally distinct from Ethics."[8] But even if the distinction between economics and ethics were accepted, the discipline must provide (if it is to permit us to choose with the "full awareness of the implications of our choice") mechanisms by which such "full awareness" choice can be made. The market alone cannot fill that bill in a modern industrial economy. Allocation and valuation are indeed different, and a discipline concerned only with the former can never permit "fully aware" choices to be made.

Those who view economics as a science of allocation customarily have argued that all participants in the economic process get their "values" from wherever they get them, that in fact societal values are of no concern to the economist. Thus all the economist need do is pontificate: "If an individual chooses to allocate his income in Direction A he must forego Direction B." "To achieve certain objectives, here is the most efficient way for society to achieve them, and here is what must be foregone in the process." Consequently, generations of economics students were taught that economics is not concerned with questions of "ought" but only with questions of "is." Economics as a science was not normative but positive.[9] Thus economics was viewed as the administrator of social options, in charge of calculating costs and predicting results, but without any normative participation in the process. The economist *qua* economist occupied a role in which normative judgments definitionally had no place. Only the economist *qua* citizen was permitted to be filled with the minimal requisite quantities of passion, prejudice, and "subjective valuation" that reside in the breast of other mere mortals.

This view of economics had some convenient side effects. For one, it enabled economic theory to blind itself to the implicit subjective valuations (previously alluded to) of what it did in the guise of pursuit of the scientific method, rigor, and precision. It therefore enabled economics to emulate the physical sciences and thus led to the coronation of equilibrium as normatively "good" in economics because in physics, from whence it came, it was "natural." If Keynes's notion of underemployment equilibrium represented a severe jolt to this notion, in microeconomics it survived because equilibrium prices led to market clearing, which was definitionally good. Finally, equilibrium could be viewed as an end in itself because the continued assumption that Adam Smith's Invisible Hand (developed for atomistic competition) could be appropriately if only approximately attached to emergent prices in actual markets rationalized away any lurking doubts about how economics disposed of the value problem. Individual selfishness was transmogrified into a process optimizing social welfare, and emergent prices did indeed express the values of society in the only way that need concern the economist.

Economics as a Science of Valuation

The simple world of the classical economist, familiar to all economists, was orderly and attractive, but unrelated to much of the economic reality even of its own time. The history of economics has shown a remarkable tendency to cling to that world, however, and to make emendations only when pushed by a variety of inexorable forces. Even in its own time, classical price theory developed with the Industrial Revolution in England, and so Smith projected his Invisible Hand on a world replete with, among other things, subhuman factory conditions, child labor, widespread poverty, great inequality in the distribution of both wealth and income, vast slums and urban ghettos, and a rigid and uncompromising class system which severely restricted labor mobility and economic opportunity. In short, it was a world with a whole host of problems with which society still copes and from all of which Smith's economics was structured to dissociate itself.

It is interesting to note that this view of economics, based on emulating the physical sciences, has in our own day seen the physical sciences come to question the rigid distinction between the normative and the positive. The dynamism of technology was such that by the 1940s the physicists had begun to realize that merely suggesting what constitutes the most efficient way to destroy the world as we know it might not thoroughly discharge the ultimate responsibility of the physicist *qua* physicist.[10] So much for the model economics chose to emulate.

To the extent that economics subsequently faced up to its value problem (as opposed to its allocation problem) at all, it did so through the introduction of the familiar notion of the Pareto optimum, which fit extremely well the notion of the Invisible Hand. Pareto optimality (however stated) never has been more than a very carefully hedged statement: With given tastes, technology, and resources, no reallocation of resources could better satisfy any member of the community without someone else being less well satisfied. Such a view, even leaving aside the old controversies about measuring satisfaction, nonetheless fits well into the conventional perspective because it does not ask how the distribution of satisfactions came to be what it is, what the rules of the game are in which satisfaction-seeking is played, and so forth. As was the case with the Invisible Hand, the Pareto optimum was an attempt to define the value problem in economics in sufficiently narrow terms to make it coterminous with resource allocation in the market via prices.

To the extent that conventional theory altered its focus to cope with imperfect as opposed to pure competition, the following conclusions seem germane to our central concern with how economics copes with its value problem. Institutionalism in the past attacked the use of "competition" in conventional theory, but failed to note that *whatever* equilibrium might mean in competitive markets, it means something different in imperfect markets. Institutionalists were thus vulnerable to the charge of beating an ill if not dead horse. However, the charge that conventional economics continues to overemphasize the competitive model because it is elegant, precise, and deterministic while imperfect models have none of these characteristics is probably a fair one. Economists cling to the competitive model, partly at least as a child to a security blanket, and rationalize its continued emphasis in academic curricula by a variety of means. These contain enough truth to avoid broadside attacks on the theory as irrelevant, but enough error to prevent economists from easily addressing the modern world in a realistic, direct, and straightforward fashion.[11]

Economists always have been remarkably unconcerned about the allocational implication of how they spend their time and energy in price theory. Here, put in language the economist is uniquely qualified to understand, the institutionalist may have had a point: Price theory devotes a disproportionate amount of the economist's resources to competitive theory and too little to theories more generally applicable in the real world. To many economists no doubt price theory has the appeal of chess, and (importantly) it does permit the mechanics of the price system to be detailed. But even in the sector of the economy in which market prices still operate it leaves many questions untouched. Despite the failure of men like Clarence Ayres to recognize the development of noncompetitive models, the institutionalists still had a point in criticizing price theory. But this was in any case not the main import of what they were arguing.

The Frontiers of Economics: Valuation in the Market

If, as I believe, economics is and always has been primarily a science of valuation rather than merely allocation, it follows that price is not the only relevant measure of value, even in the areas where the price system still serves as the sole or primary allocative mechanism. There are many questions to which conventional economics should address itself in the areas where prices in fact do the allocating, but which many economists still prefer to ignore. For example, it is by now fairly clear that assuming that consumer wants are "given" assumes away many critical problems bearing on "the meaning of the price system." The normative implications of emergent prices in a system in which large corporate businesses produce whatever they choose to produce and then persuade consumers (through advertising, appeals to snobbery or class, or whatever) that this is also what they want are most assuredly *not* what they would be in a system in which prices reflected the efforts of business firms to adapt to the "sovereign" wishes of consumers. This would, of course, be true no matter where consumer wants came from provided only that they were not created by profit-seeking business firms themselves. This charge always has been levelled at price theory by institutionalists, beginning with Thorstein Veblen and including today J. K. Galbraith. He refers to demand manipulation as "the revised sequence" and comments: "The revised sequence sends to the museum of irrelevant ideas the notion of an equilibrium in consumer outlays which reflect the maximum of consumer satisfaction."[12]

It may be that Galbraith has exaggerated the degree of demand manipulation, as some have charged, but it is unlikely that any would argue that consumers and business firms interact on terms approaching parity. The attention given to Ralph Nader in recent years is due to the fact that consumerism is still so new and immature in our economy. Its rise is recognition that manipulation of consumers by firms unmatched by organized and informed consumer manipulation of firms seriously alters the normative implications of emergent prices. Only in economics as allocation can one argue that "the work or value of a thing is determined simply by what a person is willing to pay for it."[13] There is no need here to linger over this point except to note that what lies "beyond demand," to use John Gambs's phrase, is an integral part of economics as valuation and always has been.

A second inadequacy of the economist's analysis of how markets operate is closely related to the first and involves again the tremendous concentration of power in the modern business corporation. Economics as allocation has not been unduly concerned with economic power *per se*, but only with how "market imperfections affected the allocation of resources." Economics as valuation can make no such convenient division. There is by now a vast literature dealing with the rise of the modern corporation, its basis in great wealth, its *raison d'être* in its unique ability to exploit the fruits of ongoing technological development, and the concentration of power (economic but also political and social) to which these factors led. Certainly relatively little attention has been paid by mainstream economists to the impact of concentrated power on the meaning of the price system in operation.

Adolf Berle and Gardiner Means warned in the 1930s of the implications of separating ownership and control.[14] R. A. Brady some years later warned of the implications of concentrated corporate power to the fabric of the sociopolitical as well as the economic system[15] in a view anticipating Dwight Eisenhower's celebrated warning of the dangers to democracy inherent in the military-industrial complex. Despite the effort to develop models of imperfect competition, economics as allocation has never escaped from the dilemma posed by the dynamism of technology which simultaneously destroyed the world of Smithian competition, with its convenient assumptions of the Invisible Hand, and enormously increased the efficiency and productivity (but also the dangers to "sovereignty") of the system in fact operating.

This call to incorporate the realities of corporate economic power into conventional economics thus has a very old if relatively futile history. It may even be a cliché to mention, but like many clichés it represents an obvious necessity since it is still unrealized in economic theory. It is currently being urged most conspicuously by Galbraith.[16] Thus, if institutionalists erred in failing to recognize the impact of imperfect competition theory on the normative implications of "equilibrium," this error was small in the face of the problem they did perceive in the operation of prices to allocate resources in the market. The realities of concentrated power, the implications of an allocative mechanism based on "one dollar, one vote" operating amidst tremendous inequality in the distribution of both wealth and income, the degree to which concentration exercised a pervasive influence on both the flow of information and the "wants" assumed to be given—all these and related aspects of the economy were not so much unknown to economists as simply ignored definitionally by the profession in considering economic theory. The result was that even in its *terra cognita*, the domain of allocation in markets via prices, economists could not really deal with the value problem effectively. But the greatest inadequacies resulted from concentrating the attention of the economists unduly in this corner of their field, thereby ignoring the full implications of economics as valuation.

Institutional Economics and the Valuation Process

The meaning of the price system is only part of the strategy of economic progress, and it is the latter that lies at the heart of economics as valuation. It was this view, of course, that gave institutionalism its characteristic flavor, and Ayres in particular tried to pull the separate threads together to make a complete statement of economics as a science of valuation directed at developing a strategy of progress. From Veblen came his great sensitivity to the impact of institutional forces (economic and noneconomic) in shaping the development of priorities and the resultant futility of presuming wants to be given when in fact they are shaped by the economy. From the disputes in the physical sciences came his conviction that the Newtonian emphasis on equilibrium was far less significant for economics than was the Darwinian emphasis on conflict, process, and change. From John Dewey came the instrumental theory of value, which succeeded in producing a dynamic from which the valuation process in economics could be analyzed.

What Ayres saw better than anyone else, in my judgment, was that instead of concentrating on how resources are allocated in markets via prices, economists should subsume that problem in the larger and more compelling problem, namely: How does the economy shape as well as channel human choice, both during a given period and through time? What mechanisms does it provide both for the development and for the expression of values? When Kenneth Arrow considered welfare economics, he still viewed the economy as a transmission mechanism for expressing "values" exogenously determined—hence his title *Social Choice and Individual Values.* But a more meaningful title might well have been *Individual Choice and Social Values.* It is the latter which "the economy" represents. And I dare say that the fallacy of composition scarcely could be of greater critical importance than in the placid assumption of economists that the economy is an adequate and effective mechanism for summing individual values into social values. There is clearly a complex interaction between individual and social values, but the way in which the economy directs this interrelationship is far from clear, let alone necessarily satisfactory. (And "satisfactory" here may be interpreted only as certainty that the system accomplishes what each of its participants would prefer it to accomplish if they were "suitably" aggregated.)

The major critical frontier in economics, therefore, cannot be restricted even to market valuation; it lies in a far broader perspective.

The Frontiers of Political Economy: Individual Choice and Valuation in Society

Perhaps even Ayres took too narrow a view, in the sense that the ultimate concern of economics is not merely the meaning of the price system, but the meaning of the entire allocation pattern which emerges.[17] Increasingly it seems clear that economics as valuation cannot avoid concern with nonprice phenomena. The evidence is piling up on all sides that the old view of economics (as primarily concerned with how the market allocates resources via price under rigidly given assumptions) increasingly is being pushed aside by the necessity for facing many critical valuation problems.

This necessity has, however, only exaggerated the schizophrenia in economics. It is suddenly very fashionable in economics courses to include mention of urban blight, air and water pollution, conservation, the energy crisis, the population explosion, racial and sexual discrimination, and even "the quality of life." Our elementary texts exhibit the result brilliantly. They add chapters on these topics as each is pressed upon the professional consciousness in too forceful a manner to continue to be ignored, but these concerns are almost invariably grafted on at the end, in about chapter 37. The central chapters on the operation of the market are untouched, and the inadequacy of the theoretical framework in the field for coping with the valuation problems is glossed over. Price theory, particularly competitive theory, is our rosary. Critical areas of economic valuation are each given a chapter. That is our confession. The religion is intact.[18]

Thus Gunnar Myrdal recently suggested: "Modern establishment economists have retained the welfare theory from the earliest neoclassical authors, but have done their best to conceal and forget its foundation upon a particular and now obsolete moral philosophy."[19]

No better corroboration can be found for the thrust of the argument being advanced than to consider the history of the agricultural sector during the past several decades. Such perusal shows that price is by no means the same thing as value. It should suggest that welfare economics—even of the conventional type—cannot neatly separate allocative from distributive welfare problems, although it customarily tries to do so. It should support the notion that economics as valuation cannot easily isolate utility-based welfare economics, which is conventionally viewed as more manageable, from ethically based welfare economics, considered too ambiguous to be capable of economic analysis, but clearly involved in fact in determining resource allocation and distribution in this sector. It underscores the bases of essential allocative mechanisms in *both* the decision unit of one dollar-one vote and of one man-one vote, and it illustrates the manipulation of both to reveal and shape essential societal values. Finally, in the critical area of interrelationship between the origin and transmission of individual values, on the one hand, and the origin and transmission of societal values, on the other, it reminds us how every beginning student learns to corroborate the fallacy of composition. It is with the recognition that economic analysis shows that the result of individual farmers trying to lower their prices to increase their income may lower the prices and incomes of all. That being true, why is it so difficult to persuade economists who are not beginning students that they cannot blithely assume that individual choice, let alone values, will necessarily be transformed through simple summation into harmonious societal choice, let alone values? Is it not possible that in modern market-oriented economies, so far from atomistic competition, the Invisible Hand could fall victim to the fallacy of composition? Should we not at least attempt to develop a suitable analytical framework, specifically a realistic theory of political economy, in which the question could be pursued?

In fact the necessity for such an attempt is in process of being thrust upon us. Political economy as valuation is being forced to realize by the gap between the central concerns of the conventional analytical apparatus of economics and the central concerns of the economy that they need to be fused. Welfare economics never has been comfortable with notions of Pareto optimality, although it has elaborated them endlessly, because for one thing Pareto optimality never could cope satisfactorily with the Pandora's box Marshall so innocuously called externalities. Nor could it cope with welfare in any except a highly restricted sense involving the allocation of resources by prices with all the determinants of value given. The whole of the public sector, to which attention is shortly directed, is a monument to the limitations of Pareto optimality. Critical resource allocation decisions need to be—and in fact are—made constantly that cannot revolve easily about a market-price-measurable calculus. Pareto's maxim that the improvement in any member of the community improves social welfare if no one in consequence "feels himself worse off" is already inadequate if one must consider (as in all taxation questions, for example) the decrease in welfare of those whose taxes are increased and the increased welfare of those on whom the resultant revenues are spent.

Political economy as valuation then is ultimately as closely related to political science as economics always has been to psychology. Total allocation is made by both dollar votes and man votes.[20] To the conventional concern with how to measure the choices of individuals must be added the problem of how individuals influence each others' choices.[21] Even more crucial is the question of how individual and societal choices are interrelated. We lack a coherent developed theory here for static analysis, let alone for a dynamic theory capable of coping with the notion of economic progress. These problems can best be approached in turn.

The Valuation Process and the Public Sector

From what has been said, it is clear that the meaning of the political economy as the instrument for valuation transcends the confines of economics as allocation. One clear proof is the size of the public sector in all advanced industrialized economies, even the most market-oriented—our own. (More than 20 percent of 1972 U.S. GNP originated in the public sector.[22])

Prices are utilized for the goods and services purchased in the public sector, but we do not permit the price system to do the allocation except in a trivial sense. Indeed, the public sector exists precisely because here we have chosen to express our values through resource allocation by fiat. The quintessential example always has been defense expenditures. Collective consumption of any kind reflects the value process as embedded in the political economy. Our system operates in such a manner that military expenditures far more readily can achieve a high priority justifying taxation for subsequent social expenditures without being termed inflationary or "fiscally irresponsible" than can social welfare expenditures (note the term). The latter run into far stiffer opposition. Elementary macroeconomic theory suggests that a dollar's worth of government expenditure might, as a first approximation, be viewed as being as inflationary as any other dollar's worth of government expenditure. The terminology employed is, therefore, merely obscuring differences in what one defines as "necessary government expenditures." We conclude in effect that we "need" national security "regardless of price"—a subjective value judgment. We opt for stricter controls and limits on our definition of "need" in other directions, also a value judgment and one essentially nonprice determined. This can be illustrated by Charles Schultze's comment that the 1969 Department of Defense appropriation of some $78 billion involved only 50 different appropriations of which one (for procurement and research and development), amounting to $22 billion, was justified by a single-page appropriation. In contrast, the Health, Education and Welfare budget of a mere $14.5 billion (the non-trust fund part) was covered in approximately 100 different appropriations. HEW's budget is one-fifth the defense budget, but requires twice the appropriations.[23] The same value orientation can be substantiated by dozens of comparable illustrations. The point here is neither to criticize nor approve any particular attitude toward the resource allocation involved. It is only to underscore that because it concerns resource allocation, it is indubitably economic in nature; it involves political economy as valuation, and we have virtually nothing to contribute to the analysis as political economists.

Resource allocation is being carried out via *de facto* values, which both shape and are shaped by the economy and are no less integral because economics chooses to take them as given. A mixed economy is definitionally part market and part command, but most of the efforts made to bring the value problem into economics (except for the institutionalists) have centered on value as allocation in the market. This is true (as already noted) of Pareto optimal notions of welfare; and it is true of welfare economics in the Bergson-Arrow tradition.[24] Arrow made this point absolutely unambiguous: "We will assume in the present study that individual values are taken as data and are not capable of being altered by the nature of the decision process itself. This is . . . the standard view in economic theory."[25]

In short, virtually all would agree that modern welfare economics has been deliberately restricted to the interesting but extremely limited problem of defining and measuring social welfare only in cases for which individual values are given data and in which social welfare is restricted to the summation of these individual values. The "welfare" problem is confined to how to express and communicate individual values, how to sum them, and how to interpret the results. Whether individual values even so viewed can include collective consumption is not at all clear. The "social good" is surely deliberately eschewed. This brings us to the current concern with what is called cost-benefit analysis. On the face of it, it appears a potential step forward in coping with the value problem; perhaps it could be. But of crucial importance is the fact that cost-benefit analysis customarily is referred to as an application of welfare economics, and "social betterment" is viewed in terms of "a potential Pareto improvement." In short, social betterment cannot be separated from the summation and transmogrification of given individual values, which brings us back to the fallacy of composition, already commented upon.[26]

E. J. Mishan has suggested that Pareto-improvement notions of welfare are not very adequate until the economist decides whether to ground his welfare economics in utility or ethics.[27] This seems to obscure the issue somewhat, because one certainly could subsume utility under ethics, but what is needed is some more complete calculus than "the market" for expressing the underlying value system in economic decisions. This is more than cost-benefit analysis has ever claimed for itself.

Consideration of the public sector, therefore, suggests the magnitude of the problem. The public sector represents a sizable part of the total allocation of human and nonhuman resources in all market-orientated economies. We have noted that although the resources so allocated have prices attached to them, they are not fundamentally allocated by prices, but by fiat. The fiat comes from the political economy in the form of decisions to tax and to spend which are made by various officials selected in various ways (most through election, although by appointment in many critical areas, such as the Office of Management and Budget), and by consumers and producers organized into political units. What I am suggesting is that the manner and degree to which the economy develops, conveys, reacts to, and acts on societal values is as crucial to understanding and evaluating the political economy as the psychological basis of demand theory is to considering the behavior of individual consumers. Whereas economics may worry at least on occasion about its psychological assumptions, both in demand theory and the theory of the firm (the units involved in conventional economic "value" theory), little concern is expressed for the assumptions or characteristics of the political system through which individual and societal values are intermingled in myriad complex but crucial ways. Here dollar votes often are weighted by power considerations and in any case must be combined with man votes to represent the total allocational machinery—the political economy. Economics traditionally views "the market" as the only such individual-social conduit with which it need concern itself. But while it has concerned itself with its view of the individual, it has been relatively oblivious to the character of the other end of the conduit.

Such analysis is a necessary prerequisite to a meaningful evaluation of the performance of the economy in coping with its value problem. This emphasis is what distinguishes the position taken here from that taken by radicals, liberals, or conservatives, all of whom ultimately would seem to advocate the substitution of their own values for those they perceive in the system. The radical dissent involves, it is true, much that customarily is considered out of the bailiwick of conventional economic theory (the total distribution of power, for example). To the extent that the argument here is that the political economist must focus on the total allocation system, on how the political economy both shapes and responds to emergent societal values if it is to comprehend the meaning of the economy, our view, like that of the radicals, is broader than that customarily taken. To the extent that the radical critique is based on their dislike of the results they *perceive* emerging from the system, judgments with which we may agree or disagree, the argument here is different from the radical dissent.[28]

Liberals such as Galbraith, who is disturbed by "private affluence and public squalor," object to how the public sector is being used. But he, as are radicals and conservatives, ultimately is arguing that he likes his own values better than those he views as emerging from the political economy. His impact, too, depends ultimately on his persuasiveness. But for the science of political economy, adopting the values of any participant is no substitute for developing techniques for ensuring that the economy moves in a way that is consistent with its *own* emerging values, no matter how individual participants may view them. Such a theory of political economy as valuation would suggest, incidentally, appropriate techniques to all groups for influencing it in the marketplace of valuational ideas.[29]

The same judgment is essentially applicable to the conservative critique. Milton Friedman, for example, no doubt would argue that his "positive economics" avoids subjective valuation. He has attempted, in effect, to elevate market allocation *per se* to a value premise on grounds that the results are, in his view, most efficient, or if not efficient more reliable and ultimately more in accord with his notion of what the economy should be doing than any other allocative mechanism. His argument is that one should "trust the market" because, whatever its flaws, it performs better than nonmarket mechanisms. Friedman has commented, for example, that "the role of the market . . . is that it permits unanimity without conformity; that it is a system of effectively proportional representation."[30] The word *effective* glosses over most of the problems considered earlier (the actual sovereignty of the consumer, the impact of concentration on the use of power in market allocation, and so forth) as well as being fairly irrelevant to collective consumption. The market cannot possibly allocate defense, "proportionally" or otherwise. Friedman, therefore, does find a role for political allocation (man votes). But he suggests that "fundamental differences in basic values can seldom if ever be resolved at the ballot box."[31] It seems inconsistent to place such faith in laissez-faire markets for economic allocation and so little in democratic processes for converting individual values into social policy.

In the end, reliance on the market, even if more consistent than reliance on any one individual, is no substitute for a theory of political economy as valuation. There still will be allocation for necessary collective consumption by political or administrative fiat. Social Security may be "necessary" to Galbraith, but not to Friedman.

National defense is "necessary" to them both (but how much and how to decide?). What shall be the criteria for determining "necessary"? The argument here is that these are crucial *economic* problems about which the economist remains mainly mute, that no single individual's values will suffice as acceptable criteria for these allocative decisions, and that the only solution is finally to face the total relevant value problem inherent in shaping and directing the destiny of the economy.

It might be added that Ayres's distinction between institutional and technological values was directed at just this point: that notions of welfare never can be appropriately resolved by the imposition of the "value system" of a single individual or group, nor (he argued) even of a given society. His failure was to suppose that emphasis on *process*, which eliminated the old problem of means and ends, could solve the value problem entirely. He argued that "the general welfare is not a condition; it is a process."[32] While he certainly was correct that values in this sense change, he underrated the practical need to develop an analytical technique by which emergent values in the political economy could be discerned. An adequate theory would constitute a mechanism through which emergent values are recognized, transmitted, and reflected in the ongoing operation of the economy. More important, economists then could judge both the accuracy and sensitivity with which the political economy expressed society's emerging values and how closely it conformed to any other preconceived "standard." This is why the emphasis here has been on the need to develop a more complete theory of the political economy as valuation.

The institutionalist emphasis on process was convenient in that one could assume that progressive development, as in technology, would constitute economic progress definitionally. It did not entirely serve to distinguish growth from progress, however, unless one assumes that in time society will make the "right" (that is, "technological") choices. (Ayres, of course, did indeed feel technological choices were eventually inevitable. By emphasizing the "continuum" he thought he had disposed of the value problem inherent in the notion of an end in itself ["ultimate values"].[33])

If the unsatisfactory way in which political economy currently copes with the value problem is illustrated by what it can offer in evaluating the public sector, its inadequacies for viewing the political economy through time are exemplified by considering the notion of economic progress.

The Frontiers of Dynamic Valuation: Political Economy and the Meaning of Progress

We have proceeded by stages, and we come now to the last step. We have suggested that economics has concentrated its work in welfare theory on that which is measurable within the market through prices and with individual values assumed given. Consideration of the meaning of prices limited to that framework suggests that the institutionalist charge (but only this charge) that conventional equilibrium always meant competitive equilibrium can be partially rebutted. We also have argued that the economy as an overall allocative mechanism should be the proper focus of the economist and that to do so he must once more become a political economist and cope with the meaning of total allocation—that is, the problem of value. It is here that the question of the public sector is most instructive.

If, finally, the element of time is added, as it must be if questions such as pollution, conservation, and development are considered, even a simple Pareto optimality would become quite complex. Should we try to "dynamize Pareto optimality" by saying that "a dynamic Pareto optimality implies that a change which enhances the well-being of at least one member of the next generation without reducing the well-being of a single member of the present generation shall be defined as genuine economic progress"? If strategy X enhanced the well-being of the next generations as well as the present one, but at the expense of the $n + 1$ generation (the "limiting case" being the annihilation of the race in some future generation), what then? Intergenerational trade-offs are inherently complex even in the relatively simple Paretian world because tastes, technology, and resources at the very least must become dynamic givens.[34]

But just as Pareto optima cannot serve as adequate guides to the total value adequate problem in political economy in a single period, they cannot serve as adequate guides to progress. It is important to note that the customary emphasis in economic dynamics is on growth rather than progress for precisely the same reasons that the traditional emphasis in statics is on allocation rather than valuation. Progress involves valuation through time, while growth involves simply increase in whatever it is the economy happens to be doing.[35] Paul Samuelson, for example, in the ninth edition of his basic text tries finally to suggest that progress rather than growth is what concerns us, but his approach is to introduce a version of the Nordhaus-Tobin measure of economic welfare.[36] Samuelson suggests that increases in "per capita net economic welfare" are at a slower rate than increases in per capita GNP. The Nordhaus-Tobin suggestion that growth brings "disamenities" which need consideration is constructive. Techniques for distinguishing growth from progress, let alone measuring it, have very far to go, however.[37]

In short, the strategy of economic progress clearly suggests the primacy of political economy as a science of valuation. The focus is on a global inventory of human and nonhuman resources over time, their relations to changing technology, and the processes by which human beings create political economies. The latter are thus mechanisms through which emergent goals are determined through the interaction of individual and societal valuation processes. By explicitly comprehending the mechanisms in a theory of total allocation, the political economist thereby would enable the participants to direct all resources toward the goals which emerge and to evaluate them against any external criteria they individually might choose to employ. This emphasis on progress rather than growth currently is being debated both in developing economies, where institutionalists long have had an interest, and in the developed economies.

Ayres was one of the first (and still one of the few) to concern himself with economic progress rather than economic growth.[38] Technological progress has been such that we now can view the possibilities for the future with considerably greater awareness of the full implications of alternative strategies than was possible even thirty years ago, when Ayres outlined his theory of economic progress.[39] Economists increasingly recognize the distinction between growth and progress. Political economy as dynamic valuation focuses on where economies are headed. It is allocational in the broad sense that it begins with some fundamental notions: Accessible to human beings on the earth are a number of human and nonhuman inputs which an evolving technology converts into potential resources (in Zimmerman's sense); economies exist as channelling and conditioning mechanisms to assist in both determining and transmitting individual and social values as well as to provide techniques by which analysists can study the success or failure of economies in accomplishing what their participants expect of them. Political economy will develop criteria for making such judgments and at the same time will lay bare the techniques it develops for exposing the criteria so that advocates of diverse goals for economies (that is, with different views of what constitutes progress) will be better able to assess both the economy as the valuating mechanism it is and their own views for change.[40]

Implicit in this is ultimately a noneconomic value premise—that economic progress as dynamic valuation will emerge from within the system rather than be imposed from without by elitist or authoritarian agencies. Advocates of divergent strategies for progress will need to be able to dissect the existing strategy with reasonable accuracy so as to know whether their problem is to improve the way the existing economy reflects existing values or whether the problem is to change the values so as to produce a different path into the future.[41]

It should be noted that in advocating that political economy as dynamic valuation must confront the notion of progress in meaningful terms, we are not suggesting that there is no natural division of labor between economists and philosophers in approaching value. It seems consistent with the present position to argue that economists can continue to shunt off onto philosophers the more abstruse elements of the value controversy as it affects, for example, the debate over what constitutes the good life. If, however, we accept that resource allocation is the heart of economics, then economists need to confront all the value elements that bear directly on this central problem. So viewed, economics never has been "mere allocation," that is, concerned only with resource allocation via prices in markets.

Conclusions

It is perhaps possible to summarize the essential argument in a few propositions.

(1) Economics always has recognized that its distinctive emphasis has been on the need to make choices in a world where the energy crisis is only the most recent reminder that affluence has yet to replace scarcity as a basic conditioner of human existence.

(2) While economics, therefore, indubitably revolves about allocation, it is pre-eminently a science of valuation. To say this is to say something more specific than the philosopher's more cosmic concern with the ultimate destiny of man, but less specific than, say, Lionel Robbins's definition of economics would imply. Economic theory, in which market imperfections are noted, but values are assumed given, even when termed only "benchmark theory," is inadequate theory to cope with the economic problem.[42]

(3) Ayres well may have erred in his view of the meaning of modern market equilibria, but he surely was supremely correct in arguing that the central concern of economics is not how markets allocate resources, but rather how the total allocative thrust of the economy is perceived, determined, reviewed, transmitted, and altered over time.

(4) Economics long has given in to the tendency, therefore, to convert what is essentially a complex value problem into a relatively

simple and often mechanistic allocative problem because of the advantages of the latter in developing precise and rigorous models. But this effort has produced schizophrenia which has become ever more pronounced. The disproportionate attention given to theoretical apparatus which concentrated on simplistic allocation while the economy itself wrestled with valuation increasingly is being recognized. Perusal of any basic text will underscore this discrepancy between the complexity of our apparatus to deal with "markets" and the paucity of our apparatus to deal with value (in static terms) or progress (in dynamic terms).

(5) Only when economic theory concentrates on the meaning of the political economy—the problem of value—will we be able to assess the adequacy of our current allocation (outside as well as inside the market) to accomplish the evolving ends which the participants in the economy currently set for it. Only then can we criticize either the actual functioning of the economy or the expectations of its participants in effective fashion.

(6) If we accept consumer sovereignty as the important factor in economic allocation that classical and neoclassical economists assumed, the challenge is to turn their assumption into reality by developing a theory of political economy as valuation in terms of which the evolving total allocational thrust of society (its emerging values) can be expressed. In such terms economic performance can be judged by the only criteria that ultimately make sense: How effectively and accurately does the system reflect emergent choice?[43]

(7) The frontier of the political economy, therefore, is to be found in developing criteria by which economies can be judged in terms of their ability successfully to express the emergent values of society. In dynamic terms these criteria will provide an avenue for judging the economy through time as the embodiment of the evolving values of its participants, that is, economic progress. Only then can we comment meaningfully on whether the current structures in the economy constitute a road to serfdom, a road to utopia, or some halfway road, and whether, whatever the road may be, it is what (rightly or wrongly) its inhabitants choose.

Notes

1. That there were problems with the notion of equilibrium was not denied; they were simply ignored. For example: "Equilibrium economics describes a community without economic problems, because so far as it affects him, everybody knows how everyone else is going to behave." T. W. Hutchison, *The Significance and Basic Postulates of Economic Theory*

(1938) (New York: Augustus M. Kelley, 1965), p. 164.

2. In this connection, it is instructive to consider the views of Malthus, originally expressed in 1819. "It has been said, and perhaps with truth, that the conclusions of Political Economy partake more of the certainty of the stricter sciences than those of most of the other branches of human knowledge. . . . There are indeed in Political Economy great general principles . . . [but] we shall be compelled to acknowledge that the science of Political Economy bears a nearer resemblance to the science of morals and politics than to that of mathematics." T. R. Malthus, *Principles of Political Economy* (Tokyo: International Economic Circle, 1936), p. 1.
3. Alfred Marshall, *Principles of Economics*, 8th ed. (New York: The Macmillan Company, 1949), p. 1.
4. Ibid., p. 14.
5. Lionel Robbins, *An Essay on the Nature and Significance of Economic Science* (London: Macmillan and Company, 1946), p. 43.
6. Ibid., p. 16. Robbins thus explicitly related "means and ends" in the way which Ayres, with his notion of the "means-ends continuum," was to reject. The point is discussed below.
7. I do not suggest that Lord Robbins himself assumed that his definition so disposed of all means-ends problems, but only that this is what the profession customarily permitted his definition to lead them to.
8. Ibid., p. 152.
9. This view found expression, for example, in most of the editions of Paul Samuelson's widely used text, but significantly has dropped out of the last few.
10. The peril implicit in this view was aptly summarized by Tom Lehrer in his song about the ethics of Werner von Braun: "Once the rockets are up who cares where they come down? 'That's not my department,' said Werner von Braun." Developing such awesome technology carried with it uncomfortable responsibilities that could not be consigned to "society," and the physical sciences have been far less precise and certain, and far more factionally divided, ever since.
11. I myself some years ago argued strongly that institutionalism was failing to make much impact on the profession precisely because it attacked price theory as though no changes in the apparatus had occurred since Marshall. (Compare P. A. Klein, "A Critique of Contemporary Institutionalism," *Quarterly Review of Economics and Business* 1 [May 1961].) While I have not changed my view of the validity of that charge, I have changed my view of its importance, as the text may indicate.
12. John Kenneth Galbraith, *The New Industrial State* (New York: New American Library, 1967), p. 223.
13. The words are those of E. J. Mishan in *Cost-Benefit Analysis* (London: George Allen and Unwin, Ltd., 1971), p. 31, and represented his description of conventional "normative economics," not his concurrence with the definition.
14. Adolf A. Berle and Gardiner C. Means, *The Modern Corporation and Private Property* (New York: The Macmillan Company, 1932).
15. Robert A. Brady, *Business as a System of Power* (New York: Columbia University Press, 1943). In connection with the failure of economics

as allocation ever adequately to come to grips with the value implications of emergent prices in concentrated markets, we may quote Robert S. Lynde's introduction to Brady's book: "For the most part, contemporary social scientists still exhibit toward the changing business world the encouraging moral optimism of Alfred Marshall. Nor are we helped by the fact that the crucial science of economics derives its data within the assumptions and concepts of a system conceived not in terms of such things as 'power' but of blander processes such as the automatic balancing of the market" (p. xvi). The economist would not make so simple a statement, lest he be accused of being simpleminded, but the charge strikes one as not only apt in 1942, when it was written, but discouragingly apt as well in 1974.

16. In his Presidential Address to the American Economic Association in December 1972, entitled, significantly, "Power and the Useful Economist," Galbraith reiterated the theme once more that modern corporations have obtained control of half the economic output in the United States and in the process have acquired so vast a network of control as to justify calling the result a "power or planning system." *American Economic Review* 63, no. 1 (1973): 4.
17. In this connection Allan Gruchy characterized Ayres's view as follows: "He shifts the center of attention from the individual as a choosing person to the whole economy as an evolving process in which individuals as a collective unit or body seek to cope with the problem of using scarce resources to serve culturally determined wants or needs." *Contemporary Economic Thought* (New York: The Macmillan Company, 1972), p. 95. The argument of the text is that the relationship between individuals and society cannot adequately be characterized as a one-way street in either direction, but is rather one of constant interaction through time.
18. In this connection Ayres wrote: "The truth is, it is impossible for economics to disavow the ethical implications of value theory or to dispense with the terminology in which those implications are imbedded, since economics is, and always has been, concerned primarily with the meaning of the price pattern." *The Theory of Economic Progress* (Chapel Hill: The University of North Carolina Press, 1944), p. 82. If by the "price pattern" one means the total pattern of allocation in an economy, then Ayres's view is identical with the view taken in the text.
19. Gunnar Myrdal, *Against the Wind, Critical Essays on Economics* (London: Macmillan Press, Ltd., 1974), p. vi.
20. T. W. Hutchison noted this many years ago. "The *political* side of politico-economic problems is represented sometimes as the 'weakness of the politician' in not putting through necessary but unpopular measures, or 'rigidities' or frictions. That is, the difficulties are not faced at all; it is implied simply that they ought not to be there." *Significance and Basic Postulates,* p. 165. We suggest only that the problem is not faced much more directly nearly forty years after Hutchison wrote because we still lack a coherent theory of political economy with which to view economics as valuation.
21. Game theory tends to be mechanistic rather than value oriented and to ignore the producer-consumer interractions alluded to earlier.
22. For a comparison of the role of the public sector in eleven market-oriented

economies during the 1960s, see P. A. Klein, *The Management of Market-Oriented Economies: A Comparative Perspective* (Belmont, Calif.: Wadsworth Publishing Company, 1973), Table 8-2, p. 179.

23. Charles Schultze, *The Politics and Economics of Public Spending* (Washington, D.C.: The Brookings Institution, 1968), p. 4.

This value perspective continues critically to shape allocation through the public sector. Thus a Brookings Institution analysis of the fiscal 1974 budget proposals concluded that the administration's budget proposals, "while leaving the structure of federal taxes and the current defense posture unchanged . . . recommended a sweeping series of reductions in the domestic expenditures of the federal government, including elimination or sharp curtailment of many programs." Edward R. Freed, Alice M. Rivlin, Charles L. Schultze, and Nancy H. Teeters, *Setting National Priorities, The 1974 Budget* (Washington, D.C.: Brookings Institution, 1973), p. vii. This is not Friedman's "proportional representation" through the market (see text below), but economics as valuation masquerading as mere "fiscal orthodoxy."

24. Some years ago, Arrow suggested the difference between Abram Bergson's view and his own as follows: "But where Bergson seeks to locate social values in welfare judgments by individuals, I prefer to locate them in the actions taken by society through its rules for making social decisions." *Social Choice and Individual Values*, 2d ed. (New York: John Wiley and Sons, 1963), p. 106. Arrow appears, therefore, to come closer than Bergson to avoiding the possibility mentioned earlier that the Invisible Hand might be afflicted by the fallacy of composition. Arrow came close to recognizing that the real value problem in economics needs to be faced, but in the welfare economics he developed he generally appears to *assume* that the value problem somehow has been met and overcome (see text) and then concentrated on the mechanisms of its transmission through the economy under varying circumstances and assumptions.

25. Arrow, *Social Choice*, p. 7. Arrow goes on to note that this standard view has been attacked for its lack of realism by Veblen, Frank Knight, J. M. Clark, and others.

26. For a clear current statement of cost-benefit analysis and its view of social betterment, see Mishan, *Cost-Benefit Analysis*, especially p. 8.

That efforts of this sort to develop applied welfare economics take too restricted a view of the required scope of economics as valuation may be noted in the following typical comment (this time from input-output analysis in welfare terms): "The analysis in this book has been concerned only with the implications of specifying a national objective such as maximizing production or consumption. Before one may examine how such an objective may be reached, it is first necessary to describe the actual operation of the economy in terms of a set of lagged behavior functions in market prices." Burgess Cameron, *Input-Output Analysis and Resource Allocation* (Cambridge: the Univeristy Press, 1968), pp. 94-95. Economics as valuation never can be encompassed simply by specifying a maximizing objective without some framework to suggest how specifying the character of the maxima reflects the value system, and that will never emerge from concentration on market prices alone, even if presented as a set of the most elegant of lagged behavior functions.

27. Ibid., p. 311.
28. An interesting and illuminating exchange between a radical and a mainstream economist was that between John Gurley and Robert Solow in 1971. Gurley argued that the establishment paradigm emphasized data and technique and ignored such factors as power and conflict and thereby "a large part of reality." Solow's rebuttal suggested that "knowledge of technique and acquaintance with data" was precisely what distinguished economists from others. See *American Economic Review* (May 1971): especially, 54 and 65.
29. Ayres would no doubt suggest a technique be devised for testing the degree to which the emerging societal values are consonant with evolving technological values. Sooner or later, in Ayres's view, they would have to match.
30. Milton Friedman, "The Role of Government in a Free Society," in *Capitalism and Freedom* (Chicago: University of Chicago Press, 1962), p. 23.
31. Ibid., p. 24.
32. C. E. Ayres, *The Industrial Economy* (New York: Houghton Mifflin Company, 1952), p. 315.
33. He compared our problem to that of medicine, where "health" is the only required criterion and good and bad become more or less in terms of the relevant value criterion. One wonders what he would have said about abortion and euthanasia, both currently highly debatable value propositions. If, as he argued, "as between institutional and technological systems of value, the technological values have always had the last word" (ibid., p. 314), which is the technological value side of these debates? Can one see far enough down "the continuum" to answer?
34. Institutionalists always have objected to the assumption of "given" tastes. Ayres stressed the inherently dynamic role of technology, and a fundamentally dynamic view of resources as the only meaningful one for economists to take was stressed (although rather widely underrated and/or ignored by economists) many years ago by Erich W. Zimmerman in *World Resources and Industries*. It is the technological *process* which converts matter or energy into resources.

    As Zimmerman put it, "resources are dynamic not only in response to increased knowledge, improved arts, expanding science, but also in response to changing individual wants and social objectives." E. W. Zimmerman, *World Resources and Industries*, rev. ed. (New York: Harper and Row, 1951). In short, all the parameters within which economic models customarily are developed are essentially dynamic, and economics can hold them fixed indefinitely only at the peril of not developing in the most meaningful and viable way.
35. That the distinction is now attracting attention may be seen, for example, in *The Economic Growth Controversy*, edited by Andrew Weintraub, Eli Schwartz, and J. Richard Aronson (New York: Macmillan, International Arts and Science Press, 1973). In chapter 2, "Growth and Anti-Growth," E. J. Mishan, for example, writes: "It is surpassingly convenient for the professional economist to interpret people's market choices, or their economic judgment generally, as reflecting their mature judgment about what is conducive to their happiness. But I hope he is not such a fool

as really to believe it" (p. 22). The central problem under discussion is: What can the professional economist bring to bear on perfecting the mechanisms by which market and nonmarket choices about resource allocation by individuals, and by society collectively, are directed toward any meaningful notion of what society wishes to achieve?

36. Compare P. A. Samuelson, *Economics*, 9th ed. (New York: McGraw Hill, 1973), pp. 195–96.
37. "Disamenities" is a slightly expanded view of Marshallian externalities. In view of the venerability of the notion of externalities in economics and its failure significantly to affect economic theory, one cannot be too sanguine about concern for per capita net welfare transforming the perspective or approach of economic analysis in the near future. See W. Nordhaus and J. Tobin, "Is Growth Obsolete?" in National Bureau of Economic Research Inc., *50th Anniversary Colloquium*, vol. 5 (New York: Columbia University Press, 1972).
38. It often has been said that institutionalists, including Ayres, did not develop their ideas in sufficiently precise form to command widespread acceptance among economists. Samuelson, for example, has said of institutionalism: "For the most part this school has not succeeded in reproducing itself and today it seems almost extinct." P. A. Samuelson, *Collected Scientific Papers of Paul A. Samuelson*, vol. 2, no. 125 (Cambridge, Mass.: MIT Press, 1966), p. 1736 (from an article, "Economic Thought and the New Industrialism," published in 1963). While one does not find copious references to Ayres in recent literature, there is considerable evidence that his ideas increasingly have worked themselves into current economic debate. For the views of one economist who argues this see Robert A. Gordon in Joseph Dorfman and others, *Institutional Economics* (Berkeley: University of California Press, 1963).

    An example of an unfortunate lack of specificity in Ayres in connection with his view of progress is the following: "Human progress consists in finding out how to do things, finding out how to do more things, and finding out how to do all things better." *The Theory of Economic Progress* (New York: Schocken Books, 1962), p. v of Ayres's new Introduction. That sounds more like growth. Without consideration of which, of all the things human beings can do, they should concentrate their relatively scarce resources upon (time, if nothing else), this can hardly be taken as a very useful description of progress.
39. A critical part of Ayres's theory of economic progress revolved around the dynamism which he derived from his instrumental theory of value, which was closely related to Dewey's means-end continuum. That this is closely related to the notion of progress emerging from valuation in an evolving political economy may be illustrated by Charles Schultze's comment: "We discover our objectives and the intensity we assign to them only in the process of considering particular programs of choices. We articulate ends as we indicate means." *Public Spending*, p. 38. Schultze suggests intuitively that economics is, after all, a science of value.
40. That this is the most likely perspective from which innovations in economic theory always have sprung is perhaps what Leo Rogin had in mind when he wrote that "new systems [of economic thought] first emerge in the guise of arguments in the context of social reform." *The Meaning and*

Validity of Economic Theory (New York: Harper and Brothers, 1956), p. xiii.

41. A different path, in Ayresian terms, simply would be one more in accord now with emergent technological values.
42. The term is Samuelson's. "The competitive model is extremely important in providing a bench mark to appraise the efficiency of an economic system." *Economics*, 9th ed. (New York: McGraw Hill, 1973), p. 631.
43. An implicit assumption is that these emergent choices can embody Ayres's "technological values." Whatever they embody, it appears ultimately to be the only defensible system, short of any imposed authoritarianism.

References

Arrow, Kenneth J. *Social Choice and Individual Values*. 2d ed. New York: John Wiley and Sons, 1963.

Ayres, Clarence E. *The Industrial Economy*. New York: Houghton Mifflin Company, 1952.

———. *The Theory of Economic Progress*. Chapel Hill: The University of North Carolina Press, 1944.

Berle, Adolf A., and Means, Gardiner C. *The Modern Corporation and Private Property*. New York: Macmillan, 1932.

Brady, Robert A. *Business as a System of Power*. New York: Columbia University Press, 1943.

Cameron, Burgess. *Input-Output Analysis and Resource Allocation*. Cambridge: the University Press, 1968.

Freed, Edward R.; Rivlin, Alice M.; Schultze, Charles L.; and Teeters, Nancy H. *Setting National Priorities, The 1974 Budget*. Washington, D.C.: The Brookings Institution, 1973.

Friedman, Milton. "The Role of Government in a Free Society." In *Capitalism and Freedom*. Chicago: University of Chicago Press, 1962.

Galbraith, John Kenneth. *The New Industrial State*. New York: New American Library, 1967.

———. "Power and the Useful Economist." *American Economic Review* 63, no. 1 (March 1973).

Gordon, Robert A. In *Institutional Economics*, Joseph Dorfman and others. Berkeley: University of California Press, 1963.

Gruchy, Allan. *Contemporary Economic Thought*. New York: Macmillan, 1972.

Gurley, John. "The State of Economics." *American Economic Review* 62, no. 2 (May 1972): 53-62.

Hutchison, T. W. *The Significance and Basic Postulates of Economic Theory*. New York: Augustus M. Kelley, 1965.

Klein, Philip A. "A Critique of Contemporary Institutionalism." *Quarterly Review of Economics and Business* 1, no. 2 (May 1961).

———. *The Management of Market-Oriented Economies: A Comparative Perspective*. Belmont, Calif.: Wadsworth Publishing Company, 1973.

Marshall, Alfred. *Principles of Economics*. 8th ed. New York: MacMillan, 1949.

Mishan, E. J. *Cost-Benefit Analysis*. London: George Allen and Unwin, Ltd., 1971.

Myrdal, Gunnar. *Against the Wind; Critical Essays on Economics.* London: Macmillan, 1974.

Nordhaus, W., and Tobin, J. "Is Growth Obsolete?" In National Bureau of Economic Research, Inc., *Fiftieth Anniversary Colloquium,* volume 5. New York: Columbia University Press, 1972.

Robbins, Lionel. *An Essay on the Nature and Significance of Economic Science.* London: Macmillan, 1946.

Rogin, Leo. *The Meaning and Validity of Economic Theory.* New York: Harper and Brothers, 1956.

Samuelson, Paul A. "Economic Thought and the New Industrialism." Reprinted in *Collected Scientific Papers of Paul A. Samuelson,* volume 2, no. 125. Cambridge, Mass.: M.I.T. Press, 1966.

———. *Economics.* 9th ed. New York: McGraw Hill Book Company, 1973.

Schultze, Charles. *The Politics and Economics of Public Spending.* Washington, D.C.: The Brookings Institution, 1968.

Weintraub, Andrew; Schwartz, Eli; and Aronson, J. Richard, eds. *The Economic Growth Controversy.* New York: Macmillan, International Arts and Science Press, 1973.

Zimmerman, Erich W. *World Resources and Industries.* Rev. ed. New York: Harper and Row, 1951.

2

Power and Illusion in the Marketplace: Institutions and Technology

Thomas R. De Gregori

Both in writing and in lectures, C. E. Ayres frequently quoted Thorstein Veblen's warning concerning "the triumph of imbecile institutions."[1] Our times seem to be dominated by crisis—environmental crisis, energy crisis, and so on. In the United States, domestic economy and economic policy tools, once gloried for their efficacy and precision, are failing spectacularly. Government economists advise inaction on inflation and unemployment since, as they admit, they do not fully understand the causal forces. In many ways our response to crisis is following patterns that Ayres warned against. The system of ideas that led us to these crises, rather than being seen in need of revision or rethinking, is held to more firmly by some as the answer to all of our problems. Nowhere is faith manifested more than in the ability of markets and unhindered price signals to channel resources to problem areas, and nowhere is Ayres more cogent in his strictures than against the mysteries of the price system.

In the Preface to the paperback edition of *The Theory of Economic Progress*, Ayres calls attention to his attack in the opening chapters against the "obsession with the market" of conventional economics.[2] To Ayres, this obsession with market activity diverted attention from the technological processes and implied a causal relationship between buying and selling and economic well-being. Obviously, individuals in a market economy must enter into market relations, and these relations are the major determinants of their individual wealth. Market analysis focuses on this aspect of individual economic activity to the almost total neglect of the individual skill activity, for example, of a machinist, medical doctor, or farmer. As Ayres noted, "doubtless farmers would do well to study the market, and any individual farmer who had achieved notable skill in this exercise might do better to give up farming altogether and become a broker. But a nation of brokers would raise no crops."[3] Ayres's emphasis is clear: An activity that is capable of bringing an individual wealth cannot be generalized as the primary activity that brings wealth to a community.

A major objection of Ayres's to the imputation of causal or creative attributes to markets was that such implied causality served to justify a grossly unequal distribution of income. All the institutional factors (prestige, wealth, and so on) that give market power to some individuals tend to be congealed into one explanatory factor: productivity. Such a theory, in Ayres's view, does not pass the first test of a scientific theory but is in reality a "collective representation" (Émile Durkheim's use of the term) in that it "epitomizes commercialism more completely, and no other idea carries greater weight in the exercise of rationalization by which commercial society has justified itself to itself."[4] His view is echoed in John Kenneth Galbraith's magnificent Presidential Address to the American Economic Association. Galbraith notes the neglect of a concept of power in economic theory and argues that such a theory "is not neutral. It is the influential and invaluable ally of those whose exercise of power depends on an acquiescent public."[5] If those who believe in the centrality of the logic of price theory and markets to economic analysis are committed to one thing, it is to the neutrality of their inquiries. Writers from Joseph Schumpeter to Lionel Robbins, in defending against the institutionalist critique, always have stressed that the tools of economic inquiry can be used by a socialist or a devotee of free enterprise.

Arguments about the neutrality or nonneutrality of price theory or about the significance of technology in economic change have been the root and branch of the controversy between conventional and institutional economists. The Ayresian critique takes conventional economics to task not only for implying causal efficacy to the market but also for finding moral values there. "Thus it was in medieval thought that price first assumed the role of social principle and in which society "raised the merchants' plea to the level of a doctrine of the church."[6] Today most economists would deny that they impute a moral purpose to the market, yet virtually all economists will make a normative use of markets and prices, and there are some schools of economics that have elevated market price as the sole device for resource allocation and indicator of economic preferences and well-being. The idea of "revealed preferences" implies that our modern economic society, things being as they are, is the summation of free individual choices. If the environment is being destroyed, if housing and health are inadequate while deodorants and hair sprays are abundant, or if products are unsafe, it is because people "want" it that way.[7]

It is the contention of this article that the normative interpretation of market behavior is a major element in our current ideological confusion that frustrates effective government economic and social policy. Furthermore, such normative interpretation is fundamentally in error in that, among other difficulties, it ignores the reality of modern economic life. Finally, C. E. Ayres not only correctly discerned this difficulty, but also provided intellectual guidance on critical economic and social policy issues. Let us look at each of these contentions.

As we have noted, those who would have us rely almost exclusively on market decisions neglect the role of power in shaping market behavior. The free choice mythology of market theory allows us to condone market activity that would be condemned were it carried on elsewhere.[8] As Ayres has noted, "poisoning one's wife is a mortal sin, whereas poisoning thousands of people by selling adulterated foods or drugs is a mere business misadventure."[9] Beside the fact that some people have more dollar votes than others, a fact recognized by all economists, there are considerations of power from position, prestige, and prejudice. The economic man in the marketplace of conventional economics is an individual without culture and therefore without existence. His preferences, as Ayres has observed, are merely a twentieth-century variant of the eighteenth-century innate predilections of the philosophers' natural man.[10]

One of the reasons that many economic theorists can make plausible and/or logical arguments for market solutions to problems is that they give problems a purely market definition. Needs are defined by the market, and, consequently, the market can provide for these needs. During the recent gasoline shortage, we were told by some that there would be no shortage if we raised the price high enough. "There is no long term 'energy crisis,' there is a short term problem. Economic science teaches that shortages cannot exist in free markets. In free markets prices rise in order to eliminate shortages. 'Crisis' as opposed to simple scarcity results from market disruptions; the *only* sector of society that possesses the power to disrupt a large market is the government."[11] This is the ultimate ***reductio ad absurdum*** of conventional theory, and the author cited above is not alone in proclaiming it. Human needs exist only in markets. Raising prices thereby reduces human needs.

Price theory, with its market obsession, lacks a theory of value to define human need. In fact, the very structure of the theory makes a nontautological conception of value impossible since value and price are identities.[12] Probably no term is more misused today than the word *need*. We are told that by 1980 we will "need" X barrels of oil. We continually are being exhorted as to how we will need this or that and how we will have to adjust our economy or direct massive scientific and technological efforts to fulfill this "need." Yet, on even cursory inspection, we find that our future "needs" are merely a projection of past and present consumption into the future. *Need* turns out to mean that people will be willing and able to consume a given quantity of production.

Such misuse of the word *need* comes quite easily to conventional economists since, as Galbraith has noted, practitioners have divorced "economics from any judgment on the goods with which it was concerned. Any notion of necessary versus unnecessary or important as against unimportant goods was vigorously excluded from the subject. . . . Nothing in economics so quickly marks an individual as incompetently trained as a disposition to remark on the legitimacy of the desire for more food and the frivolity of the desire for a more elaborate automobile."[13]

The divorce of economic theory from any substantive theory of needs or values makes economists' pronouncement on needs quite without content, that is, meaningless. Several vital components of a theory of needs are thereby neglected. First, as Galbraith cogently has analyzed, needs or wants cannot be separated from the process of production. There are, of course, basic needs recognized by Galbraith that exist independently of society, such as food, protection from cold, and so on, but even here culture is still the arbiter of what will or will not satisfy these basic wants. Given what Galbraith calls the "dependence effect," and "given that consumer wants are created by the process by which they are satisfied," then we no longer can speak of wants as "independently determined desires," nor can we continue to impute moral purpose to market decisions.[14] If we have crash programs to meet the energy or other "needs" of the 1980s, then it is quite likely that our prophecies will be self-fulfilling in that we will consume that energy. But it does not mean that there was a moral imperative to do so. Currently, we are gearing for massive multibillion-dollar governmental effort to meet our future energy needs so that individuals can exercise their free choice in free competitive markets to consume the energy that they innately will desire in 1980. If there is irony in massive government expenditure to fulfill a supposed free market imperative, it has not been widely commented upon.

Veblen had a concept of need that nicely complements Galbraith's: "Invention is the mother of necessity."[15] As with Galbraith's concept, Veblen thinks that the productive process satisfies basic needs and also creates further needs. Beyond that, in Veblen's framework, we adjust our lives to new technology and, within certain limits, are dependent upon it. Thus, if we continue with suburban sprawl, freeways, automobiles, and virtually no public transportation, we will "need," in a fundamental sense, more energy in 1980 than we do today. And we will "need" energy also to fulfill the reasonable expectations of many of the presently disadvantaged, who expect to participate in the utilization of many energy-using amenities that they currently are denied. But these "needs" will arise, not out of any moral purpose of the market, but out of public and private decisions that have been and are being made. Consequently, we can alter our energy "need" by changing the matrix of our decisions (other than by denying the upward expectations of the poor). Somehow, most of our energy pundits in government and industry assume that we will not (or cannot) alter our choices (without saying so), project what our "needs" will be if things do not change, and then calculate what minimal changes we can make to close this deficit. The obsession with markets of which Ayres spoke is not a minor factor in allowing such specious reasoning to prevail.

We can conclude from the foregoing that present market decisions operate in a context of past and present public and private decisions. Thus, conventional theory tends to take the impact of past experience as given, just as it takes cultural experience, power, and prestige as given. Yet, in many instances, the public action that establishes the context of decisions can be the predominant factor in shaping the social and economic pattern that emerges. We tend not to notice the public decisions if they tend to further the economic interests of the powerful, while at the same time we give free reign to the status pursuits of the populace. Our historic policy decisions concerning the automobile are a case in point. Instruments of transportation (public and private) presumably should provide people with the ability to get from where they are to where they wish or need to go, with ease, safety, comfort, and without undue costs and time. In many respects the private automobile has performed and continues to perform this task admirably. However, given the congestion of modern urban centers, factors of ease, comfort, and time rarely are satisfied for the commuter. The rising costs of cars, repairs, and insurance do not make the automobile an inexpensive mode of conveyance. And, of course, there are immense social costs, such as automobile pollution and the tearing up of cities for freeways and parking lots. Market theorists and defenders of the automobile industry argue that we are in our current state of affairs because we "want" to be.

Did, in fact, our current modes of transportation come to pass simply as a result of private, individual market choices? Obviously not! When Los Angeles, once internationally noted for its system of public transportation, gave cars the right-of-way over trolleys, the shift away from public transportation was begun. The post-World War II building of freeways constituted a subsidy for automobiles and continued the process of decline for public transit; fewer riders were followed by less service and higher costs and still fewer riders. Government at all levels continually has supported the automobile. To state the obvious, few cars and little gasoline would be bought and sold without roads to drive on. Today millions of citizens do not have effective choices in commuting to work or other destinations. Although there is growing concern, and some action is being taken for public mass transit, we are hampered by the market mythology that deifies the status quo. Past governmental actions that created the status quo are ignored; present governmental actions are distrusted and considered inferior to "free market choices." The consumer is always sovereign when casting dollar votes in the marketplace but to be feared when casting votes in the political process. Although there are other sources of inequality, at least in the voting booth each person has roughly the same voting power as his neighbor.[16]

Probably no concept is more fundamental to conventional economics than that of scarcity. Our wants are infinite, the means to satisfy them are scarce, and, consequently, economics concerns the allocation of scarce (finite) resources among alternate uses. Ayres's and Galbraith's criticism of the conventional concept of wants calls this basic postulate into question. A logical corollary of the postulate of infinite wants is what Galbraith calls the "economists's mission," namely, "to seek unquestioningly the means for filling these wants."[17] On this question Ayres would be a bit closer to orthodoxy than is Galbraith. The whole thrust of Ayres's writing (and that of the institutionalists of which he was so much a part) was toward a theory of technological change as an explanation of the process of growth. Furthermore, this process of technological change (and by implication the economic growth that it fosters) is without end. On the issue of abundance, Ayres maintained: "That the industrial economy produces all kinds of goods and services in far greater profusion than mankind has ever known before is obvious and incontestable. Not only is abundance a fact; it is one of the most conspicuous facts of modern life. Moreover, in the apprehension of the community at large it is the proudest boast of Western Civilization, and especially of the United States."[18] These remarks begin a chapter on abundance in which Ayres is clear in finding the "apprehension of the community at large" to be essentially correct. He closes the chapter with the following paragraph:

> Abundance is not good in any secondary or derivative sense, "merely" because it derives from the technological process. Nor is the technological process inherently disagreeable in itself but good in consequence of producing abundance. Both are good because they are inseparable—from each other, and from all other real goods. In a sense abundance is the aggregate of all goods and derives its goodness from all that is good. But in an equally valid sense all other goods derive their meaning from that of abundance, since a good is anything we would be better off for having more of. Thus abundance carries us back to the interrelatedness of all human experience, from which the meaning "good" derives, and it is that interrelatedness which is likewise manifest in the technological process from which abundance flows.[19]

Certainly, Ayres is close here to the basic assumption of much of microeconomics that more is better than less. The difference, however, is critical. The conventional microeconomic definition is derived solely from market actions: More is a greater sum in the marketplace. Ayres seeks to derive his definition of a good from the totality of human experience. Goods or "values derive their meaning . . . in considerable part from the human adventure itself, from the quest for knowledge and ever more knowledge, and from the never-ending struggle to harness the forces of nature to human use."[20] Those goods for which "we would be better off for having more of" need not be economic in that they are bought and sold in the marketplace.[21] Ayres, then, has a conception of values and goods that is consistent with limits of growth if such a policy ever needs to be implemented. In Ayres, economic growth and human progress have been part and parcel of one another, but with abundance it is possible to have continued human progress without economic growth.

Limits of growth theorists, environmentalists, and others raise serious challenges to modern economics. Ayres's institutional theory provides useful insights into these challenges. For, if we are to limit growth or make decisions to preserve the environment, then we need not only, as a basis for making choices, a theory of what economic goods are, but also to know what economic bads are. Ayres, in his concepts of "conspicuous waste" and in his analysis of absolute and relative wealth, provides such a theory. If there is ever a need to limit growth, we must understand the cultural forces that drive people to accumulate goods and what psychological and social purposes these otherwise superfluous items serve.

Ayres derived his concept of "conspicuous waste" directly from Veblen, who said:

> In strict accuracy, nothing should be included under the head of conspicuous waste but such expenditure as it incurred on the ground of an invidious pecuniary comparison. . . . The indispensability of these things after the habit and the convention have been formed, however, has little to say in the classification of expenditures as waste or not waste in the technical meaning of the word. The test to which all expenditure must be brought in an attempt to decide that point is the question whether it serves directly to enhance human life on the whole—whether it furthers the life process taken impersonally.[22]

Our ability to waste goods seems almost limitless. Perhaps, in that sense, our wants are infinite. But it is equally clear that insofar as "conspicuous waste" is a factor, the process of "satisfying" these wants adds little to individual or group well-being. In fact, it may detract from it. For, as Veblen observes, the purpose of "conspicuous waste" is invidious, and it is an attempt to gain status by having an object that others lack. Galbraith likens it to "the efforts of the squirrel to keep abreast of the wheel that is propelled by his own efforts."[23]

J. M. Keynes, in a passage cited by Galbraith, develops the same basic idea about the inability to satisfy the wants of conspicuous waste.

> Now it is true that the needs of human beings may seem to be insatiable. But they fall into two classes—those needs which are absolute in the sense that we feel them whatever the situation of our fellow human beings may be, and those which are relative in the sense that we feel them only if their satisfaction lifts us above, makes us feel superior to our fellows. Needs of the second class, those which satisfy the desire for superiority, may indeed be insatiable; for the higher the general level, the higher still are they. But this is not so true of the absolute needs—a point

> may soon be reached, much sooner perhaps than we are all of us aware of, when these needs are satisfied in the sense that we prefer to devote our further energies to non-economic purposes.[24]

As we plan the course of economic policy for the coming years and decades, deciding our energy "needs," our conservation "needs," our medical care "needs," and so on, it is necessary to have a theory of value that sorts out our different needs and establishes priorities other than those of the market. For the origin of our various needs conditions both the desirability and capability of meeting them. In this regard it is important to recall, in this time of economic pessimism, the prophetic words of Ayres, stated in a time of economic optimism, that abundance for all was possible, but that it could be jeopardized by other tendencies in society.

> Even so, as an idea and as a condition abundance has definite limits. It may be possible for every family in the United States to be reasonably well fed, well clothed, and well housed—far better, at all events, than they have ever been in the past. But it is not possible for every family to be better off than its neighbors. In short, abundance ends where snobbery begins. Is snobbery likely to increase as fast as our capacity to produce, or even faster? If so, all hope of future abundance might as well be abandoned. However large, the product of industry is always a finite quantity, whereas the capacity to waste has no limit. What Veblen described as "conspicuous waste" might conceivably become more and more conspicuous, with the result that all our abundance, however vast in quantity, might become as meaningless qualitatively as a sounding bell and a tinkling cymbal.[25]

In examining some facets of Ayres's institutional economic theory, we have discussed the power of ideas to shape economic policy. The ideas that Ayres criticized have drawn their sanction from tradition and still persist in their ability to misdirect public policy. Today much of the public economic policy is in disrepute. To some, as Ayres would have expected, contemporary difficulties call for a more rigid adherence to dogma, just as in primitive tribes a failure in the hunt is attributed to incorrect performance of ritual. To others, however, the time seems propitious for change, and it is possible that circumstances may be similar to those described by Keynes a generation ago. He said that "people are unusually expectant of a more fundamental diagnosis; more particularly ready to receive it; eager to try it out, if it should be even plausible."[26]

Certainly the power of vested interests and its corollary, the neglect of power by economists, is slowing the progress on economic problems that we face. But vested interests and mythopoetic economic theories survive because they are consonant with inherited institutional beliefs and practices. Their power does not exist apart from the illusions that sanctioned ideas create and, in a democracy, the susceptibility and tolerance of the population. Ayres distinguishes between the power of ideas that exists because they are right and the power of ideas that derives from their being part of the established ideology of the community.[27] To many observers the economy is moving without direction. We proclaim a commitment to the environment and do little about it. We attempt to solve one problem, unemployment in some industries, by stimulating automobile production and thereby further other problems of pollution, lack of mass transit, and the energy shortage. We face a gasoline shortage and seek as part of the solution the undoing of what little was done to protect the environment. And so it goes. We always will have problems, and today's solutions will be part of tomorrow's problems. But when today's solutions do not solve today's problems, making tomorrow's worse, then it is time to cut through the fog of ideology and illusion and rethink basic issues. There is no better place to begin inquiry, in order to find the ideas to further the human endeavor and the adventure of life, than in the writings of Clarence Edwin Ayres.

Notes

1. For example, quoted in C. E. Ayres, *The Theory of Economic Progress* (1944) (New York: Schocken Books, 1962), pp. x, 176. "History records more frequent and more spectacular instances of the triumph of imbecile institutions over life and culture than of people who have . . . saved themselves alive out of a desperately precarious institutional situation, such, for instance, as now faces the peoples of Christendom." Thorstein B. Veblen, *The Instinct of Workmanship* (1914) (New York: Norton Library, 1964), p. 25.
2. Ayres, *Theory*, pp. xiii, xiv.
3. Ibid., p. 15.
4. Ibid., p. 39. Ayres here is speaking specifically of the concept of capital.
5. John Kenneth Galbraith, "Power and the Useful Economist," *American Economic Review* 63 (March 1973): 10–11.
6. Ayres, *Theory*, p. 26.
7. Numbered among the public choice theorists are some of the extreme believers in the manifestation of moral purpose in markets. Acts in the marketplace reflect free choice; acts in the voting booth invoke coercion. In a voluminous, prestigious, and growing literature can be found arguments against government intervention (1) for product safety (let the consumer have the choice of self-insurance), (2) for licensing doctors, or (3) to eliminate discrimination. For a survey and criticism of this

literature, see my article, "Caveat Emptor: A Critique of the Emerging Paradigm of Public Choice," *Administration and Society* 6 (August 1974), in press.

8. See illustrations in my article cited above.
9. C. E. Ayres, *Toward a Reasonable Society: The Values of Industrial Civilization* (Austin: The University of Texas Press, 1961), p. 265.
10. Ibid., p. 26. This is one of the many reasons why Veblen argued that economics was pre-Darwinian and nonevolutionary. See Thorstein B. Veblen, "Why Is Economics Not an Evolutionary Science?" in Thorstein B. Veblen, *The Place of Science in Modern Civilization and Other Essays* (1919) (New York: Russell and Russell, 1961), pp. 56-81.
11. W. Philip Gramm, Professor of Economics, Texas A&M University, in the *Wall Street Journal*, 30 November 1973. For other examples of market definition of human need, see my article, "Caveat Emptor."
12. Probably the greatest contribution that Ayres made to institutional economics was his comprehensive, cogent theory of value, which formed the basic structure for his economic and social theorizing. Unfortunately, we will discuss only small aspects of it that are relevant to the issues under discussion.
13. John Kenneth Galbraith, *The Affluent Society* (Boston: Houghton Mifflin, 1958), p. 147.
14. Ibid., pp. 155, 260.
15. Thorstein Veblen, *The Instinct of Workmanship and the State of the Industrial Arts* (1914) (New York: W. W. Norton, 1964), p. 314. "And here and now, as always and everywhere, invention is the mother of necessity."
16. Part of the mystique of the market has been the association of freedom with market activity. In the eighteenth century there was undoubtedly more freedom for the middle class in economic pursuits than there was in political pursuits under monarchical forms of government. Furthermore, a good portion of economic intervention was to benefit the state and not to promote the commonweal. Today, in the United States and other countries, we are approaching a democracy. Economic intervention can be an instrument for public benefit. Frequently, where intervention is harmful, it is because of the inordinate political power of those who already have market power and seek to use government power to enhance it. In Ayres's view we have the scientific and technological means to solve the basic economic problems of food, shelter, and medical care (and clean air); only our subservience to free market ideology prevents our doing so. If Ayres is correct, and I would argue that he is, then our commitment to free markets stands in the way of the real freedom of our citizens instead of promoting it.
17. Galbraith, *Affluent Society*, p. 157. In the late 1960s, when the limits of growth theories came to the forefront, many had forgotten Galbraith's pioneering work of a decade earlier on the key element in this issue, consumption. No praise can be too extravagant for someone who was seeking solutions when virtually no one even recognized the problem.
18. Ayres, *Toward a Reasonable Society*, p. 229.
19. Ibid., p. 246.
20. Ibid., p. 6. The sentence from which this quote is drawn is framed in

terms of a question, but it is clear from the context that the question is largely rhetorical and that Ayres was making a clear affirmation.

21. There are, of course, some definitions of *economic* that apply to all goods.
22. Thorstein B. Veblen, *The Theory of the Leisure Class: An Economic Study of Institutions* (1899) (New York: The Modern Library, Random House, 1934), p. 99. Veblen further notes that "it is obviously not necessary that a given object of expenditure should be exclusively wasteful in order to come under the category of conspicuous waste. An article may be useful and wasteful both, and its utility to the consumer may be made up of use and waste in the most varying proportions" (p. 100).
23. Galbraith, *Affluent Society*, p. 154.
24. John Maynard Keynes, "Economic Possibilities for Our Grandchildren," in *Essays in Persuasion* (1931) (New York: W. W. Norton, 1963), p. 365. Keynes expressed similar ideas in *The General Theory* when he suggested that the scarcity of capital could be eliminated in a generation in "a properly run community equipped with modern technical resources." J. M. Keynes, *The General Theory of Employment, Interest, and Money* (1936) (London: Macmillan, 1947), pp. 32-33. The idea that wealth is relative goes back in economics at least as far as David Ricardo, but few have drawn the conclusions from this, as have Keynes, Galbraith, and Ayres, that absolute need may be satiable.
25. Ayres, *Toward a Reasonable Society*, p. 239.
26. Keynes, *General Theory*, p. 383. In discussing the power of ideas no statement is more appropriate than the words following the above quotation and closing the book. "But apart from this contemporary mood, the ideas of economists and political philosophers, both when they are right and when they are wrong, are more powerful than is commonly understood. Indeed the world is ruled by little else. Practical men, who believe themselves to be quite exempt from any intellectual influences, are usually the slaves of some defunct economist. Madmen in authority, who hear voices in the air, are distilling their frenzy from some academic scribbler of a few years back. . . . But soon or late, it is ideas, not vested interests, which are dangerous for good or evil" (pp. 383-84).
27. Ayres, *Theory*, pp. 286-90.

3

The Impact of Economics on Technology

Seymour Melman

Among economists and other social scientists, machine technology characteristically is viewed as an autonomously fixed condition in relation to human behavior. The typical treatment in the literature dealing with society and technology is of "the impact of technology on society." Indeed, historians of technology have noted a virtual absence of such titles as "the impact of society on technology."[1] There has been a general consensus among social scientists that technology has a direction and momentum of its own and, accordingly, that it sets limits that have a controlling effect on what is socially possible. In a volume entitled *The Technological Society*, Jacques Ellul succinctly expresses this viewpoint when he writes: "Capitalism did not create our world; the machine did."[2]

This article stands the above assumption on its head. I do not quarrel with the obvious fact that, once created and utilized, technology has wide-ranging economic and social consequences. I take issue, however, with the belief that it has an autonomous momentum and direction. Technology is man's creation. It is applied in accordance with specific social criteria wielded by those with economic decision power in the society. I propose here to indicate how the specific design and selection from among technological alternatives is controlled decisively by the industrial managers, private and governmental, on whose behalf technologies are researched, developed, and produced.

One implication of this formulation, in contrast to assumptions about an autonomous technological momentum, is that technology is subject to major alternations as a consequence of variation in the economic and social criteria that are used to decide technology.

The differentiation between science, invention, and technology is useful for our discussion. *Science* is the body of knowledge and the process of discovery concerning the characteristics of the universe. *Invention* is the application of science to artifacts and methods for performing operations; it also refers to the research and development process whereby new artifacts and procedures are produced. By *technology*, I mean the application of science and invention in the service of some social requirement. The latter differentiation is crucial since museums of technology and the engineering literature world-wide are filled with inventions that never actually have been applied. New knowledge about the universe and free invention add to the options that conceivably can be siezed upon for application in the form of technology: products, means of production, or methods of organization. The present discussion is concerned with technology, not with the processes of science or invention.

By way of illustrating the characteristics of technology, let us draw on the experience of the automobile industry in the United States and other countries. The mass utilization of automobiles, *any kind of automobile*, would have generated profound effects on the distribution of population and the associated suburban life-style. These results would have been achieved had motor vehicles been large or small, expensive or inexpensive, energy efficient or inefficient, safe or unsafe. Needless to say, highways, suburbia, and the motor vehicles themselves include a host of humanly and socially destructive features and effects. These include unsafe vehicles and highways; grossly expensive, inefficient, and air-polluting vehicles; suburban configurations that are unreachable and unusable without the automobile; and the concommitant withdrawal of public capital from metropolitan centers. None of these results sprang autonomously from machine technology. All these features and effects were preferred selectively by the economic decision makers who determined which technology, in each instance, was most serviceable to their business advantage.

Throughout its history as a quantity-produced product, the design and hence the operating characteristics of the U.S. automobile have been stamped by the requirements of the directing managements of the major auto firms. They have sought to maximize the extension of their decision power as gauged by criteria of profit, capital investment, market share, and control over workers. However, the strategies used toward these ends have varied, and the changes of business strategy have been reflected in the technologies of the auto product and of the industry as a production system as well. First, the product.

The Automobile

In the industry dominated by the Ford Motor Company until the Great Depression, the mass-produced passenger car was a simplified, standardized, functional product. By the close of World War II, the industry was dominated by General Motors, whose business strategy, different from that of early Ford, favored a product technology of growing ornateness, a price-graded product line, and annual model changes that stressed numerous cosmetic alterations and dysfunctional innovations. Product standardization was deemphasized in favor of promoting product variation both in single years and through time. Product standardization was reduced, and the idea of auto simplification virtually was abandoned.

It is significant that during the period 1919–1929 the average price of U.S.-produced cars actually fell from $830 to $630 per car. By contrast, from 1949 to 1971 the average price per U.S.-produced passenger car was increased from $1,300 to $2,500.[3]

These changes in product (and prices) do not represent, in any sense, technology with direction and momentum of its own. All the changes in auto design were the result of elaborately developed management strategies. Tailfins, meaningless trim, horsepower beyond anything that could be used on any public road, failure-prone mechanisms, and quality control to ensure limited component and vehicle life, all these were ordered as part of a top management strategy for profits and expansion of decision power. A special kind of naïveté is required to accept the explanation for tailfins once offered to me by a former president of a major auto firm: The consumer wanted it.

By 1973 one of the Big Three had 43 models in its "low cost" line. The cost of auto transportation to the user was raised by the proliferation of body types, engines, transmissions, and seat controls, and the multitude of internal fittings produced a situation in which a major auto assembly plant could complete a year of work without actually building two identical cars. This kind of diversity killed the advantages of relatively low-cost quantity production and stable design that once had been the trademark of the U.S. auto industry.

It is worth noting some of the product technology characteristics that were avoided during the last decades. Vehicle economy was foregone in favor of higher price tags and expensive maintenance. Safety considerations that would reduce highway deaths by at least half were foregone. Fuel economy was sacrificed for ever-higher horsepower. Convenient vehicle size was avoided in favor of styling considerations. Passenger comfort in the form of seating, head room, and leg room were given short shrift in preference to the "long, low look" and dysfunctional styling.

If product technology had a direction and momentum of its own, then it is unlikely that product design would have taken on precisely those characteristics that were serviceable to a particular business strategy rather than to the vehicle user. There is no escaping the fact that product technology did not just happen. It was selected, managed, ordered.

Criteria of choice play a key part in determining product design. Criteria determine the selection (and avoidance) of technology options from the array of alternatives that are available to industrial managers and to their engineer surrogates. With 97 million passenger cars in use by 1972, 83 percent of U.S. families depended on their cars. They obtained transportation at an average out-of-pocket vehicle cost of 15 cents per mile, annual vehicle costs of about $1,500, and a yearly toll of 56,000 highway deaths and 4,850,000 persons injured.[4] The medical and environmental cost of auto air pollution is unknown, but surely is large. All these costs of using conventional autos could have been diminished substantially by vehicles that were designed by engineers whose work assignments specified cheaper, safer, and less polluting passenger cars.

Imagine a row of engineers, each one given a different prime criterion for designing a gasoline-engined passenger car. The first must design with minimum money costs of operation in mind. The next with stress on safety for the driver. Another with the main emphasis on mechanical reliability, let us say, over an arbitrary period of fifteen years of use. The next must design with an eye toward maximizing fuel efficiency, another toward minimizing vehicle contribution to air pollution, and so on. The varying prime criteria of these assignments will cause the engineers to design, in each instance, a product that is manifestly different from others. By similar reasoning, change the criteria for automobile performance, and you will transform the familiar motor car.

In September 1973, the Porsche management in Germany displayed a prototype of a passenger car designed to last a full twenty years and run 180,000 miles. The car would cost about 30 percent more at the outset, but over the twenty-year period a reduction of 15 percent in full operating expenses could be expected. One of the engineers who developed this design stated that it is not based on exotic technology. "The components are either available or manufacturers will have them ready in the next several years." The car body would be aluminum, stainless steel, or recyclable plastic. Larger than normal components of many sorts would be used, and the engine would be a modest 75 horsepower with sophisticated mechanical and electrical features.[5]

Obviously, the production of such a vehicle is contrary to the U.S. auto industry's long sustained product and marketing strategy. But it reflects technological feasibility once there has been an enforced decision by a larger community that sets limits to the inefficiency of present motor vehicles. The fact is that the engineering literature includes an immense number of partial and full designs for motor vehicles that differ dramatically from the conventional products. They range from electrically driven to steam-powered cars. Whatever else, the Porsche design illustrates that management decision and not technological inevitability have determined automobile design.

In sum, several lines of evidence converge on the conclusion that auto products have no autonomous genesis or termination. Auto industry managers order their engineers to design products in keeping with their firms' general business strategy. Product designs that are not consistent with management policies are left to the limbo of office files, Patent Office drawings, engineering society papers, or museum models. All this spells product technology carrying the imprint of management's business strategy rather than any autonomous technological development. Similar patterns are visible in the shaping of the auto industry's production technologies.

Automobile Production

The belief that technology is autonomously determined generally includes the assumption that dehumanized and alienating conditions of work are intrinsic to the use of production machinery. Production work, it is assumed, must be inherently boring, dirty, and dangerous and must turn human beings into appendages of machines. Certainly contemporary conditions in the U.S. auto industry seem to be consistent with this belief. But are these conditions inevitable results of automotive production technology? Or, are they also heavily dependent on the choices of economic decision makers and hence subject to alteration given changed criteria and ways of decision making?

Managements whose traditions have included viewing the industrial worker as a species of replaceable, animated, special purpose machine have not given priority attention to the impact of the physical conditions of the workplace on human work performers. The result is a working environment that is often dangerous, or noisy, or dirty, or poorly ventilated, or too hot, or too cold, or some combination of these. Long exposure to such conditions is bound to have a degrading effect on the workers involved, especially while executive offices luxuriate in a modern, air-conditioned decor. Think of spending the work day in a place where, in order to speak to someone during working time, you must shout at the top of your voice, or of ending each day covered with grime.

As external pressures, such as liability for disabilities, have compelled managers to order the reduction of noise in the factory, for example, sustained attention has been given to developing new techniques for this purpose. True, there are bound to be some limits to what is possible in particular places. An iron foundry is certain to be dirty because of the constant handling of large quantities of fine sand. Areas around large presses are bound to be noisy and vibration filled. Batteries of automatic lathes can produce a fearful din. Even after considerable effort, a large amount of residual dirt, vibration, and noise is sure to remain in such work areas. Even with maximum effort it never will be like working in a library.

Nevertheless, very much could be done to reduce the tedium and even the monotony of many industrial jobs by redesigning them and, finally, by mechanizing difficult work hitherto done manually. In the auto industry there could be economic justification for mechanizing many monotonous jobs if the mania for annual model changes and meaningless product variety were diminished, thereby increasing the annual quantities of many components which could be standardized over several years.

A U.S. visitor to the Saab-Scandia auto factories in Sweden has commented on a four-year effort to organize automobile assembly work on a small team basis. Engines, for example, are assembled by three workers acting as a team. He further found that "the noise level of the machinery was far below the decibel level of comparable American machines . . . in contrast to the noisy and dirty conditions of comparable American plants one could not help but be astonished."[6]

The production technology of the auto industry is sensibly considered in two parts: the physical means of production and the techniques for organizing and integrating the host of production operations. In fact, these two aspects of production technology are intertwined and are separable only analytically. Nevertheless, it is useful to distinguish them for both purposes of engineering design and the present discussion. First, let us consider the means of production.

The Means of Production

The industrial manager who wants particular work done typically is confronted with the problem of choosing from among many alternative tools, devices, and machines available for accomplishing the given task. The availability of many methods stems from the accumulated body of science and invention and previous applications to technology.

Consider a very simple task, such as making a hole of specified size and shape in a one-inch thickness of wood. You immediately discover a great array of methods. You can start with a simple instrument such as a knife, advance to a device that has a drill bit, powered by hand, and move on to the same drill powered by a motor. Furthermore, the device can be held in place by a table or, beyond that, mounted on the floor. The alternatives extend to a device that automatically will put a work piece in place, perform the drilling operation, measure it for an acceptable dimension, remove the work piece, and transfer it to a stack of finished work.

To be sure, industrial managers and engineers often wish to accomplish a given task in a new manner; for example, by machine instead of human labor. Checking on the dimensions of a particular item long has been a manual task, but available knowledge and prior technology open the option for making this kind of product inspection a mechanical task. Thus new types of machines are designed and constructed to measure the dimensions of an object and segregate the bits that meet the required dimensions from those that fail. The development of new technology for production work enlarges the array of equipment options for accomplishing particular tasks. For engineers and managers the typical problem is: Which of the alternative available equipment options is most suitable to the particular work requirement?

This problem ordinarily is solved by applying a particular criterion to the range of alternatives. The usual one preferred by cost-minimizing managers is an estimate of the cost of doing the work with any particular machine. In such estimates, two factors have tended to dominate the scene in mechanical manufacturing operations: the price of the machine and the cost of labor per hour to the management. (In the process industries it is the ratio of raw materials to machinery costs.) Using these criteria, one usually can rank the alternative available machines according to the mix of labor and machinery costs involved, that is, from those using most labor and least machine cost per unit of work done to those involving most machine and least labor cost. For a given quantity of work, the machine with the least combined cost will be determined by the prevailing pattern of wages and machinery prices.

During most of the twentieth century there has been a regular pattern of development of labor and machinery costs to U.S. management. The wages of labor have tended to grow on the average more rapidly than the prices of machinery. The result of this rise in the alternative cost of labor to machinery has favored ever more intense mechanization of work by cost-minimizing managers.[7] Average growth in output per worker man-hour has been the direct result of this process. Indeed, this criterion has been used to account for the considerable variation among countries in the productivity of labor.

If it were true that technology had a direction and momentum of its own, then it reasonably could be expected that the same sort of production methods and equipment would be used throughout the world. After all, the market for production machinery has long been an international one, training about science is similar in every land, and the literature of engineering (except for the secret military type) is available everywhere. Actually, the methods of mechanical manufacture have varied considerably among economies in a way that is not at all mysterious. I can illustrate the pattern of development by drawing on some of the data from my studies of comparative international productivity.

The Ford Motor Company is one of many corporations that owns and operates factories in different countries. During the 1950s I examined aspects of production operations in the Ford factories in Detroit, Michigan, and Dagenham, England.[8] I found striking differences between the two. The Detroit factories were using much more power equipment per worker. The factories at Dagenham, outside London, produced similar products but had work methods that required much more muscle power, more use of human sensory-motor capability than did those in Detroit. Stated differently, there was a much higher intensity of mechanization of production work in Detroit than in England. The similarities among these factories included: the same kind of product, the same company, the same underlying scientific knowledge in both places, the same ample staffs of engineers and ample access to technological knowledge in both, and ample access to capital for the purpose of designing and operating production facilities in both places. The differences in degree of mechanization remained to be explained.

I found that this variation in mechanization could be accounted for by the accompanying variation in the relative cost of labor to machinery in the two countries. Thus, in 1950 in the United States it was possible for an employer, at the cost of hiring a worker for one hour, to buy 157 kilowatt hours of electricity. In England, the employer could use the cost of employing a worker for one hour to buy only 37 kilowatt hours of electricity. Hence, employers interested in minimizing the total money cost of doing particular work were required to buy more electricity and fewer man-hours in Detroit and to buy more man-hours and less electricity in Dagenham.[9] Similar contrasts showed up in the ratio of labor to machine-hour costs.

Making the usual calculations of business cost, the managers of the Ford Motor Company and their counterparts in other firms made essentially the same decision: less mechanization in England than in Detroit. That was the result of the effort to minimize enterprise production costs in each case. There is no evidence here of production methods technology having a life of its own. No mysteries of self-actuated machine processes need to be invoked to account for the observed variation in the means of production, either in one country through time or among countries at a single time. The actual patterns of technological choice lend themselves to fairly straightforward explanation. Industrial managers and their engineer surrogates selected (or developed) those means of production which best satisfied the capitalist economic criteria for the operation of their enterprises. Similar considerations apply to the other major part of production technology—the organization and integration of production work.

Organizing and Integrating Work

A division of labor is an indispensable feature of automobile production. It is inconceivable that a single person could fabricate and assemble all of the main materials and functional components of a motor vehicle. Within that limitation, however, a great many alternatives are possible for the division of labor, both in ways of organizing and integrating the specialized work and in the decision processes that are needed to integrate the division of labor. To consider this matter, it is first necessary to overcome a considerable intellectual bias, namely, the assumption that the division of labor and the accompanying decision processes that have been characteristic of the auto industry are in some way integral to and essential for the utilization of any kind of machine technology.

The main elements of division of labor are, for each person, the task to be performed, the physical means to be used to perform it, the variability that is possible in the performance of the work, the frequency of performance, and the ways by which the work of each person is linked to the work of others. In the auto industry (but also in mechanical manufacturing generally), the most characteristic pattern for division of labor has included three elements. The first is work simplification, which has meant ever smaller work tasks and more finely delimited work methods. The second is more specification, which has lessened variability in the ways of performing a work task. The third is maximum removal from the production worker of responsibility and authority for integrating his work with that of other workers. Terms such as *mass production* and *assembly line* have come to be used as generalized descriptions of this set of conditions.

The division of labor technology that selectively was installed and that operated for many years in the U.S. auto industries was particularly suited to the main objectives of managers who directed industrial operations. Thus, the micro division of unchanging work tasks first instituted by Henry Ford lowered production costs by raising the productivity of both capital and labor. More than that, by these means Ford was able to hire and quickly train workers with virtually no prior industrial experience. A new occupational category was invented: "semi-skilled." Getting work done with these rigorously controlled workers of limited skill broke the decision power of craft workers and craft unions in the industry. Management reigned supreme and unchallenged (until the CIO organizing of the 1930s) in its control of the growing industry, while being hailed as an industrial benefactor for paying the highest industrial wages and mass-producing the cars that transformed the U.S. life-style.

The U.S. auto industry's managers long were able to draw upon a large, new, industrially inexperienced work force from rural America, North and South. As its labor force increasingly comes from a more educated population, it is more than likely that the managers will confront increased worker opposition to their traditional pattern of work simplification plus mechanization plus work intensification plus work discipline policed by an ever-growing supervisory staff. New forms and intensities of worker resistance to these management policies manifested themselves recently in the General Motors factories in Lordstown, Ohio, where from 1972 on, a young, unusually well-educated work force rebelled against the managers of a much heralded showplace factory.

So common have work simplification and allied practices become in industry, and so dominant in the literature of industrial engineering, that they typically are assumed to be inevitable parts of industrialism. That is far from the truth. The progressive restriction of work tasks (work simplification) and repetition of identical tasks by workers are only two of many alternative ways of dividing work. Work tasks can be varied in content. Allocation of work tasks can be varied through time for each worker. Work tasks can be designed for performance by single workers or by small and large groups. Methods of working can include variations in the particular techniques employed. Workers can be decision makers in integrating their work tasks, including varying work assignments. Work simplification and task repetition have been preferred strategies of the auto industry managers bent on achieving both low production costs and maximum control over industrial workers. But there is no evidence of an autonomous technological imperative that has dictated these choices in division of labor.

Neither is there assurance that industrial productivity has been optimized by managerially controlled work simplification strategies. There has been little attention given to alternative conceivable ways for division of labor and decision making on production, within constraints of given intensities of mechanization.

The Locus of Decision Making

The prevailing methods of industrial decision making in the auto industry have led to little or no sense of connection or pride in the product and to alienation from the management and from the workplace. "Pride?" said one auto worker recently. "Nobody's proud of anything anymore. It's a job they come to because no one else will pay them more money." And further: "I think all blue-collar workers are taken for granted. I think deep down, most workers want to do a good job and take pride in their work, and if they're taken for granted this hurts them. If a car is built good, it's 'GM this and GM that,' but if something goes wrong it's always the fault of the workers."[10]

In the litany of the technology determinists, such worker attitudes derive from the mass-production process. The thrust of the present analysis is to distinguish between the methods of production and the decision processes that govern their characteristics and their use. The evidence from communities and industrial situations where workers have a substantial voice in industrial decisions indicates that both the reality and collateral feelings of alienation do not derive from the use of powered equipment in production or from a division of labor. Rather, alienation is traceable to the absence of workers' decision power over their work.

There is no characteristic of industrial products or of production processes that vests decision-making authority over production in managerial occupations. The idea that there are many conceivable ways of dividing and organizing work is reflected in a growing literature that seeks to open new options for *Work in America.*[11] An increasing number of industrial consultants has been focusing on the feasibility and effects of widening and varying work tasks (job enrichment). There is evidence too of the feasibility of workers' mutual and democratic decision making over their own work rather than control over workers by separate managerial occupations operating through authoritarian hierarchies.

During the 1950s I examined and reported in some detail on the internal decision-making processes of workers and managers in the factories of the Standard Motor Company in Coventry, England. These factories employed thousands of workers and mass-produced passenger cars and tractors. An innovative top management and the local unions formalized the operation of a "gang system" of production organization for the factories in their collective bargaining agreements. Under the system a worker group rather than a single individual was responsible for the output. Payment varied with the output of the group rather than with the individual. Under the gang system as practiced in the Standard Motor Company, the size of particular work tasks could be regulated by a worker group. Management typically was agreeable to modification in tooling for work as the easing and the mechanization of work contributed to higher labor and capital productivity. Management substantially reduced its supervisory effort over the workers; in fact, these factories operated without supervisory foremen.

All these arrangements functioned within a framework of an agreed "price" per tractor or per car produced. This price was expressed in number of man-hours worked in the factory per vehicle completed. Hence, at the close of a week if the output was, for example, 50 percent greater in relation to man-hours worked than agreed upon labor times per unit, then a wage bonus of 50 percent was paid to all workers and other employees in the bargaining unit. These conditions gave the workers not only high pay but also a substantial voice in the detailed allocation and conduct of their work. Management agreed to this development in return for the high productivity of labor and capital and lowered administrative costs which accompanied the gang system of production organization.[12]

The successful operation of these factories under these conditions casts doubt on the assumption that work simplification enforced by authoritarian managerial control is a necessary condition for quantity production of motor vehicles. More recently, renewed interest in alternatives to work simplification has drawn attention to efforts by the managements of the Swedish Volvo and Saab companies to organize parts of the vehicle assembly operations on a group responsibility basis instead of on the basis of the traditional management-enforced, simplified, repetitive jobs performed along an assembly line.

The above examples of important variation in work organization have occurred within the framework and at the side of managerial-capitalist control over the enterprise. It is worth noting, however briefly, that there is evidence of the viability of industrial enterprises in which there is no formal separation between final authority over the enterprise and the performance of production work. The evolving industrial development in Israeli *kibbutzim* represents more than 200 factories in which control over the division of labor and the ways of integrating it is vested finally in the industrial workers themselves. Furthermore, an investigation of the relative efficiency of these enterprises has shown them to be as good or better than conventional capitalist enterprises in terms of productivity of labor and capital.[13] This experience from larger and smaller industrial enterprises is not accounted for by the conventional wisdom that says mechanized work only can be performed to the accompaniment of job simplification, or that a division of labor only can be organized and integrated by managerial controllers.

Conclusion

Drawing on the record of the prototypic industry of twentieth-century mass production, I have tried to respond to the mystique of technology which holds not only that society is powerfully affected by technology, but also that man and society have become the creatures of the machine. Fortunately, the reality is that our machines can be given varying characteristics by our machine designers and builders.[14] Technology, within the limits set by nature, is man-made and hence variable on order. If one wants to alter our technologies, then the place to look is not to molecular structure but to social structure, not to the chemistry of materials but to the rules of man, especially the economic rules of who decides on technology.

Man's social—especially economic—relations are imprinted upon technology. It cannot be otherwise because there is no way to make technology that is abstracted from human choice, hence from society. Given variety in our knowledge of nature, choices must be made by and criteria for choice come from man and not from nature. Thus the product and the production system technologies of the auto industry have built into them the preferred economic criteria of the industry's decision makers.

It is therefore a warranted inference that technology does not, indeed cannot, determine itself. The physical and chemical properties of materials do not cause them to leap into the shape of man's artifacts. Only man, in fact, designs and shapes every particular technology. Once created and used, the given technologies have important bearing on man's life. But the location and direction of decisions to make particular use of our knowledge of nature derive from the power relations and the values which prevail in a given social system.

Notes

1. See the review article by George H. Daniels, "The Big Questions in the History of American Technology," *Technology and Culture* (January 1970), and the following papers.
2. Jacques Ellul, *The Technological Society* (New York: Vintage Books, 1964).
3. Emma Rothschild, *Paradise Lost: The Decline of the Auto-Industrial Age* (New York: Random House, 1973).
4. U.S. Bureau of the Census, *Statistical Abstract of the U.S., 1974*, pp. 550–53.
5. *Business Week*, 15 September 1973.
6. *New York Times*, 3 July 1974.
7. Seymour Melman, *Dynamic Factors in Industrial Productivity* (Oxford: Basil Blackwell; New York: John Wiley, 1956).
8. Ibid.
9. Ibid.
10. *Boston Globe*, 16 July 1972.
11. *Work in America: Report of a Special Task Force to the Secretary of Health, Education, and Welfare*(Cambridge, Mass.: The MIT Press, 1973).
12. Seymour Melman, *Decision-Making and Productivity* (Oxford: Basil Blackwell; New York: John Wiley, 1958).
13. Seymour Melman, "Managerial Versus Cooperative Decision-Making in Israel," *Studies in Comparative International Development*, vol. 6, 1970–1971, no. 3 (New Brunswick, N.J.: Rutgers University Press, 1971).
14. For numerous illustrations of the variability of design according to the criteria used, see Victor Papanek, *Design for the Real World* (New York: Pantheon Books, 1971). See the following Ph.D. dissertations which illustrate the detailed role of economic factors as determinants of design: John E. Ullmann, "Criteria of Change in Machinery Design," Columbia University, 1959; and George E. Watkins, "Cost Determinants of Process Plant Design—Central Station Boilers," Columbia University, 1957.

4

Confronting Power in Economics: A Pragmatic Evaluation

Philip A. Klein

All social sciences have in common their preoccupation with human interaction. Mainstream economics has traditionally preferred to assume that such interaction is essentially harmonious, if not because of the intrinsic nature of human beings, at least by virtue of their subservience to the Invisible Hand. Generally, institutionalists, following Charles Darwin, have always assumed that human interaction is essentially based on conflict; therefore, the pursuit of power by participants in the economy—the ability to prevail over others—must always be assumed.[1] Coping with this pursuit must, therefore, be a major concern of any social science.

Mainstream economics confronts the implications of concentrated power from two perspectives, one theoretical and the other applied. Formal theory was amended many years ago to incorporate oligopoly as a market structure intermediate between competition and monopoly. This effort to inject "realism" into economic theory remains to this day, we shall see, one of the least satisfactory aspects of conventional theory. In applied economics, the field known as industrial organization has attempted to measure concentration and to explore its implications for resource allocation via markets. It has led to a variety of possible evaluative insights—workable competition, interproduct competition, and countervailing power are among the better known—and all ultimately rationalize the status quo.

Outside the mainstream, radical economists have attempted to confront power in various neo-Marxist models of a class-based economy. Whatever else these efforts may have accomplished, they have not customarily focused directly on how resource allocation operates—by what criteria and with what results—in sufficiently precise a manner to permit evaluation of economic performance or confrontation of the policy problems the economy must face.

This article will approach the analysis of power and its economic impact from the perspective of institutional or evolutionary economics. Viewing the economy as both shaping and being shaped by societal values, it will, in effect, attempt to turn Anthony Downs's *An Economic Theory of Demrocracy* on its ear.[2] That book tried to use economic logic and economic methodology to dissect the operation of the political system. We shall argue that the perspective and approach of political science may be fruitful in studying the effect of power on the operation of the modern market-oriented economy.

Other social sciences have developed a perspective and vocabulary for considering the impact of power on human interaction. Mainstream economics, alone, we shall see, has developed a perspective and vocabulary, as well as a methodology, for avoiding the consideration of this issue. While, therefore, almost any social science appears to have taken a more realistic approach to power than has economics, the lessons of political science appear to be particularly pertinent and less often noted than, say, those of psychology.

The approach here involves a pragmatic evaluation in the sense that the initial assumption is that any theory must be judged against its usefulness in developing policy with which to confront perceived public problems. We shall argue that none of the approaches to power in contemporary mainstream economic analysis has significantly improved our ability to develop economic policy. Economics has continued to avoid the challenge that constellations of power present. Unlike democratic theorists within political science, who recognize concentrated power as a clear danger to the operation of the polity in conformity with the democratic ideal, economic theorists have either rationalized the danger that economic power presents to the competitive ideal, or more often have simply assumed away the problem. The implications of this state of affairs will be explored, and some possible approaches to improved economic analysis will be considered.

Defining Economic Power

Power can most simply be defined as disproportionate control over the decision-making process. Thus, "powerful" participants in an interactive process exercise more control than their numbers would suggest, and "powerless" participants less. As we have already noted, most other social sciences revolve around the myriad and complex consequences of this disproportionate deployment of power.

The distribution of both concentrated power and powerlessness, therefore, conditions the way in which the economy functions. Mainstream economics has customarily avoided consideration of the implications of power because it assumes that the distribution of income is given. Since the participants deploy power by using "dollar votes," the households and firms exercise power in accord with their control over dollars. In quite a different way, standard theory could be more realistic were it to consider the power relationships *within* households and firms. Economics has never been terribly interested in the interrelationships among members of households, and standard theory has customarily ignored most intrafirm relations as well. The field of industrial organization has considered, albeit fitfully, the implications of the separation of ownership from control. If applied economics has never been clear about what public policy was designed to achieve, it may be partly because it derives from pure theory, which has stopped short with the substitution of notions of Pareto optimality for the comfort of the Invisible Hand. Either way, power was no problem because the selfish pursuit of self-interest was conveniently transmogrified into optimal, if not socially harmonious, courses of action.

Many psychologists or sociologists are principally concerned with why individuals and groups fail to get along and with how they use power to achieve their own objectives. These objectives could be social or antisocial—both disciplines devote considerable resources to defining these parameters. Similarly, political science is most especially concerned with how power influences the outcomes of the interactions of actors on the political stage. A dictionary definition of *power* defines it as "capacity for action," the very quality which, while it might be equally distributed, is clearly *unequally* distributed among the participants in social interaction in the real world as viewed from the perspective of *all* the social sciences. That distribution, we reiterate, is in reality the principal focus for analysis in all the social sciences except economics, where the studious avoidance of that reality has been honed, polished, and embroidered into a fine art. It remains enshrined there, rationalized as "a simple and logical starting point" and as the "norm" beyond which the overwhelming thrust of standard theory almost never succeeds in moving.[3]

An Economist's View of Political Science

There is a commonality in the view taken by evolutionary economics toward political economy and the view of standard political science toward the analysis of the polity. A major theme to be developed here is that if standard economics were to adopt the general perspective of the dominant group in political science, one of the consequences would be not only greater realism, but also specific attention to the effect of power as, in fact, it is deployed in the functioning of the economy.[4]

One cannot fail to be struck by the preoccupation of political science with power. One of the better known political scientists, roughly comparable to Paul Samuelson in the basic text field, begins a major early section of his book with the caption, "Politics as Power."[5] More recently, a basic political science text was begun with this introductory comment: "This book is about politics and power. It is designed to give the reader some understanding of the basic nature of politics and government and of the role of power in political processes."[6]

Is there anywhere a basic economics text which begins: "This book is about economics and power. It is designed to give the reader some understanding of the basic nature of economics and of the role of power in economic processes"? The political scientist just quoted, Eugene J. Kolb, is following the basic approach developed by and associated with David Easton, who has argued that political analysis essentially involves the study of interactions. "Furthermore, what distinguishes political interactions from all other kinds of social interactions, is that they are predominantly oriented toward the authoritative allocation of values for a society."[7] And what do political scientists mean by "values"? Kolb defines *value* as "an object of human desire, something human beings pursue, and with varying degrees of intensity strive to attain."[8] They can be either "ego-centered acquisitive values" (wealth, power, respect, affection) or "moral values" (justice, welfare, and so forth). This view is a linear descendant of the perspective of John Dewey's instrumental theory of value, from which institutionalism has also drawn. It suggests that values refer to the attitudes drawn by participants in the social process from the institutional structure. Values (of both the sorts referred to by Kolb) clearly concern "what individuals and groups hold dear or prize."[9] What this view of a political system or of government implies, therefore, is that fundamentally the function of governments is to make "binding (authoritative) allocation of values."[10] This notion would appear to suggest that the political system both influences and is influenced or shaped by the values (priorities) of its participants and has the authority to force all participants in their roles in the system to abide by the commonly held emergent values. The power system must reflect the value system. Presumably, then, the political system is judged by how well or how poorly it reflects the contemporary value system, and over time it is judged by its ability to reflect changing values. That the system is a participant in the process by which values change is evident.

In the United States several years ago, we often heard that Watergate proved that the system could work. Presumably this meant that values were advanced which had not been socially legitimized (or about which there was at least some controversy concerning their legitimacy), and that the political process worked in such a way as to deny them legitimacy. (Executive privilege was perhaps an example.)

Such a view of political science is today not uncommon, and it is very much like the perspective taken by evolutionary economics. Eugene Meehan argues, for example, that "facts and values form an integrated unit that is broken only analytically," and that there are "remarkable similarities between the instruments used for explanation and the instruments used to make value judgments or choices."[11] He adds that to deny the possibility of defending value judgments with reasoned argument leads to what he calls "normative 'know-nothingism.' "[12] That is a quite reasonable description of what "positive economics" strives for.[13] If, indeed, economics is a "science of value," as Clarence Ayres insisted long ago, then Meehan's view of political science is essentially compatible with Ayres's view of economics.

In short, there is an ironic situation. Standard political science as viewed by most of its practitioners can at least attempt to deal realistically with power, because it, along with many other social sciences, does not make the normative-positive dichotomy as rigid as does standard economics. The result is that the discipline which prides itself particularly on the precision of that distinction cannot, in its "positive" guise, deal with the real world. Institutionalists follow the political scientists and so attempt to confront the real world, power included, far more explicitly than do mainstream economists. (We do not claim that mainstream political science has made spectacular progress. Much of its current thrust seems crude indeed. All that is claimed is that it appears to ask a number of pertinent questions, and that is a necessary first step.)

Defining Political Science

It is true that political scientists do not appear to define their field as explicitly as, or with the near unanimity of, mainstream economists. One recent definition, for example, states: "Political science is the study of men related by authority. Put another way, it is the study of who says what the issues are, what is to be done about them, and by whom."[14] Another argues that political science studies political systems and defines the latter as "any pattern of human relationships that involves, to a significant extent, control, influence, power or authority."[15] These definitions, whatever else one may say of them, lack anything approaching the specificity of, say, Paul Samuelson's well-known definition of economics.[16]

With the temerity of the *Auslander,* I venture to suggest that political science could be defined as routinely as is economics. Political science is concerned with the interactions involved in determining and channeling the evolving values of the polity, and with the distribution of the benefits, costs, and sanctions determined in the process of defining the rules of the game for living within a societal unit. Political systems are judged by their ability to achieve their objectives. In a democratic system, this means by how well or how sensitively the governance system reflects the current collective values of the participants in the polity. Similarly, an authoritarian system would be judged by how sensitively the system reflects the values of the authority.

Such a view of political science appears to reflect the current behavioralist view in that discipline. There are, of course, other views. As do all social sciences, political science has a conservative wing, a "positivist group," a new left wing, and so forth.[17] Clearly, defining "the collective will" or the public interest is difficult and perhaps impossible.[18] But the view of political science expressed by most contemporary practitioners at least forces the discipline to begin by analyzing precisely those aspects of the polity that economists, for their part, in the parallel situation prefer to assume away. Political scientists, despite the democratic espousal of "one man, one vote," appear to *know* that power is not equally distributed. They know that voters do not have perfect knowledge, even if a voter's knowledge of alternative candidates may perhaps be somewhat more complete (at least part of the time) than a consumer's knowledge of alternative products. Even if the public interest is difficult to define, political scientists have never, to my knowledge, alleged it useful to proceed as if there were abroad in the land any mechanism capable of automatically transmogrifying self-interest into the public interest. They *assume* from the outset that power constellations can thwart the political system in achieving its professed objectives, whatever they may be.

No political scientist would, I suspect, begin by declaring: Political scientists argue that given the existence of one vote per person and the principle of voter sovereignty—the principle that individuals should be free to use their vote as each sees fit—the play of open electoral competition will result in the most efficient allocation of values within the polity.[19] I suspect political scientists would not let this pass without questioning what "efficiency in the allocation of values" meant, and this would lead to some consideration of evolving societal objectives. Indeed, in terms of the prevailing view in postwar political science—that of David Easton—we noted previously that he regards political science as being concerned with the *authoritative allocation of values.* Instead of *assuming,* however, that the polity is making this allocation in any predetermined or predefined efficient way, Easton appears to believe the proper focus for political science is on precisely how *in fact* the polity does make such allocation so that, presumably, emergent societal values can make whatever changes in the political structures and/or their functioning that the participants in the polity deem appropriate.

Even the political scientist's assumption of one man, one vote is less troublesome normatively than the economist's customary assumption of a given income distribution (votes presumably are distributed more evenly than is income); furthermore, standard political science appears closer to the mark than standard economics. Assuming a "given income distribution," as institutionalists have said many times, renders Pareto optimality normatively sterile. Meehan understands this very well: "Pareto optimality, the condition in which any change or modification of the existing distribution of goods would increase or create social inequities, is a mathematical ideal and not an observed social fact. It is an appropriate assumption only when society can dispose of all the resources needed to meet the basic requirements of the population . . . without exception."[20]

In short, modern political science appears to grant that it is a "science of value"—that its chief role has to do with analyzing how values are determined in the polity and how, in fact, they are allocated. We have noted that the field is not explicitly defined—not with the precision of standard economics—and it is true that it has no neat body of assumptions and logical propositions flowing from them comparable to the paradigm admiringly called mainstream economic theory. But it tends to ask somewhat more realistic questions. It confronts (however imperfectly) the major problems and challenges thrust upon it by the actual functioning of the polity. It most particularly confronts the effect of power on the operation of the system.

Some time ago I commented that "political economy as valuation . . . is ultimately as closely related to political science as economics has always been to psychology. Total allocation is made by dollar votes and man votes."[21] This suggests that perhaps the alternative paradigm, which standard economists never tire of demanding of those who feel mainstream economic theory is inadequate for confronting economic problems, could emerge if institutionalists considered more closely than they have the political scientist's approach to understanding the evolving polity.

Social Scientists qua Scientists

It is worth pausing to ask why mainstream economists continue to be unable to incorporate power as it is exercised in our economy into their formal thinking on economic problems. The mainstream model continues unchallenged largely because economists regard any model less internally rigorous than their own as untenable. But other social sciences, typified by political science, manage to make some progress in analyzing their problems with less rigorous models. In this respect, much of modern political science appears to be closer to the other social sciences than does economics. Moreover, most social sciences appear to recognize more clearly and consistently than does "positive economics" that "the initial choice of a problem for investigation by the social scientist is often value laden."[22] In anthropology, for example, a recent and widely used textbook states: "When Malinowski called for anthropology to become an applied science in 1938, he began the debate over anthropological ethics that still continues, centering around two basic issues: objectivity and relevance . . . a growing number of 'action anthropologists' [argue that] refusal to become involved is tantamount to supporting the status quo."[23]

A similar debate about objectivity, relevance, and value judgments appears to be going on in sociology. A recent textbook comments: "Efforts to make sociology contribute to the solution of social problems are as old as the discipline itself, but the societal crises of recent times have given such efforts a new urgency."[24] This new urgency in sociology starts considerably ahead of the prevailing position in mainstream economics. The same authors quote the warning of a founder of modern sociology, Lester Frank Ward, written seventy years ago: "Sociology, which of all sciences should benefit man most, is in danger of falling into the class of polite amusements, or dead sciences."[25] Would any mainstream economist term the competitive model a "polite amusement"?

In short, it is not that the other social sciences do not distinguish normative from positive, insist on rigorous scientific procedures insofar as possible, or make appropriate efforts to separate fact from opinion. Rather, they recognize that prevailing community values are part and parcel of the problems they confront. These values are more than mere data—they enter into the analytical process. In this regard, therefore, political scientist Meehan was probably speaking for most social scientists when he wrote that "social science must . . . deal directly with the values that are accepted in society, seeking gaps and inconsistencies that can be resolved or eliminated, examining the justifications offered for existing standards, and accumulating evidence relating to the consequences of accepting particular standards for dealing with particular situations. Systematic criticism and correction of the operative normative structure is an essential and unending task."[26]

Economists would accept part of this view, but certainly not the conclusion, namely, that systematic attention to the normative structure is any part of their responsibility. Here, mainstream economists still follow Lionel Robbins very closely: "The fundamental concept of economic analysis is the idea of relative valuations; and . . . while we assume that different goods have different values at different margins, we do not regard it as part of our problem to explain why these valuations exist. We take them as data."[27] It is this view of economics as a "positive science" that prevents, among other things, confronting power in the real world in economic analysis. At issue is more than insistence that economic analysis should proceed by deduction from a simplified model that will be regarded as a benchmark. In the analysis of income distribution, no one objects to the use of a Lorenz curve; the 45° line serves a purpose. It is a benchmark, but it is customarily regarded as devoid of normative implications. If the analyst, however, devoted 80 percent of his attention to the 45° line and scarcely ever got around to the curve, one would be justified in declaring the discussion irrelevant, dull, or both. It is a reasonable institutionalist charge that mainstream economists devote too much attention to the benchmark and too little to reality. Their treatment of power—charitably described as elliptical at best—is a significant case in point.

Many of these weaknesses are revealed in the difficulty mainstream economics has in analyzing the public sector, an area in which theory provides few if any benchmarks. The size of the public sector has made it increasingly difficult for economists to ignore public goods, but they have no neat criteria for judging the results emerging from the public sector comparable to the presumed normative implications of private sector prices.[28]

The Paradigm Is the Problem

The perennial charge to institutionalists is to develop a better paradigm. This originally grammatical term refers to "a set of forms all of which contain a particular element," in short, the economist's penchant for model-building. Of all the models built by economists, the competitive model is the most fundamental. Our consideration of the approach of political science leads to one clear conclusion. In economics, as Figure 1 will try to establish, the paradigm is not the solution, it is the problem. Because power and power constellations do not fit the paradigm, economists focus their analysis on the functioning of the economy, as though power were atomized; in fact, it is anything but.

Economics has been led into this trap because, unlike other social sciences, which appear to focus directly on their problems and grope, however imperfectly, toward their solution, economists prefer to cling to a paradigm that reflects to them the economy in manageable form. Instead of analyzing the actual economy, they manipulate variables in the paradigm to approximate coping with real economic problems. Because power does not fit neatly into the paradigm, most economists usually simply ignore it.

Had political science developed a paradigm of the ideally functioning democratic system, it undoubtedly would have been constructed on a set of assumptions that combined, ideally, responsiveness to the collective wishes of its participants, as expressed in freely cast votes (one per participant), with some technique for ensuring that the collectivity and current expertise on each issue would be brought into unison. One could not have an ideal democracy if the majority could be in error! Political scientists then could simulate "real political problems" by manipulating variables in their paradigm. Obviously, this is not typically what they do. If, for example, they are concerned with the effect of corporate or union power on decision making through elections, or through congressional activity, they collect evidence of how such power has been used to manipulate the decision-making process. I doubt that political science students are asked to forget about lobbying, bribery, and so forth, for three-quarters of a term while an "ideal democratic polity" is carefully considered.

Were economists to confront their problems directly, there would be room for much of the conventional analysis. U-shaped cost curves, economies of scale, and a host of similar conventional constructs would prove valuable in analyzing how the economy does function. These techniques would be applied to real problems, instead of to ideal types in a world in which all the critical imperfections have been swept under the *ceteris paribus* rug.

A Tale of Three Paradigms

Since institutionalists, as already noted, are always being exhorted to "produce a new paradigm" if they do not like the conventional one of mainstream economics, I have tried to oblige. Figure 1 presents three paradigms—the mainstream, institutionalist, and political science paradigm. We have considered some of the implications that appear to emerge from Figure 1. Its essential message is clear and the conclusions obvious. First, if one compares the structures of mainstream microeconomic theory, institutionalism, and mainstream political science, one finds very many striking parallels between the assumptions, perspective, attitudes, and presumed results emerging from the latter two. Second, whatever bows to reality conventional economic theorists may have made, they have never rid themselves of the theory-as-benchmark psychology that prevents economic theory from confronting the critical reality of economic power. Third, whatever the faults and flaws of both institutionalism and modern political science, both attempt to confront the world as it is. This means, preeminently, that they begin by seeing the deployment of power in the economy and the polity as it is—not as one might wish it to be.

The remainder of this article considers the problem of confronting power in economics and pursues the notion that the example of the political science paradigm might be a good one for political economy as well.

The Normative Implications of Market Clearing Prices

If economics customarily assumes away most of the implications of power, mainstream political science appears to begin by assuming that the distribution of power is the preeminent conditioner of how the political system operates. Power is the prime determinant of most of the decisions that lead to particular market prices. Power and wealth are mutually supportive. One is used to acquire more of the other. Together they seep through most of our attitude-forming institutions and, in the process, affect mightily what consumers want, whether and to what extent pro-

Figure 1. *Three Social Science Paradigms*

	Political Economy		
	Mainstream economics	*Institutionalism*	*Political science*
Basic outlook	1) Invisible Hand (with imperfections) 2) Harmony	1) Cultural conditioning with technological dynamic 2) Conflict	1) Cultural conditioning 2) Conflict
Basic function of system	Allocate scarce resources	Express emergent values of participants through allocative decisions	Allocate values authoritatively
Basic mechanism	Market prices	Interactive value system	Interactive value system
Assumptions:	1) Primarily competitive interaction 2) Automaticity	1) Power distorts value system 2) Values result from interaction of system and participants	1) Power distorts value system 2) Values result from interaction of system and participants
Motivation	Self-interest	Perceived self-interest	Perceived self-interest
Assumed distribution of decision-making authority	One dollar = one vote	Control over constellations of dollar votes, reflecting concentrated wealth and power	Control over constellations of one man, one vote reflecting concentrated wealth and power
Objective of system	The end: market equilibrium (all markets cleared)	End-in-view: progress of economy consonant with emergent community values	End-in-view: progress of polity consonant with emergent community values
"Ideal" system	Pure competition	Decision-making process sensitive to changing views of participants in economic process	Decision-making process sensitive to changing views of participants in the political process

Ultimate arbiter of actual system	Consumer sovereignty plus technological progress	Technological change limited by concentrated power and big producer sovereignty	Concentrated power and big unit sovereignty
Result:	Efficiency and progress through producer acquiescence	Manipulated consumer	Manipulated voters
Basic units in system	Households, firms	Individuals	Individuals
Corollary:	Households and firms express demands (wants) and supplies (costs) through prices with optimal technological productivity	Both households' and firms' decisions are the result of power deployment by individuals	All political units' decisions are the result of power deployment by individuals
Result:	Socially ideal resource allocation	x-inefficiency; x-disutility Corrupt results of ideal systems (above)	Actual allocation of values deviates from ideal system (above)
Obstacle:	Imperfect knowledge of households and firms	Power blocs deliberately distort information flows	Power blocs deliberately distort information flows
Solution:	Assume it away	Improve information flows to individuals	Improve information flows to individuals
Welfare assumption	Competitive market equilibria define community welfare (subject to Pareto optimality constraint)	Community welfare as an "end" cannot be defined. The means for moving in the direction of greater community welfare can be discerned in the process	The public interest as an "end" cannot be defined. The means for moving in the direction of greater public interest can be discerned in the process
		There is a means–end continuum that enables the polity or the economy to progress along the continuum despite the absence of a definable absolute end.	

ducers will produce efficiently, and for whom products will be produced. Power constellations determine the information that flows through all the communications media. It is power that conditions economic participants' views as to what shall be regarded as "needs"—what must be acquired "regardless of price," and so forth.

It is clearly misleading to say that "the market" determines resource allocation, since power constellations have previously conditioned the market and determined the manner in which it will present choices. The manner of presentation frequently, if not usually, determines the choices made.

Economics has always set much store by the normative implications of market clearing prices. It is almost a cliché to note that certain areas, such as national defense, are customarily roped off from the "market test." More recently, it has become clear that the debate about energy cannot be resolved "in the market through prices." Public sector allocations are determined by a complicated political and economic process. The hallmark of that process, however, is that concentrated power plays a preeminent role. National defense and energy are merely dramatic examples of the fundamental normative failure of market clearing to render the judgments we customarily attribute to them. Or, if they render judgment, it is at the most trivial level. The questions "the market" poses for consumers are essentially rigged. In the final analysis, it is the distribution of economic power that sets the parameters for the market—that determines how the market will structure the choices offered consumers.

Political science, at least so far as I understand it, attempts to confront the impediments to the functioning of the polity as delineated in political theory. Political scientists focus on *precisely* those things economists customarily prefer to assume away—the ignorance of voters, the effect of vested interests on campaigns, the possibility of bribery and corruption, and so forth. Economists profess to be unconcerned "qua economists" about the economic counterparts to these concerns. Why consumers and producers vote as they do, how they make their decisions, all are aspects of consumer (or producer) decision making that economists prefer to assume away or ignore. Yet, the political scientist, for all the discernible faults in "the system," is forced (or simply prefers) to begin by considering precisely the questions that, in comparable situations, the economist shuns.

None of this should be taken to mean that nonmarket allocation decisions have any innate normative advantages. One might well be as uneasy with emergent allocation from a Gosplan as from "the market." Neither need be sensitive to the ideals of a democratic polity or economy.

Political scientists do not imbue with virtue the winners in political contests simply because they are winners. Why should economists applaud winners in the market? In both cases, one wishes to know how well, if at all, the winners conform to a slippery ideal—the collective judgment of well-informed choosers, all of whom have had some appropriate and meaningful voice in the selection process. It is in comprehending that voice that the major challenge lies, both in formulating welfare economics and in judging the results of resource allocation in markets.

Confronting Power in Economics: Two Other Approaches

It is clear that the very paradigm from which mainstream economics confronts its tasks prevents it from tackling realistically the implications of concentrated power for the economy's functioning. It is not surprising, therefore, that the principal applied field in economics in which power might be considered, industrial organization, has been mired in debate almost from its inception.[29] An applied field attempting to apply murky theory can be no better—it will emerge murky as well. What was the intent of the Sherman Act? Is bigness as such bad? Are there insuperable conflicts between size relative to the market (that is, concentration) and efficiency? Can one settle for a "workably competitive" performance-based economy and forget all these disturbing questions?

These and a host of related questions not only blunt the implications of power even as it might conceivably be included in conventional economic reasoning (for example, oligopoly theory), but also totally ignore their significant implications for what might be called the central allocative thrust of the economy. Industrial organization as a field does not worry about the political implications of power as it impinges on the economy.[30] It is not concerned with J. K. Galbraith's "revised sequence," or indeed about any of the myriad ways in which, for mainstream economics, the tail wags the dog. If institutionalists are correct in their view that emergent values condition the way the economy performs its essential functions, then surely one cannot avoid the implications of concentrated power for shaping and reshaping the emergent values.

There is one other approach in economics, in addition to institutionalism, that dissents from the mainstream: radical economics. Not surprisingly, radical economists' concern with concentrated economic power overlaps, to a considerable extent, that of institutionalists. They customarily refer to this power as monopoly capital. (In the United States it is more accurately called oligopoly power, but presumably this is hair-splitting.) We cannot here consider the difference between radical economists and institutionalists in any detail. From the outset, the two groups have moved in different, if occasionally parallel, tracks. Thorstein Veblen was no Marxist. He might have characterized Marxist theory as unduly teleological—at least, Marx appeared surer of where capitalism was going and what would succeed it than did Veblen.[31]

Today, the primary differentiation between radical economists and institutionalists would appear to be that the two take quite different attitudes toward the system we have and toward what changes they might proffer. Radicals denounce the system categorically, wish to overthrow it, and want to replace it with a socialist system. Institutionalists point the way in which the prevailing system, most especially its power constellations, prevent it from reflecting sensitively or accurately the emergent values of all its participants as they might develop in a freer economy. Institutionalists continue to take no position on what must inevitably replace capitalism, preferring to work on ways to open the information, communication, and influence channels of the economy so that, in the manner of the modern political science approach, something closer to economic democracy as a decision-making system can be achieved.

Power and the Economic System: A Final Assessment

We have discussed the customary approach to the deployment of power and its effect on the economy's operation by mainstream economists. Competition exists scarcely anywhere, but competitive theory provides benchmarks for what happens in actual markets. With a relative minor addition of ancillary attention to conglomerate mergers, and a few other new factors, the state of debate—whether in theory or in application—appears to have changed scarcely at all in many years. The situation has never been expressed more eloquently or more explicitly than it was by Robert A. Brady in 1943: "Democracy has slurred over the challenge to its very existence inherent in growing economic power."[32] Brady noted that "monopoly-oriented groupings" seek ever to enhance their leverage through more collusion rather than competition. They use political as well as economic means to achieve greater domination. He noted, too, that early orthodox economists (in the days, one supposes, of "political economy") understood all this, but that after the "lame synthesis" of John Stuart Mill, "the separation of economics and politics became an issue as important as the separation of church and state."[33]

I believe that Brady was absolutely correct, but neither his thesis nor his conclusions have been especially influential. The two major exceptions have been Dwight Eisenhower's celebrated farewell address, in which he warned of the dangers inherent in the "military-industrial complex,"[34] and the writings of Galbraith. Concerning Eisenhower, his words have rapidly taken on the aura of the Bible, which people regard as of some significance but rarely read, let alone ponder or act on. Galbraith is more complicated. In his Presidential Address to the American Economic Association in 1973, he suggested the critical importance of power—what he called "the planning system"—along with the market system. Galbraith contends that the "greatest debate in economics," that concerning the role of the state, is necessitated by "the power of the planning system." This position is not unlike that he has taken in a number of his recent books, but it leaves unanswered a question raised in earlier Galbraithian pronouncements. His invocation of "the conventional wisdom" as an at least mildly pejorative term for the views inspired by the system as we know it (including concentrated power) always sidestepped the question of how one differentiated "true" from "conventional" wisdom. This controversial question is an old one, and Ayres solved it, however controversially, by distinguishing the universality of the technological continuum (with its inherent compass for distinguishing progress from retrogression or stagnation) from ceremonialism. Galbraith has no such device, and one is left with the uneasy feeling that only Galbraith might be able to tell conventional from real wisdom. Of course, Galbraith himself is presumably immune from analytical distortions through the conventional wisdom.

One is left with the disarming question of where societal values legitimately come from, how they change, and how their evolution can be tracked. A number of writers have addressed these issues,[35] but the essential point is that the deployment of power plays a very large part. Power surely is a critical factor in comprehending the role of both the corporations and the state in structuring emergent modern societal values. That much of the story Galbraith was surely correct about when he wrote: "When we make power and therewith politics a part of our system, we can no longer escape or disguise the contradictory character of the modern state. Yet on all the matters mentioned—the restrictions on excessive resource use, organization to offset inadequate resource use, controls, action to correct systemic inequality, protection of the environment, protection of the consumer—remedial action lies with the state."[36]

What is not generally recognized is that the full implications of this state of affairs affect the operation of the economy in almost every dimension. It is not just that large corporations can restrict output and raise price from what "it otherwise would be"—the competitive norm. Indeed, the qualifiers which must be added to that case, including economies of scale, render the norm quite meaningless ("what otherwise would have been" is an uneconomically small unit of production in many or most cases, at least in the manufacturing sector).

Similar distortions emerge when power is factored into household analysis. We have already suggested that power *within* firms and households can well lead to what Harvey Leibenstein calls "x-inefficiency," to which may be added "x-disutility."[37] In this way power can distort the results emerging in the world on which mainstream theory has concentrated.

What attention economists have paid to power has generally been paid to differential power among firms. When evolutionary economists question the consumer sovereignty assumption of conventional theory, one factor they have in mind is that the differential power of firms to influence demand creation, as expressed by households, emerges in ways that cannot be predicted clearly. But it is obvious that firm-household interaction is not based on the independent self-interests of two presumably equal agents in market interactions. The normative implications of market clearing prices are surely affected thereby. Within households, too, individual members have disproportionate power ("x-disutility"), and the consequences of this for the normative analysis of emergent prices in markets has never been explicitly considered by economists. Who controls the purse strings in the American family? How have changing patterns of life, as in nonfamily households, altered power as deployed within the household, and how have these changes affected the economy's performance or its emergent values?

One is left with a complex situation. Power as exercised by agents in our economy affects not only the offerings of firms and the demands of households, but also the way in which the government is involved in the resultant economic interactions. It is frequently asserted, for example, that governmental regulatory agencies are themselves co-opted by the private units they presumably oversee. In short, virtually all economic decisions are affected by concentrations of wealth and power, either indirectly, directly, or both.

If the benchmark notion is all but useless, what remains? We must develop techniques for assessing the emergent values of the economy so that economic performance can be compared to those values. This is not so tall an order as it may appear. Political scientists do not spend their time exclusively preoccupied with the mechanics of elections. They are primarily concerned, or so it seems to me, with analyses of our current political system in the light of a perhaps vague but more than merely "positive" standard—that of representative democracy. And they concern themselves with what power concentrations do to the presumed equality of one man, one vote as an integral part of representative democracy. They know that political competition (free elections) does not automatically lead to the ideal of representative democracy, because the power over voters of various groups within the polity makes "representativeness" itself a complex norm.

There are critical differences as well as similarities between the challenges confronting political science and political economy. One critical similarity is that it is as difficult to define the public interest as it is to define community welfare. Still, most political scientists do not *assume* that what emerges from the political process *is*, definitionally, the public interest. They focus on imperfections in representative democracy, however slippery that concept may be. In assessing how choosing mechanisms actually function, political scientists can at least begin with a presumed equality in the distribution of votes. A preeminent factor complicating welfare analysis in economics is the inequality in the distribution of dollar votes.

Evolutionary economists have traditionally concerned themselves not only with what the economy was producing, but also with where the economy was going, or at least its direction. Assuming we could achieve the stable, full employment growth rate that both mainstream and evolutionary economists agree is "ideal," evolutionary economists would go still farther and ask where the fully employed economy is headed—at whose behest, and with what results? In this they echo concerns of modern political scientists concerning where democracies are headed.

Any economy at any given time operates as it does because of a vast network of decisions. This much is a commonplace and leads mainstream economists to argue that knowledge of how prices are set stands all economists in good stead, because even in nonmarket economies a central planning board would use prices to achieve its objectives. But such a board's planning objectives are—or can be—clearly stated, and the results emerging from the economy can be compared to that set of goals. There is a concrete way to judge the performance of that economy. In the modern market-oriented economy, such a standard simply does not exist, and we continue to muddy the waters by insisting that the "competitive ideal" can serve as a benchmark. As we have stressed here, when virtually none of the decisions are made as they would be made were power distributed in the economy as implied in the case of a truly competitve economy, mainstream economists have no way of knowing what a truly "representative" economy would look like. Who can say what goods and services would be demanded and at what rate, and at what costs in future goods and services, were allocative decisions free to emerge from participants, no one of whom had more influence than another? The problem is perhaps easier to see in the reverse situation; it is the distribution of powerlessness—widespread to be sure—that is reflected at least as much as the distribution of power in the operations of our economy.

In the final analysis, I think evolutionary economists do not argue for a system of imposing values from normative Big Brothers on the rest of the community. They argue for developing a system in which information flows are open, discussion is free and candid, alternatives are presented and known, and decision-making channels can reflect the outcome of all these deliberations. That would produce the economic equivalent of representative democracy. In such a system, political economists would be in the position of political scientists in that they could concentrate on the distortions the process might still reflect, and they could analyze the quality of the emergent system.

Conclusion

Watergate, we were told, vindicated the ability of our political system to "work." It is difficult to produce similar evidence concerning the ability of the economic system to work, for economists tend to accept the results that emerge as proof the system is "working." True, an occasional antitrust case arises, but economists generally do not ask whether the economy is performing as its participants would wish it to perform were all of them empowered in any "representative" sense to affect the outcome.

The economy itself and the choices it offers its participants are both affected by power concentrations. Moreover, the total choosing system is partly economic (dollar votes) and partly political (ballot box votes), and *both* operate differently than they would were power and wealth not concentrated. It is as inappropriate to focus on "free markets," as though markets really were free (making a few ancillary comments about "imperfections"), as it would be to focus on "free elections," making a few anciliary comments about "imperfections" in the democratic process. Economists focus on the free market, but political scientists do not devote themselves to "representative democracy"; they focus on the imperfections. In fact, it would appear that optimal progress in both political economy and political science could be made were the theoreticians as well as the "applied specialists" to concentrate on the imperfections. One writer, observing that decisions are made on a basis combining individual votes with the changes wrought by concentrated wealth and power, has suggested that the system we have might well be called a "plutodemocracy," suggesting the role of both individuals and "plutos," or wealth.[38]

If, as I believe, the proper study of political economy is the economy we actually have, then the perspective of political science would appear to point the way toward a reorientation of much of what the economist does. Anthony Downs may have shown what economic logic can do for political science; the potential in the reverse direction may well be far greater.

Notes

1. Many years ago, John Gambs noted that mainstream economics regarded coercion and exploitation as "atypical." He added: "The entire basis of economic theory is changed when coercion, or aggression, instead of competition becomes the dominant theme of economics" (*Beyond Supply and Demand* [New York: Columbia University Press, 1946], p. 13). At about the same time, Clarence Ayres wrote of "the sinister fact of economic power" (*The Divine Right of Capital* [Boston: Houghton Mifflin, 1946], p. 172). Even earlier, R. A. Brady wrote an entire book entitled *Business as a System of Power* (New York: Columbia University Press, 1943).
2. New York: Harper and Row, 1957.
3. The terms could be from almost any conventional microeconomics theory text, but they happen to come from Richard Leftwich, *The Price System and Resource Allocation*, 7th ed. (Hinsdale, Ill.: Dryden Press, 1979), p. 31.
4. We refer to the "dominant" group in political science because that field is methodologically and ideologically no more monolithic than any other. This point is amplified below.
5. V. O. Key, *Politics, Parties, and Pressure Groups*, 4th ed. (New York: Thomas Y. Crowell, 1962), p. 4.
6. Eugene J. Kolb, *A Framework for Political Analysis* (Englewood Cliffs, N.J.: Prentice-Hall, 1978), p. x.
7. David Easton, *A Framework for Political Analysis* (Englewood Cliffs, N.J.: Prentice-Hall, 1965), p. 50.
8. Ibid., p. 3.
9. John Dewey, "Theory of Valuation," in *International Encyclopedia of Unified Science* (Chicago: University of Chicago Press, 1939), vol. 2, no. 4, p. 58.
10. The phrase, as already noted, is that of David Easton, whose views are discussed further below.
11. Eugene J. Meehan, *The Foundations of Political Science, Empirical and Normative* (Homewood, Ill.: Dorsey Press, 1971), p. 144. Easton's view is only slightly different: "Ethical valuation and empirical explanation involve two different kinds of proposition that, for the sake of clarity,

should be kept analytically distinct. However, a student of political behavior is not prohibited from asserting propositions of either kind separately or in combination as long as he does not mistake one for the other" (*Framework,* p. 7).

12. Ibid., p. 145.
13. The classic distinction between normative and positive economics is that of Lionel Robbins: "Economics deals with ascertainable facts; ethics with valuations and obligations. . . . Propositions involving the verb 'ought' are different in kind from propositions involving the verb 'is' " (*An Essay on the Nature and Significance of Economic Science* [London: Macmillan, reprint ed. 1946], pp. 148–49).

    More recently, Milton Friedman, in *Essays in Positive Economics,* expresses this view of economics, insisting on a rigid distinction between what "is" and what "ought to be." He concludes: "I cannot remember when policy questions did not present themselves to me as dilemmas, which I would have to go outside formal theory to get my bearings on, and even then would find very heavy going" (reprinted in *Readings in Economics and Politics,* 2d ed., edited by H. C. Harlan [New York: Oxford University Press, 1966], p. 772). In recent years, Friedman has seemingly found the going less heavy, to judge by the profusion of policy statements he has made.

    Meehan's view of economics can be compared with the institutional view. See, for example, my "Economics: Allocation or Valuation?" *Journal of Economic Issues* 8 (December 1974): 789–811.
14. D. A. Strickland, L. L. Wade, and R. P. E. Johnston, *A Primer of Political Analysis* (Chicago: Markham Publishing Company, n.d.), p. 1.
15. Robert A. Dahl, *Modern Political Analysis,* 3d ed. (Englewood Cliffs, N.J.: Prentice-Hall, 1976), p. 3.
16. "Economics is the study of how people and society end up choosing, with or without the use of money, to employ scarce productive resources that could have alternative uses, to produce various commodities and distribute them for consumption, now or in the future, among various persons and groups in society. It analyzes the costs and benefits of improving patterns of resource allocation." Paul M. Samuelson, *Economics,* 11th ed. (New York: McGraw-Hill, 1980), p. 4.
17. Conservative political scientists follow in the footsteps of Leo Strauss, who charged "generous liberals" with appearing "to believe that our inability to acquire any genuine knowledge of what is intrinsically good or right compels us to be tolerant of every opinion about good or right or to recognize all preferences or all 'civilizations' as equally respectable." He himself favored "natural right" (*Natural Rights and History* [Chicago: University of Chicago Press, 1953], p. 5).

    At the other extreme are new left political scientists such as Alan Wolfe, who has written a book on repression in America in which he charges that "the traditional social sciences have ignored the problem, as part of their presumed objectivity, [which] indicates that a more accurate assessment of this phenomenon can come only through a commitment to substantial political changes" (*The Seamy Side of Democracy: Repression in America* [New York: David McKay, 1973], p. 23).

There also are positivists, not unlike Robbins in economics. Herbert A. Simons, for example, has written: "Factual propositions are statements about the observable world and the way in which it operates. . . . It is a fundamental premise of this study that ethical terms are not completely reducible to factual terms. . . . The task of ethics is to select imperatives—ought sentences; and this task cannot be accomplished if the term 'good' is defined in such a way that it merely designates existants" (*Administrative Behavior,* 3d ed. [New York: Free Press, 1976], pp. 45–47).

Clearly, there are diverse schools in political science, but the view alluded to in the text appears to be dominant today.

18. There are political scientists who argue that the public interest "is so vague a term as to be virtually useless" and so recommend abandoning it. See, for example, Frank J. Sorauf, "The Conceptual Muddle," in *Nomos V, The Public Interest,* edited by Carl J. Friedrich (New York: Atherton Press, 1962), pp. 183–204.
19. This is a slight rewording of Richard A. Musgrave's view of economics: "Economists have argued that given the state of income distribution and the principle of consumer sovereignty—the rule that individuals should be free to use their income as they see fit—the play of free competition will result in the most efficient use of resources" ("The Public Interest: Efficiency in the Creation and Maintenance of Material Welfare," in *Nomos V, The Public Interest,* edited by Friedrich, p. 107).
20. Meehan, *Foundations,* p. 234.
21. Klein, "Economics," p. 795.
22. The sentence appears in Nicholas Hobbs, "Ethics in the Social Sciences," in *Encyclopedia of the Social Sciences,* vol. 10, pp. 160–61, and is a view attributed to Edward Shils.
23. Fred Plog and Daniel G. Batos, *Cultural Anthropology* (New York: Alfred A. Knopf, 1976), pp. 70–71.
24. Melvin L. DeFleur, William V. D'Antonio, and Lois DeFleur, *Sociology: Human Society,* 2d ed. (Glenview, Ill.: Scott, Foresman, 1976), p. 21.
25. Lester Frank Ward, *Dynamic Sociology,* 2d ed. (New York: Appleton, 1911), vol. 1, p. xxvii; quoted in ibid., p. 17.
26. Meehan, *Foundations,* p. 208.
27. Robbins, *Essay,* pp. 94–95.
28. It should be noted that some analysts have considered the public sector and the process of choosing public goods. One of the major figures, already mentioned, is Anthony Downs, who in *Economic Theory of Democracy* attempted to apply the logic of economic theory to decision making in the public sector (toting up costs and benefits—preferably at the margin). This approach has been called a "positive" rather than "normative" view of government actions by Randall Bartlett, *Economic Foundations of Political Power* (New York: Free Press, 1973), p. 16. Downs has attempted to apply economic logic to political decisions in the public

sector. We are suggesting that considering resource allocation from the perspective of political science might be a valuable approach for political economy.

Recent efforts to appraise public sector resource allocation include Richard Musgrave, *The Theory of Public Finance* (New York: McGraw-Hill, 1959); James Buchanan and Gordon Tullock, *The Calculus of Consent* (Ann Arbor: University of Michigan Press, 1962); and James Buchanan, *Public Finance in the Democratic Process* (Chapel Hill: University of North Carolina Press, 1967). While most of this literature regards itself as positive rather than normative, it appears most often to conclude (normatively) that the role of government is "limited."

29. Writing of the situation some years ago, Carl Kaysen and Donald F. Turner commented: "Economists and economic theory offered little guidance to the courts. There had been little systematic thinking about oligopoly" (*Antitrust Policy, An Economic and Legal Analysis* [Cambridge, Mass.: Harvard University Press, 1959], p. 240).

A recent comment typifies the view taken in intermediate microeconomics theory texts: "The solution to the oligopoly model (that is, equilibrium price and output) depends critically upon the assumptions the economist makes in regard to the behavioral reaction of rival entrepreneurs. Since many different assumptions can and have been made, many different solutions can and have been reached. Thus there is no 'theory of oligopoly' in the sense that there is a theory of competition or monopoly" (C. E. Ferguson and S. Charles Maurice, *Economic Analysis, Theory and Application,* 3d ed. [Homewood, Ill.: Richard D. Irwin, 1978], pp. 397–98).

30. John Kenneth Galbraith has made this point repeatedly; for example: "The public policy which derives from the present view of price making in the industrial system involves the same contradictions as the theory and a roughly similar resolution. Monopoly is illegal. The market power associated with oligopoly or small numbers is not, in principle, presumed to yield different results. It is viewed with suspicion. But since it serves quite well, nothing is done about it. This evasion is then disguised by a great deal of peripheral litigation, and by the well-understood tendency for any learned discussion, if sufficiently voluminous, to obscure the issue" (*The New Industrial State* [Boston: Houghton Mifflin, 1967], p. 194).

31. As Allan Gruchy has said, "unlike Karl Marx, Ayres finds no laws of capitalist development leading to the inevitable demise of capitalism and the transition to socialism. Neither Veblen nor Ayres duplicates Marx's interest in the laws of capitalist development . . . both substitute a logic of capitalist development which is nonteleological in nature. Veblen asserted that the demise of capitalism was inevitable, but what came after capitalism was not inevitable. It could be either facism or socialism. [For] Ayres, the next stage in capitalist development is uncertain" (*Contemporary Economic Thought* [Clifton, N.J.: Augustus M. Kelley, 1972], p. 123).

32. Robert A. Brady, *Business as a System of Power* (New York: Columbia University Press, 1943), p. ix.

33. Ibid., p. 298.

34. I am told it was written by a political scientist.
35. See Klein, "Economics."
36. J. K. Galbraith, "Power and the Useful Economist," *American Economic Review* 63 (March 1973): 10.
37. Harvey Leibenstein, *Beyond Economic Man* (Cambridge, Mass.: Harvard University Press, 1976). Also see Figure 1, above.
38. Maurice Duverger, *Modern Democracies: Economic Power versus Political Power* (Hinsdale, Ill.: Dryden Press, 1974), p. 5.

Bibliography

Bartlett, Randall. *Economic Foundations of Political Power.* New York: Free Press, 1973.

Brady, Robert A. *Business as a System of Power.* New York: Columbia University Press, 1943.

Buchanan, James. *Public Finance in the Democratic Process.* Chapel Hill: University of North Carolina Press, 1967.

———— and Gordon Tullock. *The Calculus of Consent.* Ann Arbor: University of Michigan Press, 1962.

Dahl, Robert A. *Modern Political Analysis,* 3d ed. Englewood Cliffs, N.J.: Prentice-Hall, 1976.

DeFleur, Melvin L.; William V. D'Antonio; and Lois DeFleur, *Sociology: Human Society,* 2d ed. Glenview, Ill.: Scott, Foresman, 1976.

Dewey, John. "Theory of Valuation." In *International Encyclopedia of Unified Science.* Chicago, Ill.: University of Chicago Press, 1939. Vol. 2, no. 4.

Downs, Anthony. *An Economic Theory of Democracy.* New York: Harper and Row, 1957.

Duverger, Maurice. *Modern Democracies: Economic Power Versus Political Power.* Hinsdale, Ill.: Dryden Press, 1974.

Easton, David. *A Framework for Political Analysis.* Englewood Cliffs, N.J.: Prentice-Hall, 1965.

Ferguson, C. E., and S. Charles Maurice. *Economic Analysis, Theory and Application.* 3d ed. Homewood, Ill.: Richard D. Irwin, 1978.

Friedman, Milton. *Essays in Positive Economics.* Chicago: University of Chicago Press, 1953.

Friedrich, Carl J. *Nomos V, The Public Interest.* New York: Atherton Press, 1966.

Galbraith, John Kenneth. *The New Industrial State.* Boston: Houghton Mifflin, 1967.

————. "Power and Its Uses." *American Economic Review* 63 (March 1973): 1–11.

Gambs, John S. *Beyond Supply and Demand.* New York: Columbia University Press, 1946.

Gruchy, Allan G. *Contemporary Economic Thought.* Clifton, N.J.: Augustus M. Kelley, 1972.

Hobbs, Nicholas. "Ethics in the Social Sciences." In *International Encyclopedia of the Social Sciences.* Chicago: Crowell Collier and Macmillan, 1968. Vol. 10, pp. 161–66.

Key, V. O. *Politics, Parties, and Pressure Groups.* 4th ed. New York: Thomas Y. Crowell, 1962.
Klein, Philip A. "Economics: Allocation or Valuation?" *Journal of Economic Issues* 8 (December 1974): 785–811.
Kolb, Eugene J. *A Framework for Political Analysis.* Englewood Cliffs, N.J.: Prentice-Hall, 1978.
Leftwich, Richard H. *The Price System and Resource Allocation.* 7th ed. Hinsdale, Ill.: Dryden Press, 1979.
Leibenstein, Harvey. *Beyond Economic Man.* Cambridge, Mass.: Harvard University Press, 1976.
Meehan, Eugene J. *The Foundations of Political Science, Empirical and Normative.* Homewood, Ill.: Dorsey Press, 1971.
Musgrave, Richard. *The Theory of Public Finance.* New York: McGraw-Hill, 1959.
Plog, Fred, and Daniel G. Batos. *Cultural Anthropology.* New York: Alfred A. Knopf, 1976.
Robbins, Lionel. *An Essay on the Nature and Significance of Economic Science.* London: Macmillan, 1946.
Samuelson, Paul M. *Economics.* 11th ed. New York: McGraw-Hill, 1980.
Strickland, D. A.; L. L. Wade; and R. P. E. Johnston. *A Primer of Political Analysis.* Chicago: Markham, n.d.
Ward, Lester Frank. *Dynamic Sociology.* 2d ed. New York: Appleton, 1911.

5

Power and Economic Performance

Wallace C. Peterson

The problem of power and the economy is largely neglected in conventional economic analysis, the reason being that the classical heritage abstracts power from the picture. When competition reigns, power appears as an occasional aberration, not something worthy of serious and prolonged study. The viewpoint of this essay is different. It rests upon the proposition that power exists, that it is widespread, and that it is a phenomenon as "natural" to our economic order as is competition. Furthermore, it is maintained that power has been a factor of far greater importance than competition in shaping the post–World War II economic order in the United States. Thus, if we want to know how the economy works, we must understand both how power enters into the economic process and how it affects that process. Moreover, we cannot get to the roots of the crisis in contemporary market capitalism—a crisis dramatized by persistent and simultaneous excesses of inflation and unemployment—until we come to terms with economic power and its uses.

Power does not exist in a vacuum. What it is and how it works can be understood only if it is seen in the context of other crucial forces that have shaped the economic system in the last three decades. The two most important of these other forces are economic growth and the ongoing struggle over the distribution of income. The nature and interaction of growth and income distribution provide an essential backdrop for the analysis of power and how it comes into play in the economy. This view also dictates organization of this essay, which begins with a panoramic view of the economy's growth after World War II. Then, by linking income distribution to economic growth, the essential conditions are established for showing how power enters into the process and how it affects the economy's performance. It is the critical interplay among economic growth, income distribution, and power as it operates in the market side of the economy that has been the major source of the economy's unsatisfactory performance for more than a decade. This is the essay's fundamental theme.

Economic Growth in the "Age of Keynes"

The years from 1945 to 1970, dubbed the "Age of Keynes" by Sir John Hicks, represented for the U.S. economy a period of extraordinary growth and prosperity, a time when there seemed to be no limit to the material abundance the U.S. economy could attain. Sooner or later, everyone would share in the American dream—a home in the suburbs, two or more cars in the garage, a college education for one's children, vacations, and plenty of leisure time to enjoy boating, golfing, tennis, or any activity one fancied.

So accustomed are we to material abundance, it is difficult to appreciate fully the magnitude of the changes a quarter-century of virtually uninterrupted growth brought to American life. When World War II ended, only one-half of American families owned an automobile; now more than 90 percent have cars, and the two- and three-car family is no longer a novelty. It is the same story with practically all of the other durable consumer goods that have become commonplace necessities for the American life-style, one which is still being widely imitated across the globe. Television was virtually nonexistent in 1945, but now 97 percent of American families have sets, and 61 percent of them in color. Ownership of clothes dryers, room air conditioners, and dishwashers was negligible as the war ended, but today these are found in from one-third to one-half of American homes. Mechanical refrigeration is found in nearly every home, although in 1945 only one-half the families had such an appliance. Because of the transistor, radios are everywhere.[1]

In addition to the durable goods explosion that transformed the American home, postwar affluence brought other and drastic changes in the way we live. Superhighways and jet airplanes, also virtually unknown as World War II ended, made us a "society on the move," so much so that now it is more the exception than the rule for children, upon reaching adulthood and marriage, to settle in the community where they were born. The two- or three-week packaged vacation tour to Europe or other faraway places is not beyond the reach of middle income and working class families, although before World War II only the rich dared contemplate such a journey. The jet airplane has all but eliminated the ocean liner as a means of travel abroad and the passenger train as a means of travel within the nation. Along with the durable goods explosion came an explosion in higher education, fueled in part by the postwar "baby boom" and in part by a growing conviction that college was the magic key that would open the door to a good job, a good income, and the good life. Throughout the 1950s and 1960s it appeared as if there were no limits to job opportunities for the college trained, especially engineers, physicians, lawyers, businessmen, administrators, and even teachers. No more. As the boom in higher education collapsed in the 1970s, the economic worth of a college education came under attack.[2] Nevertheless, the vast transformations wrought in both the world of work and the world of leisure by the quarter-century of near boom conditions are not likely to be undone, even though they face drastic modifications as a result of market capitalism's current crisis.

There is no question that sustained economic growth became a material economic fact during the Age of Keynes. Less understood, perhaps, is that it also became a major psychological fact. By this is meant the belief not only that as a society we *can* grow more or less indefinitely, but also that we *must*. This idea has become deeply embedded in the nation's consciousness. As George Katona, a leader in the development of consumer survey techniques, observes: "In the twenty-five years after World War II continuing growth and a steady improvement in our standard of living were viewed as our *natural* destiny. In those years thousands of people reported to our interviewers that their living standard was better than that of their parents and grandparents, and they expressed confidence that it would continue to improve both for themselves and their children."[3] It is quite possible that modification of our faith in the psychological fact of growth will prove to be an even more difficult problem than adjusting to the growing energy and material shortages that impinge upon the real foundations of growth.

Before so many things began to come apart in the 1970s, there seemed little reason to question the doctrine of unlimited material progress for mankind, certainly not in the United States. The idea of material progress as a continuing process was born in the Enlightenment, took root in the nineteenth century, and reached its zenith in the 1960s. Fueled by the continued application of science and technology to economic production, more output and a rising material standard of life for everyone seemed assured. Economists added their prestige to the popular belief that a continued scramble for more production and more consumption was necessary, possible, and beneficient. In 1967, Walter Heller said he saw no reason why the economy should not grow in the decade ahead at an average annual rate of between 4 to 4.5 percent, a figure well above the economy's long-term historic real growth rate.[4] He was mistaken.

A major consequence of the emergence of the psychological fact of growth in the post–World War II era was the preeminent place growth came to occupy in the policy agenda of all modern industrial states, especially the United States. As E. J. Mishan, British economist and leading advocate of the viewpoint that growth is neither socially nor environmentally benign, points out, growth in the postwar era was not just one of a number of policy goals for society. It became the paramount goal, the one to which all others were necessarily subordinate.[5] Problems of unemployment, the distribution of the national income, the balance of international payments, and even inflation had to be handled within the context of their effect upon the pace of economic growth, regarded as the primary long-term objective for society.

After the exuberance of the early 1960s, disquieting signs appeared with increasing frequency, signs which cast doubt upon the possibility for continued material growth. Although scorned by mainstream economics, two reports by the Club of Rome argued that attempts to continue growing at the rates characteristic of the postwar era were doomed to failure, either because of the barrier of a finite supply of material resources or uncontrollable pollution. Among economists, Mishan has continued his struggle to persuade a profession wedded to a "more is better" ethic that the collective pursuit of economic growth has serious adverse effects upon the physical, biological, and social environment.[6] It has also been suggested that the long surge of real growth after World War II was a unique event, one which resulted from a special combination of circumstances. Among the latter were the availability of vast quantities of cheap energy and a "storehouse" of technology left over from the war.[7]

For whatever reasons, the engine of economic growth began to slow in the 1970s, not just in the United States, but globally. In this country, the most disturbing aspect was the sharp drop in the rate of growth of productivity. From 1970 through 1979, output per manhour grew at an average rate of only 1.4 percent annually, compared to 3 percent in the 1960s and 3.1 percent in the 1950s. The reasons for the productivity slowdown remain baffling, and no one knows whether or not the trend is permanently downward.[8] If the decline reflects a growing scarcity of primary products and the disappearance of cheap energy, then the future for material progress is not bright. There are troubling signs that these sources of growth may have run their course, even though Americans still have faith that technology will ultimately bail us out of our difficulties.[9]

Despite many disquieting signs, faith in growth as the ultimate solution to our problems, including inflation, remains strong, especially among the nation's policy makers. This was apparent, for example, in the 1979 *Economic Report of the President* and the response of the Joint Economic Committee of the Congress to it. For the first time in two decades, the minority and majority members of the Joint Economic Committee were in agreement, both in their reaction to the *Economic Report* and in the conclusions reached in their own report on the state of the economy. What brought about this unusual consensus was the committee members' belief that "modern economists have rediscovered the supply side of the economic model."[10] The practical meaning of this is that the ultimate solution to our problems is to increase productive capacity and put more goods on the shelves for consumers.[11] How is this to be done? The committee answer is conventional: The slowdown in productivity can be reversed if the rate of capital formation is stepped up, an objective easily attained if the profit prospects of the business community are improved. The rightness or wrongness of the Joint Economic Committee's analysis is not the major issue here.[12] What their attitude illustrates is the persistence and strength of the psychological fact of growth, an unshakable faith that, despite a growing sense of unease about our situation,[13] everything will ultimately work itself out if we can just get the economy back onto the track of sustained growth that prevailed during the Age of Keynes.

What the conventional wisdom about growth, rooted as it is in both material and psychological fact, fails to consider is that growth will no longer suffice to solve our problems. This is true *even* if the increasing physical and environmental obstacles to growth can be overcome, in itself a dubious proposition. To understand why, we must look again at how economists define their subject. Most textbooks start from the proposition that the material wants of human beings are unlimited, whereas the resources necessary to satisfy those wants are scarce. Thus we have the *raison d'être* for economics. Interest in growth naturally flows from this definition. After all, if human beings are to make headway in satisfying their endless list of wants, they must produce in ever greater abundance, which is what growth is all about.

Yet, such a definition leaves one uneasy, even if nearly all textbooks say that human wants are virtually without limit. Our common sense tells us that the gap between wants and resources ought to begin to narrow as a society grows richer, as more and more goods and services become available to its citizens. It is true that, since the Industrial Revolution, economic growth has lifted the vast majority of people in Western nations to undreamed of levels of material prosperity. We need not deny this fact, nor is there anything to be said in favor of the kind of wretched poverty that still exists in much of the world, including parts of the United States. The only cure for such poverty is more output, making more goods and services available to consume. But having said this, there appears to be a time in the life of advanced industrial societies when this common sense idea—that more output ought to lessen the overall intensity of the basic economic problem—does not seem to work. Things get topsy-turvy. More output fails to add to our satisfaction.[14] Furthermore, it is possible that growth makes the basic want-means dilemma worse rather than better, that growth spawns new demands faster than old demands are being satisfied. This is the darker side of economic growth, the paradox that makes it a source of the economic problem as well as a solution.

Probing the Paradox of Growth

Exploration of the foregoing proposition involves a venture into virgin territory, primarily because conventional economic analysis rarely questions its most fundamental proposition, namely, that wants are a "given" and virtually unlimited. But if this is not so, and if, as argued here, attempts to bridge the continuing gap between wants and their satisfaction widens rather than narrows that gap, a fundamental dimension to the science of economics is missing. Economists must try to account for the fact that no matter how great our material progress, the solution to the economic problem seems to recede farther and farther from our reach.[15] Let us begin to correct this situation by examining two important developments in the post–World War II era of affluence. The first involves the kind of economy that evolved during the long postwar boom, and the second concerns subtle but significant transformations in the nature of our wants during this same period. When viewed together, these developments take us a long way toward understanding why growth has become a chimera, why satisfying our wants remains such a will-o'-the-wisp. This analysis, in turn, sets the stage for explaining the strategic role that income distribution and economic power play in our continuing inflation and unemployment crisis.

The High-Pressure Market Economy

By any reasonable standard of comparison, the U.S. economy is enormously productive, a fact stressed in prior comments about the material transformation of the society during the Age of Keynes. Despite current problems, it spews forth a dazzling array of consumer goods and services at rates that would dumbfound the fathers of classical economic science. In 1979, for example, $6,844 worth of consumer goods and services were produced for every man, woman, and child in the nation. This could have provided the hypothetical family of four with a bundle of consumption goods worth more than $27,000, an amount far in excess of requirements for survival or subsistence. Of course, consumer goods and services are not distributed equally, but the figure is useful in offering some insight into the sheer power of the economy to deliver the goods.

In the process of getting to where we are now, however, we created an economic machine that works smoothly only within the confines of a "high intensity" market environment.[16] The system functions well, breakdowns are avoided, only so long as the economy continues to offer to the consumer an ever-increasing array of goods and services, many of which are unrelated to any major and important needs. A troublesome aspect of this situation is the close link between production—any sort of production—and income, a fact strongly emphasized by John Kenneth Galbraith some years ago.[17] When production falters, incomes falter, and the society is in trouble. However, more is at issue. The post–World War II production explosion, which, *pari passu*, allowed a greater and wider range of wants to be satisfied, brought with it more than just the economic transformation of society. Vast and profound cultural changes also took place as a consequence of the long postwar boom. In the high-intensity market setting now characteristic of our society, the entire culture has become strongly oriented toward production. The reason, according to William Liess, political scientist and professor of environmental studies, is that modern society represents the first "large-scale attempt to found stability and authority not upon . . . patterns of inherited privilege or traditional associations, but rather directly on the achievements of economic production and the satisfaction of needs."[18] This process, which began with the emergence of capitalism, reached its apogee about the time the long postwar boom began to falter in the late 1960s. What is most significant is that the dominant cultural thrust, strongly reinforced by all the media of mass communication, is for people to find satisfaction for their needs almost exclusively through consumption, especially of commodities. Possibilities through which the individual might achieve self-fulfillment in ways which do not involve the direct consumption of commodities and related services are tacitly discouraged. In the mass consumption, high-intensity market society, the behavior of an affluent minority is constantly held out as the "ideal" of a high-consumption life-style that everyone should emulate.[19] Even a casual observation of the "message" continuously hammered home by the advertising on commercial television will verify the validity of this observation.

Another major consequence of this transformation is a loosening of the link between the goods and services produced and the wants they are supposed to satisfy. Contemporary market capitalism produces such an enormous number and variety of complex commodities that it is extremely difficult in many cases to discern exactly what human want is being satisfied. There is not only complexity, but also excessive fragmentation of wants through the continued appearance of "new" commodities, each one only slightly different in either a real or imagined way from an existing commodity.[20] Today's leading washday detergent, the television commercials tell us, is always a drastically "new and super improved" product as compared to the detergent we bought last week, last month, or last year. This litany is reiterated for nearly every known consumer product.

The significance of the foregoing is twofold. First, it means that growing numbers of commodities are produced that do not correspond to any deeply felt need on the part of the consumer. Rather, they are being produced with the expectation that the necessary want can be generated once production of the goods is under way. In his *Economics and the Public Purpose,* Galbraith characterizes this as the "management of the private consumer," pointing out that it is a task of no small sophistication and one to which the giant corporations devote a significant portion of their resources. Through advertising (especially high-powered television advertising), through market research, and through vast sales and merchandising staffs, they push and cajole the consumer into buying the goods they produce.[21] Second, the consumer is left in a state of continuous agitation and dissatisfaction. No sooner is one set of wants satisfied by highly advertised goods or services, than new commodities and services appear, cleverly designed, packaged, and promoted to make consumers once again unhappy with their lot. This is not a matter of new wants emerging as a consequence of old wants being satisfied. Rather, it is a built-in characteristic of the high-intensity setting of contemporary market capitalism, a major contributing factor to the growing ambiguity between output and wants. Since it is obvious that the possibilities for product variation and minor change are almost endless, it seems inevitable that the consumer is kept in a state of permanent dissatisfaction. Therefore, the product becomes the determinant of the need, not, as traditional economic analysis puts it, the other way around.

If we accept this perspective on our wants and how they come into existence, it is difficult to argue seriously that a wealthy society like ours is grappling with a fundamental scarcity of resources. It is not a credible argument to apply to an economy capable of churning out almost $7,000 worth of consumer goods and services per person, even in a year of high inflation and less than full employment. Resources are not unlimited, here or anywhere else on earth. Nevertheless, it is plausible to argue that our basic "scarcity of resources," the stock-in-trade of the beginning economics text, springs from our high-pressure, market-intensive economic structure. This is just as persuasive as the more traditional view that resource scarcities are somehow inherent in the fundamental human condition.

Anthropologist Marshall Sahlins, in an essay entitled "The Original Affluent Society," challenges conventional economic thinking on this point. Although his main interest is to demonstrate that the usual historical view about the precarious existence and dire poverty in primitive hunting and gathering societies is incorrect, he also argues that capitalistic societies, no matter how wealthy, dedicate themselves to "the proposition of scarcity."[22] What he means is that in the modern industrialized market economy, scarcity is institutionalized; it is not an objective fact, an unalterable feature of the human condition. Rather, it emerges from the special characteristics of the market society. When almost all production and distribution take place through prices and the institution of the market, and when everyone's livelihood depends upon getting and spending, then a continued insufficiency of material means becomes the starting point of all economic activity.[23] In this environment,

> consumption is a double tragedy: what begins in inadequacy will end in deprivation. Bringing together an international division of labor, the market makes available a dazzling array of products: all of these Good Things within a man's reach—but never within his grasp. Worse, in the game of consumer free choice, every acquisition is simultaneously a deprivation, for every purchase of something is a foregoing of something else, in general only marginally less desirable, and in some particulars more desirable, than could have been had instead.[24]

These observations about wants and scarcity point up the fundamental dilemma of the high-intensity market economy. Bluntly put, it is that continued growth cannot resolve our problems. The faster we grow, the faster is the growth in our wants, as an ever greater array of commodities and services spews forth from the economic machine. Rather than mitigating the problem of scarcity, the high-intensity market setting exacerbates it. Thus, there is built into our situation a permanent contradiction between expanding total wealth and the continued escalation of material demands by individuals because of that expanding wealth. As long as there exists an increasing ambiguity between output and wants, and as long as a growing proportion of our wants are generated by production itself, we shall remain upon a treadmill, unable to quiet the increased feelings of dissatisfaction that now accompany more consumer affluence. This basic dilemma, this built-in contradiction of the system, is reinforced by the transformation of wants in the post–World War II era, a topic to which we now turn.

The Transformation of Wants

The problem of the high-pressure economy is not simply that wants accelerate more rapidly than output, that the "scarcity" problem remains, no matter how rich we are. It is also that a fundamental qualitative change in the nature of our wants takes place as growth proceeds. Six years before *The General Theory* was published, J. M. Keynes, in a little known essay, touched upon this possibility.[25] Human beings, he said, have two kinds of needs: those "which are *absolute* in the sense that we feel them whatever the situation of our fellow human beings may be, and those which are *relative* in the sense that we feel them only if their satisfaction lifts us above, makes us feel superior to, our fellows."[26] Keynes admitted that "relative" wants might be insatiable, but not "absolute" needs. The latter could be satisfied, perhaps within a hundred years, and thus the economic problem would be solved; it was not, as Keynes said, "the permanent problem of the human race."[27] Unhappily, the economics profession paid little attention to Keynes's insights, which, if pursued, might have permitted questions pertaining to wants and how they are determined to be brought into the body of the science. This was not to be. His 1930 essay had little immediate impact, since thereafter the energies of most economists were absorbed in coping with the depression.

As a matter of fact, the issue lay dormant until 1976, when the late Fred Hirsch, former Research Fellow at Nuffield College, Oxford, and former staff member of the *Economist*, published an analysis of why economic growth, although a compelling social and private goal in Western economics, often yields bitter disappointment and popular disillusionment when it is achieved.[28] In Hirsch's study, *The Social Limits to Growth*, there are strong echoes of Keynes's intriguing suggestion about two classes of human needs, although Hirsch's analysis is not descended directly from Keynes's rather casual observations in his 1930 essay. Hirsch's objective is much more ambitious. He attempts to show why, once the mass of the population in an industrial society has satisfied its basic biological and physical needs for life-sustaining food, shelter, and clothing, traditional ideas about economic growth lose much of their clarity, force, and significance. Consequently, the classical faith that an increasing material abundance for mankind will yield greater happiness and a more satisfying life is illusory.

Hirsch's main argument rests upon the proposition that the modern market system produces two major kinds of output (goods and services). In the first category are what he describes simply as *material* goods (and services), normally dealt with in conventional economic analysis. They consist primarily of products (and services) that will satisfy individual wants independently of the number of people consuming the same good or service. Thus, the satisfaction one gets from eating a meal, wearing warm clothing on a cold day, or being sheltered from the rain is not affected by the satisfactions others get from consuming the same things. Material goods fill Keynes's *absolute* needs, those that people feel irrespective of the situation of their fellow human beings. Since the availability of material goods depends directly upon resource supply and the efficiency with which resources are used (productivity), their supply is increased by economic growth. The *material* economy consists of "output amenable to continued increase in productivity per unit of labor input . . . . The material economy embraces production of physical goods as well as such services as are receptive to mechanization or technological innovation without deterioration in quality as it appears to the consumer."[29] Contemporary economists generally approach the questions about growth within this framework.

There is, however, a second category of goods, one which is largely unrecognized in standard economics, but which opens the door to understanding why affluence often breeds more discontent than happiness. These are what Hirsch describes as *positional* goods (and services). Simply put, their worth to any individual depends upon the extent to which the same goods and services are being consumed by others in the economy. They are akin to Keynes's notion of *relative* needs in that they exist only if, in the process of satisfying them, we are lifted up, or made to feel superior to our fellow human beings. A weekend home in the country, an exclusive model of a sports car, a rare painting, or even a college degree are positional goods whose value and satisfaction for the user derive from their scarcity, not in an absolute sense, but relative to other persons having access to the same good.

Unlike material goods, the supply of positional goods is not linked directly to the resources needed to produce them. A more subtle process is involved, because we are dealing more with social than physical scarcity. Two factors are at work. For some goods—rare paintings, antique furniture, or access to a unique landscape—there is an absolute physical scarcity. These goods cannot be produced as other goods and services are produced even if the demand is intense. The condition that makes the good important is socially imposed. Antique furniture is a case in point. Its value for want satisfaction—its emergence as a positional good, in other words—is a consequence of changing cultural and social values with respect to the usefulness and desirability of old furniture. The fact that the market cannot respond and "produce" more antique furniture simply adds the special dimension of physical scarcity to the broader fact of "social scarcity." Hirsch says that goods for which there is an absolute limit to the physical supply represent "pure" social scarcity.

The second factor involves both the intrinsic characteristic of the good itself (a weekend house) and the extent to which the good is available and in general use. The more widely used or available a particular good (or position) happens to be, the less are the advantages to the individual (and the worth) of having that good or position. To illustrate, when only a few persons have a college degree, it is a great advantage in competing for a job. But if everyone has the degree, this advantage disappears. The crucial point is that social considerations rather than material economic resources and their availability determine both the volume and ultimate worth of positional goods.

Hirsch links his ideas to economic growth and its frustrations by sketching out what happens when it takes place. Growth means there will be an increase in the output of Hirsch's first category, namely, *material* goods. There is nothing extraordinary in this. More output means more income, also a standard interpretation of the economic process. But higher income brings opportunity for persons to increase and widen their range of consumption, and here trouble occurs. As the real income of a society rises because of increases in the production of *material* goods, the pattern of consumption shifts toward *positional* goods. Hirsch does not specify the precise degree to which consumption becomes "positional" with growing affluence. He simply asserts that this happens as a society moves beyond devoting most of its energy and resources to the satisfaction of basic biological and physical needs.

Two important things happen as the nature of wants is transformed in a growing economy. First, prices for positional goods that are absolutely limited in supply inevitably rise. The demand for them increases with rising affluence, but rising prices choke off the excess demand. Thus, goods characterized by pure social scarcity remain beyond the reach of large numbers of people, even though the society is becoming more affluent. This will be a source of frustration for many. A different process occurs in the case of positional goods for which scarcity (and hence level of satisfaction from use) is largely determined by their extensiveness in use. Rising real income increases the demand for these goods, usually in disproportion to the rise in income. Goods and services in this category include education, vacation homes, travel, dining out, and a variety of other leisure time activities and personal services. Of course, prices for these goods rise under the stimulus of higher demand, just as is the case for positional goods in fixed supply. However, more than price increases are at stake. When growing numbers of people demand positional goods not in absolutely fixed supply (expensive cars, vacation houses, trips to Europe, and so forth), the phenomenon of "crowding" appears. Because many more people are able to purchase goods and services once available to a few, the "quality" of these positional goods is seen by consumers as declining. Increased consumption of positional goods by ever larger numbers of people causes them to lose their uniqueness, which is to say that the individual can no longer feel superior to others by consuming them.

Herein lies the false hope of economic progress. The implied promise of growth is that, in time, the majority will be able to enjoy the same level of satisfaction that the minority derives from access to positional goods limited primarily by social rather than material considerations. All individuals cannot have what at times is available only to a few individuals—at least without seeing the anticipated satisfaction slip away as their aspirations are realized! All too often, the fruit of material economic progress is frustration, despite the fact that market capitalism has been extraordinarily successful in satisfying basic material needs, the kind Keynes dubbed absolute. Yet, this material success, in combination with the transformation of wants into those that require *positional* goods for their satisfaction, has aroused expectations that cannot be fulfilled, no matter how great the material progress. This is the basic thrust of Hirsch's analysis.

The Distribution of Income

As the preceding discussion shows, economic growth brings in its train both an explosive expansion in new wants and a transformation in the basic nature of many of our wants. These developments alone are sufficient to pose some searching questions about the continued viability of a system strongly oriented toward a growth ethic. What makes the situation more serious is that the material development of the economy and the transformation of wants increasingly into positional goods has taken place against the backdrop of a pattern of money income distribution essentially unchanged since World War II. Table 1 shows the proportion of money income received by each quintile of families in the United States for selected years since 1947.

The story told by these figures is plain. Money income in this professed egalitarian society is badly distributed. The richest 20 percent of families take home slightly more than 40 percent of all money income generated in the economy, but the poorest 20 percent must be content with a mere 5 percent. This pattern has been unchanged since the end of World War II, although for a while the myth that incomes were becoming more evenly distributed gained currency.

Table 1. ***Percentage Distribution of the Money Income of U.S. Families, Selected Years, 1947–1978***

Quintile	*1947*	*1956*	*1966*	*1978*	*Dollar range, 1976*
Lowest fifth	3.5%	5.0%	5.6%	5.2%	(Under $8,720)
Second fifth	10.6	12.5	12.4	11.6	($8,720 to $14,700)
Middle fifth	16.7	17.9	17.8	17.5	($14,700 to $20,600)
Fourth fifth	23.6	23.6	23.8	24.1	($20,600 to $28,632)
Highest fifth	45.6	41.0	40.4	41.5	($28,632 and up)
Top 5 percent	18.7	16.4	15.5	15.6	($44,878 and up)

SOURCE: U.S. Department of Commerce, Bureau of the Census, *Money Income and Poverty Status of Families and Persons in the United States*, 1978, P-60, No. 120 (Washington, D.C.: November 1979), and *Historical Statistics of the United States, Colonial Times to 1970* (Washington, D.C.: 1975).

How money income is distributed—who gets what and why—is important in any society, but it is of near transcendent importance in the high-intensity market economy in which we live. There are several reasons for this. Most obvious, of course, is that a family's positioning in the income distribution pyramid determines what its share of the economy's output is going to be, the level of its *real* standard of life. More fundamentally, however, money in our society is more than a "means of exchange," a ticket of entry into the market. As sociologist Robert K. Merton maintains, "money has been consecrated as a value in itself, over and above its expenditure for articles of consumption or its use for the enhancement of power."[30] It is important to understand this, particularly in view of recent efforts by some conservatives to argue that, because of large-scale "in-kind" transfers to low income families (food stamps, housing subsidies, and medical care), income is, in fact, distributed much more equally than is commonly believed.[31] What counts for a family in this culture is the money income it receives. Monetary success is an entrenched goal in American culture, continuously reinforced by the family, the schools, and the workplace, institutions that are of major importance in shaping the personality and goals of every American. Money is the key to the American Dream, a dream for which there is no stopping point.[32]

One would normally think that the richer the society becomes—the greater the *real* income of the society—the happier it ought to be. If money and the things it buys are the ultimate measure of success in our society, it is natural to assume that growth will bring a greater sense of well-being and contentment. As Tibor Scitovsky observes, this rather obvious principle is basic to much of the economist's work: "The higher one's income, the more one can spend, and the more one spends, the more satisfied one should be."[33] However, this is not the way things work, a fact of paramount significance for the line of analysis pursued here.

There is, of course, no objective measure of happiness, but it is possible to find out how people rate themselves. One recent survey has done just this, not only for the United States, but also for numerous other developed and less developed nations.[34] Its findings, plus the evidence from modern psychology, underscore a crucial paradox about the relationship between money and happiness, one which throws light on the puzzle examined earlier, namely, why the fruits of economic growth so often are disappointing. It turns out that individuals equate more money with more happiness, but raising the incomes of all individuals does not increase the happiness of all individuals. Furthermore, the evidence shows that, by and large, there is no relationship (positive or negative) between happiness in a country and the level of its national income. But within any one country, and between different income groups, people in the upper brackets are, on the average, much happier than those lower on the income scale.[35]

The true significance of the unchanged distribution of money income that has existed since 1945 (and before) in the United States is that what counts for the individual or the family is *relative* income, the place one occupies in the income distribution pyramid. Only if the individual or family improves its relative position will its happiness level increase. A mere increase in absolute income will not do the trick, especially if it results from economic growth that raises the income level of everyone in society, but does not necessarily change the distributional pattern.

Now the stage is set for understanding a key element in the dynamics of the contemporary economy. Relative income is more important than absolute income for understanding the working of our high-intensity market system because people evaluate their achievements, status, and general material well-being, not in terms of the goods they have, but in comparison to the goods (and services) they think they should have.[36] What people think they should have is a social norm, derived from the cultural setting of which the economy is a part. An individual's consumption behavior is never independent of the consumption behavior of other families and individuals. By emulating the consumption of people higher up the income scale, individuals and families tell the world that they, in effect, have joined a higher status group. Remember, too, that the social norm—the goods and services people think they ought to have—continuously expands, partly because growth always spawns new wants, and partly because of the transformation in the nature of wants as growth proceeds.

When this process occurs with no significant changes in the distribution of income, the situation becomes explosive, almost certain to result in disappointment, anger, tension, and frustration. Why so? What emerges out of the combination of a static distribution of income and deep and widespread feelings about the importance of one's *relative* income position is an *aspiration gap*.[37] This is the distance between the standard of living people have and the one they think they ought to have. Its size depends upon the "changes experienced by individuals, groups, and nations relative to those of their 'reference groups,' i.e., those with whom they normally compare."[38] Some such gap has always existed, but it is only relatively recently that it has emerged as a factor of major importance in explaining endemic inflation. Its roots lie in two major developments. First, the success of growth in raising material standards of life, both in the advanced nations and across the globe, generated the so-called revolution of rising expectations. This is the belief that the process of growth will continue and that its benefits will be spread ever more widely. Second, vast changes in communications (especially television and the cinema), massive improvements in education and literacy, the development of low cost transportation and the ensuing movement of people, and the pervasive spread of high-pressure advertising have combined to make people everywhere keenly aware of the life-style of the affluent. Given this awareness and an unchanged income distribution, it is inevitable that the aspiration gap widens, especially in advanced societies. In this concept is the crucial link between income distribution and inflation. The greater the intensity of feeling people have about where they are and where they think they should be, the more they struggle to increase their share of the income pie. As a consequence, money claims run ahead of capacity, making inflation inevitable. Economic power makes this possible, the subject to which we now turn.

The Nature of Economic Power

In the analytical framework developed in this essay, economic power is significant for one primary reason: It is the major means whereby people and business firms gain control over their incomes. The struggle for more income, the striving to move up the income scale, is a crucial determinant of what the individual and the family get out of the economy, of how they share in what is produced. For the business firm, especially the giant corporations that dominate key sectors of the economy, control over income is the key not only to survival, but also to growth and expansion, the building of bigger business empires. Thus, if we want to comprehend how the economic system works, we have to understand the intensity of the struggle for income, and this we cannot do without coming to terms with power and the way it enters into the economic picture.

Power, according to Max Weber, resides in the capacity of a man or number of men to "realize their own will in a communal act *even* against the resistance of others who are participating in the same act."[39] For Weber, the essence of power is the potential to act. Furthermore, it is primarily a group action, even though the potential for action may be lodged in a single individual. Adolph A. Berle, who regards power and love as the oldest known phenomena involving human emotions, uses the word *power* to mean the "capacity to achieve intended results."[40] This definition is clear and straightforward, although it is only a starting point for understanding a matter of considerable complexity.

We not only must know what power is in the generic sense, but also must see how it comes into existence. This is necessary for understanding how economic power is used in our society. Basically, power originates in one of two ways. The first is based upon fear and brute force. This is the kind of power exercised by a bandit with a gun or a dictator with an army to command. This variety, although unhappily far too prevalent in our world, is not our major concern. The second form is the power that grows out of the allegiance, loyalty, and cooperation that people in any group accord to those who exercise leadership. This notion applies to groups ranging in size and nature from the family to the nation.[41] What is of key importance is that the *means* through which power comes into existence and is made effective is an *organization.*

We cannot overstress the importance of this point. It is especially significant for understanding the nature and origin of economic power in our society. The power we are talking about, the kind that makes a difference in the way the world and the economy works, is the power flowing out of the way in which we organize ourselves, our activities, and the social, political, and economic institutions that reflect organizational action. As Berle says in his monumental study, "power is invariably organized and transmitted through institutions . . . . There is no other way of exercising power—unless it is limited to the power holder's fist or gun"[42]

For the individual, this means that power is acquired only by reaching a position of authority and control within an important political, social, or economic institution. Power essentially is an attribute of the role people occupy in the key institutions of society. C. Wright Mills puts the matter as follows: "No one . . . can be truly powerful unless he has access to the command of major institutions, for it is over these institutional means of power that the truly powerful are, in the first instance, powerful."[43] Sometimes there is confusion on this point, especially in economics. Does this view mean that skilled and talented persons, especially those in the performing arts, in letters, and in organized sports, have no power? Not necessarily. However, we must distinguish between the persuasive influence exercised by talented people in any field and effective power, which is the capacity to make decisions involving control over the conduct and lives of others. Talent, skills, and other personal characteristics often are the basis for playing an influential role in society (as when a movie star endorses a presidential candidate) as well as being highly useful in gaining positions of power.

In economics, this confusion between influence and power usually centers around people with great wealth. The phrase "the rich and powerful" reflects such confusion, suggesting that great wealth always represents great power. In the late nineteenth century, and even the early years of the twentieth, great wealth and power were, perhaps, synonymous. The Rockefellers, the Vanderbilts, the Morgans, the Whitneys, and others of vast personal wealth did, in fact, also effectively control banking, railroads, mines, utilities, and much basic manufacturing in this country. This is no longer the case. Great family fortunes still exist, but many of the descendants of the robber barons of the last century no longer exercise effective power in the enterprises that evolved from the handiwork of their forebears.

These comments do not mean that in the corporate world, the prime focus of our concern, there does not exist an elite that wields power because it has effective control at the points at which crucial decisions are made. In this context, "elite" simply refers to the fact that, in all large-scale organizations, key decisions are made by a small number of people. It is thus in business, in the military, in governmental bodies, in political parties, and even in trade unions. As far as the modern corporation is concerned, members of the governing elite no longer belong to a readily identifiable class of the propertied and wealthy, as was the case in the nineteenth century. Today, the ruling elite of corporate America comes from a mostly middle class background. In achieving power, possession of the "correct" talents for moving up within the corporate hierarchy is far more crucial than circumstances of birth, upbringing, or social connections.[44] What counts, basically, is not necessarily who has the power at any one time, although obviously we cannot discount entirely the strengths, character, and personality a particular individual brings to a key decision-making position. What ultimately counts are "the chairs in the top offices," that is, those positions in the corporate hierarchy in which the crucial and strategic decisions are made. These are not so immediately obvious as one might think. Galbraith, for example, believes they reside in the technostructure, the complex of scientists, engineers, market experts, specialists in public relations, lobbyists, and managerial executives, all of whom make up "the guiding intelligence of the business firm."[45] Others limit them to the highest echelons of management, including a relative handful of wealthy shareholders who are also active managers or exercise a powerful influence over corporate boards.[46] In any event, locating the centers of power in any institution is not primarily a matter of identifying specific people, but the roles through which power is exercised.

Let us now be more specific. As noted, the object of power is control over income. In the economy, this pivots around four major areas of decision: (1) determining prices for the product or services sold, as well as the prices paid for goods and services used in production; (2) accumulating money capital and investing it; (3) innovating, that is, controlling the introduction of new products and technologies into the economic process; and (4) shaping the future direction of society itself, a power largely derived from the first three.[47] In the world of classical economics, these decisions are supposed to be made entirely in an impersonal way through the interplay of supply and demand in competitive markets. In that world, power simply does not exist. Reality is vastly different. The giant managerial corporation has captured effective control over these key areas of decision in the economic process. As Berle observes, the twentieth century brought with it one of the greatest shifts in the structure of economic power for which mankind has any record: away from the market, as conceived by Adam Smith and the classical economists, to the "bureaucracies of the vast private collectives called corporations."[48] Furthermore, power within the corporation has passed from the nominal owners (the shareholders) to the elite occupying strategic positions in the corporate bureaucracy. William T. Gossett, former general counsel for the Ford Motor Company, captured the essence of this shift: "The modern stock corporation is a social and economic institution that touches every aspect of our lives; in many ways it is an institutionalized expression of our way of life. During the past 50 years, industry in corporate form has moved from the periphery to the very center of our social existence. Indeed, it is not inaccurate to say that we live in a corporate society."[49]

The Concentration of Economic Power

Given the fact that, with the possible exception of government, the big corporation has become the dominant economic and social institution, we must answer two questions. What gives the business corporation its power? To what extent has power become concentrated in the corporation in this society?

First and foremost, economic (or market) power is an attribute of size. It stems both from *absolute* size, as measured by sales, assets, or any other of the usual economic variables, and from *relative* size, that is, size in relation to the market in which a corporation operates. Both enter into the power equation, although most efforts to measure economic power concentrate on relative size.

To define power as an attribute of size and to measure its pervasiveness through concentration stand the classical view on its head. Classical economics abstracts power from its analysis. It does so by assuming a world in which firms (in any market) are so numerous and so small that no single firm has any power over the outcome of economic events. But if this thesis is valid, in theory if not in reality, then its converse must also be true. Whenever firms are few and large, then necessarily they have power. We need not dispute this as an abstract proposition.

If size is the crucial determinant of economic power, the logical step is to examine the extent to which assets and production in the economy are concentrated in the hands of a relatively few business firms in crucial sectors of the economy. The reason is plain: Size and concentration are necessarily closely correlated. Thus, by examination of the facts on concentration, the pattern and structure of economic power in the nation is revealed.

Concentration of economic power and its effect upon the economy is not a new subject. In the late 1930s, President Franklin D. Roosevelt, alarmed by the mounting evidence of economic concentration, launched a massive investigation. The vehicle was the Temporary National Economic Committee, usually described as the TNEC. In his message calling for an inquiry, Roosevelt said: "The liberty of a democracy is not safe if the people tolerate the growth of private power to a point where it becomes stronger than their democratic state itself. That, in its essence, is fascism—ownership of government by an individual, by a group, or by any other controlling private power. . . . Among us today a concentration of private power without equal in history is growing."[50]

The TNEC investigation was probably the most exhaustive inquiry into concentrated economic power ever undertaken in this country. Yet, little changed as a result of the committee's work. In part, this was because the final report was neither forceful nor far reaching in its recommendations for change in the structure of the economy. Also, by the time the report was released in 1941, problems associated with World War II absorbed the interest and energies of the Roosevelt administration, Congress, and the public.

Aside from a brief flurry of interest after Roosevelt's 1938 comments on the dangers of concentrated economic power, the public has generally been indifferent to the subject. In the long post–World War II boom, economic concentration failed to arouse any passion, even among liberal and leftist elements in the Democratic Party, although they traditionally have taken the lead in movements toward economic and social reform. The situation remains unchanged, although the worsening crisis cannot be resolved without ultimately confronting the issue of concentrated economic power.[51]

What are the facts on concentration in the U.S. economy? Even though economists disagree on the precise way in which economic concentration is to be measured, the massive evidence accumulated by the TNEC and subsequent investigations shows a high degree of concentration and that the tendency is increasing. A simple but dramatic picture emerges from an examination of *Fortune* magazine's data on the nation's largest industrial and nonindustrial corporations. In addition to its well-known list of the 500 largest industrial corporations, *Fortune* publishes similar statistics on the 50 largest banks, life insurance companies, retailing concerns, transportation companies, and public utilities. These 750 corporate giants number less than one-hundredth of one percent of the more than 14 million business firms in the United States. Yet, this tiny fraction has assets worth more than *$2.4 trillion*, almost 40 percent of the national wealth.[52]

In 1978, these firms employed 22.4 million workers, or approximately one-fourth of the U.S. work force. Their combined gross sales totaled $2,191.6 billion, more than the gross national product. The *Fortune* list includes the names of companies that produce, sell, finance, or transport virtually every product or service known and consumed by the American public. These firms represent an accumulation of physical and financial wealth, productive capabilities, and private economic power unmatched in history or anywhere on this planet.

A special comparison helps to highlight the distance separating these 750 firms from the rest of the economy, even including firms with average assets of more than $1 billion. *Fortune* compiles similar data on the second 500 largest industrial corporations, a list also containing many firms that are household names. But these, large as they are in their own right, are dwarfed by those on the list of the largest. For example, the total assets of the first 500 industrial corporations are nearly 12 times greater than those of the second 500. Their sales are 12 times greater, and they employ 9 times as many people.

These comments suggest the extent to which the economy is dominated by a tiny proportion of the nation's business population, but they do not show another important aspect—the degree to which, *within* each of the major categories, a tiny handful of firms dominate. This information is contained in Table 2, showing the percentage of assets, gross sales, net income, and employees accounted for by the ten largest industrial corporations and by the five largest in each of the other major categories—banking, insurance, retailing, transportation, and utilities.

An examination of Table 2 reveals that the concentration of wealth and power in the hands of a relatively few corporations is far more pronounced than the totals drawn from the *Fortune* data indicate. In the industrial sector, a handful of megacorporations—only 2 percent of the *Fortune* 500 population—account for more than one-third of sales, one-quarter of the net income, almost one-quarter of the assets, and 17 percent of the employment. *This is concentration within concentration.* Similar patterns prevail in the other categories, where 10 percent of the firms are responsible for impressive percentages in all of the economic variables considered: assets, gross and net sales, and employment. An even more significant point is that this concentration among giant firms is an across-the-board feature of the U.S. economy. No aspect, from retailing to transportation, to power production and communication (utilities), to finance, and to industrial production is free from domination by corporate giants. Intense concentration is not limited to the industrial sector.

Table 2. ***Concentration among the Ten Largest Industrial Firms and Five Largest Firms in Other Sectors: 1978***

Category	*Assets*	*Gross sales*	*Net income*	*Employees*
		(in percentage)		
Ten largest industrials[a]	23.6	36.9	25.9	17.0
Five largest commercial banks[b]	41.9	42.3	39.0	36.3
Five largest life insurance companies[c]	50.2	42.5	49.4	42.4
Five largest retailing companies[d]	42.3	37.6	45.0	36.9
Five largest transportation companies[e]	19.9	28.8	25.5	34.1
Five largest utilities[f]	48.3	48.7	51.5	75.4

SOURCE: *Fortune*, 7 May 1979 and 16 July 1979.

[a]General Motors, Exxon, Ford, Mobil, Texaco, Standard Oil of California, IBM, General Electric, Gulf Oil, and Chrysler.

[b]BankAmerica Corp., Citicorp., Chase Manhattan, Manufacturers Hanover Corp., and J. P. Morgan.

[c]Prudential, Metropolitan, Equitable Life Assurance, New York Life, John Hancock.

[d]Sears Roebuck, Safeway, K Mart, J. C. Penney, Kroger.

[e]UAL, Trans World Corp., Union Pacific, United Parcel Service, American Airlines.

[f]American Telephone and Telegraph (Bell System), General Telephone & Electronics, Southern Company, Pacific Gas and Electric, American Electric Power.

Figures in the *Fortune* surveys are useful in providing an overall picture of the role giant firms play in the economy, but they do not tell the full story. For this we need additional measures. Two such are in common use, even though economists continue to differ with respect to their accuracy and how they should be interpreted.[53] The measures are *aggregate concentration* and *market concentration*. The former shows the proportion of the productive capacity or financial resources in a broad segment of the economy (such as manufacturing) that is controlled by a relatively few corporations. The latter shows the extent to which control in a particular industry is concentrated. The usual method is to show the proportion of production or sales in an industry accounted for by the four largest firms. The four-firm ratio is the best known and most widely used measure of concentration for particular industries. It is important to understand the distinction between aggregate and market concentration. The first is the broader of the two, providing an overview of power as it exists in major segments of the economy, whereas the second focuses on power in a particular industry or market.[54]

Now we come to two crucial questions. (1) What is the overall picture with respect to concentration in manufacturing in the U.S. economy? (2) What is the degree of concentration present in specific markets or industries within manufacturing?[55]

Data drawn from studies by John Blair, Willard Mueller, and others on overall (or aggregate) concentration point to one clear conclusion: Concentration is high in the economy and is growing. The well-known 1969 Federal Trade Commission study reported that in 1929 the 200 largest industrial corporations owned 45.8 percent of all manufacturing assets; by 1968, the 200 largest firms had increased their share of manufacturing assets to 60.8 percent. Other data show the same long-term trend. In his monumental treatise, *Economic Concentration*, the late John Blair examined seven separate statistical series that measure overall concentration. Spanning various periods between 1909 and 1968, the trend for each series was upward, thus lending strong support to the argument that the U.S. economy is not only highly concentrated, but also is becoming more so.[56]

The second question involves market (or industry) concentration. The standard practice is to calculate the percentage of shipments accounted for by the four largest firms. An industry is highly concentrated if the four largest account for 50 percent or more of shipments, moderately concentrated if the percentage is between 25 and 49, and unconcentrated if it is below 25 percent. Using these criteria, Blair reported in 1963 that approximately one-third of manufacturing industry fell into each of these categories, a finding that agrees with other studies. Until recently, the prevailing view has been that, despite an overall trend toward more concentration in manufacturing, there was no clear movement to more or less concentration in other sectors. Except for manufacturing, in the economy as a whole, industries with increasing concentration, as measured by the four-firm ratio, were offset by those in which concentration had declined.

This generalization no longer holds. Recent studies show that the average four-firm concentration ratio has risen since 1947, which means that market concentration at the industry level is rising along with overall concentration. This increase has been especially pronounced in the consumer goods industries, a development attributed primarily to advertising, especially on television. As the authors of a recent study observe, "high market concentration pervades much of American manufacturing. Some may quibble over the precise level and trend of concentration. But the indisputable fact of life is that in many industries production is concentrated in a few hands, has been concentrated in a few hands for many decades, and will in all probability remain so unless some explicit public policy initiatives are taken to change things."[57]

There is another reason to believe that actual concentration at the industry level is much higher than the standard studies indicate. The reason is that concentration ratios usually are based upon "raw" census data. These are not adjusted to take into account geographical limitations for particular markets, to provide a more accurate definition of market boundaries than is found in the census data, and to correct for the effect of imports.[58] When these adjustments are made, the "real" degree of industry concentration is much higher. University of Michigan economist William G. Shepherd believes this to be the case. For example, the raw data from the 1972 *Census of Manufactures* show that the average concentration ratio for all manufacturing industry is 39.9. But if the adjustments as described above are made, the ratio for all industries jumps to 58.7.[59] What does this number signify? Simply put, it means that, on the average and for *all* manufacturing in the economy, the four largest firms in each industry account for almost 60 percent of the output. Rather than only one-third of U.S. industry being highly concentrated, as earlier findings indicate, high concentration is a fact of life in almost all industries.

It is, of course, true that statistical evidence in economics is rarely conclusive, yet the data strongly support the judgment that roughly 1,000 corporations are responsible for at least one-half the private output of goods and services in the United States. Concentration of economic power and its continued increase is, in the judgment of Mueller, pushing us toward a "closed economic system, one in which price and other business decisions are made, as in the *Zaibatsu* apparatus of the Japanese, by giant conglomerate firms operating largely outside the disciplining influence of a competitive market economy."[60] We now turn to the effects of the trend toward concentration on the economy's performance.

Market Power and Economic Performance

There is little doubt about the widespread existence of market power in this economy, concentrated primarily in the giant corporation, but also present in lesser bodies, especially trade unions.[61] Our task is to analyze how market power is linked to the economy's chronic crisis, especially its systemic inflation. The crucial linkages are corporate pricing policy and the wage-price spiral.

It is no great secret that across a wide spectrum of economic activity prices and wages are "administered," or, as some may prefer, "managed." Alfred E. Kahn, chairman of the Council on Wage and Price Stability, described our situation succinctly when he said: "The fact is that most people in this country don't like the way a truly competitive economy operates, and have found ways of protecting themselves from it. . . . In much of the economy, for example, wages and prices are not determined by a process of competitive demand interacting with competitive supply."[62] The late Arthur Okun concurred: "Most of our economy is dominated by cost-oriented prices and equity-oriented wages. Most prices are set by sellers whose principal focus is on maintaining customers and market shares over the long run."[63] The widespread presence of administered prices (and wages) is a reflection of the pervasiveness of market power. Without it, management could not set prices, and labor could not negotiate wage rates.

What is not so obvious is the exact way in which market power in the corporate-dominated sectors is linked to pricing behavior. Given the fact that corporations possess substantial market power, it is tempting to conclude that there is a simple direct line between concentrated power and inflation. Unfortunately, this is not the case. The link is there, but it is neither simple nor direct. For more than four decades, controversy involving this issue has raged in economics journals. It is by no means settled—perhaps it never will be—but the dispute has brought a better understanding of the role of market power in the economy's chronic inflation. It now seems clear that the process linking power to inflation is deeply bound up with the behavior of the two key price- and wage-making institutions of this society, the giant corporation and the big trade union.

Gardiner Means and Administered Prices

Because of research by Gardiner C. Means in the 1930s, economists probably began to think seriously about the fact that there are *two* (not just one) processes by which prices are determined in the modern economy.[64] They can be set in a free market as a result of interaction between large numbers of buyers and sellers, or they may be set by *administrative* decisions, influenced to a greater or lesser extent by market conditions. Originally, Means tried merely to distinguish between prices which did and did not change frequently, describing the former as "market-determined" and the latter as "administered." He did not attempt initially to establish any relationship between seller concentration and administered prices, particularly because he found that inflexible or administered prices often exist in nonconcentrated sectors of the economy, such as retail trade. Later, in a more comprehensive analysis of the U.S. economy, Means concluded that the major factor which made many industrial prices insensitive to collapsing demand in the 1930s was administrative power over these prices. Furthermore, the source of this power was found in the "relatively small number of concerns dominating particular markets."[65]

By the end of the 1930s, Means had worked out the broad outlines of his "administered price hypothesis." Its main feature is the argument that the observed stability over the business cycle of many industrial prices stems directly from the exercise of economic power by large firms. Industrialization leads to an increase in the concentration of economic power; therefore, administrative control over prices gets built into the economy. At first glance, price stability should be a good thing, but it is not. In a recession, the downward insensitivity of administered prices aggravates the situation. It does so by shifting the impact of falling demand from prices to output and jobs. Thus, big firms in their struggle to maintain profit margins keep prices up but lay off workers and cut back production.

Interest revived after World War II in Means's administered price arguments, especially when the economy of the late 1950s confronted for the first time the baffling experience of rising prices during a recession. In contrast to the 1930s, when the hypothesis was called upon to explain why prices in some industries did not fall when demand dropped, Means and others used the assumed relationship between market power and administered prices to explain why prices would rise even when total—or Keynesian—demand is deficient. Means began using the term "administrative inflation" to describe *any* upward movement of the price level arising out of the exercise of market power, irrespective of whether the economy is in a recession, a period of stagnation, or a state of recovery.[66] In this context, administrative inflation can be applied to any specific initiating cause, such as an increase in wages, a decision of management to widen profit margins, or higher energy costs caused by OPEC. What counts is the fact that management has the power to respond to specific events by *administratively* raising prices. Since administrative inflation, according to Means, is endemic to modern industry, the only way that it can be dealt with ultimately is by confronting the fact and use of power in the concentrated industries.[67]

As can be easily imagined, the belief that administered prices were a source of price stability and output instability (before World War II), as well as a source of inflation (after World War II), and that they spring from concentrated economic power aroused a storm of controversy in the economics profession. One reason for the intensity of the long, complex, and even bitter debate is that Means's hypothesis challenges the most fundamental proposition of neoclassical economics. Basically, this states that, despite concentration, the economy remains essentially competitive, the "laws" of supply and demand are at work, and thus resources are efficiently coordinated and allocated by impersonal market forces. But if Means and others are correct in their view that crucial resource coordination and allocation decisions are made *administratively* through large firms with substantial market power, then neoclassical ideas about the nature of the economy and how it works have little relevance. They do not help us either understand the real world economy or devise the kind of policies required for effective economic performance under conditions as they actually exist. This is the theoretical crux of the conflict.

A major spinoff from this controversy has been the numerous studies that have tried in different ways to test statistically the validity of the administered price hypothesis.[68] The crucial issue has been whether significant statistical correlation exists between market power and the way in which administered prices behave. As often is the case with statistical attempts to test theoretical propositions in economics, the results have been relatively inconclusive. One economist has written: "The debate over administered prices was one of the less distinguished episodes in the history of economic thought. It was attended by much sound and fury, many attacks by critics who had not bothered to study carefully what they were assailing, and considerable jumping to conclusions based upon ill-conceived or faulty analyses."[69]

Two critical problems confronted these efforts. The first was the use of the four-firm concentration ratio as *the* measure of market power. Concentration ratios are a useful but limited measure of market power; they can never capture its full essence. Power is an institutional phenomenon, and understanding its full scope and deployment requires a thorough knowledge of the qualitative peculiarities of particular industries, as well as their quantitative characteristics. It may not be possible to develop broad generalizations that apply in all situations. Second, even the best price data available are far from exact. Most statistical studies of concentration and price behavior use Bureau of Labor Statistics wholesale price indexes. These are the most accurate figures available, yet they do not always represent faithfully what is happening to prices. Actual prices may be quite different from reported prices because many sales also involve a variety of price concessions and discounts, particularly when large firms are involved.[70]

Out of this controversy and the statistical evidence, three findings emerge. First, in the long run (itself a vague notion), there is little statistical correlation between market power (as measured by concentration ratios) and the inflation rate.[71] This conclusion is not especially important in view of the imprecise nature of the long run and the fact that over several decades a variety of forces in addition to concentrated power affect the economy's performance. Since 1945, the U.S. economy has been buffeted by two wars, vastly expanded federal spending in pursuit of the Great Society, and increasing concentration of economic power in the hands of a relatively few supercorporations. Second, during a business cycle, prices in concentrated industries behave differently from prices in the more competitive parts of the economy. During a downturn, prices in the concentrated industries fall less or increase more than do competitive prices, and in an expansion they rise less. The tendency of prices in the concentrated industries to *rise* during a recession was first observed in the 1950s and has become progressively stronger ever since.[72] Generally speaking, these findings tend more to support than disprove Means's hypothesis, although in no instance is the statistical correlation between concentration and price behavior strong. Finally, firms in concentrated industries show more willingness than other firms to accede to generous wage boosts, a factor that bears significantly on the wage-price spiral.

What are we to conclude? Certainly not that power is unimportant; quite the contrary. Market power exists, it is formidable, and, as the evidence indicates, it is growing in importance. The lesson to be drawn from the inconclusive results of years of statistical testing is that market power cannot be related to inflation in a simple, mechanical fashion. The exercise of market power is a discretionary act, one which varies with time and circumstances. This is why the construction of, say, a theory of market power is such a difficult task, one which continues to elude the economist. Economic theories are basically broad general statements to identify and explain observed relationships. Because of the discretionary element in market power, the relationships between concentrated power and inflation cannot be readily compressed into a single general statement.

Target Return Pricing

There does exist an appropriate framework—some call it a theory—into which both market power and the different circumstances that bring it into play can be fitted. This is the concept of target return pricing, a model of how large firms in concentrated industries establish prices, and it fits the observed behavior of administered prices over the business cycle.[73] The main thrust of this argument is that big firms do not try in textbook fashion to "maximize" their profits all the time. Rather, over both the long and the short run, their goal is to secure a particular rate of (or target) return on the firm's investment. This objective is possible only if firms have significant power to set their prices. The means to attain the target rate of return is a price markup, the addition of a specific percentage figure to raw material, labor, and other costs to arrive at a price that will ensure enough profit to attain the target rate of return. This process, also called full cost pricing, means that large firms set price markups in order to attain a targeted rate of profit, adjusting them as necessary and as the level of sales changes.[74]

The clue to what happens to prices in concentrated industries over the business cycle lies in the relationship of price markups to business costs. When demand and sales fall because of a recession, sooner or later the business firm will be faced with higher costs. This is due in part to the drop in productivity, which almost always happens in a recession, and also to the fact that the firm's fixed or overhead costs are spread over less and less production. Wages simply do not drop anymore in most industries, and material costs may or may not, depending upon whether the industries supplying raw materials are concentrated. Rising costs and falling sales squeeze profits, thus threatening the target rate of return. At some point, the firm responds by raising its price markup to protect the target rate of profit. Such behavior makes perfectly good sense for the business firm, although it is perverse from the standpoint of the whole economy, namely, raising prices when demand is falling.

When recovery comes and the economy begins to expand, there will be an approximate reversal of this scenario, but not quite. Recovery from a recession normally leads to some decline in costs, the reason being better productivity and spread of the overhead over a larger output. But since firms in concentrated industries are notoriously loath to reduce prices, markups automatically tend to increase during recovery. This creates price stability in the concentrated industries, since no pressure is generated to reduce markups. They may remain unchanged until the expansion has been under way for a long while. Costs then begin to rise. Material shortages emerge, labor becomes scarce and expensive, and efficiency declines as firms press against capacity limits; all these factors combine to push up costs, once again squeezing profit margins. Firms respond with markups in order to maintain the target rate of return.

Two important consequences for inflation emerge from this behavior pattern. The first is a ratchet effect, which pushes the price level continuously upward from one cycle to another. Prices rise in a recession, stabilize briefly during the recovery, rise in the late stage of an expansion, and then take another jump in the ensuing downturn. Because of the strategic importance of the concentrated sectors—which includes most manufacturing—what happens there reverberates throughout the economy, working its way into the cost structure of every activity, including services. The second consequence concerns unemployment. The only way to slow this process is to raise unemployment, for at some point the drop in demand that is tied to higher unemployment will have a feedback effect upon demand in the concentrated industries. This, of course, will tend to curb the power to increase price markups. But the more concentrated the industry, the deeper any recession will have to be before the anti-inflationary effects of rising unemployment make themselves felt. Thus, stagflation worsens as the economy drifts from one cycle to the next.

Is this the way the economy actually behaves? The evidence that this is an accurate picture is impressive and growing. In a 1976 study prepared for the Joint Economic Committee of the Congress, economists Howard Wachtel and Peter Adelsheim examined the price and markup behavior for 100 major industries during the five business cycles between 1948 and 1970.[75] Two main conclusions emerged. First, in all the recessions during this period, save the 1969–1970 downturn, a majority of industries in the high concentration sectors exhibited "perverse economic behavior," meaning they raised their price markups and hence their prices. Wachtel and Adelsheim used a four-firm concentration ratio of 50 percent or more as their measure of high concentration, the same used by Blair and others. What made the difference in the 1969–1970 recession was the intense foreign competition faced by the automobile industry, which caused producers to reduce the size of their markups. If the automobile industry is eliminated from the high concentration group, the average markup increased, as it did in all prior recessions. Second, this kind of behavior—higher markups and prices in recession—is spreading into the medium and low concentration industries, a development Wachtel and Adelsheim attribute to the growth of conglomerates. Since these tend to spread themselves across the whole spectrum of industry, they need not limit a pricing strategy involving higher markups in a recession to their activities in the high concentration sectors. Thus, the inflationary bias inherent in markup pricing spread throughout the economy, a development even the *Wall Street Journal* noted in 1976. "Get 'em up and keep 'em up," is the way one story opened, adding: "That order pertains to prices and it's coming from the highest levels of corporate management these days. There is no parallel with the traditional cry of bandits and holdup artists, businessmen contend." The reason for this push, the story explains, is to protect traditional profit margins.[76] Conclusions similar to those of the Wachtel-Adelsheim analysis have been reached by other economists, particularly John Blair and Alfred Eichner.[77]

The merit of the target return analysis is that it provides a logical framework into which one can fit a variety of specific events that "trigger" the inflationary exercise of market power, even when the economy is in recession. The downturn, as we have seen, may cause the firm in the concentrated industry to raise its prices, but other events may unleash the firm's power, including negotiated wage hikes in excess of productivity growth, or sharp increases in energy costs because of OPEC decisions.[78]

The Wage-Price Spiral

Turning from corporate pricing policy, we shall conclude with an analysis of the wage-price spiral, the other primary linkage between power and the current crisis. The term has become a shorthand expression for describing the way in which wages and prices continue to leap-frog each other, a process that occurs in both good and bad times. In a broad sense, the wage-price spiral exists because major corporate businesses normally have little difficulty in passing on (or initiating) large wage increases, and trade unions are able to push up wages despite rising unemployment. Its roots, in other words, lie in the interaction between corporate and trade union power. There are, of course, limits to the exercise of price-setting and wage-making power by these institutions, but currently these limits have little practical significance because they lie beyond the tolerable boundaries for recession and unemployment. Thus, the wage-price spiral acquires a life and momentum of its own, immune to standard Keynesian and monetarist policy remedies.

While it is generally correct that the wage-price spiral is a result of the interaction between corporate and trade union power, this does not tell us enough about the process, about how it works and why it has acquired such a momentum. As with the deployment of corporate power to increase prices, a variety of events may affect the way in which trade unions use their power in wage settlements. What is crucial is not the specific event bringing this power into play, but the extent to which wage settlements made in an institutional setting characterized by corporate and trade union power *exceed* annual gains in worker productivity. This is a delicate and explosive issue. Any attempt to point out how wage settlements are linked through productivity gains to wage costs and inflation invites gross misunderstanding. Since trade unions use their power to negotiate substantial wage settlements, some seek to make them the scapegoat for the wage-price spiral. But whether wages lead prices or prices lead wages is not the fundamental issue. What is basic is the fact that wages and salaries make up about 75 percent of the national income. Therefore, money wages are, as Joan Robinson has said, the main influence on the general price level.[79] Wage increases that *continually* exceed productivity gains are translated through markup pricing into higher prices. This statement is not antilabor; it flows from the simple arithmetic of wages, labor costs, and prices. Wages may still lag behind prices, as happened in the late 1970s.[80] When this is the situation, the scramble by workers to recoup real income losses pushes money wages up at an accelerated pace, thereby exacerbating the wage-price spiral.

Table 3 contains data from 1960 through 1979 that illustrate this process. If the current wage-price spiral can be said to have a "beginning," it was in 1966, when compensation per manhour jumped ahead of the growth in productivity. This reflected a breakdown in the Kennedy-Johnson "Guideposts," which, like the Carter "Guidelines," tried to control inflation by linking increases in money wages to productivity changes. Increased spending for the Vietnam War without a compensating tax increase triggered the initial inflationary surge, which gave birth to the wage-price spiral traced out by the data in the table.

Although the beginning of a continuing wage-price spiral is not without interest, of more immediate and practical concern is the question of why the spiral continues, particularly in view of the two fairly sharp recessions in the 1970s. As the figures in Table 3 show, however, wage gains (as reflected in the compensation rate) accelerated in both recessions, a clear indication of market power at work. The data also point up vividly the deteriorating state of productivity as a major factor in the worsening of the inflationary situation in the last half of the 1970s.

Unfortunately, there is no simple or single explanation for the persistence of the wage-price spiral. It appears, however, that power almost always enters into the way in which the key elements in the process interact. Scitovsky argues, for example, that our economy responds to virtually any shock involving costs with an inflationary upward drift in the price level because of power conflicts in different markets.[81]

What is clear is that wage increases in excess of productivity gains induce cost increases, and these, given target return pricing practices by large corporations, inevitably lead to higher prices. What is not so evident, however, are the mechanisms involved in the opposite situation, that is, how price increases initiated by firms in concentrated sectors spread throughout the rest of the economy. It is not the problem of rising prices in an expansion that is so baffling; it is the problem of rising prices in recession, even a recession as severe as the one experienced in 1974–1975.

As already suggested, a recession is the trigger that causes firms in the concentrated industries to raise their prices, which evokes a trade union response. In the high concentration sectors, where a rough parity of bargaining power exists between corporations and trade unions, corporate pricing practices always are a factor entering into wage negotiations. Since

Table 3. *Unemployment, Inflation, Productivity, and Labor Costs: 1960–1979*

Year	*Unemployment rate*	*Inflation rate*	*Productivity*[a]	*Compensation*[b]	*Unit labor costs*[b]
1960[c]	5.5%	1.6%	1.0%	4.2%	3.4%
1961	6.7	1.0	2.6	3.3	0.6
1962	5.5	1.1	4.3	4.0	–0.3
1963	5.7	1.2	3.4	3.5	0.1
1964	5.2	1.3	3.6	4.6	1.0
1965	4.5	1.7	3.4	3.5	0.1
1966	*3.8*	*2.9*	*2.5*	*6.1*	*3.5*
1967	3.8	2.9	1.6	5.5	3.8
1968	3.6	4.2	3.2	7.3	4.0
1969	3.5	5.4	–0.3	6.3	6.7
1970[c]	4.9	5.9	0.1	6.7	6.5
1971	5.9	4.3	3.1	6.7	3.5
1972	5.6	3.3	3.7	6.5	2.8
1973	4.9	6.2	1.7	7.8	6.0
1974[c]	5.6	10.9	–3.1	9.1	12.7
1975[c]	8.5	9.1	1.9	9.9	7.9
1976	7.7	5.8	3.5	8.3	4.7
1977	7.0	6.5	1.6	8.0	6.3
1978	6.0	7.7	0.5	8.6	8.0
1979	5.8	11.3	–1.2	8.9	10.2

SOURCE: *Economic Report of the President* (Washington, D.C.: U.S. Government Printing Office, 1980), pp. 237, 247, 259.
NOTE: All figures except unemployment represent annual rates of change.
[a]Output per man-hour in the nonfarm business sector.
[b]Per man-hour in the nonfarm business sector.
[c]Recession year.

changes in wage bargains usually have to be justified by changes in circumstances, when corporations raise their prices it is comparatively easy for trade union leaders to argue that it is only fair that wages also be increased. Ever since Walter Reuther demanded that General Motors "open its books," the intertwined issues of fairness and ability to pay have entered into wage negotiations between big firms and big unions.

What is crucial is how these wage increases spread across the economy, especially since workers organized into trade unions are in a minority in the United States. Several factors are involved. First, it is well established in all major industrial countries that wages in the nonunionized sectors rise roughly in parallel with wages for organized workers.[82] This means that wage negotiations in the concentrated sectors influence far more workers than those immediately involved. Second, the "communications revolution" makes almost everyone, everywhere, aware of what is happening throughout the economy, especially who is getting what through collective bargaining. Finally—and this is, perhaps, the most important factor—the notion of "fairness" has become a crucial element in explaining what happens to wages. Fairness is not easily defined or readily measured, but that does not mean we should underestimate its force in wage settlements. Nobel Laureate John Hicks says that its essence lies in the worker himself feeling that he is being treated fairly.[83] It is "unfair" if prices are rising and wages are not rising in the same proportion; it is "unfair" if wages go up for some workers and not for others. What this means is that labor scarcity is no longer a key factor in explaining why wages in so many industries continue to rise, even during a slump. Whenever wages rise in the dominant sectors—where the big trade unions hold sway—workers elsewhere feel they are being left behind and therefore unfairly treated. As a consequence, enormous social pressures are generated for them to catch up, creating a situation in which wages rise in slumps just about as much as they do in booms. This is how Hicks sees fairness working to spread wage increases, irrespective of market conditions prevailing in particular industries. Both the uniformity and rapidity with which wage increases spread across all sectors in most noncommunist industrialized states are thoroughly documented.[84] Furthermore, a kind of reverse money illusion speeds the process. This is the common belief that prices are rising even faster than is actually the case, which leads people to believe they are falling behind ever more rapidly.[85]

The rapidity with which wage increases spread out from the concentrated sectors, especially when they run well ahead of productivity gains, provides the necessary link to price inflation in other parts of the economy. That inflation is particularly felt in industries supplying basic necessities (food, shelter, energy, and health care), where prices have been rising more rapidly than prices in general. Since parts of these basic industries are competitive, it is important to understand the exact nature of this link. True, only firms with substantial market power can raise prices administratively in a recession, but market forces work to push prices up for virtually *all* firms when they are confronted with a *general* increase in costs. Even conventional economic theory says this will happen. Once we admit power as well as competition into the picture, prices acquire another function, one not usually stressed in the textbooks. Prices become a "cost coverer" as well as a "resource allocator."[86] The textbooks have much to say about the latter function, but virtually ignore the former. Yet, we cannot make sense of the wage-price spiral without taking the cost-covering function into account. Price increases originating in the concentrated sectors generate an upsurge in wage costs, and this spreads throughout the economy, even into those areas where prices are competitively determined, as is the case for many services. Everywhere, prices respond. In the background stands the commitment to high employment, which ensures that unemployment and the deflation of spending will not be allowed to go far enough to end or reverse the wage-price spiral. This commitment, in other words, provides the necessary elbow room for the exercise of power. Paradoxically, the fact of power and its use has largely rendered ineffective the traditional monetary and fiscal instruments for economic management.

A Concluding Comment

It is worth noting that the purpose of economics involves more than seeking to unravel the complexities of the world in which we live. As John H. Williams, a former president of the American Economic Association, once said: "Economic theory seems pointless unless it is aimed at what to do."[87] What do we do? Obviously, the end of a long diagnostic and analytical essay is not the proper place for a list of specific proposals for coping with our economic malaise; that task deserves a much fuller treatment. But it is appropriate to say a word or two about the direction any proposals must take.

In retrospect, the element in the picture drawn here that is of overriding significance is income and its distribution. It is the static distribution of income, in juxtaposition to exploding and changing wants brought about by economic growth, that makes power and its deployment so important. Power in the corporations and power in the trade unions are in collision, pushing the economy into a wage-price spiral from which there is no easy escape, even when the slump comes. Concentration in corporations and in the ownership of wealth go hand in hand, tending to keep the distribution of income unequal and static. Society is being pulled in opposite directions by spreading notions of "fairness," especially in the matter of wages. Thus, the struggle over income intensifies. We lack understanding and viable proposals in two critical areas. First, we have not yet found an effective means for bringing private corporate power under social control; second, society lacks a meaningful consensus on income distribution, a consensus embodying the belief that it is being distributed justly although not perfectly. In these areas there is crucial work for the economist in the 1980s.

Notes

1. Figures are for 1974 and are taken from *Statistical Abstract of the United States* (Washington, D.C.: U.S. Government Printing Office, 1979).
2. See, for example, Richard Freeman and J. Herbert Hollormon, "The Declining Value of a College Education," *Change* 7 (September 1975): 24–31; and James O'Toole, "The Reserve Army of the Underemployed," *Change* 7 (May-June 1975): 26–33.
3. George Katona and Burkhard Strumpel, *A New Economic Era* (New York: Elsevier, 1978), p. 46, italics added.
4. Walter W. Heller, *New Dimensions of Political Economy* (New York: W. W. Norton, 1967), p. 105.
5. E. J. Mishan, *The Economic Growth Debate: An Assessment* (London: George Allen & Unwin, 1977), p. 26.
6. As Mishan argues, the issue is not, and never has been, whether or not people as individuals are better off by having more worldly goods in their possession than fewer, whether or not it is better to be nonpoor than poor. The fundamental issue is whether or not the collective pursuit of growth results in such damage to the environment that the social costs exceed the benefits.
7. See Fred C. Allvine and Fred A. Tarpley, Jr., *The New State of the Economy* (Cambridge, Mass.: Winthrop Publishers, 1977).
8. See *Economic Report of the President* (Washington, D.C.: U.S. Government Printing Office, 1980), p. 247. Also see Edward F. Denison, "The Puzzling Drop in Productivity," *Challenge* 22 (May/June 1979): 60–62; and Campbell McConnell, "Why Is U.S. Productivity Slowing Down?" *Harvard Business Review* 57 (March-April 1979): 1–8.
9. See Lester R. Brown, *The Twenty-Ninth Day* (New York: W. W. Norton, 1978), pp. 182ff.
10. Joint Economic Committee, Congress of the United States, *Joint Economic Report 1979*, Senate Report No. 96-44 (Washington, D.C.: 1979), p. 87.
11. Ibid., p. 45.
12. For a sharp and bitter criticism of the conventional wisdom on the critical nature of the lag in productivity, see Richard D. DuBoff, "Productivity crisis—economists ride again," *In These Times*, 23–29 May 1979, p. 17.
13. For example, the Survey Research Center, University of Michigan, reported that increasingly, beginning in the early 1970s, consumers reported no greater feeling of satisfaction, even though the quantity of consumer goods possessed by them grew. See Katona and Strumpel, *New Economic Era*, p. 47.
14. Several important economists have reached this same conclusion from a number of different deductions. The findings of George Katona have already been cited. E. J. Mishan believes this, as do Fred Hirsch and Tibor Scitovsky. See, especially, Hirsch's *Social Limits to Growth* (Cambridge, Mass.: Harvard University Press, 1978); and Scitovsky's *The Joyless Economy* (New York: Oxford University Press, 1976).

15. Some may argue at this point that it is an error to suggest that the economic problem might ever be solved, that anything of the sort is implied by the conventional definition of economics. Perhaps, but it is well to remind ourselves that Keynes believed the *economic problem* might be resolved within a century, that the want-means dilemma was not the permanent condition of the human race. See his essay, "Economic Possibilities for Our Grandchildren" (1930), in *Essays in Persuasion* (New York: W. W. Norton, 1963), p. 366.
16. See William Leiss, *The Limits to Satisfaction* (Toronto: University of Toronto Press, 1976), p. 7.
17. John Kenneth Galbraith, *The Affluent Society* (Boston: Houghton Mifflin, 1958), p. 292.
18. Leiss, *Limits to Satisfaction,* p. 4. Much of the discussion which follows draws upon Leiss's study.
19. Ibid., p. 100. In a way there is nothing extraordinary in this. In a market society the primary social bond, the "glue" that holds society together, is the clear identification of the self-interest of the individual, which is expressed through maximizing his needs, with the self-interest of society as a whole. In this way, individual well-being is directly linked to more production, that is, a rising GNP. This, of course, is another way of saying that Adam Smith's invisible hand will, if allowed to work, maximize both private and social welfare. This also fits neatly into economists' definition of their subject and their implied faith in continued output as the ultmate answer to the economic problem. What is important to understand is the broader social significance of the belief in a permanently rising level of consumption. The latter has become the key principle of legitimacy for the modern market system, by which is meant the basic rationale for the continued acceptance of the *existing* distribution of wealth, income, and power. But if continuing escalation in the real levels of consumption is a proposition whose validity is increasingly open to question, then we cannot continue to avoid distributional questions.
20. Ibid., p. 26.
21. John Kenneth Galbraith, *Economics and the Public Purpose* (Boston: Houghton Mifflin, 1973), p. 137.
22. Marshall Sahlins, *Stone Age Economics* (New York: Aldine-Atherton, 1972), p. 3. What Sahlins argues is that, in general, the hunter-gatherer societies maintained an adequate level of satisfaction for their members and did so with a much shorter workday than is common today. Of course, their real level of living was low by modern standards, but it was not a substandard existence on the edge of starvation.
23. Ibid., p. 4.
24. Ibid.
25. Keynes, "Economic Possibilities for Our Grandchildren."
26. Ibid., p. 365, italics added.
27. Ibid., p. 366.
28. Hirsch, *Social Limits.* In 1958, the British economist Sir Roy Harrod touched upon this theme briefly in an essay written for the Committee for Economic Development. He suggested that there were certain types of

economic wants that would go unmet no matter how long economic growth continued. He never returned to the theme, however, in any of his subsequent writing.

29. Ibid., p. 27.
30. Robert R. Merton, *Social Theory and Social Structure* (Glencoe, Ill.: The Free Press, 1957), p. 136.
31. See, for example, Edgar K. Browning, "How Much More Equality Can We Afford?" *Public Interest* (Spring 1976): 90–110; and U.S. Congress, Congressional Budget Office, *Poverty Status of Families Under Alternative Definitions of Income* (Washington, D.C.: U.S. Government Printing Office, 1977).
32. Merton, *Social Theory*, p. 137.
33. Scitovsky, *Joyless Economy*, p. 134.
34. See Richard A. Easterlin, "Does Economic Growth Improve the Human Lot? Some Empirical Evidence," in *Nations and Households in Economic Growth: Essays in Honor of Moses Abramovitz*, edited by Paul A. David and Melvin W. Reder (New York: Academic Press, 1974).
35. Ibid., p. 119.
36. Richard A. Easterlin, "Does Money Buy Happiness?" *Public Interest* (Winter 1973): 4.
37. Milivoje Panic, "The Inevitable Inflation," *Lloyds Bank Review*, no. 121 (July 1976): 5.
38. Ibid.
39. Hans Gerth and C. Wright Mills, *From Max Weber* (New York: Oxford University Press, 1946), p. 180, italics added.
40. Adolph A. Berle, *Power without Property* (New York: Harcourt, Brace, and World, 1959), p. 83.
41. Berle says that the division of power into these two basic categories traces back to the seventeenth century and the writing of John Althans, an Emden (Germany) magistrate who discussed the problem of power in his *Systematic Politics.*
42. Adolph A. Berle, *Power* (New York: Harcourt, Brace and World, 1967), p. 92.
43. C. Wright Mills, *The Power Elite* (New York: Oxford University Press, 1956), p. 9.
44. Andrew Hacker, *The End of the American Era* (New York: Athenaeum, 1970), p. 60.
45. Galbraith, *Economics and the Public Purpose*, p. 82.
46. James B. Herendeen, *The Economics of the Corporate Economy* (New York: Dunellen, 1975), p. 5.
47. These aspects of power are discussed in detail in Berle, *Power*, pp. 199–216.
48. Ibid., p. 190.
49. Quoted in Arthur Selwyn Miller, *The Modern Corporate State* (Westport, Ct. Greenwood Press, 1976), p. 19, italics added.
50. Franklin D. Roosevelt, Message to the Congress of the United States, 29 April 1938. The TNEC was unique in its organization, consisting of three Senators, three Representatives, and members from six executive agencies:

the departments of Justice, Treasury, Labor, and Commerce, plus the Federal Trade Commission and the Securities and Exchange Commission. The hearings filled more than 20,000 pages in 15 volumes. In addition, 43 monographs were published as part of the investigation. Although it was Roosevelt's message that got the project started, the TNEC was actually created by a joint resolution of the Congress, approved 16 June 1938 (Public Resolution No. 113, 75th Congress).

51. There is irony in the fact that 1976, the year of the nation's bicentennial, also marked the bicentenary for Adam Smith's *Wealth of Nations*. The irony lies in the fact that the highly concentrated character of the U.S. economy bears only a faint relationship to Smith's "model" for organizing economic activity by means of decentralized, highly competitive markets. Yet, we constantly clothe our actions in the ideology of Smithian economics, even though the reality is far different.

52. The most recent Bureau of the Census figure for the national wealth is for 1975, at which time it totaled $5,587.6 billion. The percentage figure cited here is an estimated update, based in part on growth rates in the national wealth prior to 1975 and on inflation rates since then.

53. See William G. Shepherd, *Market Power and Economic Welfare* (New York: Random House, 1970), p. 16.

54. The most detailed information on concentration is available for the manufacturing sector of the economy and the individual markets in that sector. The reason is that the Bureau of the Census publishes, at five-year intervals, a detailed *Census of Manufactures*, which also includes calculated concentration ratios for the whole spectrum of manufacturing industries. These ratios are based upon the value of shipments by each industry, this being the best measure of the industry's output. Unfortunately, similar comprehensive information about other major sectors of the economy is not available from government sources, although, as we have seen, the data from the *Fortune* reports provide significant insight into concentration found in the nonmanufacturing parts of the economy. Because manufacturing accounts for about one-third of the economy's output as measured by the GNP, the data on concentration in this sector take us a long way in understanding the overall concentration picture. The comments that follow apply primarily to manufacturing.

55. Ever since the TNEC investigation, a massive amount of statistical information on concentration (especially in manufacturing) has been accumulated. There are, however, two major studies recognized as classics in this area. They are the 1969 study by the Bureau of Economics, Federal Trade Commission, *Economic Report on Corporate Mergers*, by Willard F. Mueller, formerly Chief Economist, Federal Trade Commission, and *Economic Concentration* (New York: Harcourt, Brace, Jovanovich, 1972), by the late John M. Blair, formerly Chief Economist, U.S. Senate Anti-Trust Subcommittee. These two works are the primary source for the detailed discussion on aggregate and market concentration as applied to the U.S. economy.

56. Blair, *Economic Concentration*, pp. 61ff. The seven series are: total assets, 200 largest nonfinancial corporations; total assets, 100 largest manufac-

turing, mining, and distribution corporations; net income, 200 largest nonfinancial corporations; net working capital, 316 largest manufacturing corporations; total assets, 100 largest manufacturing corporations; value added by manufacture, 200 largest manufacturing corporations; and total manufacturing assets, 200 largest manufacturing corporations.

57. Willard F. Mueller and Larry G. Hemm, "Trends in Industrial Market Concentration," *Review of Economics and Statistics* 56 (November 1974): 519.
58. The census data pertain to national markets, but many industries serve distinct local or regional markets in which their concentration far exceeds the national ratio. An example is newspapers. In 1972 the *national* four-firm ratio was 14 percent, which meant that the four largest newspapers accounted for only 14 percent of total sales nationally. Locally, there are many markets in which the concentration ratio is 100 percent because there may be only a single newspaper. Imports have the opposite effect because they add to the total amount of a product available.
59. William G. Shepherd, *The Economics of Industrial Organization* (Englewood Cliffs, N.J.: Prentice-Hall, 1979), p. 280.
60. Willard F. Mueller, "The Rising Concentration in America: Reciprocity, Conglomeration and the New American 'Zaibatsu' System," *Antitrust Law and Economics Review* 4 (Summer 1971): 103.
61. As the reader has no doubt noted, emphasis has been on corporate power. The reason is simply that the corporation is the most important institution through which private power is organized in our society. Trade unions are next in importance. The powerful trade unions that dominate the key manufacturing sectors of the economy sprang into existence primarily as a reaction to power concentrated in giant corporations. Trade union power, in other words, is seen as both a consequence and a countervailing force to corporate power. Without the one, we should not have the other.
62. Alfred E. Kahn, speech to the Economic Club of Chicago, 13 March 1979.
63. Arthur Okun, "Sticks with Two Short Ends," *Challenge* 22 (July-August 1979): 47.
64. Gardiner C. Means, "Industrial Prices and Their Relative Flexibility," Senate Document 13, 74th Cong., 1st sess., 17 January 1935.
65. Gardiner C. Means, *The Structure of the American Economy* (New York: Augustus M. Kelley, Publishers, 1966 [1939]), p. 43.
66. Gardiner C. Means, "Simultaneous Inflation and Unemployment: A Challenge to Theory and Policy," in *The Roots of Inflation*, edited by John M. Blair (New York: Burt Franklin & Co., 1975), p. 11.
67. Ibid., p. 28.
68. No single definitive survey summarizes all these tests, but one of the most comprehensive is by Allen H. Spencer and Reuben Kyle, *The Administered Price Thesis: Reflections on Forty Years of Empirical Study* (Murfreesboro: Business and Economic Research Center, Middle Tennessee State University, 1974). This and other literature cites 14 studies; there are undoubtedly more.

69. F. M. Scherer, *Industrial Market Structure and Economic Performance* (Chicago: Rand McNally, 1970), p. 284.
70. Ibid., p. 294.
71. L. W. Weiss, "Stigler, Kindahl, and Means on Administered Prices," *American Economic Review* 67 (September 1977): 619.
72. Ralph E. Beals, "Concentrated Industries, Administered Prices, and Inflation: A Survey of Recent Empirical Research," a study prepared for the Council on Wage and Price Stability, June 1975.
73. In recent years, Blair was a leading exponent of this concept. See his article, "Market Power and Inflation," *Journal of Economic Issues* 8 (June 1974): 453–78. The pioneer work in this area appeared in a 1955 Brookings Institution study, *Pricing in Big Business*, by A. D. H. Kaplan, Joel B. Dirlam, and Robert F. Lanzillotti. See also the article by Lanzillotti, "Pricing Objectives in Large Companies," *American Economic Review* 48 (December 1958): 921–40.
74. See Horace Wachtel and Peter Adelsheim, *The Inflationary Impact of Unemployment: Price Markups during Postwar Recessions, 1947–70* (Washington, D.C.: Joint Economic Committee, 1976).
75. Ibid.
76. *Wall Street Journal*, 7 December 1976, p. 1.
77. See Blair, "Market Power and Inflation"; and Alfred Eichner, "A Theory of the Determination of the Mark-up Under Oligopoly," *Economic Journal* 83 (December 1973): 1184–1200.
78. An intriguing explanation of how market power may come into play during a slump is found in the financial instability hypothesis developed by Hyman Minsky. Drawing upon neglected elements in Keynes, Minsky argues that the market economy is beset by a *systemic* instability rooted in the periodic financial crises that beset the large business firm. These occur whenever the firm is unable to meet large cash commitments resulting from a combination of debt obligations contracted during a boom and a decline in cash flows (revenue) during a slump. From the 1960s onward, firms found themselves increasingly in this situation because the nation's financial system underwent a transformation from a "robust" to a "fragile" state. This came about because the large reserves of liquidity (assets readily converted into cash) carried over from the wartime era became exhausted. As a result, the corporate economy found itself having to depend more and more on borrowed funds to finance its holdings of assets. When the firm confronts a "liquidity" crisis in a slump, it is forced to try and increase its cash flow. For the large corporation, the best way to do this is to raise prices. Thus, the slump and the ensuing financial crunch bring market power into play, leading to rising prices and higher markups. For full details, see Hyman Minsky, *John Maynard Keynes* (New York: Columbia University Press, 1975).
79. Joan Robinson, "The Second Crisis in Economic Theory," *American Economic Review* 62 (May 1972): 5.
80. For example, *real* weekly earnings (before taxes) of workers in the private nonagricultural economy in 1979 were $101.02 (in 1967 prices), which was below the 1970 average of $103.04 and only a penny more

than the 1965 average of $101.01. Thus, real earnings hardly changed at all in almost 14 years. They reached a high of $109.26 in 1972 and have declined steadily since then. This shows that, on the average, money incomes have failed to keep pace with the price level.

81. Tibor Scitovsky, "Market Power and Inflation," *Economica* 45 (August 1978): 227.
82. Ibid., p. 224.
83. John Hicks, *The Crisis in Keynesian Economics* (New York: Basic Books, 1974), p. 64.
84. John Eatwell, John Llewellyn, and Roger Torling, "Money Wage Inflation in Industrial Countries," *Review of Economic Studies* 41 (October 1975): 515.
85. Peter Wiles, "Cost Inflation and the State of Economic Theory," *Economic Journal* 83 (June 1973): 381.
86. Ibid., p. 386.
87. John H. Williams, "An Economist's Confessions," *American Economic Review* 52 (March 1962): 10.

6

Power: An Institutional Framework of Analysis

William M. Dugger

The problems of power and of individuality are intertwined in such a complex fashion that one cannot be understood without understanding the other. Each is rooted in the institutional structure of a going society. Let me preview my approach to the problem of power by asking several questions. Where does one start an analysis of power? An institutional analysis cannot start with power itself. Rather, the place to begin is with the question of why individuals, often physically and mentally stronger than their rulers or leaders, willingly obey orders or instructions. That question leads to another: How do individuals acquire motives, goals, ideals, and means? The answer to this takes us down to bedrock, the institutional structure in which the individual is embedded. Institutional structure is the source of power, for individuals learn motives, goals, ideals, *and means* from their participation in society's institutions. In the family, church, school, military, corporation, and government, we learn what is expected of us, and we learn how to do it. *Some* of us also learn how to exercise power, and how to back it up if need arises.

The following is an attempt to construct a holistic (institutional) framework for analyzing power. Footnotes are minimized, and useful works appear in an annotated bibliography.

Any discussion of power should first define it. Here, *power shall refer to the ability to tell other people what to do with some degree of certainty that they will do it.* When power wielders must coerce others, power is tenuous and obvious. When coercion is unnecessary, power is secure and unnoticed. In twentieth-century America, coercion is minimal. This is because power is relatively secure, except during times of overt crisis and war. Twentieth-century Americans, usually, submit to power voluntarily. Individuals often do not even consider their behavior as submissive. Rather, they "choose" to do what is expected of them. They do not even notice power. Instead, they consider themselves as free, exercising individual initiative.

These illusions of individual choice and autonomy make it very difficult to see, let alone analyze, power. The following framework will place great emphasis upon the institutional structure and the individuals it produces. Only after grasping the relation between institutional structure and individuality can power itself be analyzed.

Institutional Structure

A society is a network of institutions, each linked more or less tightly to others. An institution is two things. First, it is an organized pattern of roles, often enforced with positive and negative sanctions. Second, it is the patterned habits of thought learned by individuals performing those roles. Institutions, as both these patterns, are clustered around general functions. Each functional cluster is linked to the dominant cluster. In the American case, economic institutions dominate, for ours is a pecuniary civilization. The corporation and the labor union are the primary institutions within the economic cluster. But as organized labor has come to represent an increasingly smaller percentage of the work force, the corporation has become paramount. It increasingly gives order to the American institutional structure by linking other clusters of institutions to itself.

Institutional Hegemony

American society contains six clusters of institutions: (1) Economic institutions produce and distribute commodities; (2) educational institutions produce and distribute knowledge; (3) military institutions prepare for and conduct war; (4) kinship institutions produce children; (5) political institutions make and enforce laws, with recourse to the ultimate sanction—violence; and (6) religious institutions instill faith in a system of supernatural doctrines [contrast with Gerth and Mills 1953, pp. 26–29].

Each of the noneconomic clusters is linked to the dominant economic institution, the corporation, in a kind of means-end continuum. That is, the corporation uses other institutions as means for its own ends. This is important, because it provides the first glimpse at the true source of power.

Educational institutions, particularly public schools and state universities, produce an ample supply of trained and disciplined specialists for corporate employment. In addition to serving their "educational" function, high schools, junior colleges, and universities are extensions of the corporate personnel office, grading the human capital for easier processing. Most high school drop-outs become drudges, criminals, or unemployables. High school graduates are earmarked for blue-collar jobs. Junior college graduates are slated for clerical use. University graduates become either management material or specially trained corporate experts in this or that technique. Hence, educational institutions produce the means for pursuit of corporate ends. Of course, some elite (adequately endowed) educational institutions can exercise a degree of autonomy and pursue their own ends. Nevertheless, the main thrust of education is not education, but the production of suitable graded employees with suitable knowledge. Educational institutions can ignore this corporate imperative, but only at their own risk *and expense.*

The military occupies a unique position within our institutional structure. During a cold war, it protects corporate interests at home and abroad, by underwriting corporate research and development and by buying corporate commodities. During a hot war, military institutions become dominant. Instead of being means for corporate ends, they become the ends, and corporations temporarily become the means. Yet, hot wars are infrequent and are the occasional price paid for the more useful periods of cold war.

The major kinship institution in twentieth-century America is the family. It serves two major functions for the corporation. First, as a household, it is the major outlet for corporate commodities. It is the terminal point in the Galbraithian revised sequence. If that sequence breaks down, as it occasionally does, the fault often lies within the household for failing to follow the corporate imperative: "Thou Shalt Consume." Because it is the weak link in the revised sequence, tremendous corporate pressure (in the form of advertising) and corporate investigation (in the form of market research) is directed at the household. Second, as a family, the major kinship institution produces the semiprocessed materials used as inputs into educational institutions. Children must be instilled with respect for authority lest school officials find them unduly active and irreverent. Children whose ultimate destination is corporate management (future technocrats) must also be instilled with a desire to succeed. If families fail in this general child-molding function, resort is often made to psychotherapy (drug abuse, either professionally applied or self-administered), corporal punishment, or incarceration.

Political institutions—parties, state and federal legislatures, executive and judiciary branches—are, in a sense, the most unruly of all twentieth-century American institutions. This is because they sometimes pursue ends that are not corporate means. The roles of persons in political institutions are of very ancient origin. They evolved long before the corporation. The people performing these roles often acquire motives, goals, ideals, and means that took concrete form in the Age of Enlightenment rather than in the Age of Corporate Capital. Some judges seek justice; some legislators seek equality, liberty, and fraternity; some presidents seek basic social reforms. The institutional roles they perform not only teach them these noncorporate habits of thought, but also provide them with the *means* to follow them. Such individuals possess power, that is, they can tell others what to do with some degree of certainty that they will do it, but most political officials exercise their power in the service of corporate ends. After all, corporations usually fund the higher educational institutions they attend, employ their fathers, give them their first jobs, finance their campaigns, provide them with the information they need to perform their public duties, and hire them when they tire of "public" service. In short, the habits of thought of most political officials are those learned in performing, or in preparing to perform, corporate roles. These political officials are *not corrupt*. They are *not conspirators*. They do not have to be. They simply follow the motives, goals, and ideals they have learned, and in doing so they also use the means they have learned.

The last major cluster of American institutions are those that pursue religious ends. But they employ economic means, and there is the rub. Most American religious denominations employ various functionaries and officials. These employees must be paid, or at least fed, clothed, and sheltered. Most denominations also use various and assorted houses of worship. These must be of a substantial nature, for they serve a substantial purpose. In short, religious institutions must be financed, and without the power to tax, financing comes from voluntary contributions. If a religious institution pushes too hard against the sensibilities of its financiers, it loses their support. Sad, perhaps, but the bottom line is brutally clear. Most religious institutions cannot aggressively attempt to change the habits of thought of their lay supporters for fear of losing their support. By and large, this means that most religious institutions have little autonomy. Even if religious leaders want to instill certain habits of thought in their lay supporters, the best they can do is legitimate or reinforce those habits of thought already held. If they preach against them, they may lose the means necessary to do so. Ours is a secular society.

In summary, at the close of the twentieth century, a structure of institutional hegemony clearly can be discerned in the United States. With a few exceptions, noneconomic institutions are either ineffective (religious) or perform functions linked to the corporation, the dominant economic institution. Most institutions are means to corporate ends. People performing roles in these subordinate institutions may possess power, but it is usually exercised in such a way that it serves corporate ends. Their power, such as it is, is not autonomous. Rather, it is literally and figuratively incorporated into an institutional structure of corporate hegemony.

Instruments of Hegemony

This corporate hegemony is not held together by a conspiracy. Several social mechanisms simply operate in such a way that they become instruments of hegemony, means of corporate domination, and, ultimately, the social cement holding the edifice together. These social mechanisms may be termed the superstructure, but the name is unimportant. Four of them are important to an understanding of power: subreption, contamination, emulation, and mystification.

In legal terms, subreption is unfair or unlawful representation through suppression or fraudulent concealment of facts. In this article it refers to the process whereby the function performed by one cluster of institutions becomes the means of another cluster of institutions. Thorstein Veblen's *Higher Learning in America* is perhaps the best study of subreption ever written. According to Veblen, higher learning has its own means and ends: the increase and dissemination of knowledge. The major institution performing this function is the university, but American universities are not autonomous. They are run by and for businessmen. As a result, the end of higher learning has become subrepted into a business means. Universities became "practical" and began producing practical knowledge (how to get something for nothing) and practical men. Knowledge for knowledge's sake faded into the background.

It is through subreption that the allegedly autonomous clusters of American institutions have become linked to one dominant institution, the corporation. Subreption is one of the least studied social phenomena of the twentieth century. The reason is simple. Subreption destroys the foundation of a pluralistic society. That is, subreption replaces institutional autonomy, a half-truth so near and dear to the hearts of mainstream liberals, with institutional hegemony, the foundation of corporate power and the reality of twentieth-century America. It is through subreption that the functions (ends) of our major institutions have become *incorporated* as the means of one dominant institution. In the process, the power of the subrepted institutions has either declined or has become an extension of corporate power. "Eat your breakfast, Johnny, or you won't grow up to be a successful businessman like your father."

Contamination occurs when the motives appropriate for the roles of one institution spread to the roles of others. Religious institutions in the United States are contaminated with corporate (pecuniary) motives to the extent that the acquisition and display of wealth (conspicuous consumption) has become *the* motive of many religious officials. To the extent that they are judged by and judge themselves by their moral and theological stature, they are free of contamination. To the extent that they judge themselves and are judged by the stature of their real estate, they are contaminated. That is, their motives are those of business.

The same applies to people in other institutional roles. "Vote for John Doe and put sound business practices to work in city government." "This university should be run according to sound business principles." "What this family needs is a business manager!" Although obvious, it seldom consciously occurs to people in their roles as political official, university administrator, or parent that governments, universities, and families are not business corporations. As a result, motives appropriate for corporate roles have contaminated the roles performed in other institutions, giving corporate roles and those performing them far more weight than noncorporate ones.

Contamination is akin to emulation. Emulation, as used here, occurs when one institution or cluster successfully denies the prestige claims of other institutions and successfully realizes its own claims, becoming the fountainhead of social value. That is, emulation occurs when one institution becomes *the* source of status. Acquisition of status then comes from performing the top roles of the dominant institution and from displaying that successful performance. In our society, one must earn and then spend big money.

One earns it performing a top corporate role of one form or another. One spends it, not just in conspicuous consumption, which is a bit gauche, but also in "public service." A choice ambassadorial post is an excellent way to turn corporate cash to public account (acclaim). Philanthropy is also a suitable activity, for educational and religious institutions are always in need of the businessman's pocket *and the businessman's animus*. Furthermore, he who throws his bread upon the water receives it back a thousandfold.

Through emulation, two things happen. First, corporate leaders cash in their corporate status by becoming leaders of other institutions. Second, and more important, people performing roles in other institutions do *not* object to the usurpers. Instead, they wish to be like their corporate benefactors. Through emulation, strong and proud men *willingly* accept the status claims of others and *willingly* denigrate their own. After all, if you have never met a payroll . . . .

Mystification is the emulation and distortion of symbols. It occurs when one institution produces the most important or the most valued symbols of a society and other institutions attempt to emulate or support them. Such symbols as "free (corporate) enterprise," "private (corporate) property," and "individual initiative" are examples of two things. First, they are very important symbols to most Americans. These symbols all originate in the corporate sphere of life and are actively disseminated by that sphere and by its outlyers. They represent or purport to represent things of great value to Americans in all walks of life. Second, these symbols are mystifications, distortions. In the twentieth century, free enterprise, private property, and individual initiative no longer mean what they purport to mean. Instead, they are mysteries or talismans of immense ceremonial potency. These symbols are used as weapons, both offensive and defensive. When used defensively, they rally public support for free enterprise (that is, corporate power to administer prices) in the oil industry, for example. When used offensively, they rally support for individual initiative (that is, union busting and right-to-work laws) in the southern textile mills, for example. Of course, the symbol "private property" is so powerful that its potency even protects *corporate* property from abuse at the hands of the profane (socialists and national planners).

In short, corporate hegemony is maintained, not through a conspiracy, but through four social mechanisms. Subreption ties all institutions together so that noncorporate institutions are used as means to corporate ends. Contamination puts corporate role motives into noncorporate roles. Emulation allows corporate leaders to gain acceptance, even respect, in noncorporate leadership roles. And mystification covers the corporate hegemony with a protective (magic) cloak of the most valued American symbols.

Individuality and Power

Individuality

The source or foundation of power should now be clear. It is institutional position, not individual strength, will, or cunning. But this statement may simply beg the question, for do not strong, willful, and cunning individuals rise to high positions and then use those positions for their own ends? The answer is no, because the question contains a false premise. The question assumes, incorrectly, that powerful individuals acquire their ends *independently* of the institutional roles they performed on their way to the top. This is not true. Prefabricated individuals are not simply selected to perform certain roles. Instead, as individuals perform certain roles, they are shaped by the roles they play.

An institution is an organized set of roles *and* the habits of thought people learn as they perform them. Furthermore, our current institutional structure is one of corporate hegemony, which means that in the family, the school, and then in the corporation proper, individuals are shaped by the roles they play in each institution, and each institution is itself linked to the corporation. For the individual who passes through the family and school on his or her way to the corporation, this institutional shaping produces the motives, goals, ideals, and means of the individual.

Veblen surely would have called the shaping process habituation to the corporate way of life, for that is exactly what it is. Individuals who pass through this habituation process and find themselves chief executives for the largest corporations are very powerful men. But they do not exercise *individual* power.

Power

The power of corporate executives is not individual but institutional, in both its source and in its direction. In other words, both the ends and the means of their power are institutionally determined. The ends of power are institutionally determined because the motives, goals, and ideals of the powerful have been learned in their role-by-role climb to the top. From the role of father's little man, through teacher's star pupil, to chief executive's protégé, the powerful executive learns how and why to act, how and why to think.

Furthermore, if he is religious, then God provides him with the ultimate sanction. If he has been in the military, then as chief executive of XYZ corporation, he performs his patriotic duty. If he has served in government, then political doors and regulatory rules are open to him. Such access helps him prevent unfair competition and unbusinesslike principles in government. In short, other institutions are his means. But his ends are corporate, not religious, not military, not political.

The means of power are also institutionally determined because, as a corporate executive, religious, military (outside of hot war), educational, and political ends are all available to him as means. The leaders and followers of the other institutions depend upon him for material and immaterial support. He is not depended upon as an individual, but as head of an institution. His power, and the willing obedience to it, are institutionally determined. Another can easily fill his shoes. This is because both individual power and what individuals do with it are determined by the institutional roles performed. Institutional roles, then, and the "superstructure" supporting them, are the ultimate source of power.

Conclusion

The top roles in the top institutions of any institutional structure (society) are supported by certain social mechanisms, by a substructure. This is what reinforces the power of a top role, whether that role be in second-century Rome or twentieth-century America. But in the former case, power is easy to see and to analyze because it was tenuous and based on coercion. In the latter case, power is difficult to see and to analyze because it is secure and based on voluntary compliance. Institutional analysis is the key to understanding power based on obedience or compliance. It is from institutionally organized roles that we, in twentieth-century America, learn the habits of thought conducive to getting along in the institutional structure into which we are born.

Getting along means adjusting to our position in life. We are aided in this adjustment process (Veblen's habituation) by four social mechanisms. These not only support and reinforce the top roles in our top institutions, but also help all of us, including the performers of the top roles, accept the situation, perhaps even enjoy it. Through subreption, the ends of teachers and students, parents and children, military officers and enlisted men, elected officials and bureaucratic staff, nicely mesh into a means-ends continuum. They provide the means, the corporation the ends. And he who serves best is happiest. Through contamination, a churchman can work for a huge building fund and feel good about it; a student and her teacher can work for a good job offer and feel the same. In short, people in all walks of life can acquire and follow a pecuniary animus, even though in doing so they are borrowing corporate motives and applying them to noncorporate activities. Nevertheless, they do so willingly. They individually and freely want to, therefore it is right and good; or so they think.

Being contaminated with the motives of corporate business, very few people notice that the values and prestige claims of corporate life are emulated in *all* walks of life, allowing successful performers of top corporate roles to cash in their claims by becoming leaders of noncorporate institutions. All this is done, not in the name of the corporation, but in the name of free enterprise, or private property, or individual initiative. Mystification allows (some of) us to think that individual initiative is served by union busting, to believe that private property is protected by fighting land use planning, and to believe that free enterprise is served by dismantling government regulation of corporate power.

These processes and the structure of power that they support (corporate institutional hegemony) are laid bare through an *institutional* not an individual framework of analysis. If we are to change that structure, and surely we must, because it is inconsistent with democracy, with liberty, equality, and fraternity, then we must first change the institutions and social processes that create and support it. Simply calling for a revival or a renewal of the individual human "spirit" will not suffice. That spirit is a pattern of learned habits of thought, and through institutional analysis, we know where those habits of thought are learned.

Annotated Bibliography

Arnold, Thurman W. *The Folklore of Capitalism.* New Haven: Yale University Press, 1937. Excellent work on mystification.

Berle, Adolph A., and Gardiner C. Means. *The Modern Corporation and Private Property.* Rev. ed. New York: Harcourt, Brace and World, 1968. Authoritative work on separation of ownership from control.

Coleman, James S. *Power and the Structure of Society.* New York: W. W. Norton, 1974. Discussion of the power of a new creature, the corporation.

Commons, John R. *Institutional Economics.* Madison: University of Wisconsin Press, 1961. Going concerns, working rules, and foundations of institutional analysis.

Dahl, Robert A. *Who Governs?* New Haven: Yale University Press, 1961. Pluralist social theory and empirical support.

Dowd, Douglas F. *The Twisted Dream.* 2d ed. Cambridge, Mass.: Winthrop Publishers, 1977. Institutional analysis from an evolutionary and radical perspective, focused on the United States.

Galbraith, John Kenneth. *The New Industrial State.* Boston: Houghton Mifflin, 1967.

———. *The Affluent Society.* 2d ed. Boston: Houghton Mifflin, 1969.

———. *Economics and the Public Purpose.* Boston: Houghton Mifflin, 1973. A grand summary of Galbraithian economics.

Gerth, Hans, and C. Wright Mills. *Character and Social Structure.* New York: Harcourt, Brace and World, 1953. Superb discussion of institutional roles and their shaping of individuals.

Kanter, Rosabeth Moss. *Men and Women of the Corporation.* New York: Basic Books, 1977. Excellent case study of corporate behavior.

Maccoby, Michael. *The Gamesman.* New York: Simon and Schuster, 1976. Psychological study of character types in the corporate world.

Melman, Seymour. *The Permanent War Economy*. New York: Simon and Schuster, 1974.

Mills, C. Wright. *White Collar*. New York: Oxford University Press, 1951. The social life of the middle class.

———. *The Power Elite*. New York: Oxford University Press, 1956. Classic study of power in the higher circles.

———. *The Sociological Imagination*. New York: Oxford University Press, 1959. Exploration of the relations between personal biographies and social forces.

Pirsig, Robert M. *Zen and the Art of Motorcycle Maintenance: An Inquiry into Values*. New York: Bantam Books, 1974.

Tool, Marc R. *The Discretionary Economy*. Santa Monica: Goodyear Publishing Company, 1979.

Veblen, Thorstein. *The Theory of the Leisure Class*. New York: Macmillan, 1899. Discussion of emulation.

———. *The Theory of Business Enterprise*. New York: Charles Scribners Sons, 1904. The means and ends of business.

———. *The Instinct of Workmanship*. New York: Macmillan, 1914. Discussion of the Veblenian dichotomy, pecuniary versus industrial.

———. *The Higher Learning in America: A Memorandum on the Conduct of Universities by Business Men*. New York: B. W. Huebsch, 1918. The subtitle is explanatory.

———. *The Place of Science in Modern Civilization and Other Essays*. New York: B. W. Huebsch, 1919. Collection of classic essays.

Whyte, William H., Jr. *The Organization Man*. Garden City: Doubleday, 1957.

PART II

THE CORPORATE SYSTEM

Introduction to Part II: The Corporate System

The lead paper in this section, by the late Gardiner C. Means, is at once a sobering comment on the continuing archaic status of economic inquiry and a testament to Mean's astute grasp of economic reality. After two decades, his analysis retains its vitality and relevance as a critique of mainstream analysis and as a characterization of the actual, corporation-dominated economy. Means saw the New Deal as a revolutionary departure from "the principles and policies of private capitalism." Rejected was the presumption that full employment was automatic, that individuals received income in proportion to their contribution, that unemployment reflects individual laziness, that supply and demand forces would keep a balance between farm and industrial prices, and that imbalances in international payments would not persist. Orthodoxy failed utterly to recognize "two great institutional changes . . . that destroyed the validity of classical assumptions." Small private enterprise had been substantially displaced by "big modern corporations," and "flexible market prices" have generally given way to administered pricing. In "administered competition, . . . a price (or wage rate) is not set by the equating of supply and demand but by administrative action. . . . Actual price becomes . . . a matter of arbitrary use of pricing power within the limits, often broad, set by demand and costs." Corporations are "great collectives"; we have evolved to a system of "collective capitalism." Means calls for a fundamental change in the research program of economists so that the five major problems that old orthodox theory cannot resolve—unemployment, administered inflation, imbalance in international payments, flawed allocation of resources, and inequality of income distribution—may be addressed more constructively and successfully. He concludes with a recommended policy agenda for these problem areas reflecting this new (institutionalist) perspective.

However, in the following paper by Daniel R. Fusfeld, the corporate revolution is generalized to encompass the whole social order. He contends that "the United States has moved well down the path toward a corporate state." His purpose is to demonstrate that "economic power is concentrated in the hands of a relatively few supercorporations that are now moving toward a dominance in the world economy"; that "political power has shifted heavily into the hands of the executive branch of the federal government"; that "these two centers of economic and political power have developed a growing symbiosis"; and that "the self-selecting elite of the supercorporation dominates the decision-making process, while lesser centers of power in labor unions and the universities are drawn into the system as junior partners." Moreover, "an economic and political compromise" has been struck "between those who hold power and those who do not." "As long as the economic system provides an acceptable degree of security," and "growing material wealth, . . . the average American does not ask who is running things or what goals are being pursued." The economic and political symbiosis derives from interdependence—big business needs big government to help sustain economic growth, and big government needs big business to provide modern armaments. The "self-selecting economic elite" shares behavioral modes, values, and goals, including the creation and extension of national power. But conflicts within the corporate state threaten continuity of the social order. What is needed is the restructuring of "our economic institutions" to "disperse economic and political authority." "We need more than prosperity, economic growth, and stable prices. We need a redistribution of wealth to achieve greater equality and freedom. We need a world at peace."

Where Fusfeld sees the concentration and use of political and economic power as having mainly negative and threatening consequences, Robert A. Solo, in the next article, although readily acknowledging the presence and use of power, offers analysis of how to recast its character, redirect its use, and achieve more rationally acceptable outcomes. Initially responding to President Nixon's introduction of direct wage and price controls in the early 1970s, Solo considers them to have been devoid of "a conceptual base and without coherent and accepted values"; they were "unworkable." He argues, even so, that "direct controls are inescapable in the modern economy . . . the fundamental issue is not whether to control, but how to control." He disclaims any intent to provide a comprehensive, coherent, and rational "system of control" reflecting "accepted criteria of justice and equity." Such a system, he contends, "cannot be predesigned; it must evolve through an extended process of social learning and value formation." However, in two areas he offers extensive analysis culminating in the following summary recommendations: First, "that the political authority . . . act upon the determination of prices and wages by reference to accepted norms for the relative distribution of income and the intersectoral allocation of resources." Second, "that it must plan, program, and promote technological advance sector by sector." "Under certain market conditions the latter would require that the political authority finance the transformation of technology" with certain guarantees. What is sought is the integration of "motivation and skill in the management of enterprise with informed control in the social interest." However, movement toward such "control capability" would require "a new ideological consensus . . . a new breed of public servant operating from . . . a new knowledge base . . . and new institutional arrangements for participatory planning."

Following Solo's consideration of relations between the public government and corporate enterprise, the focus shifts to an examination of the transformation of the corporate structure itself over recent decades with a paper by William M. Dugger. Dugger sees "the development of corporate hegemony," the domination of the economy at large by one institution—the imperial corporation—as the primary locus of economic power in the United States. Building on his earlier paper in Part I, Dugger updates the evidence of concentration of economic power (giant corporations "account for nearly three-fourths of all corporate assets, over half of all corporate receipts, and over two-thirds of all corporate income"). He demonstrates the need for increased control by tracing the transformation of organizational types from the old U form (unitary organization) to the M form (multiple divisions), and the latter's adaptation to megacorp or imperial conglomerate corporate institutions. Their size has now reached the point where they are no longer dependent on external sources of finance. Moreover, modern information technology is used extensively, but not exclusively, to organize and control people. Effectual control of such large organizations has driven corporations to develop "common corporate cultures"—a set of shared beliefs and values inculcated in the corporations's employees"—as a means of unifying its diverse and semi-autonomous divisions. Dugger explores the motives and practices of establishing conglomerates through reference to the Boston Consulting Groups counseling to manipulate subsidiaries and acquisitions as "cash cows" to be milked, "stars" to be supported in growth, "dogs" to be disposed of as necessary, and "cats" to be promoted if market shares can be enhanced. But a final and major focus for Dugger is the examination of the emergence of corporate power through the establishment of internalized control over its managers and employees. The goal is to increase hegemony over insiders by deliberate alteration of their value structure through "contamination, subordination, emulation, and mystification." Such control is directed primarily to the "single-minded pursuit of short-run profits."

Rick Tilman explores diverse views concerning the emergence of corporate power in the next paper. More particularly, he contends that "theories of social value (criteria of choice), perspectives of corporate power, and interpretations of political elites are closely linked in contemporary American political economy." Although these linkages are often noted, they are not "self-evident." His "central thesis is that the acceptance of a particular social value theory such as the utilitarian, Marxist, or instrumentalist fosters a mind set or ideological syndrome that results in a particular view of corporate power and political elites." His demonstrative vehicle is an assessment of the reaction of critics—libertarian, conservative, liberal, and radical—to Charles Lindblom's recent *Politics and Markets.* Libertarian critics exhibit the utility theory of value with its deference to subjective preferences expressed in free markets. The preeminance of business power is denied; markets, not corporations, govern; and only the elitist elements of government are cause for concern. Conservatives add certain ethical absolutes to the relativistic utility value principle—status, order, tradition, religion, for example. The "invisible hand joins incongrously with an organic view of the social order." Significant private corporate power is exaggerated. Liberals retain the utility theory of value but are much less deferential to market processes—negative externalities, market imperfections, and market failures are significant departures. The political reality of interest group politics is the counterpart of the free market; it holds achieved power somewhat accountable. Radicals, whether Marxist, instrumentalist, or humanist, share a concern for the values of "equality and community." "All see the major industrial and financial corporations as the center of the American power system, and all believe political elites achieve their dominance from their relation to the system of corporate enterprise and the class structure it has produced." Utility value theory is abandoned in favor of labor theory or of instrumental self-correcting value judgments. In sum, "the more . . . the critic is the ideological captive of utilitarian theory, the more likely he or she will be to deny the dominance of corporate economic and political power . . . the more the critic subscribes to the Marxian labor theory of value or the neoinstitutionalist instrumentalist theory of value, the more likely he or she will be to emphasize the political and economic potency of the corporation and business-oriented elites."

Where the previous papers in this section have addressed the emergence and potency of corporate power in a generalized theoretical way, the following papers offer extensive empirical analyses of the emerging character and increasing complexity of corporate control of the economy. David Bunting and Mark S. Mizruchi, in the first of these latter papers, describe the transfer of control of large corporations from finance capitalist to corporate managers in the period 1905–19, in the United States. Arguing that the simple owner-manager divorcement and dichotomy is not a sufficient account of the evolution of control, Bunting and Mizruchi show that corporate directors had the basic discretion to direct the use of the corporations' assests and that this discretion was exercised, in the context of, and through the instrument of, extensive interlocking directorates among major corporations. Anticipating later work [below] by John Munkirs, these authors demonstrate that "between 1905 and 1919 a large fraction of large American companies were connected together into a formal network." Directors were diplomats; it was their function, via interlocks, "to resolve disputes" among competing firms, "as well as protect their [own] interests, signal rivals, and generally survive in a hostile environment." Formal relationships among companies were established "to create a basis for harmony and commonality." This interlocking directorate network provided "a practical solution to the theoretical problem of oligopolistic interdependence." However, finance capitalists did not recreate their successors; they appeared vulnerable to "public attacks or restrictive legislation." Control passed "mostly by default to subordinates who had been retained to manage particular companies. However, while financial control disintegrated into managerial control at the level of the individual firm, the intercorporate network established by the finance capitalists persisted"; it "seems to have continued to this day."

John R. Munkirs, the author of the next paper, would agree. It is Munkirs's contention, guided by his acceptance of the Veblenian dichotomy, and as demonstrated by extensive empirical analysis and matrix construction going back over a decade, that "the theory of Centralized Private Sector Planning (CPSP) is a more accurate description and explanation of extant economic institutions" in the United States than any other. Indeed, "the cumulative effect of changes in our economic institutions over the last half century . . . have created a fundamentally different type of economic system." So profound and pervasive is this structural transformation that the solutions to most of our continuing problems of instability, slow growth, inequitable distribution and the like must await the recognition and incorporation into analysis of this transformation. Munkirs defines the CPSP "as *a process whereby the production and distribution activities of the economy's key corporations and industries are* organized and coordinated *so as to bind these corporations and industries together into a functionally integrated production and distribution system.*" [Author's emphasis]. The CPSP model includes "those industries that actually perform the production and distribution functions, and the Central

Planning Core (CPC)." The integration of corporate institutions is accomplished through "formal and/or legally binding instruments," and through "informal and/or influential planning instruments." Of the former, stock holdings, boards of directors interlocks, and debt access and control are primary. In its several roles as information center, trustee, transfer agent, registrar, and general power center, the CPC, consisting of "seven banks, four insurance companies, and one diversified financial institution," uses direct and indirect directorate interlocks and stock, debt, and trustee (among other) intracore interlocks to bind these institutions "into a cohesive and solid structural and functional unit." Munkirs offers no conspiracy theory: "In a very real sense, the CPC's planning instruments are simply modifications of traditional business devices—modifications made in such a way as to *simulate*, from an administrative perspective, the concentration, or consolidation, that technological advances made possible in the country's production processes." They have been motivated by "their entirely *conscious, logical, and rational* pursuit of monetary gain, or profit." (Author's emphasis)

However, as the following article by Munkirs and Michael Ayres makes clear, given the absence of accountability instruments, there is no necessary assurance that the pursuit of private CPC planning interests will also serve the public interest. The difficulties in achieving accountability are multiple and diverse: Government officials, who because of an uncritical belief in laissez-faire, are unable "to envision government institutions as a countervailing force" to private power, reflect an "ideological self-encapsulation." "This encapsulation is viewed by those in power in the private sector as a trait to be sought in those who seek public office" and as a criterion to determine who is "to receive campaign support." The corporate community has been successful in this century in seeing that such persons dominantly staff major government implementing and regulating agencies. In consequence, while at times "grass roots pressures" have succeeded in getting legislation passed "that, if enforced, would have made it impossible for an institutional arrangement such as the Central Planning Core to exist, . . . the government's enforcement efforts . . . especially in relationship to the Centralized Private Sector Planning (CPSP) . . . have been little more than an elaborate charade." Of equal importance, moreover, is the CPC's pursuit of "governmental policy influence-peddling through the establishment of private organizations that operate" to generate conservative elitist concurrence on major policy issues, act as informational conduits for conveying such consensus positions to public and governmental bodies, and serve "as screening mechanisms for potential candidates for public office." The authors then examine private organizations that frame governmental policy proposals in international affairs, especially the Trilateral Commission, and such bodies that recommend on domestic policy—especially the Business Roundtable. The above mentioned sources of power and influence are shown to be of such significance as to absolutely require a "two-tiered approach in the formulation and application of governmental public policies" in the areas of environmental control, "foreign trade, price accountability, employment, and monetary or fiscal policy": one tier is the CPSP sphere; the other tier is the non-CPSP sphere. The former requires direct and continuing public control; the latter needs less extensive accountability mechanisms, since it is heavily influenced by the CPC.

John R. Munkirs' analysis of the locus and use of corporate power is continued in a third article, here with James I. Sturgeon as coauthor, in theoretical and empirical considerations of "oligopolistic cooperation." While many scholars agree that most finance, mining, and manufacturing industries are oligopolistic in market structure, they tend to the view that such firms are competitive, though not necessarily in pricing practices. In contrast, Munkirs and Sturgeon show that a "more accurate description . . . of the industrial core is 'oligopolistic cooperation'." Such cooperation "goes beyond coordination or 'unconscious parallelism'," (the Machlup-Chamberlin characterization of "structural independence, psychological interdependence, and rivalry") to the creation of "specific, legally binding, quasi-permanent, organizational structures." Oligopolistic cooperation reflects "structural *intradependence* as opposed to *independence*." Among several forms of such intradependence, this paper considers administrative, ownership, and stock control intradependencies. Empirical evidence and analysis are illustratively presented on banking and insurance in the financial markets and petroleum in industrial markets. Central to their analysis is the contention "that a qualitatively different 'rational' course of administrative action emerges when day-to-day interaction among corporate employees replaces the more or less psychological guessing game created by mutual interdependence." Policy implications of this view of oligopolistic enterprise include the necessary abandonment of laissez-faire and antitrust approaches as irrelevant. "New forms may require (1) changing the elements of structural intradependence so that they cannot serve as a basis for cooperation or (2) that the public take a more direct role in the affairs of business enterprises while leaving the existing elements of intradependence largely intact. The latter approach depends upon the recognition and demonstration that cooperation is superior to competition in some areas of production." "Cooperation . . . cannot be left unattended or attended only by private interests." Also eroded by this analysis are the adequacy of empirical analyses confined to concentration ratios, and the relevance of tacit assumptions of competitive solutions being realized even by oligopolistic structures.

David S. Schwartz, in considering issues of the locus and use of economic power in the regulation of electric power and gas industries, addresses "a number of generic pricing policies and market structure issues that affect utility performance and consumer equity" in the next article. At the outset, he distinguishes between market values and social values in industries "affected with the public interest." He argues that the social values of the public interest are served by regulation that provides for "adequacy and availability of service, consumer protection from exorbitant prices, and protection against price discrimination in inelastic residential markets . . . that deal with basic necessities." "The traditional view of economic regulation of public utilities is that it exists to achieve direct control of prices and earnings of monopolistic or oligopolistic firms. In addition, in order to achieve economies of scale and adequacy of service, commissions have authority over the entry and exit of firms in the regulated markets." In focusing on the period since 1969, Schwartz observes that the regulation process has become subject to devastating criticisms from regulated firms over cost recovery and "archaic" regulations, consumer groups over rising prices, and environmentalists over pollution. Proposed solutions have ranged from improved regulatory processes to total deregulation. Given the dominion of orthodoxy and the influence of the Chicago school, the pressure for a "return to reliance upon market solutions" has been substantial, and, in the case of natural gas, partially successful. But Schwartz's main concern is not to respond to the bias and naivete of the orthodox but "with the criticism of regulation, and with the failure of government interevention, which has provided its critics the ammunition for such damaging impact." The bulk of the article explores the controversies surrounding the regulatory commissions' "ratemaking process and the procedures reflected in the cost of service, rate base, revenue requirements, and rate design" deliberations in the electric-power industries, and the pressures to deregulate the natural-gas industry to allow private planning of gas rates and service through joint ventures and interties with petroleum industries. Schwartz concludes by urging that the public's control over its own energy destiny be accomplished by legislation prohibiting oligopolic concentration and by a diversification of ownership forms, and therewith discretion, including both public and private institutions. He concludes that "if we are to be successful in pragmatically implementing and broadening the regulatory framework for social control, then we must gain access to the centers of power."

This volume concludes with two papers by Walter Adams and James W. Brock that address directly how achieved economic power wielded by the giant corporations is used contrary to the public interest. The authors are not content with mere assertions; they include case studies of actual private-power decisions made and of adverse consequences experienced. In the lead paper, Adams and Brock draw on Henry C. Simons for their concept of "economic sabotage" as one form of misused power. In a mature economy with an extensive division of labor and functional interdependence, "every large organized group is in a position at any time to disrupt or to stop the whole flow of social income." The economy cannot survive "if groups persist in exercising that power, of if they must continuously be bribed to forego its disastrous exercise." No government can allow any such group significantly to impair the flow of real income, to engage in economic sabotage. Adams and Brock pose these questions: "Is economic giantism relevant to an understanding of the shape and practical consequences of government policies? Does the power of gigantic . . . organizations . . . include the capacity to compound, frustrate, and subvert rational public policy? Does it include the capacity to elicit counterproductive and antisocial government intervention?" They answer in the affirmative. To what extent are the failures of public policy attributable to disproportionate size and its capacity to practice economic sabotage? To a considerable degree, they insist. The case studies that culminate in these responses include the automobile industry's subversion of national regulations for fuel economy in new vehicles; the steel industry's successful quest for protection, via congressionally established quotas, from foreign steel suppliers; and the ability of giant corporations to render ineffective national macroeconomic stabilization policies. In conclusion, they recommend that the explicit and extensive power of the noncompetitive industrial sector be recognized; that note be taken that such power extends well beyond the "capacity to influence price in an isolated market"; and that a renewed and energized structural antitrust policy be employed to hold the achieved power of giant corporations more accountable.

The second paper by Adams and Brock returns to the question and problem of corporate size and economic power. However, in this case the focus is on the ability of giant corporations "to demand—and to obtain—government bailouts." The advantages of this use of power are singularly overlooked in the usual debates over bigness: size fosters efficiency, technological advance, and impressive performance versus size undermines efficiency, aborts innovation, and subverts performance. As John Kenneth Galbraith observes, "roughly speaking, if you are in trouble and big enough, you will be rescued and recapitalized in one way or another by the government." As Adams and Brock make clear, the "advantage of bigness seems obvious: by virtue of *disproportionate* (author's emphasis) size, the giant corporation vitally affects the fortunes of broad segments of society. . . . They come to be perceived as too big and too important to be allowed to fail. Acting through government, society then feels compelled to guarantee the survival of corporate giants almost regardless of how inefficient, unprogressive, or mismanaged they may be. . . . Society becomes a hostage to bigness." In considerable detail and with compelling examples, the authors "analyze *direct* government bailouts, such as those involving Lockheed and Chrysler," and *indirect* bailouts of giant firms through "a variety of other . . . equally potent ways, including protection from foreign competition, regulatory delays and dispensations, privileged government procurement practices, state-sponsored promotion, tax favors, and exemption from prosecution for illegal acts and practices." The parade of these examples of deference and subsidy arrangements for the already power-advantaged is disturbing to the authors. They draw the following implications from their analysis: the bailout factor does demonstrate that 'mere' size does, in fact, matter; that it transforms an "onstensibly free enterprise society in a subtle but profoundly radical way. It privatizes profit while socializing losses–provided the latter are large enough"; when "disproportionate size converts private mistakes into social catastrophes, the community's capacity to absorb private error is corroded"; "the bailout factor obviously repudiates the . . . New Economic Darwinism, and its central precepts that only efficient firms survive." In consequence, "antitrust policy is infused with heightened importance" because it will serve both a corrective and a preventitive role in combating corporate bigness and the abuse of achieved power.

7
The Problems and Prospects of Collective Capitalism

Gardiner C. Means

Thirty-six years ago, our system of private capitalism was in a state of collapse. A quarter of the labor force was unemployed, the economy was operating at less than two-thirds of its capacity, business enterprises were failing on all sides, farms were being foreclosed on a mass scale, and money, the medium of exchange which is at the heart of capitalism, was being wiped out by the closing of banks until the whole banking system ceased to operate. The collapse of the capitalist system predicted by Karl Marx seemed to be taking place before our eyes.

THE GREAT REVOLUTION

Then came a revolution. It was not the Marxian revolution in which labor seizes the instruments of production, but a more basic and less obvious revolution which rejected the principles and policies of private capitalism and made a start toward developing a new set of principles and policies applicable to a new type of capitalism.

This revolution rejected the principle that under capitalism automatic forces would tend to maintain full employment and that any significant departure from a prosperous condition is only temporary. It rejected the principle that automatic forces would tend to bring to each individual an income in proportion to his contribution to production, and that unemployment is the product of an individual's own laziness or moral lack. It rejected the principle that automatic forces of supply and demand would tend to maintain a fair balance between farm and industrial prices. At the London Conference of 1933 this revolution rejected the principle that automatic forces would correct any persistent unbalance in international payments.

These rejected principles were a fundamental part of the warp and woof of private capitalism. For more than one hundred years, these principles had been accepted as valid and had provided the basis for national policies.

Why this sudden wholesale rejection? The easy answer is to say that the policies based on these principles were not working. But why were the policies of private capitalism which had worked reasonably well for over a century failing to work? The principles on which they were based had been developed and refined by a host of able economists. Their logic had been epitomized by Léon Walras in his beautiful system of equations. Their validity for the economy of private capitalism was well established.

THE BASIC CAUSE OF FAILURE

The answer is to be found in two great institutional changes which had taken place that destroyed the validity of the classical assumptions. One was a change in the characteristics of the predominant form of enterprise, and the other was a change in the characteristics of the predominant form of market.

For most of the nineteenth century, the predominant type of enterprise was the small private enterprise. Such enterprise was the basic concept of classical economic theory, and the economic system was analyzed as a system of small private enterprises interrelated through markets in which no individual enterprise had significant market power. Monopoly was recognized as an aberration to be broken up or regulated while prices in the competitive markets were presumed to adjust freely and flexibly to equate supply and demand. Thus, the policies of private capitalism were based on the twin assumptions of small private enterprises and flexible market prices. It was these policies that had failed 36 years ago.

By the 1930s, these assumptions had ceased to apply. The United States had become one in which the big modern corporation played a predominant role, and the great bulk of commodities and services entering the market were exchanged at inflexible, administered prices.

E. Chamberlin and Joan Robinson in 1933 made it clear that lying between the classical conception of competition and the classical conception of monopoly there is an important type of competition to which the conclusions of classical competitive theory did not apply. Adolph Berle and Gardiner Means established the predominant importance of the big corporation and its non-private character. My own writings established the major role played by administered prices and their relative inflexibility. As we look back on the 1930s, it is easy to see why the policies of private capitalism were not working. The economy was not predominantly one of small private enterprise nor was it one of flexible prices making swift and automatic adjustments.

THE NEW PERSPECTIVE

The revolution which took place at that time was a revolution in point of view. In place of looking backward and describing our economy in nineteenth century terms, we turned around, looked forward and began to describe our economy in more realistic terms.

Today we see in the foreground the big modern corporation. Obviously it is not a private enterprise. There is nothing private about a corporation with a hundred thousand stockholders, a hundred thousand workers, hundreds of thousands of customers and thousands of suppliers. Also obviously, such a corporation is not government. It is an institution standing midway between private enterprise and public government.

In a very real sense, the modern corporation is a great collective. Its management tends to be a self-perpetuating body in control of the enterprise and the enterprise itself consists of all those participating in it—some supplying capital, some supplying manpower, some supplying raw materials and some providing the market. The responsibilities of management can no longer lie solely with the stockholders. Within the wide limits set by the new type of competition, management has the power to affect the interests of all the participants in the enterprise and the responsibility to use this power to balance these interests. The long-run survival of the collective as an independent institution is likely to depend on management's maintaining an effective balance between these often conflicting interests which give the collective its life. The very legitimacy of the power wielded by management depends on its achieving such a balance.

Also in the foreground of our real economic world is what I have called "administrative competition". It, like collective enterprise, lies outside the principles and policies of private capitalism. Administrative competition is a form midway between classical competition under which no one has any market power and classical monopoly in which pricing power is unique. Whether we call this "competition among the few" or administrative competition or use such misleading terms as "monopolistic competition" or "imperfect competition,"[1] it is essentially a form of competition in which a price (or wage rate) is not set by the equating of supply and demand but by administrative action, and held constant for a period of time and through a series of transactions.

Under administrative competition, demand and costs influence price but do not determine it. Demand can change without producing a change in price. Costs can change without producing a change in price. And a change in price can be made with no initiating change in demand or costs. Actual price becomes in some degree a matter of the arbitrary use of pricing power within the limits, often broad, set by demand and costs. At the same time, demand and costs tend in part to be a product of how this arbitrary power is used.[2]

By the time of the great depression, the institutional changes of the preceding fifty years had converted a system of private capitalism into a system predominantly made up of huge collectives and markets in which prices are determined by administrative decision. The great evolution from private capitalism has given us a new form of the free enterprise system which may be called *Collective Capitalism*. It is a form of capitalism lying

[1]The terms "monopolistic competition" and "imperfect competition" are misleading because by implication they deny the presence of something which is *neither* classical competition nor classical monopoly and is not technically a blend of the two. One cannot have selling by a *single* seller when there are two or more sellers. And imperfect competition does not differ from classical competition if "perfect" competition has never existed.

[2]For example, a high price and much advertising versus a lower price and less demand but lower costs.

entirely outside the conceptions of John Stuart Mill and Karl Marx, and, of course, outside the conceptions of Adam Smith.

CONFIRMATION OF THE DIFFERENCES

When I was drafting this paper, two items came to my attention which underlined this difference between private capitalism and collective capitalism.

The first was a recent comment by *Business Week*[3] which started off, "There's a new impetus to the search for a more general managerial objective than that of making as much money as possible. Doubts about profit maximizing as the ultimate business objective are increasingly being voiced by friends of the free enterprise system." *Business Week* goes on to say, "Classically, management serves as trustee for the owners. The modern idea is that the professional manager serves as trustees for all parties connected with the enterprise: owners, employees, customers, suppliers, creditors, government, and the public." *Business Week* then points out that not everyone agrees with this view, and quotes Milton Friedman as writing in 1963, "Few trends could so thoroughly undermine the very foundations of our free society as the acceptance by corporate officials of a social responsibility other than to make as much money for the shareholders as possible." Friedman is then quoted as calling the concept of a wider responsibility "a fundamentally subversive doctrine."

The second item deals with prices and also involves Milton Friedman. The September issue of the *Journal of Economic Abstracts* summarizes an attack by Abba Lerner on Friedman's 1967 presidential address to the American Economic Association on the ground that Friedman assumes a degree of flexibility of prices and wages which is seldom met with in practice.[4]

These comments dramatically illustrate the dichotomy between the theories based on private capitalism and the reality of collective capitalism. If Friedman had said that the modern corporation and administered prices are subversive of classical theory, one could heartily agree. And if Friedman should advocate a return to classical conditions by breaking up corporate enterprise and union organization to the point that *no one had significant pricing power* and to the point that administered prices were few and far between, his classical theory and his policy would be consistent. But collective capitalism has created a new set of problems with which classical theory is not competent to cope.

[3] *Business Week,* November 2, 1968, p. 71.

[4] *Journal of Economic Abstracts,* September 1968, p. 675.

A REVERSAL OF FOCUS

The first of the set of problems, and I think the most important, is the way we think about our economic system. There is a great and understandable tendency to describe the present day economy as a private enterprise system, though with some important modifications. This tendency appears both in the teaching of economics and in the theorizing about the system. I believe the time has come to reverse our field and describe our system as a collective enterprise system which has some elements of both private enterprise and government enterprise.

When we follow the implications of this reversal, the beginning theory course will describe our present economy as one in which big collective enterprises play a major role with the remainder of production carried on, for the most part, by government on the one hand and by private enterprise on the other. Similarly, price and wage analysis would first focus on administrative competition and the indeterminacy of prices and wage rates. Then classical monopoly and classical competition would be considered as special cases.

This procedure would be in sharp contrast with much of present day teaching. For example, Samuelson's *Economics* starts the section on price determination with four chapters primarily devoted to the determination of price by supply and demand, followed by a chapter on equilibrium of the firm devoted mostly to pricing by a monopolist, and a final weak chapter on "imperfect competition."[5] Since the great bulk of commodity and service transactions take place at administered prices, this approach from classical competition to administrative competition clearly leaves a false impression.

We do not yet know as much about administrative competition as we do about classical competition. Points that need to be covered are the indeterminacy of prices, their insensitivity to changes in demand and in costs, and the possibility of arbitrary prices changes. We also need to cover the possibility that administrative competition may result in higher cost as well, or intead of, lower prices. And one can question whether the neat curves of marginal cost and marginal revenue have much relevance to practical pricing decisions where pricing is aimed at a target rate of return. What is of major importance is that administrative competition should be the central focus of teaching.

Likewise in theoretical analysis there is need to posit in place of the simplified classical model of an economy *solely* involving classical competition and perfectly flexible prices and wages, a simplified model in which all production is carried on by collectives and all prices are administered prices. The theoretical implications of such an economy could then be adjusted to apply to an economy which has some classical competition and some government production.

[5]Paul A. Samuelson, *Economics,* Fourth Edition, New York, pp. 367-498.

I do not believe that we can fully understand the practical problems of collective capitalism or develop the best policies for dealing with them until we have made this revolution in teaching and theory. But already some of the practical problems are apparent and we are moving toward solutions. I will consider here five of the major problems created by collective capitalism, indicate some of the steps we have already taken toward their solution, and point the direction in which a satisfactory solution seems to me likely to lie.

MAINTAINING FULL EMPLOYMENT

The first practical problem is, of course, that of maintaining full employment. Under the theory of private capitalism, there was a price-adjustment mechanism which would automatically tend to maintain that level of aggregate demand necessary to eliminate involuntary unemployment and assure reasonably full employment. If aggregate demand was deficient, a fall in the price-wage level would increase the real value of the outstanding stock of money, making it greater than the public would choose to hold at the lower level of prices. This redundancy of money would restore real aggregate demand.

Under collective capitalism, the price-wage structure does not have that degree of flexibility necessary to allow this classical mechanism to work. Instead of a general fall in price level, a deficiency in aggregate demand creates a fall in employment and incomes which more than offsets the stimulating effect of any increase in the real stock of money.

The need for positive government action to maintain aggregate demand was fully recognized in the Employment Act of 1946, and there has been general agreement that monetary and fiscal measures should provide the primary means. But the twenty years of experience still leaves us with neither the institutions nor the policies which allow a fine tuning of aggregate demand, or even a reasonable certainty that coarse tuning can be maintained.

It is my own opinion that monetary measures can be a powerful tool for maintaining the appropriate level of aggregate demand, but we have not yet learned how to use them effectively. I cannot see any justification for last summer's 1968 policy which stimulated demand by increasing the total money supply at the rate of 11 percent a year at the same time that we put into effect the surtax aimed to cut demand.[6] In a whole year the tax could be expected to take only $11 billion of income out of the private sector; yet in just four months, monetary policy allowed $6 billion of extra money to be created, or at the rate of $18 billion a year. This provided the economy with the immediate effect of $6 billion of extra credit and the continuing effect of the extra $6 billion in the stock of

[6]From April to July 1968 the total of demand deposits and currency (adjusted for season) increased 2¾ percent or an annual rate of 11 percent.

money. No wonder the surtax has seemed to have no effect in the third and fourth quarters.

Notice that here I am taking issue with the Keynsian doctrine that the only significant way money affects aggregate demand is through its affect on interest rates. Classical theory assumed, and the statistical evidence indicates, not only that money has a direct effect on aggregate demand, but that this effect can be substantial. Because the Keynsian analysis neglects this direct effect of money, it tends to over-emphasize fiscal policy and underestimate the potentials of monetary measures.

However, I reject the classical assumption that there is a fairly stable relation between the amount of money the public would choose to hold and incomes. Therefore I reject the proposal that the stock of money should be increased at a steady annual rate corresponding to the growth in potential real income. Unfortunately for this proposal, the amount of money the public would choose to hold at full employment tends to vary for a variety of reasons. It varies with the seasons; with short-term interest rates; with shifting attitudes toward the future; and with international developments. For an economy predominantly of administrative competition, these variations in the demand for money balances would mean fluctuations in employment if there were no short-run fluctuations in the stock of money.

Clearly we need to know more about the actual effect of monetary and fiscal policy on aggregate demand, and also to revise our monetary and fiscal institutions so as to be able to adjust aggregate demand to the level called for by our productive capacity. When I first introduced the concept of administered prices, I pointed out their implications for monetary policy,[7] and more recently I have suggested how to reorder our monetary institutions to make them more effective instruments for regulating the level of aggregate demand.[8] Once we get away from the overemphasis on fiscal policy and the interest effect of money, I believe we will develop a set of monetary institutions and monetary policies which will allow the fine adjustment necessary for maintaining the appropriate level of aggregate demand.

ADMINISTRATIVE INFLATION

A second major problem of collective capitalism is a new type of inflation unknown to private capitalism. The inflation of classical theory was a demand inflation with a general rise in prices and wage rates. The inflation represented too much money chasing too few goods, and at least for a single country, it could be prevented by the fine tuning of aggregate demand to give both full employment and stability in the price level.

[7] "Price Inflexibility and the Requirements of Stablizing Monetary Policy," *Journal of the American Statistical Association,* Vol. 30, June 1935, pp. 401-413.

[8] "Monetary Institutions to Serve the Modern Economy," in *Institutional Adjustment,* Austin, Texas, 1967, pp. 151-177.

The new type of inflation arises from the indeterminacy of administered prices and wage rates, and from the market power they involve. It is sometimes called "cost-push" inflation with the implication that it results from labor's use of its power to push wage rates up faster than productivity. This is a theoretical possibility. But so also is it a theoretical possibility that business price administrators raise prices arbitrarily, without any increase in units costs or in demand. This could be called a "profits-push" inflation. Because this new type of inflation could be either a cost push or a profits push inflation and because it could only come where prices or wages are administered, I have chosen to call it "administrative inflation."

A characteristic of demand inflation under the conditions of collective capitalism shows itself first in the prices subject to classical competition, but only with substantial lag for administered prices and wage rates. It is also characteristic that it can occur only when aggregate demand is in excess of that needed for full employment. This was true of the inflation which followed the removal of price controls after World War II and of the Korean War inflation. Both were clearly demand inflations.

In contrast, an administrative inflation shows itself first in a rise of administered prices with no rise or fall in classically competitive prices, and it can occur whether or not there is full employment. The 1953 to 1958 price rise was clearly of this character. In that period, the bulk of the 8 percent rise in the wholesale price index was in administered prices, while the indexes for such categories as textiles and farm products went down, a finding that was inadvertently confirmed in a statistical analysis developed by proponents of the Chicago school.[9] This 1953 to 1958 inflation occurred in a period of slack demand, as is indicated by the average unemployment of over 5 percent and the large amount of idle industrial capacity. When the Federal Reserve Board sought to control this inflation on the assumption that it was a demand inflation, it created the depression of 1957 to 1958. Throughout the period a paradox to classical theory existed: simultaneous inflation and underemployment. The inflation was clearly not the result of excess demand.

In recent months, I believe we have been seeing an inflation which is a compound of an excess in aggregate demand due to the rapid increase in the money stock and an administrative inflation which would have occurred in the absence of an excess in demand. Once we adjust our monetary and fiscal institutions so that we can fine-tune the level of aggregate demand, we can prevent *demand* inflation. But this in itself will not prevent administrative inflation.

It has been suggested that administrative inflation can be controlled by maintaining a substantial cushion of unemployed labor and capital. But the

[9]Hearings before the Subcommittee on Antitrust and Monopoly of the Committee on the Judiciary, U. S. Senate, Part I, 1964, Appendix 10 (material by Horace J. DePodwin and Richard T. Selden, with comment by G. C. Means).

administrative inflation of the 1950s occurred with 5 percent of the labor force unemployed. Even if such a cushion could be successful, full employment and creeping inflation would seem to be a more economic alternative than to force more than a million and a half of extra unemployment on those least able to bear the burden. Undoubtedly a system of price and wage controls could prevent administrative inflation, but again, the remedy would seem to me worse than the disease. I do not believe we have yet given the guide-line approach an adequate test. Once the problem is fully understood, I believe that guide lines worked out by the government with the assistance of the leaders of enterprise, labor and consumers could eliminate administrative inflation, or keep it to an acceptable minimum. If not, more drastic measures would be needed.

THE EXTERNAL BALANCE OF PAYMENTS

A third problem created by collective capitalism concerns the external balance of payments. Under private capitalism and the gold standard, flexible prices and wage rates were expected to adjust automatically so as to correct any fundamental imbalance in payments between countries.

With the inflexibility of prices and wages under collective capitalism, the old gold-flow mechanism simply could not work. If prices and wage rates were flexible, a fall in the stock of money in the gold-losing country could be expected to bring a reduction in aggregate demand with a corrective effect of a reduced internal price level. But where prices are insensitive to declining demand, the reduced aggregate demand would result in unemployment. The old gold mechanism could have corrected an imbalance in payments, but it would do this by creating a depression in one country and a boom in the other.

The institutions set up at Bretton Woods are effective in prolonging the period in which change or special measures can correct an imbalance in payments and special drawing rights can extend the period, but neither can correct a fundamental imbalance except by abrupt and painful changes in exchange rates. Of course, we would have an automatic mechanism if we dropped the objective of exchange stability and let exchange rates work themselves out in the market, but this would set up speculative movements and lose the very real values of short-run exchange stability.

I believe that this problem will ultimately be solved by an intermediate course which gives short-run stability in exchange rates and long-run, but gradual, flexibility. Most of the advantages of exchange stability could be obtained if exchange rates were kept within a known narrow bracket for six months or one year at a time. For example, if periodic small changes in the bracket were made in the light of current balances but announced, say, six months or a year in advance, such a forward peg could give short-run stability of rates, avoid speculative pressures for change and yet over a period of years, allow very considerable but gradual changes in exchange rates.

Just what form the intermediate mechanism may take I cannot foresee. But it seems to me clear that changes in internal levels of employment as a method of exchange adjustment will not be tolerated; and that neither freely floating exchange rates nor fixed exchange rates with occasional exchange crises provides a satisfactory basis for adjusting the balance of payments.

THE ALLOCATION OF RESOURCES

A fourth problem arising from collective capitalism has to do with the allocation of resources. According to the theory and principles of private capitalism, a country's resources would tend to be best used if each small producer sought to maximize his profits. Competition would keep prices in reasonable relation to costs and the unseen hand would guide individuals into the most economic use of the resources available to them.

But the large collective enterprise and administrative competition do not fit into this beautiful picture. The powers of corporate management are only crudely controlled by the unseen hand. To maximize profits is often to make less than the most effective use of resources. And mistakes in a single management that would be of negligible importance in a small enterprise can affect the lives of tens or even hundreds of thousands of individuals in a big collective.

The answer to this problem is not to break up collective enterprises into such small pieces that classical competition can prevail. The affluence of our society arises in large part from the high productivity of our big collectives. We do need our antitrust laws and agencies to prevent monopoly where administrative competition can prevail, but these agencies cannot enforce classical competition. Nor is it a satisfactory answer to regulate these collectives except where technology requires monopoly, as in the case of the public utilities, for regulation involves a degree of centralization which tends to be deadening to initiative.

There are, however, two lines of development which are wholly compatible with our free enterprise system and could be expected to make collective capitalism operate more effectively in using our resources.

The first is to forge a criteria of performance for the management of our big collectives. It is an appropriate function of the big collectives to make profits. But the objective of *maximizing* profits is no longer appropriate. In my book on *Pricing Power and the Public Interest,*[10] I examined this problem and suggested certain lines of approach based on target pricing and incentives to performance. Whether these or some other lines of approach are finally adopted, the managements of the big collectives do need a clarification of what constitutes good performance and incentives to stimulate such performance.

[10]Harper Brothers, New York, 1962.

Also, the public needs a great deal more information on costs and volume in order to judge performance. I believe that all corporations controlling half a billion assets or more, and many smaller corporations, are so far removed from the status of private enterprise that they should be given a new legal status and be required to make public the kind of information on costs and volume that is necessary to appraise economic performance.

The second line of development which I believe would make the policy decisions of both the managers of collective enterprises and government more effective has to do with economic planning. Economic planning of the Russian type would clearly be incompatible with our free enterprise system. But advisory planning can provide business and government with valuable background against which to make specific decisions.

I will give you a simple example. Toward the end of World War II, the Committee for Economic Development carried out a piece of advisory planning with profound results. It is a long story which I will not go into now, but through the use the CED made of its advisory planning publication, *Markets After the War,* it raised the sights of the business community and helped to prevent a major depression right after the war. This planning action was entirely advisory. It did not force anyone to act in any particular way. But organized information and estimates were brought to the attention of business men in such a manner that their decisions were altered. The businessmen were influenced in ways that brought their interest and the public interest more nearly together.

How far such advisory planning can go in improving the working of collective capitalism we will not know until we try. And whether the planning is headed by government or by research foundations is secondary, though government would seem to be the natural agent. In either case, such planning should bring together the economic experts of business, labor, consumers, government and the universities. It presumably would include estimates of the general magnitude of consumer demand for different categories of products at full employment over a period of years: the consequent need for capital expenditures and the directions they might well take; estimates of the best uses of our land and water resources; and estimates of the magnitude of the need for different types of manpower skills and training.

Such advisory planning would not dictate to business management. Actual decisions would be in the hands of the individual policy-makers of enterprise. But the broad and approximate plans would, I believe, facilitate management in making better decisions, would provide a better basis for defining performance, and would make easier the appraisal of performance.

The combination of criteria of performance and advisory planning should help to canalize the use of management's power in the great collectives, and bring its exercise closer to the public interest. This would increase the legitimacy of corporate power. If these do not suffice, again more drastic measures would be needed.

INCOME DISTRIBUTION

The final problem I plan to discuss, but only briefly, is that of income distribution. Under the theory of private capitalism, the unseen hand was expected to bring about an equitable distribution of income. That this does not happen under collective capitalism is abundantly clear, a fact that is explicitly recognized in such social legislation as unemployment insurance and the progressive income tax. Furthermore, an affluent society which can afford to eliminate poverty cannot afford not to. We have made important progress in reducing inequities but we still have a very considerable distance to go.

SUMMARY OF MAJOR PROBLEMS

Here, then, are five major problems facing collective capitalism: full employment, administrative inflation, the external balance of payments, effective allocation of resources and equitable distribution of income. To list them seems almost trite. But the theory of private capitalism says that the unseen hand will take care of each, while both the theory of collective capitalism and actual practice say that automatic forces will not suffice. Where the economy is predominantly one of collective enterprise and administrative competition, market forces alone will not serve, or serve only in a very gross and unacceptable degree.

In the 36 years since capitalism was in near collapse and the principles of private capitalism were rejected, we, as a society, have moiled and toiled to solve these problems. In spite of the interference of a world war and two regional wars, we have made important progress. For a democratic society as large as ours to reject one set of principles and develop a new set to guide policy is a major undertaking and takes time. And until the new set is clearly delineated and accepted and working successfully, the society will be in some degree at sixes and sevens. There will be much frustration and disagreement, and unfairness and injustice. Will this frustration become endemic and force a change-over to a radically different system, or will collective capitalism develop into a viable and continuing system?

AREAS OF PRIVATE ENTERPRISE

Before I attempt to answer this question I want to point to two sectors of our economy in which private enterprise is the prevalent form.

The first is agriculture. The great bulk of farm production today is carried on by family farms and the efficiency of this form of organization, with its close tie between incentive and reward, is attested by high and increasing yields in this country. Both Russia and China have sought to get efficient farm production through collectives and have failed. Indeed, in Russia, nearly half the livestock products and a third of total agricultural output now come from the private enterprise of peasants on individually operated farm plots. I do not expect that agriculture in this country will lose its private-enterprise character for years to come.

A second major segment of our economy which is predominantly a matter of private enterprise is urban rental housing. In contrast to the efficiency of private enterprise in agriculture, the results of private enterprise in our inner city housing have been far from satisfactory. Private enterprise in agriculture would seem to be compatible with a successful system of collective capitalism. The same cannot be said for private enterprise in urban housing, except as it is substantially modified or canalized in the public interest.

THE RUSSIAN ALTERNATIVE

I must also consider the Russian alternative to collective capitalism, which is based primarily on three propositions: first, that capital is not productive; second, that government centralization of control over production can be more productive than the decentralized control of capitalism; and third, that the inequity in the distribution of income will be at a minimum under government ownership of productive resources.

The first of these, that capital is not productive, has already been disproved by the behavior of Russia and its satellites. In each, capital is closely rationed as a scarce resource and some economists in these countries are beginning to admit that Marx was wrong on this point.

The second proposition, that government-centralized control over production can be more productive than free enterprise, still remains to be proved and the evidence so far does not seem to support it. While Russia was introducing western technological advances, the catching up could be more rapid; but recent rates of growth of production have been slower, and part of the increase in per capita output has resulted from the greater agricultural efficiency in that third of farm production which has been transferred to the private enterprise of individual peasants, a direct reversal of centralized control.

The third proposition, that income can be more equitably distributed than in a free enterprise system, is closely bound up with incentives and risk taking. If all saving and all risk and all production is carried on by government, it can set the pattern of income distribution that it chooses. Under free enterprise, initiative, saving and risk-taking are left primarily to private and collective enterprise, and incomes are a part of the incentive system. Under this system, income distribution can be influenced, but not dictated, by government. Increasing the equity of income distribution, particularly to the disadvantaged, is and should be an important government function under collective capitalism. But all inequities in income distribution cannot be eliminated under either system. If, as I believe, collective capitalism is both more productive and gives the individual greater freedom, somewhat greater inequity in income would be a small price to pay for these advantages, so long as the inequity comes out of the greater production and is not at the expense of the disadvantaged. The problem is to keep the inequity to a minimum.

THE FUTURE OF COLLECTIVE CAPITALISM

This brings me to the question: What is the future of collective capitalism? On this I am an optimist. I do not see this country reverting to private capitalism. Nor do I see us following the path of Russia. The major problems of collective capitalism are not the product of internal contradictions in our system, but the product of contradictions between collective capitalism and the set of policies appropriate to private capitalism. We have already made important progress toward developing new policies. As we come to recognize more thoroughly the imperatives of collective capitalism, I believe we will solve the major problems which it has created. I do not suggest that we will produce a perfect system. Nor do I suggest that the improvement in the workings of collective capitalism can be brought about easily. Resistance to change and the pressures of immediate self-interest will stand in the way. But I believe that the general interest in a well-running economy will override these resistances.

Thus I envisage a system in which fine tuning of aggregate demand, principally through monetary policy, will maintain a high level of employment of both men and machines; in which administrative inflation will be under practical control through advisory planning, wage-price guidelines and perhaps specific controls for strategic commodities; in which an external balance of payments will be maintained through exchange rates which are relatively fixed for short periods of time, but gradually change to correct fundamental imbalances; in which business decisions (as well as those of government) on the allocation of resources will be brought into closer relation to the public interest through advisory planning and clarification of what constitutes economic performance; and a complete system of government measures to support incomes of the disadvantaged at an acceptable minimum level, while above this level inequities are kept to a minimum through better operation of the economy and through the continued use of taxation.

I would expect such an economy to yield a steadily rising level of incomes, greater leisure and the funds to enjoy it, and the resources to help in the development of less developed countries. Whether the affluent life can also be a good life will be a real problem, but not one I will deal with here.

8

The Rise of the Corporate State in America

Daniel R. Fusfeld

Every society contains within itself the forces that create its own future. The social order is always in the process of becoming, and the future inevitably must be different from the past. The processes of change are rooted in the past, operate in the present, and thrust into the future. Social scientists have to develop a triple vision; they must look backward to the world we came from, analyze the world in which we live, and try to discern the future into which we will inevitably be cast. The crisis that came upon the world in the mid-1960s—Black revolt, the youth culture, disaffection of the intellectuals, turmoil in Southeast Asia, continuing peasant revolts in many parts of the world, the breakdown of the international financial system—compels us to look for the sources of the crisis, and ask where are we going and what forces propel us. We must look at the past to understand the present and divine the future.

The thesis of this paper is that the United States has moved well down the path toward a corporate state. Economic power is concentrated in the hands of a relatively few supercorporations that are now moving toward a dominance in the world economy to match their position in the domestic economy. Political power has shifted heavily into the hands of the executive branch of the federal government as the positive state has taken on an increasingly significant role. These two centers of economic and political power have developed a growing symbiosis. The self-selecting elite of the supercorporation dominates the decision-making process, while lesser centers of power in labor unions and the universities are drawn into the system as junior partners by a variety of economic and political mechanisms. Because of the tremendous economic strength of the United States, these domestic developments have tremendous import for the rest of the world. They enable American economic and political power to be used in the world at large in the interests of those who manage the emerging American corporate state.

The corporate state in this country involves an economic and political compromise between those who hold power and those who do not. As long as the economic system provides an acceptable degree of security, growing material wealth, and opportunity for further increase for the next generation, the average American does not ask who is running things or what goals are being pursued. The system and those in power remain unchallenged as long as the material payoff is sustained. The elite is free to use the great wealth of America to preserve and extend its power, and to use its power to preserve and extend its wealth.

Three Long-Term Trends

Three great long-term trends have dominated the development of American economic institutions in the twentieth century: the continuing growth of giant corporations, the rise of the positive state, and a move toward American dominance in the world economy. Together they converged in the quarter century after World War II to create the basic outlines of the emerging American corporate state.

The Giant Corporation

The chief outlines of the rise of the giant corporation to a position of dominance in the American economy are familiar to all. Three merger movements, at the turn of the century, in the 1920s, and after World War II, created the pattern of big enterprise oligopoly that dominates those sectors of the economy to which we look for the products and services of the affluent economy and the sinews of national power. In manufacturing, for example, the 100 largest firms in 1968 held a larger share of manufacturing assets than the 200 largest in 1950; the 200 largest in 1968 controlled as large a share as the 1,000 largest in 1941. This aggrandizement of the giants is matched by similar, but less well-documented, trends in other sectors of the economy where big enterprise finds its home.

Increased concentration is supplemented by ties that bind large corporations into communities of interest, based on stockholdings by wealthy families, interlocking directorates, and financial connections with large banks. The trust activities of banks and trust companies add another dimension to linkages within the corporate community and strengthen the strategic position of financial institutions. In addition, trade associations promote common policies in both economic and political activity, and strengthen the leadership of large firms within their industries.

Several aspects of the large corporation merit further exploration. First, giant international firms have appeared. The international corporation was made possible by advances in the technology of transportation and communication after World War II (jet aircraft and automatic data communication, for example). U.S. corporations were able to take advantage of the new technology much more readily than foreign corporations, in part because much of that technology was developed here, but chiefly because of the predominance of the United States in world trade and international finance. The result is that U.S.-based corporations dominate the population of giant international corporations and provide an organizational expansion of the U.S. economy that supplements its outward thrust of trade and finance.

Second, the internal organization of the giant corporation is authoritarian, hierarchical, and bureaucratic. It is run from the top by a management that is largely self-selecting. Separation of ownership from control may have spread ownership very widely, although that conclusion remains controversial, but it has enabled managements to free themselves from control by owners to a considerable degree. The chief force with which they must contend is the influence of financial institutions that dominate access to the capital markets. The combination of the rise of giant firms of an authoritarian nature with separation of ownership and control brought a self-selecting business elite whose influence over economic affairs increases with the growing dominance of the firms they manage.

Third, giant corporations become private governments, in the sense that their actions and policies govern the alternatives open to millions of people and thousands of communities. Prices, investment policy, product development, location of plants, wage and employment policies—the whole range of corporate policy—are decisions of national importance because of the size and significance of the organizations that make them. In that sense much of our life is governed by the decisions made by a small group of men who are responsible only to themselves, who select their successors, and whose organizations continue for an indefinite time. A pattern of economic decision making has emerged that is only imperfectly controlled by market forces and which has questionable legitimacy and limited accountability.

The Positive State

The rise of the positive state is the second major trend that is transforming our economic institutions. Its distinguishing feature is new and expanded functions for the federal government. Starting with the Federal Reserve Act of 1914 and continuing through the Employment Act of 1946 to the full-scale adoption of Keynesian macroeconomic policy in the 1960s, the national government has taken on the function of stabilizing the economy and fostering full employment growth. Simultaneously, it has socialized many of the economic risks of a self-adjusting system of markets through unemployment insurance, workmen's compensation, old age and survivors' insurance, mortgage guarantee programs, guaranty of bank deposits, stabilization of farm prices, and a host of other programs that reduce or shift economic risks that formerly were borne by individuals and business firms. Resolution of conflicts between labor and management is the object of a series of laws related to labor relations. Another area of conflict, that between consumer and seller, has been the concern of legislation at both the federal and state level, starting decades ago with regulation of public utilities and expanding to other areas of regulation decade by decade. Governments at all levels foster the education and training needed to keep a complex economy functioning and growing. All of these measures share a common characteristic. By intervening in the mechanism of the self-adjusting market, they are designed to create a framework within which the modern economy can flourish. They are positive action to achieve designated goals by a positive state, in contrast to the laissez-faire state.

A shift in constitutional law accompanied the functional change taking place in the role of government. The laissez-faire state's constitutional framework of limited powers permitted the federal government to do only those things specifically designated in the Constitution. In a series of path-breaking decisions over a five-year period in the mid-1930s those limitations were set aside: the federal government was enabled to use its taxing and spending powers to further the general welfare, and the general welfare was to be defined by Congress. We moved from a constitution of limitations to a constitution of powers, to use Arthur Selwyn Miller's expressive phrase.

These functional and legal changes were accompanied by a shift in the locus of political power. The New Deal years, with their enlarged federal functions and increased federal budgets, initiated a long-term shift of power from local and state governments to Washington. Within the federal government power tended to shift from the legislative to the executive branch. This change occurred partly because the departments of the executive branch had more funds to spend; the ability to allocate and use those funds increased the power of the administrative bureaucracy. Congress lost control of many programs because they were set up on a continuing basis that seriously reduced the freedom of Congress to restructure the budget. In addition, new programs or changes in old ones originated in the executive departments; they had the experts and the experience necessary to determine what was necessary to achieve policy goals. Finally, power shifted to the executive branch because the new programs were national in scope. The president and the executive departments had a national constituency, while Congress was an agglomeration of local constituencies. Initiatives for the solution of national problems were bound to come from those with a national political base.

During World War II the locus of power within Washington shifted further, to the military and the national security managers. They had vastly increased funds to spend; they had a technical competence in an area that was a *terra incognita* to most Americans; they had a near monopoly on information; and they held national survival as a hostage. After World War II, when military spending was sharply cut, it seemed as if the power of the national security managers was waning, but events quickly changed their position. The Cold War, the Korean War, McCarthyism and anticommunism, the missile gap of 1960, the rise of Fidel Castro in Cuba, and the Vietnam War pushed military and related spending to new heights. The militarization of America over the last two decades kept the military and the national security managers firmly in positions of great power.

Throughout this period the role of the chief executive also was growing. The president, not Congress, was responsible for the formation of economic policy under the Employment Act of 1946. In addition, foreign policy and international affairs became almost totally the responsibility of the president and the executive branch. As those issues came to dominate postwar federal policy, the president inevitably became the focus of government.

In this fashion, over a period of forty years the locus of power shifted to Washington, within Washington to the executive branch, and within the executive branch to the president and to those policy makers concerned primarily with military and national security affairs.

America and the World

Concurrently with the rise of the giant corporation and the positive state, the United States moved to a position of economic and political dominance in world affairs. It is now the largest single participant in world trade, accounting for over 6 percent of world exports and imports. It is the largest supplier of capital to the world economy, generating more than 50 percent of the world's savings. After decades of foreign investment and an outward flow of capital, the U.S. balance of payments shows an annual net income on private international investment of about $6.4 billion, as compared with about $1.6 billion for the nine next most important trading countries combined (1968 figures). U.S. economic growth and high living standards have made it the world's most important market and the most important source of capital in the world.

The U.S.-based international corporation is in a special position of prominence. In 1970, U.S. direct investment abroad reached $78 billion in book value, and is expected to total $85 billion in 1971. The market value is undoubtedly much greater. Sales from U.S.-owned overseas production facilities are about $68 billion, which is more than double total U.S. exports of about $27 billion. Profit rates earned by overseas facilities generally exceed those from U.S. facilities, which partially explains why foreign operations of U.S. concerns are expanding more rapidly than domestic investment. IBM, for example, earned more total profits in 1970 from its international operations than it did from those in the United States, while Dow Chemical expects its foreign sales to equal its domestic sales sometime during the 1970s.

American economic penetration of the world economy was strengthened by the international financial system established at Bretton Woods in 1944. Under that system each nation's central bank was required to maintain the value of its currency within 1 percent of par. That innocent provision, when combined with a persistent U.S. balance of payments deficit, resulted in an annual shift of assets from foreign to U.S. ownership of from $1 billion to $3 billion annually, which was financed not by U.S. savings, but by foreign central banks. It also created inflationary pressures abroad that had to be countered by macroeconomic policies which tended to restrain economic growth in the countries in which they were applied. Meanwhile, the flow of additional assets to American ownership aided the international growth of U.S. corporations and helped the U.S. government to pay for some of its military commitments abroad.

This system finally collapsed in 1971, under the impact of U.S. inflation and expanded military spending abroad. The inflation brought our seemingly permanent favorable balance of trade to an end, while the Vietnam War escalated our overseas military spending. When foreign central banks indicated unwillingness to finance the resulting $22 billion deficit in the U.S. balance of payments, we were forced to float and then devalue the dollar. The fundamental reality of U.S. economic power politics was revealed by Secretary of the Treasury Connolly, however, who told the Group of Ten at Geneva that the new currency relationships we sought would have to provide a favorable balance of trade for the United States of $13 billion annually, to finance our "normal" foreign investments and overseas military spending with $2 billion to spare for emergencies. He was proposing, in essence, that the contribution of foreigners to U.S. world dominance be shifted from the international financial system to the international trade system, and that it be made permanent rather than subject to the discretion of foreign central banks.

In passing, we should note that Connolly's proposal was equivalent to an annual tax of $13 billion on the U.S. economy, in real terms. Yet neither the public nor Congress were consulted on the American position, which illustrates how much power has shifted into the hands of the executive. We also should note that the agreements reached in mid-December of this year reconstitute the Bretton Woods system with a somewhat greater degree of flexibility, but leave it equally vulnerable to the same forces that brought its downfall.

American economic expansion had political allies. Economic predominance in Canada came from the flow of capital and proximity of markets. Those forces plus the Monroe Doctrine and military and diplomatic intervention brought Latin America under U.S. economic influence. The rest of the world was to be available to American economic interests through the Open Door policy, enunciated first with respect to the Congo in 1884 and later for China in 1895–1900. We even tried colonialism in the Philippines and Cuba, but those were aberrant experiments for a nation whose Manifest Destiny lay in the pervasive spread of its financial strength and the attracting force of its great market. It is not necessary for the United States to have colonies, or even political spheres of influence, as long as its more than 200 million people consume more than half the world's production of raw materials and manufactured goods, and generate over half the world's savings. It is only necessary that the rest of the world be open.

World War II brought political and military predominance as well. American technology achieved an initial monopoly of nuclear weapons and methods for their delivery. The war had left no nation in Western Europe with the strength to counter the USSR, so we filled the vacuum with troops, economic aid, and military alliances. Liquidation of the British and French empires in Africa and southern Asia brought U.S. military and political power to predominance there. In the Far East our military victory over Japan left us in command. Aside from the Soviet Union, Eastern Europe, and China, world power lay in Washington.

The international thrust of American political and economic power is of the greatest significance for the rise of the American corporate state. The interests of big government and big business coincide most strongly in the international sphere, where the political and military strength of the one supports and is supported by the economic power of the other. For example, U.S. oil companies in North Africa and the Middle East produce crude oil essential to the economic life of Europe and Japan, and they profit accordingly. A U.S. fleet in the Mediterranean not only maintains U.S. power and supports our Western European allies, but also maintains the existing political situation in the area and helps to stabilize economic arrangements there. It is one of the clearest examples of the symbiotic relationships between U.S. political and economic positions around the world. As America moved toward military and political predominance in the years after World War II it finally was able to achieve an Open Door policy that gave U.S. trade and U.S. capital full access to the world.

The Merging of Public and Private Power

Concentration of economic power and the emergence of executive power in a positive state were not independent of each other. There has been a growing tendency for them to merge. Economists are familiar with an early manifestation, the regulation of utilities and other industries "affected with the public interest." What began ostensibly as protection of the public was gradually transformed into protection of those presumably being regulated, with the power of the state united behind the economic power of industry.

The petroleum industry is the classic example of the cooperative use of public and private power for private gain. It is the second largest industry in the country and its fuel products are essential to a modern economy. The federal and state governments cooperate with the large integrated oil companies to maintain a complex system of market control. The domestic market is protected from foreign competition by federal legislation that restricts and licenses imports of crude oil. The states, under the Interstate Oil Compact Commission, regulate domestic output on the basis of quotas that, in effect, maintain current prices. The quotas are enforced by federal prohibition of transportation in interstate commerce of oil produced above the quotas. Control of crude oil pipelines by the industry giants, validated by an antitrust consent decree, enables large firms to profit from transporting the raw material of smaller competitors. Finally, the industry as a whole is given a favored tax position through its large depletion allowance. This system stabilizes prices and protects the existing firms. The industry charges prices that not only produce a normal profit, but also provide, in normal times, almost all the capital needed for expansion. Existing stockholders can monopolize the gains from economic growth and new technology rather than sharing those gains with suppliers of new capital. Capital for expansion comes from the taxpayer and from the consumer of the industry's products.

On a much larger scale the symbiosis of big business and big government encompasses the whole economy. Big business needs big government and the services it performs. Modern macroeconomic policies provide the economic growth that large corporations need to satisfy their own desires for growth. Full employment stability provides the security and makes possible the long time horizons that enable giant firms to carry out long-range plans. For example, in 1971 the automobile companies begin planning for the automobiles that will be marketed in 1978; they can be relatively secure in their expectations about total purchasing power and automobile demand because they know the federal government will assure relatively full employment. Assurance of full employment growth provides the lush economic environment in which the supercorporation flourishes.

Big business needs big government for a second reason. Socialization of risks, social insurance, and welfare programs resolve some of the personal problems inherent in a market economy. By bringing greater security to people these programs stabilize the social order. They give the ordinary man a stake in the status quo, and they allay some of the discontent that otherwise might lead to social and political change. A similar point might be made about labor legislation and resolution of the conflict between labor and management, but more about that in a moment.

Finally, big business needs big government to educate the technical and managerial cadres that staff big enterprise. Most of the investment in human capital required by the giant corporation is made by governments when not by individuals. Much of the basic scientific research that lays the groundwork for technological change is carried out under public auspices.

On the other side of the bargain, big government needs big business, particularly in a nation that has the position of world power of the United States. The technology of modern warfare is provided by giant firms. Modern weaponry implies such firms as Lockheed Corporation. Faced with this need, the Department of Defense consciously set out to create, foster, and succor such firms during and after World War II. The recent rescue operation for Lockheed is only the latest and largest example of many similar situations in the past. The military-industrial complex, with its intricate and interwoven relationships between public officials and private firms, between public needs and private gain, is the offspring of the dependence of national power upon the economic base provided by big business.

Big government needs big business in an even more fundamental sense. Giant corporations now are so important that government must preserve them in order to keep the economy functioning. The case of the Penn Central Railroad is instructive. That corporation occupies two strategic positions in the economic landscape. Its transportation function is essential for the proper functioning of the industrial economy of the northeastern states; remove the Penn Central and the entire economy must falter. In addition, the financial obligations of the railroad constitute an important share of the assets of many leading banks and insurance companies, and its debts are owed to many municipalities and industrial firms as well. A financial breakdown of the Penn Central could bring with it a succession of other bankruptcies. For these reasons the federal government had to intervene to keep the railroad operating and to enable it to pay its most pressing debts. The entire economy was the Penn Central's hostage, and the federal government responded accordingly.

The mutuality of interest and symbiotic relationship between big business and big government is assuming formal organization. The most recent step in this direction is the system of economic controls instituted by the Nixon administration in its effort to halt inflation. An organization combining representatives of business, labor, and the public, under the leadership of government officials, seeks to define national economic policy with respect to wages and prices, makes decisions that bring those policies into effect, and has the legal sanctions necessary to enforce its decisions.

Whatever one may think of the wisdom or effectiveness of the policies and their administration, we must recognize here both the philosophy and the mode of operation of the corporate state: individual interests are subordinated to the common good, which is determined by representatives of the chief economic interests affected, and the decisions are enforced by the state. It echoes the style pioneered by Fascist Italy and tried once before in this country by the NRA of the 1930s. We do not know what the ultimate pattern will be, but the chances are good that some form of incomes policy embodying those principles will emerge as a permanent feature of the American economic constitution.

Big Business and Big Labor

The emerging corporate state creates a subtle mutuality of interest between big business and big unions, despite the contest between the two in collective bargaining. The pattern of labor–management relations established under the umbrella of federal law helps to preserve and stabilize the positions of big business and big unions. Long-term contracts, industry-wide bargaining, grievance procedures and arbitration, even the process of collective bargaining itself, contribute to the security of both sides. If corporations gain uniform wage rates throughout the industry, one source of cost differences between firms is eliminated and maintenance of common prices in oligopolistic industries is facilitated. Long-term contracts assure large corporations of known wage costs over a period of one to three years, facilitating the planning that gives large firms an advantage over small. Firms protected against unauthorized strikes and work stoppages need not contend with disruption of production lines. As long as reasonable collective bargaining agreements are reached, the industry is protected against government intervention in determining wages and working conditions.

Unions as organizations also benefit. Exclusive bargaining agreements protect the union from having its membership raided by other unions. Grievance procedures and arbitration are means to channel members' discontent into agreed-upon settlement procedures, thereby reducing internal pressures. Even union dues often are collected by the firm and paid directly to the union. Finally, a wise business management will protect a "reasonable" union leadership by seeing to it that its constituents obtain sufficient economic gains to keep it contented with that leadership as well as with their jobs.

In recent years this growing mutuality of interest has been disturbed by the process of inflation. As long as the economy expands at a rate fast enough to maintain reasonably full employment, and government fiscal and monetary policies provide the necessary level of total spending, both unions and management can seek gains that promote inflationary price increases. As long as wage increases plus fringe benefits do not exceed productivity gains, there is no internal cost pressure on the business firm, but it is tempting for unions to push for greater gains, particularly in oligopolistic industries in which administered prices can be moved upward without damaging profits. As long as government stands ready to maintain aggregate demand at full employment levels, the burden is shifted to the general public, to the mutual benefit of workers and business firms. Inflation validated by macroeconomic policy can be a safety valve that eases the conflict between unions and management.

When inflation is caused by excessive aggregate demand, as during the escalation of the Vietnam War, and government imposes fiscal and monetary policies designed to halt the rising prices, the conflict between unions and management is intensified. Union members press for wage increases to compensate for the rapid rise in prices, while management is faced with both rising costs and government pressures to keep prices from going up. These were the conflicts, coming to a head in the summer of 1971, that forced the Nixon administration to take a further step toward the corporate state by imposing controls on prices and wages. It now seems that the controls will succeed in rescuing the corporate community from the pressures of union demands on the one side and deflationary macroeconomic policy on the other.

Clearly there are conflicts within the pattern of mutuality of interest. Inflation created by the state's thrust toward world power disrupts the tripartite relationship between state, corporation, and union. The problem is resolved by a greater dose of economic planning and further development of the corporate state.

The Universities

American universities long have functioned as training grounds for the business elite, particularly schools of law, engineering, and business administration. This function has grown steadily, as technology has become more complex, as the scope of the giant corporation has expanded, and as the legal niceties of corporate relations with government and labor have become more intricate. In recent decades a close relationship between universities and government has arisen to supplement the ties with business. The center of this new relationship was military needs and international affairs: universities did much of the basic and applied research on development of new weapons, and they trained the experts in overseas areas required by the nation's expanded international commitments.

Development of military technology involves a symbiotic relationship between government, universities, and military contractors. Government supports weapons research in the universities; the enterprise hires professors as consultants and sends its personnel into the university's classes; and everyone involved receives some kind of payoff. Roswell Gilpatric, then deputy secretary of defense, described an ideal relationship of this sort in a 1962 speech at South Bend, Indiana, to an audience of midwestern businessmen and university people.

> What Bendix has been doing in this field deserves mention. Bendix personnel, I am informed, have worked closely with the University of Michigan faculty, sharing the use of the University's nuclear reactor in significant research. The Bendix Systems Division, the University, and the Federal Government have been associated in joint meteorological programs in field tests.
>
> Bendix has employed consultants from the University faculty; Bendix technicians have given part-time service as faculty members; and Bendix personnel are encouraged to take advanced courses and to secure degrees from the University—with 30 percent of all company engineers having taken some courses.
>
> I am pleased, also, to learn that Bendix maintains contacts with other great educational institutions in this area, including Michigan State University, Wayne State University, and South Bend's own Notre Dame. These activities may help to explain why Bendix received $172 million of prime military contract awards in Fiscal 1961 and an even larger total in Fiscal 1962.

Sometimes research is done by university departments. Sometimes it centers in quasi-independent research units such as the Lawrence Laboratories (University of California), Willow Run Laboratories (University of Michigan), Lexington Laboratories (MIT), Applied Physics Laboratory (Johns Hopkins), Forrestal Laboratories (Princeton), and Aeronautical Research Laboratory (Cornell). This organizational device partially removes administration of military research from academic controls, and creates an academic vested interest in military programs.

Much university activity outside the sciences is also caught up in the military-industrial-academic complex. International programs and training of foreign language experts are funded heavily by federal fellowships or grants from foundations designed to promote the international interests of the federal government. For example, the Foreign Area Fellowship Program was originated by the Ford Foundation to help the State Department find expertise "required for the effective discharge of this country's increased international responsibilities." The National Defense Education Act also served to move the entire university community toward the goals of national policy.

The Managerial Elite

A self-selecting economic elite dominates the emerging corporate state. There always have been economic and political leaders, but in a world in which power is dispersed an elite is not possible. In modern America, however, power itself is concentrated, both in a relatively small number of giant corporations (200, 250, 500, 750?), and in a small number of executive positions in the federal government. The supercorporation and the positive state have created an institutional structure readily controllable from a small number of strategic positions. How many positions? Perhaps several thousand at the most. Certainly no more than ten thousand business and financial leaders, military men, and federal administrators constitute this power elite.

There have been enough studies of the American managerial elite to give us a rough idea of its nature and changing scope. As a group, it comes predominantly from an urban, white, Protestant, upper or upper-middle income background. Studies of the social and economic characteristics of post-World War II business leaders by W. Lloyd Warner, C. Wright Mills, and G. William Domhof, building on studies of earlier periods by Frank Taussig and William Miller, show very few immigrants or sons of immigrants, small numbers from farm, worker, or lower white-collar backgrounds, relatively few Catholics and Jews, and no Blacks. About 10 percent inherited their top positions by moving into family-dominated companies; about 5 percent are entrepreneurs who built their own companies; some 10 – 15 percent are professional men, mostly lawyers, who moved into top business positions after professional success. Some 70 percent, however, moved to top positions by working up through the business hierarchy, which is a much greater proportion than in the past. Seventy years ago the entrepreneurs and family-connected managers were far more important (68 percent), the career executive much less important (18 percent), and the proportion of lawyers and other professionals was about the same.

These data suggest that the business elite is a relatively open one. It recruits from outside the existing group, and this tendency appears to be increasing. The major source of recruits is the system of higher education; the business elite always has had more education than the average, and today that is more true than ever. The educational system is a primary screening mechanism and partially explains why so many of the business elite are from upper and upper-middle income groups. They tend to be drawn heavily from the Ivy League colleges (where most of the managers from "old wealth" families graduate) and from the large state universities (where most of the career executives receive their educations).

This first level of screening is supplemented by executive training programs and on-the-job training. There the aspiring top manager is indoctrinated with the business point of view and the ideology of management, there he learns to fit in with those already at the top, and there he develops the good judgment that top management requires. Since advancement depends on the judgment of those already at the top, a premium is placed on development of the viewpoints and styles of life that prevail. As Mills put it, "in personal manner and political view, in social ways and business style, he must be like those who are already in, and upon whose judgments his own success rests."

The business elite is a self-perpetuating and self-selecting group which develops a common set of values, an accepted mode of behavior, and an unspoken but recognizable set of goals. The value system, in particular, stresses the desirability of wealth, both for the individual and the nation, and accepts as generally beneficent the institutions of private property and the national state. Indeed, strengthening and preservation of those institutions seems to be the fundamental point of agreement among the business elite, irrespective of their political persuasions. Their value system embraces the slogan of the Medici family in fifteenth-century Florence: "Money to get power, power to protect the money."

The business elite is supplemented by a group of military leaders whose socialization occurs in the military academies. There they learn the values of national power and respect for the status quo, attitudes that are reinforced by the selection process for high command within the military itself and by contact with the leadership of the industrial part of the military-industrial complex.

The managerial elite of the executive branch of the government is another matter. We tend to think of that group as having risen from the political ranks, moving into top governmental positions from governorships, mayoraltys, or other elected posts. While that is true for some, the great majority are drawn from the business world, as studies by the Brookings Institution, Gabriel Kolko, and Richard Barnet have amply shown. In particular, the national security managers of the federal government are drawn almost wholly from the executives of large corporations, large financial institutions, and the large law firms that do their legal business. A similar situation prevails throughout other branches of the federal government, but not to the same extent. Nevertheless, one of the close ties between the positive state and the supercorporation is the presence of a managerial group in government that is drawn in large part from the top ranks of business leadership itself.

Within the managerial elite a complex set of relationships oriented toward achieving a consensus in national policy is at work. Much of what is taken for pluralist determination of policy by political scientists is, in effect, a pluralism of the managerial elite. A sketch of the process, which is quite familiar to all once we stop to think about it, will clarify the point.

Corporation managers, their bankers and lawyers, and the wealthy families associated with them dominate the boards of trustees of the great private universities scattered from Cambridge to Palo Alto. They also dominate the large foundations, which had their origins in the wealth of an earlier elite generation. The foundations, in turn, provide funds for the "think tanks" staffed by professors and researchers from the academic world and often affiliated with the private universities. The think tanks provide expert advice and advisors directly to government agencies, and also create an expertise used by a wide variety of policy planning groups dominated by foundations and corporate managerial elite, such as The American Assembly, the Committee for Economic Development, and the Council on Foreign Relations. Ideas and personnel from these organizations and think tanks flow to the federal government, particularly the executive branch, and to federal task forces, commissions, and working parties, composed in large part of the managerial elite and its expert advisors. These groups examine problems and make policy recommendations, with the result that national goals and federal policy strategies are derived from a pluralist consensus of the elite. Specific policy programs come from the political hurly-burly of Congress, but the goals of national policy are seldom determined there.

The Political Economy of Our Time

The corporate state in America rests on a complex political economy. Its power base is the supercorporation and the executive branch of the positive state. Its goals are strongly oriented toward national power, partly as an end in itself, and partly to preserve the existing structure of wealth. It is directed by a self-selecting and self-perpetuating elite. Its military power and economic strength are used to create a world in which it flourishes.

The power base is narrow, however, as any elite's must be. Control can be retained only by appeal for support, or at least acquiescence, to millions who do not share directly in either wealth or power. Two methods are used: the growing affluence derived from economic growth, and psychological appeals that seek support on emotional grounds.

First, affluence. Economic growth maintained at rates that exceed the growth of population provides rising real incomes for the great majority of Americans. As long as the system has a material payoff for the average person, little question is raised about who controls power or who has great wealth. This fundamental characteristic of our political economy helps to explain the great emphasis placed on full employment and economic growth as goals of national policy, why the principal representatives of big business embraced Keynesian economics in the 1950s, and why President Nixon could say in 1970, "I am a Keynesian." Keynesian macroeconomic policy is essential to the political compromise that enables an elite-managed corporate state to survive.

The vital importance of the materialist payoff to middle-income America is illustrated by the reaction of public opinion to the Vietnam War. The war brought taxes and inflation that gobbled up real income, and the military draft began to take sons and husbands. The American middle class first became restive and then opposed the war. The material payoff stopped, the political compromise was broken, and opposition spread. Opponents of U.S. expansionism recognized this strategic weakness of the American corporate state relatively early. Che Guevarra, for example, called for "a thousand Vietnams" to put such great strain on the system that it could not continue.

The U.S. response to that threat is just emerging. Initially, we are Vietnamizing the war in Southeast Asia to reduce the loss of U.S. manpower and placate the suburbs. Inflation is being halted by controls. For the longer strategy, however, we are developing a new type of capital-intensive warfare using electronic sensing, automatically controlled weapons, saturation bombing, and new types of chemical warfare that are designed, with the help of Lockheed's famous C5A, to fight limited wars on a moment's notice in any part of the world with few men and a great deal of materiel. Simultaneously, we are moving to a volunteer army to eliminate the draft. In the future, wars like those in Vietnam will be hardly distinguishable from peacetime. In both war and peace there will be plenty of jobs in military production, and active warfare on a Vietnam scale will disturb us hardly more than our intervention in the Dominican Republic or Guatemala.

Second, psychological appeals. The corporate state needs more than neo-Keynesian economics and a capital-intensive military technology. It needs spirit, belief in its righteousness, enemies. They are provided. All Americans, rich or poor, are taught the trappings of nationalism from an early age. Much of the teaching of history in our primary and secondary schools performs that function. Stephen Decatur's toast, "My country, right or wrong," is part of our heritage. Lyndon Johnson could appeal to a sense of national honor to justify his Vietnam policy. We are trained from childhood to see national goals as our individual goals, psychologically to identify ourselves with the nation, to feel a warm, emotional attachment to Old Glory. If the conditioning is successful the national goals designed by an elite to advance their wealth and power become the individual goals of millions.

For those who need more we provide a messianic democracy, the idea that the United States has a unique political and economic system more beneficent than any other, and it is the duty of America and Americans to spread that system to less fortunate people around the globe. From this chauvinism springs not only our well-known feelings of superiority to the rest of the world, but also such programs as the Peace Corps, foreign aid, and a series of quasi-charitable efforts that appeal to liberals and reformers.

For the fearful there is anticommunism. It identifies a known enemy of unknown dimensions, an external and internal threat that can never be fully countered. Anticommunism provides an excuse for American world hegemony, a rationale for huge military expenditures and space adventures, reasons for going to war against peasant revolutionary movements in the Third World, and justification for internal surveillance, mass arrests, and political trials.

Every fascist nation developed emotional appeals designed to gain loyalty to the regime. Japan deified the emperor, hated the westerner, and asserted the superiority of the Japanese race. Germany used anticommunism and anti-Semitism in combination with the appeal of Aryan superiority. Spain advertised a "Catholic state," whatever that may be. All were emotional appeals, irrational in their content, to gain acceptance for national goals selected by an elite that were opposed to the best interests of the mass of the people. The corporate state in America follows in the same path.

What Is to Be Done?

The American corporate state is torn by conflict. A broad malaise affects a society in which the great majority of people do not control the decisions that structure their lives. The U.S. position in the world is not sustainable without huge military expenditures, and it leads us into periodic wars that stop the domestic payoff of material gains and break up the political compromise between the haves and have-nots. We have been unable to maintain growing affluence without suffering from inflations that unsettle both domestic and international economic relationships. We have captive nations in our midst, the minority groups we crowd into low-wage, menial, service occupations. Our national goals are seen by increasing numbers of young people and intellectuals as essentially irrational, however rationally we may pursue them.

Our conflicts demand order. A society in turmoil reacts by seeking to impose new systems of control. The only other alternative is drastic change in the structure of society and the locus of power. We face the classic dilemma of the industrial society of the twentieth century. Will we opt for preservation of the existing structure by imposing the controls that keep the system's turmoil in check? Down that path lies the continuing development of our emerging corporate state into a full-blown fascism, the Leviathan of the future.

At the present moment the tacit agreement between those who hold power and those who do not has broken down under the combined impact of the war in Vietnam, the turmoil in our cities, and recognition by many that American society is malign, not benign. The Nixon administration seeks to patch up the cracks and rebuild the political compromise; it seeks a return to the days when the goals of the managerial elite were not seriously questioned; it is doing so by moving closer to the formal organization of the corporate state.

The far more difficult task is to restructure our economic institutions in the direction of a humane society. We need more than prosperity, economic growth, and stable prices. We need a redistribution of wealth to achieve greater equality and freedom. We need a world at peace. Those goals will not be achieved unless we can take the guns away from the generals and power from the managerial elite. We must disperse economic power and governmental authority. We must move to nothing less than a revolutionary transformation of our economic and political institutions.

Bibliography

The leading works on the American corporate state are those of John Kenneth Galbraith, *American Capitalism: The Concept of Countervailing Power* (Boston: Houghton Mifflin, 1952); *The Affluent Society* (Boston: Houghton Mifflin, 1958); and *The New Industrial State* (Boston: Houghton Mifflin, 1967). Charles A. Reich, *The Greening of America* (New York: Random House, 1970) presents a related analysis. Other works that deal with the institutional structure and political economy of the contemporary American economic system, from a variety of viewpoints, include Robert T. Averitt, *The Dual Economy* (New York: W. W. Norton, 1968); Michael D. Reagan, *The Managed Economy* (New York: Oxford University Press, 1963); David T. Bazelon, *The Paper Economy* (New York: Vintage Books, 1965); and Morton S. Baratz, *The American Business System in Transition* (New York: Thomas Y. Crowell, 1970). A Marxian view, now a classic, is Paul A. Baran and Paul M. Sweezy, *Monopoly Capital* (New York: Monthly Review Press, 1966). An earlier version of some of the ideas developed in this paper is found in Daniel R. Fusfeld, "Fascist Democracy in the United States," *Conference Papers,* Union for Radical Political Economics, Philadelphia, December 1968 (Reprint No. 2, URPE, Ann Arbor, Michigan).

Three recent books provide a systematic analysis of the place of the large corporation in the economy and related problems of public policy: H. H. Liebhafsky, *American Government and Business* (New York: John Wiley and Sons, 1971); William G. Shepherd, *Market Power and Economic Welfare* (New York: Random House, 1970); and Frederic M. Scherer, *Industrial Market Structure and Economic Performance* (Chicago: Rand McNally, 1970). Broader issues of social policy are developed in Robin Marris, *The Economic Theory of "Managerial Capitalism"* (New York: Basic Books, 1968); Richard J. Barber,

The American Corporation: Its Power, Its Money, Its Politics (New York: E. P. Dutton, 1970); Morton Minitz and Jerry S. Cohen, *America, Inc.: Who Owns and Operates the United States* (New York: Dial Press, 1971); Edward S. Mason, ed., *The Corporation in Modern Society* (Cambridge, Mass.: Harvard University Press, 1959); and Harry M. Trebing, ed., *The Corporation in the American Economy* (Chicago: Quadrangle Books, 1970). Interlocking directorates are documented in the *Report of the Federal Trade Commission on Interlocking Directorates* (Washington: U.S. Government Printing Office, 1951). The classic study of corporate interest groups is National Resources Committee, *The Structure of the American Economy* (Washington: U.S. Government Printing Office, 1939), chap. 9 and Appendixes 7-13. There are earlier classic studies: Adolf A. Berle, Jr., and Gardiner C. Means, *The Modern Corporation and Private Property* (New York: Macmillan, 1932); other works by Means collected in *The Corporate Revolution in America* (New York: Collier Books, 1964); Robert A. Brady, *Business as a System of Power* (New York: Columbia University Press, 1943) with its great foreword by Robert S. Lynd; and the series of monographs of the Temporary National Economic Committee (Washington: U.S. Government Printing Office, 1939-41).

The multinational firm is becoming almost a separate field of study. Some of the leading pieces are Charles P. Kindleberger, *American Business Abroad* (New Haven: Yale University Press, 1969); Stephen H. Hymer, "The International Operations of National Firms" (Ph.D. dissertation, Massachusetts Institute of Technology, 1960); and Jack N. Behrman, *National Interests and Multinational Enterprise* (Englewood Cliffs, N.J.: Prentice-Hall, 1970). Louis Turner, *Invisible Empires* (New York: Harcourt Brace Jovanovich, 1970) is a popular account. Two other useful books are Mira Wilkins, *The Emergence of Multinational Enterprise: American Business Abroad from the Colonial Era to 1914* (Cambridge, Mass.: Harvard University Press, 1970); and James W. Vaupel and Joan P. Curban, *The Making of Multinational Enterprise* (Cambridge, Mass.: Harvard University Press, 1969).

The legal basis of the corporate state is admirably treated in Arthur Selwyn Miller, "Toward the Techno-Corporate State?—An Essay in American Constitutionalism," *Villanova Law Review* 14, no. 1 (1968): 1-73; and "Corporate Gigantism and Technological Imperatives," *Emory University Law School Journal of Public Law* 18, no. 2:256-310.

The best material on the military-industrial complex and the militarization of the American economy is the work of Seymour Melman, *Our Depleted Society* (New York: Dell, 1965), *Pentagon Capitalism* (New York: McGraw-Hill, 1970), and the book of readings, *The War Economy of the United States*. They should be supplemented by Richard J. Barnet, *The Economy of Death* (New York: Atheneum, 1970). Three more popular books are Fred J. Cook, *The Warfare State* (New York: Macmillan, 1964); Sidney Lens, *The Military-Industrial Complex* (Philadelphia: Pilgrim Press, 1970); and Ralph Lapp, *The Weapons Culture* (Baltimore: Penguin Books, 1968). A more establishment-oriented treatment is Adam Yarmolinsky, *The Military Establishment* (New York: Harper and Row, 1971), while Michael Kidron, *Western Capitalism Since the War*, rev. ed. (Baltimore: Penguin Books, 1970) argues that modern capitalism cannot survive without "an arms economy." Murray L. Weidenbaum, "Arms and the American Economy: A Domestic Convergence Hypothesis," *American Economic Review* 58, no. 2 (1968): 428-37; and Walter Adams, "The

Military-Industrial Complex and the New Industrial State," ibid., pp. 652–65 are key articles on the institutional relationships between government and the military. Another very valuable collection is Herbert I. Schiller and Joseph D. Phillips, *Super-State: Readings in the Military-Industrial Complex* (Urbana: University of Illinois Press, 1970).

Very little is available on relationships between the universities and big business–big government. A useful survey is James Ridgeway, *The Closed Corporation: American Universities in Crisis* (New York: Random House, 1968). Chemical warfare research at universities is documented in Seymour M. Hersh, *Chemical and Biological Warfare* (Indianapolis: Bobbs-Merrill, 1968; Anchor Books edition, 1969). Cases of university involvement in the cold war are described in Irving L. Horowitz, ed., *The Rise and Fall of Project Camelot* (Cambridge, Mass.: MIT Press, 1967); and Robert Scigliano and Guy H. Fox, *Technical Assistance in Vietnam—The Michigan State University Experience* (New York: Frederick A. Praeger, 1965).

There is a wealth of material on American expansionism. I have found the following books particularly helpful: William A. Williams, *The Contours of American History* (Cleveland: World, 1961), *The Roots of the Modern American Empire* (New York: Random House, 1969), and *The Tragedy of American Diplomacy* (Cleveland: World, 1959); Richard W. Van Alstyne, *The Rising American Empire* (New York: Oxford University Press, 1960); Albert K. Weinberg, *Manifest Destiny* (Baltimore: Johns Hopkins Press, 1935); Ronald Steel, *Pax Americana* (New York: Viking Press, 1967); Claude Julien, *America's Empire* (New York: Random House, 1971); Sidney Lens, *The Forging of the American Empire* (New York: Thomas Y. Crowell, 1971); Lloyd C. Gardner, ed., *A Different Frontier* (Chicago: Quadrangle Books, 1966); Julius W. Pratt, *Expansionists of 1898* (Baltimore: Johns Hopkins Press, 1936); and Gene M. Lyons, ed., *America: Purpose and Power* (Chicago: Quadrangle Books, 1965). American imperialism in the post-World War II era is treated by Harry Magdoff, *The Age of Imperialism* (New York: Monthly Review Press, 1969); K. T. Fann and Donald C. Hodges, eds., *Readings in U.S. Imperialism* (Boston: Porter Sargent, 1971); Andre Gunder Frank, *Capitalism and Underdevelopment in Latin America* (New York: Monthly Review Press, 1969); and Bahman Nirumand, *Iran: The New Imperialism in Action* (New York: Monthly Review Press, 1969; German ed., 1967). The relationship between business and foreign policy is discussed in David Horowitz, ed., *Corporations and the Cold War* (New York: Monthly Review Press, 1969). The international trade in armaments is examined in George Thayer, *The War Business* (New York: Simon and Schuster, 1969). An interesting treatment of communications technology and American expansion is Herbert I. Schiller, *Mass Communications and American Empire* (New York: Augustus M. Kelley, 1969).

The American economic elite can be studied in F. W. Taussig and C. S. Joslyn, *American Business Leaders* (New York: Macmillan, 1932); William Miller, ed., *Men In Business*, new ed. (New York: Harper and Row, 1962); Lloyd W. Warner and James C. Abegglen, *Big Business Leaders in America* (New York: Harper and Row, 1955); C. Wright Mills, *The Power Elite* (New York: Oxford University Press, 1956); E. Digby Baltzell, *An American Business Aristocracy* (New York: Collier Books, 1962; originally published in 1958 as *Philadelphia Gentlemen: The Making of a National Upper Class*); Floyd Hunter, *The Big Rich and the Little Rich* (Garden City, N. Y.: Doubleday,

1965); G. William Domhof, *Who Rules America?* (Englewood Cliffs, N. J.: Prentice-Hall, 1967); and two classic studies by Ferdinand Lundberg, *America's Sixty Families* (New York: Vanguard Press, 1937), and *The Rich and the Super Rich* (New York: Lyle Stuart, 1968). The theoretical literature on elites is summarized by T. B. Bottomore, *Elites and Society* (Baltimore: Penguin Books, 1966). Joseph Schumpeter, *Imperialism and Social Classes* (New York: Augustus M. Kelley, 1951; Meridian Books edition 1955) is also useful. Books that are particularly useful in relating the economic elite to the structure of power are James Burnham, *The Managerial Revolution* (New York: John Day, 1941); and Robert S. and Helen M. Lynd, *Middletown* (New York: Harcourt Brace, 1929), and *Middletown in Transition* (New York: Harcourt Brace, 1937). Two older classics should also be mentioned: Gustavus Myers, *A History of the Great American Fortunes* (New York: Modern Library, 1936; originally published 1909); and Matthew Josephson, *The Robber Barons* (New York: Harcourt, Brace, 1934).

Literature on the ideology and value system of the American economic elite includes Richard Hofstadter, *Social Darwinism in American Thought*, rev. ed., (Boston: Beacon Press, 1955); Sidney Fine, *Laissez Faire and the General-Welfare State* (Ann Arbor: University of Michigan Press, 1964); James Weinstein, *The Corporate Ideal in the Liberal State, 1900–1918* (Boston: Beacon Press, 1968); Moses Rischin, ed., *The American Gospel of Success* (Chicago: Quadrangle Press, 1965); Edward C. Kirkland, *Dream and Thought in the Business Community, 1860–1900* (Ithaca, N. Y.: Cornell University Press, 1956); James W. Prothro, *Dollar Decade: Business Ideas in the 1920's* (Baton Rouge: Louisiana State University Press, 1954); Francis X. Sutton, Seymour E. Harris, Carl Kaysen, and James Tobin, *The American Business Creed* (Cambridge, Mass.: Harvard University Press, 1956); John R. Bunting, *The Hidden Face of Free Enterprise* (New York: McGraw-Hill, 1964); and David Finn, *The Corporate Oligarch* (New York: Simon and Schuster, 1969).

My treatment of national goals and the elite follows G. William Domhof, "How the Power Elite Set National Goals," in Kan Chen, ed., *National Priorities* (San Francisco: San Francisco Press, 1970), pp. 51–60. The place of the business elite in the executive branch of the federal government is documented by David T. Stanley, Dean E. Mann, and Jameson W. Doig, *Men Who Govern* (Washington: Brookings Institution, 1967); Gabriel Kolko, *Roots of American Foreign Policy* (Boston: Beacon Press, 1969); and Barnet, *The Economy of Death*.

Finally, two important books document and describe the larger trends in relationships between government, business, and labor, and their ideologies: W. Lloyd Warner et al., *The Emergent American Society*, volume 1, *Large Scale Organizations* (New Haven: Yale University Press, 1967); and R. Joseph Monsen, Jr., and Mark W. Cannon, *The Makers of Public Policy: American Power Groups and Their Ideologies* (New York: McGraw-Hill, 1965).

9

Organizational Structure, Technological Advance, and the New Tasks of Government

Robert A. Solo

It is strange that an administration more committed to orthodox laissez-faire than any since Herbert Hoover, and that a president who daily denounced the evils of government interference, should, for the first time in American history except in a major war, have installed a general control of wages and prices by the dictate of the political authority. It cannot be gainsaid, however, that in instituting a general system of wage and price control Mr. Nixon acted with cause. The failure of the prior economic policy, wherein his administration witnessed a steady rise both in unemployment and in prices, generated a turbulence that threatened to become an electoral storm. Another administration of a different political coloration no doubt would have been forced to do the same. Basically, the failure was not one of politicians, but of ideas. To the question of how to maintain full employment and price stability, no school of economists had any viable answer. When inflation and unemployment became politically intolerable, no recourse was open to the politicians other than the blind wage-price freeze.

Will the controls work? I predict they will fail until they are discarded. When fiscal and monetary compensatory techniques are resumed, they too will fail until controls are reinstalled. So we shall go, between frying pan and fire, until at last we develop a system of acceptable and workable controls. Direct controls are inescapable in the modern economy, and the fundamental issue is not whether to control, but how to control. It is not that controls cannot work, but that the present system is unworkable; it is without a conceptual base and without coherent and accepted values in reference to which essential judgments can be made. It is, rather, the instinctual rigidification and paralysis of a society in panic. There is no consciousness as yet on the part of politicians, bureaucrats, or the public that the question is not one of sitting tight, but of how to re-create the entire system of resource allocation, economic incentive, and wealth and income distribution (for that, precisely, is what the control of prices and wages means).

It is not the purpose of this article to propose any total, coherent, and rational system of control in relation to economic objectives that satisfies accepted criteria of justice and equity. In our view such a system cannot be predesigned; it must evolve through an extended process of social learning and value formation. We hope, however, to highlight two important and hitherto virtually neglected facets in the conceptualization and development of a viable system of control. The article will be divided into three parts.

Macro theory has conceived of the economy as a homogeneous substance with a uniform response to fiscal and monetary stimuli or constraints. This is a basic error. The private economy is composed of divers organizational forms that respond in radically different ways to a given stimulus or constraint. Part I will use a simplified model of multisectoral interaction to explain and to suggest the importance of these interactions for a system of control.

Inflation is produced by the pressures of groups to satisfy expectations beyond the production capabilities of the economy. And inflation leads to social crisis because it perpetually frustrates the expectations of social groups. In either case, the most satisfactory resolution is to satisfy expectations by increasing the productive capacity and real outputs of the economy. The rate of growth is at the heart of the matter, and the *sine qua non* of growth is technological advance. Therefore, a primary objective of any viable system of planning and control must be to maintain or accelerate the pace of technological advance. Part II will focus on the role of the political authority *vis-à-vis* the rate of technological advance in a multisectored economy. In particular, a diagnosis of and recommendations for dealing with lagging technology in heavy industry in the United States, a matter which should be of immediate concern, will be made.

Part III will consider, very briefly and tentatively, the implications of the aforementioned tasks for the institutional organization, cognitive capabilities, and ideological understructure of the political authority in the United States.

Part I. Price-Employment Control in a Multisectored Economy

The Schizoid Vision of John Maynard Keynes

The Great Depression forced capitalism to shed certain inhibitions of laissez-faire. In the desperation produced by that catastrophe, governments unbalanced their budgets to counteract mass unemployment by augmenting the flow of aggregate national expenditures. Keynes rationalized this policy *ex post facto.* As far as political action was concerned, he did not lead, he followed. His positive proposals were significant only in contrast to the obscurantism of neoclassical orthodoxy. Central to the Keynesian rationale is the assumption of a set of prices that are not responsive to changes in supply or demand, but are determined in some other way. The major tenet of neoclassical theory was and is that prices universally are free moving and flexible. They are an automatic and autonomous response to conditions of supply and demand, and the free moving pattern of prices directs the allocation of resources and determines the distribution of income throughout the economy. Thus the fundamental assumptions of Keynesian and neoclassical economics are opposite and contradictory. Keynes did not resolve the contradiction, but hid it away in the labyrinthine convolutions of his argument. Academic economists seized upon his theory because it apparently permitted them to cling to an entrenched image of a decentralized, competitive economy directed by the free and autonomous movements of price without being obliged to deny the very possibility of a general and perennial condition of mass unemployment.

Nor is the issue resolved by substituting for the notion of a price-directed market the concept of an economy of autonomous organizations where price is set as a matter of trade union and corporate choice. Both forms of economic organization (and others as well) exist in the modern economy. To be effective, a system of control must take into account the coexistence and interaction of diverse forms of economic organization.

A Multisector Model

Consider this interaction in a simple, two-sector model. Assume a price-competitive sector where sellers have no significant power or control over price, and where there is no significant barrier to the inflow of labor or investment and no significant constraint upon their use. This sector coexists with an organizational sector dominated by large corporations that have and exercise the power to determine the price of product outputs and by trade unions that have and exercise the power to determine the price of labor inputs.

In the price-competitive sector, output is a function of availability of resources, and price is the mechanism that brings production and consumption into balance. What can be produced is produced and is sold for the price it will bring. In the organizational sector, conversely, the quantum of resources used (that is, the manpower employed) is a function of the price at which outputs are offered, and price is a function of corporate and trade union policy. What then determines corporate price and trade union wage policies?

No *a priori* answer is possible, but the fallacy of one approach must be disposed of. The large organization (corporation or trade union) is *not* an individual, and its behavior is not to be understood as the expression of individualized choice. "It" has no preference function, no integral interest, and no psyche; hence it has no utility-maximizing mechanism built into its psyche. It is no more a monopolist than it is a pure competitor. The behavior of *all* large organizations—public or private—emerge out of a diversity of interests and outlooks that mingle and interact in the framework of conventions, institutionalized habit and ritual, and imageries and ideologies that are the source of coherence and cohesion for all functional groups. The prevailing images, imageries, and ideologies at the root of organizational behavior change with experience. In that sense, organizations learn, and organizational behavior or policy evolves as a consequence of learning. The "hold tight" price and wage rigidities of the thirties and forties were learned during the long years of depression. In the postwar years the old fears faded, and a new outlook and a different pattern of organizational behavior emerged.

In the first instance, however, let us suppose the policy of trade unions is to keep wages constant except to protect the *real* wages of their members (demanding a wage increase only to offset a rise in the cost of living), and the policy of corporate enterprise is to hold prices stable except to attempt to offset a decline in profits per unit of output. Assume that government, committed to maintaining full employment *and* stable prices, will use fiscal and monetary means to hold aggregate national expenditure at an appropriate level. Also suppose that there is a continuous increase in manpower resources as a consequence of increasing population and of advancing technology. Measuring resources by their potential contribution to output values, for example, if the real output per hour of labor input is doubled because of technological advance, then the manpower resource becomes twice as great although the number of available man-hours of labor remains as before. Suppose, finally, that the spontaneously generated secular increase in aggregate demand is insufficient to employ the annual increment of manpower resources *at constant product prices*. Hence there must be a constantly growing accumulation of *surplus* manpower resources, using surplus in the special sense of those who cannot be absorbed into employment at constant product prices. What then will be the consequence of such accumulating manpower surpluses on the two sectors of the economy?

Since product prices remain constant in the organizational sector, the surplus manpower (as defined) cannot be absorbed into employment there. This surplus may, and to some extent will, congeal as pools of the unemployed seeking work in organizational enterprise. In the price-competitive sector, where product prices are not constant and where output is a function of the availability of resources, surplus manpower can be absorbed into employment. As a result, output in the price-competitive sector will be increased, prices there will be reduced, and factor incomes in the competitive sector likewise will decline relative to output, price, and factor incomes in the organizational sector. Given this response of the two sectors, and taking equal marginal factor productivity as a criterion of optimal resource distribution, production will have been carried *too far* in the price-competitive sector and not far enough in the organizational sector. Unemployment in the latter sector will be matched with overemployment in the former. The outcome is not only unemployment, but also malemployment, misemployment.

Output volume, in turn a function of wage-price policy, controls the entry of additional manpower into the organizational sector. But the influx of additional investment into that sector is not excluded in the same sense. With no change in product prices and no rise in output levels, so long as higher profits are being earned there, investment (particularly the reinvestment of corporate earnings) will continue to infiltrate organizational industry; it will seek a piece of the pie, even though the size of that which is to be divided remains the same. Such investment, manifested as greater advertising, accelerated style changes, and a wider margin of excess plant capacity, may continue long beyond the point where increments of investment have a negative effect on the aggregate net value of industrial output, that is, where the effect of incremental investment is to increase costs and reduce profit margins without any addition to the real value of output. Investment then will have been carried too far in the organizational sector relative to the price-competitive sector, widening the margin of excess capacity in the former. Hence the paradox: overinvestment and underemployment in the organizational sector, and underinvestment and overemployment in the price-competitive sector.

The government, committed to maintaining full employment, is confronted with the growing mass of unemployed manpower waiting at the gates of organizational enterprise. Acting in the accepted conceptual framework, and with no other techniques of implementation at its disposal, government augments aggregate spending through monetary and/or fiscal devices. It thus increases job opportunities by inducing a rise in the output levels in the organizational sector, and for a time this policy succeeds. Employment in organizational enterprise increases, while wages and prices in that sector remain unchanged.

No increase in trade union wages is required to attract the additional manpower needed by corporate enterprise to satisfy the increased demand for its outputs. Labor can be drawn from among the unemployed and from among those who hitherto have been less remuneratively employed in the price-competitive sector. Labor already employed in organizational enterprise will enjoy higher earnings through full-time and over-time employment and through greater opportunities for promotion in supervising less experienced labor recently brought in from the outside. Given a prior accumulation of excess capacity, corporations will increase their outputs for a considerable time with an actual decrease in per unit costs and, conversely, with a rise in per unit profits.

The government-induced increase in aggregate spending will have its effects not only on the organizational but also on the price-competitive sector. It must increase directly the demand for the outputs, and (by drawing its manpower to more remunerative employment in organizational enterprise) must reduce indirectly the availability of resources and hence lower its level of output. In this form of economic organization, where output is a function of available resources and price is a function of output and demand, with demand greater and output less, prices must be forced upward. The decline in output and the increase in prices would be tempered somewhat by an influx of investment. It would be drawn in by rising factor income and generated through the reinvestment of higher earnings, and would lead to the installation of available new technologies with the consequent rise in productivity offsetting, to some degree, the outflow of labor.

A vicious cycle begins. Higher prices in the competitive sector will increase the costs of some of the goods and services procured by organizational enterprise. Also, by increasing the cost of living, the price rise in the competitive sector will reduce the real wage of workers in organizational enterprise. The trade unions will respond (following the assumed determinant of trade union wage policy) by forcing an increase in organizational wage rates. Higher wages and high prices for goods and services procured from the price-competitive sector will boost costs and, eventually, will reduce the per unit profits of organizational enterprise. Following the assumed determinants of corporate price policy, organizational enterprise will raise prices to protect per unit profits. Higher prices for the output of organizational enterprise further will increase the cost of living and hence will lower the real wage of unionized workers. Trade unions will respond by forcing wage rates upward again. The corporations will offset the rise in wage costs with a rise in product prices, and so on.

As prices and wages rise in the organizational sector, a greater and greater infusion into the expenditure flow becomes necessary in order to absorb surplus manpower into organizational employment. Larger increments to the level of aggregate demand accelerate the upward movement of prices regardless of the numbers remaining unemployed. Previously, government was confronted with rising unemployment; now it is faced with accelerated inflation. If it ceases to induce any further rise in spending, then the margin of surplus manpower widens and shows up as unemployed labor in the organizational sector and as overemployed, underremunerated manpower in the price-competitive sector. Should the government reduce the level of aggregate spending, prices and factor incomes in the price-competitive sector would be forced down, and there would be a cumulative increase in the numbers of the unemployed at the gates of organizational enterprise. Eventually, rising unemployment would force the political authority again to induce an increase in aggregate national expenditure, and once again the cost/price, price/cost spiral would be set in motion.

Nor need we assume a trade union policy of real wage stability, nor a corporate policy of price and/or unit profit stability. During affluent postwar decades, the rising expectation of all economic groups has been expressed in the periodic forcing up of wages and prices in the organizational sector. More recently, trade unions have learned to anticipate rather than merely respond to inflation and require that an automatic offset to any rise in the cost of living be built into wage contracts. Corporate enterprise has learned to keep ahead of anticipated price rises. The Keynesian conceptualization fails as a workable hypothesis for economic control.

What can be deduced that is relevant to the design of a general system of control? Perhaps the following. At one pole of the spectrum of market organizations, the large corporation and the trade union set prices and wages as a matter of policy. When a certain pattern of organizational behavior prevails in that sector, the political authority may treat price as a parameter and act upon employment by influencing the level of aggregate annual expenditure. But at the other end of the market spectrum, price moves autonomously, and the price level is a function of aggregate spending. From the viewpoint of the government planner operating from the Keynesian paradigm, the price response of the price-competitive sector is simply an ineradicable nuisance; it repeatedly throws spanners into the works and prevents the achievement of full employment through a rational policy of compensatory finance.

One must look beyond the Keynesian paradigm with its simplistic price stability norm, that is, from the criterion of holding prices as they are whatever they are, to the fundamental purpose of a pricing system. That purpose is to attain a full and efficient utilization of resources and an *equitable distribution* of income. The response of the price-directed market to the stimulus of increased spending then appears in a different light, as tending to equalize both the marginal value of factor inputs and the income of manpower of the same quality in both sectors. Hence, the price-directed market's response is eminently desirable when judged by the criteria of efficiency and equity.

Part II. Technological Advance in a Multisectored Economy

A Policy Designed to Inhibit Technological Advance

The importance of the relationship between price and employment and technological advance can be illustrated by the consequence of a policy that ignores it. It is now difficult to recall the noisy and ludicrous controversy between the two schools of true believers at the onset of the Nixon administration. The battle raged between fiscalists and monetarists, on the one side the cohorts of James

Tobin and against them the armies of Milton Friedman, about which of two ways to skin a dead cat.

The monetarists won the day and the government launched into those hoary transactions intended to reduce the supply of money. They produced an unprecedented rise in interest rates, thus imposing a heavy tax particularly on the construction of housing and on industrial investment (the revenues of this strange tax to go to banks and to lenders rather than to government). The effect on housing was so catastrophic that the government was obliged to offset the consequences of its own policy with housing subsidies of unprecedented magnitude. The whole burden was on industrial investment. The effect had to be to depress the rate at which industrial technology is transformed (through investment) to higher levels of productivity. The central target and the prime casualty of Nixon's anti-inflationary policy (and of the Friedmanite formula) was the economic capability for upgrading technology and increasing productivity, hence for a larger real output of goods and services to satisfy rising expectations without an inflationary pressure on demand. If the purpose had been to check the rise in productivity and to inhibit the growth of real output, then government policy could not have been better designed nor more successful. During 1970–1971 we witnessed a positive decline in the real value of output per capita, in its way a quite rare and remarkable feat. Both the neoclassicists and the Keynesians conceived of inflation as the response of free moving price to aggregate demand rising more rapidly than total output. What is inexplicable and inexcusable is that, even within their own paradigm, both schools of thought were concerned only to suppress demand. Neither took any account of the means of increasing supply as anti-inflationary policy.

If, through its anti-inflationary policy, the Nixon administration inhibited technological advance, it also threw away a rare opportunity to promote technological progress with the instruments at hand. The administration should (in my opinion) be praised and credited for drastically phasing down the enormous annual research and development expenditures in aerospace and weaponry. But the means of disposing of those great public and quasi-public organizations, destroying and debilitating capabilities that had been acquired over decades, and the dispersion of scientific and research cadres without provision or concern for their alternative employment was gravely in error. Neither in the administration, in Congress, in the universities, nor elsewhere was there any evident realization that those special skills and organizational capabilities are rare and costly; that they are at the heart of the capacity for technological progress in the modern economy; and that rather than destroying the means for producing technological progress, it would have been rational to give them a new direction. They could have been used to raise industrial productivity and to resolve those technological problems that plague us in respect to the natural environment and social organization, or improve progressively the basic systems of transportation, communications, and power that constitute the industrial infrastructure.

Technological Lag in the American Economy

The task of maintaining or accelerating the pace of technological advance is different for each sector of the American economy: between agriculture (where success has been so pronounced) and the small enterprise markets such as construction, textiles, and services (where failure has been so complete); and between the massive research and development under the control of the political authority and the heavy industry of the organizational sector where technology has been dangerously laggard. We will take as our example heavy industry in the organizational sector, where the problem is immediate and critical, and where the cause and cure of laggard technology both are obscure. Before World War II American industry and technology were in every way supreme. During the war the capital equipment and industrial infrastructure of erstwhile competitors, particularly of Germany and Japan, virtually were obliterated, but those of the United States emerged unscathed and, indeed, greatly enhanced. Yet, in only a few decades, the technology of those competitors has, in important instances, overtaken and outdistanced that of the United States, particularly in those high technology areas (like steel) characterized by heavy investment in producer durables. The United States seemingly is replicating Great Britain's nineteenth-century industrial decline from the heights of technological supremacy, recalling Thorstein Veblen's forewarnings about the dangers of being ahead.[1]

Without pretending to enter into the comparative measurement of productivity nor to pass judgment on industrial particulars, of this there can be no doubt: The relative position of American technology, and especially productivity in the high technology, capital-intensive industries of the United States, has changed rapidly and radically, to our detriment. Only that fact can account for an increasingly unfavorable balance of payments that finally forced devaluation of the dollar. It is significant, too, that American export strength is no longer in high technology industry, but is in agriculture. Beyond question, the United States is, relatively speaking, poorer and industrially less strong than before.

The lag in American industrial technology, in part at least, can be accounted for as the price we must pay for having diverted the great bulk of our research and development manpower during the postwar decades into the tasks of weaponry and space exploration. Moreover, there seems to be a barrier to the upward transformation of technology built into the form of economic organization that characterizes heavy industry in the modern capitalist economy. Our concern is with this barrier and its relationship to the development of a viable system of public control.

The Hypothetical Case

Let us hypothesize a steel industry in two economies and call them Japan and the United States. The management of each is equally skilled, foresightful, and unbiased; variations in the skill, energy, and wages of labor can be disregarded. Investible funds are mobile, and investment in the transformation of industry in either country can draw upon the savings of both. The structure of producer durables in the United States is intact, but in Japan virtually has been destroyed by the depredation of war. Suppose that the intact technology of the United States produces steel at an average cost of $100 a ton, including a return on prior investment of 8 percent. Suppose that a new technology is in the offing that can produce steel at an average cost of $50 a ton, including a 12 percent return on the investment required to install the technology. The intent is to postulate an extreme case where, on rational grounds, taking the net increase in the real value added as the criterion, the installation of the new technology will be absolutely in the public interest (Pareto optimal). The question is, given this opportunity, whether Japan, or the United States, or both will install the new technology.

Japan's choice is inevitable. If it is to rebuild its industry at all, it would do so by installing the new and advanced technology. The cost of producing steel in Japan, relative to costs of the prior technology, would be reduced correspondingly. What of the United States? With cost saving being so greatly in excess of the discounted value of the cost of replacing the existing installation, rational choice *should* be equally unequivocal. The social interest and a Pareto optimal decision would require that the old be scrapped and replaced. The United States would have an advantage over Japan, since the junk value, and/or the possibility of depreciation without replacement of elements of the old capital structure would reduce transformation costs as compared to installation costs in Japan.

Resistance to Technological Transformation

Would the transformation to the more advanced technology take place in the United States given pure competition, or monopoly in the classical conception, or socialism? In the case of pure competition, or the closely related Schumpeterian model, innovators enter the industry, introduce the new technology, and force prices down to an equilibrium at the lower average cost level through competition. Consumers would benefit and innovators would reap a windfall gain the magnitude of which would depend on the time lag before prices dropped to the new equilibrium level. On the other hand, equity ownership in those operations that the technological transformation had rendered obsolete would suffer losses. What Alfred Marshall would have called their quasi rents would be eliminated. The rational monopolist and the socialist planner immediately would transform operations to the more advanced technology, bearing the costs and appropriating the more than compensatory benefits of change.

In all of the aforementioned cases, given rational choice, a new technology that brings savings greater than the costs of transformation, including the opportunity costs of using the old technology with a zero return on investment, would be installed at once. For pure competition, pure monopoly (or oligopoly or monopolistic competition in micro analytic conception), or socialism, the technological choice would be the same, although in each instance costs and benefits would be shared differently. It now will be argued that an intact capital structure will prevent or significantly delay the installation of new, more advanced technology, no matter by how much the cost savings overbalance the costs of transformation, given the pricing conditions characteristic of large-scale enterprise in the modern organizational sector.

Assumptions

Several assumptions are made. (1) The entry of new firms into the market is difficult and rare, so that technological transformation depends necessarily on the policies of firms already established in the industry. (2) In managerial anticipation, the political authority can be relied on to protect the industry's domestic market against competitive incursions by foreign producers when the latter offer their outputs at prices below average domestic costs. (3) Prices on the domestic market will (and management expects that they will) find an equilibrium at anticipated average costs for the prevailing technology, including in costs the conventionally acceptable return on the investment required to install the technology.

The last assumption is critical. It suggests that the pricing behavior of organizational enterprise approximates that associated with the regulated public utility where rates are held to the level of average costs, including a fair return on investment. That is the only price that can be justified before the bar of political authority and public opinion and that can be maintained without tempting key producers to shade prices, major suppliers or buyers to integrate backward or forward, or trade unions to accelerate the upward thrust of wage rates. Suppose that management does anticipate that future prices will settle at that level of costs, whatever it might be. What will be its rational response to the opportunity of adopting a new technology that will greatly reduce production costs and that will require a massive influx of new investment for installation?

Suppose the transformation of technology is financed through the sale of additional common stock and debentures, and, in line with management's expectations, price is stabilized at the lower level of average costs at the new, prevailing technology. Who benefits? Who suffers? Consumers enjoy lower prices; workers probably receive higher wages; certain investors are better off because of the incremental investment opportunity. But what of established ownership whose prior investment had financed the replaced technology and to whom a stream of dividend and interest payments previously had been forthcoming? They must lose. The technology whose installation they had financed and the capital structure to which, on that account, they might lay claim, has gone into limbo. The real values of their ownership have been reduced to nothing. Prices would drop to average costs at the prevailing technology, including a return only for those who had financed its installation. Under the postulated conditions, the prior investors' losses would be equivalent to those which would occur under pure competition.

Joseph Schumpeter called this elimination of equities attaching to a displaced technology the "gales of creative destruction." The difference is that producers in pure competition cannot resist those gales of creative destruction. In the organizational sector, they can. The former have no defense against the hurricane of change. The decision to transform is not made by them but by others, by infiltrating innovators to whom great new prizes go. But in a large part of modern enterprise, where entry is rare and its significance is marginal (the great companies that control the steel industries of the world have not changed in generations), it is the existing community of producers that makes or refuses to make the decision to transform technology. It permits or it excludes the influx of new investment. It has and it exercises power to resist technological change. Unlike pure monopoly, it cannot capture for ownership the net increment of value attributable to technological advance, but unlike pure competition it can resist that advance. Under circumstances where prices can be expected to follow average costs of the prevailing technology, existing ownership must suffer from the transformation to a more advanced technology, no matter how great the net saving in costs and no matter how great the net gains in GNP. The community of producers can resist, and, in the interest of ownership, management will resist, the transformation of technology whenever a significant influx of new investment is required to cover the costs of transformation.

In these terms, in our hypothetical example, the acceptance of a new steel technology in Japan and its rejection in the United States follows as the consequence of rational business choice. In Japan, where the capital structure had been obliterated, the option of avoiding an influx of external investment by perpetuating the old technology does not exist; in the United States that option remains. In these terms it is possible to explain why Japanese and German steel technology has raced ahead relative to that of the United States, while in those postwar industries where the United States also started from scratch, such as electronics and computers, American technology remains supreme.

It is not only the ownership interest that enters into corporate decisions; there are other incentives and pressures for technological transformation that may countermand that interest. Nevertheless, if our assumptions and their consequences are, in fact, characteristic, then a built-in bias against technological advance in the organizational sector has been identified.

The problem can be simply stated. In this form of organization the system of pricing externalizes the benefits and internalizes the costs of technological change; the costs must be borne by those who make the decisions, and the benefits accrue to others. No matter how great the gains to consumers, workers, and new investors, the quasi rents of prior investors and present owners will be jeopardized. Nor is management culpable in seeking to fend off windfall disaster for the ownership interest. If prior ownership and a management that acts in its interest are not motivated to transform technology because they cannot benefit, it is not inadmissible that the public at large should pay for the installation of that technology as long as it is fully assured that it will receive the benefits thereof.

Part III. Institutional Implications

Tasks and Instruments

We have argued that a rational and coherent system of economic control appropriate to the conditions of the modern economy would require that the political authority must act upon the determination of prices and wages by reference to accepted norms for the relative distribution of income and the intersectoral allocation of resources, and that it must plan, program, and promote technological advance sector by sector. Under certain market conditions the latter would require that the political authority finance the transformation of technology with a guarantee that future prices will not exceed the lower operating costs of the new technology, including in cost a fair return on prior investment, but with no return allowed to equity ownership on the public investment required for the installation of the new technology.

These tasks fall within the encompassing need to integrate motivation and skill in the management of enterprise with informed control in the social interest into an effective and coherent system of participatory planning. Such a system would require significant changes in the competencies, structure, and organization of government and in the ideological underpinnings of society. Whatever the difficulties and uncertainties the achievement of an effective system of control might pose, governmental control of industry in the modern economy is not to be avoided. The political authority already is involved, pulled into participatory planning helter-skelter, by the seat of the pants. The question is whether that involvement will be better or worse, rational or irrational, in *ad hoc* response to crisis or purposive in the light of a coherent theory.

A blueprint for governmental reform is beyond the scope of this article. Nevertheless, we will venture to suggest that the following are essential for the achievement of a control capability: (1) a new ideological consensus; (2) a new breed of public servant operating from (3) a new knowledge base; and (4) new institutional arrangements for participatory planning.

The Ideological Understructure

In the regulation of prices and wages, the political authority now is conceived as an arbitrator. Its aim is to produce a series of *ad hoc* extra market bargains between private interests—between trade unions, industry, agriculture, and consumer representatives—entirely without reference to equity or efficiency, with no objective save holding on the lid, and with no achievement possible save slowing down the wheels. On the other hand, any coherent, efficient, just system of control that might conceivably go beyond the mere balancing of power and pressure must be based on a general consensus as to what is just and equitable. It must operate in relation to an accepted conception of how the economy works, how it should work, and how it can be made to work. Without that ideological underpinning the political authority can be no more than a power broker.

To what extent will one group yield its claims in favor of another? How far can the political authority go in the imposition of controls? More than a century ago, Abraham Lincoln had the answer. "Public sentiment is everything. With public sentiment nothing can fail. Without it, nothing can succeed. Consequently he who molds public sentiment goes deeper than he who enacts statutes or pronounces decisions. He makes statutes and decisions possible or impossible to be executed."

Individuals and groups will make sacrifices, will submit to constraint and hardship, will permit and support change that places them at a relative disadvantage. Basically, the answer to what constraints and controls will be accepted is always a matter of ideology, depending *not* on what seems right and reasonable to an academic elite, but on that which is understood and accepted by affected groups and the public at large.

The Cognitive Capability

Government in the United States lacks the cognitive capabilities that are needed to deal with the problems here at issue. Consider what is required of the political authority in the proposed control function. There must be an evaluation of performance, of efficiency in the allocation and utilization of resources, of equity in the distribution of income, and of technological advance and productivity. The evaluation must be made section by section, industry by industry, and great firm by great firm. It must be made in reference to the moving patterns and changing parameters of price, employment, resource allocation, income distribution, and technological opportunities at the level of the national and world economies. Beyond evaluation there must be participatory planning of change and adjustment.

Consider, for example, a public authority which must take into account the motivation to innovate and the processes of technological transformation as an aspect of (since they are inextricably linked to) any rational control of prices. Under the conditions specified in Part II, that authority would be obliged to decide what expenditures of public funds should be made in support of what technological transformation and what the subsequent cost basis of price should be. Such decisions would require a conceptual framework, a knowledge base, and a judgmental capability quite beyond that of the public administrator, lawyer, legislator, economist, corporate executive, engineer, manager, or academic scientist. These decisions properly would draw upon the range of social values, the parameters of science and technique, and upon an intimate understanding of a universe where the horizons of time, the levers of power, and the processes of choice are of another order than those found in the corporation or the marketplace. There is a need for a breed of civil servant different from those who presently bustle through the corridors of power.

An Institutional Framework for Participatory Planning

Whatever its limits and incapacities, French indicative and modernization planning suggests at least a rational institutional means of integrating those responsible for the efficient organization and operation of the firm and those responsible for the stability and growth of the economy into a process of participatory industrial-*cum*-social choice and action. The French schemata carries information, influence, and pressure from the political authority down to the decentralized base of the firm's investment, output, and technology choices, and carries information, influence, and pressure from the firm and the industry up to the centralized apex of national policy and planning.

The political authority will fail in its efforts if the most competent among those who perform its tasks are siphoned off into the private sector, or are quickly captured, corrupted, and/or controlled by those private agencies and interests which they are supposed to control. The danger would be particularly acute where public officials simultaneously would engage in planning the extension of profitable activities, reducing the costs to and otherwise in servicing industry, and yet have the power and obligation to confront and control industry where its objectives conflict with what is conceived as the public interest. Against this danger there are three possible safeguards: (1) politics rooted in an effective interaction with and a real answerability to, an electorate; (To break through self-enclosed, self-perpetuating political organization and to re-establish communication with and electoral influence upon the public officaldom is surely the crux of the current movement for political reform.); (2) professionalism in the public service developed through selective recruitment, promotion from within, and the cumulative development of competencies and a knowledge base specific to the decisions of the political authority that stands apart from and is not readily transferable to decision processes in the private sector; and (3) legal constraints and moral pressure against the changing of hats, the easy slipping back and forth between positions of public authority and positions of corporate power.

Note

1. *Imperial Germany and the Industrial Revolution* (New York: Macmillan, 1915).

10

An Institutional Analysis of Corporate Power

William M. Dugger

As institutional economists, skeptical descendants of the German Historical School, it is our duty to describe what is really going on in our economy. What is going on in the U.S. economy at the close of the twentieth century is the development of corporate hegemony. That is, our economy is becoming dominated by one institution—the giant corporation. The growth in size of the U.S. corporation is described in Table 1. The table includes data from corporations filing tax returns with the U.S. Internal Revenue Service. The very largest corporations classified by the I.R.S. are those with assets of $250 million or more. They accounted for only 0.06 percent of all filing corporations in 1965 and 0.11 percent in 1982, the latest year for which the I.R.S. has published the data. The table begins with the year 1965 because in that year the total assets and the net income of the very largest corporations were just one-half of assets and income of all filing corporations. Since 1965, however, the scales have tipped increasingly toward the side of the very large corporation. No matter which I.R.S. measurement of corporate size is used—assets, receipts, or income—the very largest corporations have grown to dominate all the measurements. The giant corporation now dominates the U.S. economy to an extent undreamed of in earlier years. They account for nearly three-fourths of all corporate assets, over one-half of all corporate receipts, and over two-thirds of all corporate income. Corporate enterprise is now a system wherein a relatively small number of giant corporations compete against a relatively large number of small enterprises, and against the rest of us. The small enterprises may be more flexible and innovative, but the large ones have been able to more than make up for it with sheer size and power. To continue growing, the very large corporation has had to adopt a new structure, and the new structure has been forcing a new kind of adjustment of its own—a cultural adjustment. Power and size interact with each other in a cumulative fashion. The drive for power leads to a growth in size, while the growth in size causes a need for more power to hold the larger organization together and to make it manageable. So, in a reinforcing spiral toward corporate hegemony, more corporate power leads to larger corporate size and larger size leads to more power. Walter Adams and James W. Brock, in their *The Bigness Complex,* provide ample evidence of the circularity of power and bigness.[1]

The Corporate Need for Control

Continued growth has forced the large corporation to experiment with a new, more powerful organization structure, a structure more capable of dealing with the problems brought on by its increased size and diversification. Some of the very early attempts at restructuring occurred at DuPont and General Motors in the 1920s. These pioneers in corporate restructuring began with what business managers call U-form organizations and turned them into what business managers call M-form organizations. (U-form stands for "unitary form;" while M-form stands for "multiple division form.") Top managers at GM became famous in managerial circles for their pioneering work in corporate restructuring.

The early U-form corporation was divided into "unitary" departments. Each department performed only one (unitary) function of the organization. The functional units of the pre-World War I corporation were usually finance, production, and marketing. All managers involved with the finance function were grouped together into one (unitary) finance department. So all finance people were united administratively and they all ultimately reported to the same finance head. Likewise, all marketing people were united administratively and all of

Table 1. ***Total Assets, Total Receipts, and Net income (less deficit) of All Reporting Corporations and of the Largest Corporations with Assets of $250 million or more, 1965–1982 (In Billions of Dollars)***

Year	Total Assets		Total Receipts		Net Income	
	All Units	*Largest Units*	*All Units*	*Largest Units*	*All Units*	*Largest Units*
1965	1,724	862 (50%)	1,195	374 (31%)	74	37 (50%)
1966	1,845	945 (51%)	1,307	420 (32%)	81	41 (51%)
1973	3,649	2,275 (62%)	2,558	1,056 (41%)	120	69 (58%)
1974	4,016	2,586 (64%)	3,090	1,426 (46%)	146	93 (64%)
1975	4,287	2,790 (65%)	3,199	1,451 (45%)	143	90 (63%)
1976	4,721	3,105 (66%)	3,635	1,679 (46%)	185	122 (66%)
1977	5,326	3,544 (67%)	4,128	1,926 (47%)	219	141 (64%)
1978	6,014	4,078 (68%)	4,715	2,210 (47%)	247	157 (64%)
1979	6,835	4,748 (69%)	5,599	2,743 (49%)	285	192 (67%)
1980	7,617	5,358 (70%)	6,361	3,229 (51%)	239	158 (66%)
1981	8,547	6,165 (72%)	7,026	3,675 (52%)	213	147 (69%)
1982	9,358	6,881 (74%)	7,025	3,647 (52%)	154	113 (73%)

SOURCE: U.S. Internal Revenue Service, *Statistics of Income, Corporate Income Tax Returns,* various years. (1982 returns are the latest available as of April, 1987)

them ultimately reported to the same marketing head. So too with all the production people. Each functional group was united, hence the name, "U-form." At least in principle, the U-form held managers strictly accountable. Those responsible for production were accountable to the head of the production department. Those responsible for marketing were accountable to the marketing head, and so on for each function performed by the organization. But as these U-form corporations grew during and after the first World War, their functionally united groups became large and cumbersome with many layers of management. The larger the U-form grew, the harder it became to hold any single manager responsible for the profitability of a particular product because the financing, producing, and marketing of each product were the responsibilities of different functional departments.

If something went wrong in a particular product line, marketing would blame production for inadequate quality control. But production would blame marketing for poor sales performance. And finance would blame everybody else for lack of cost control. So the department heads struggled against each other, either to avoid responsibility for failure or to claim responsibility for success. As a result, in the early years of GM and DuPont, the top managers and owners (the DuPont family) were increasingly frustrated in their attempt to make the two giant corporations more profitable. Other corporations that grew into very large diversified organizations, usually through consolidation and merger, ran into the same organized irresponsibility problems with their U-form organizations.[2] That is, the organization itself seemed to build in a lack of managerial responsibility. Business organization had become a hindrance to further corporate growth. The "U-form" had become obsolete.

The more advanced "M-form" structure, on the other hand, separates its functions into multiple divisions. Ideally, each of these multiple divisions is a more-or-less autonomous operating group responsible for the production and distribution of a particular product or product line. Each autonomous division performs its own operating functions, so that the head of each division can be held responsible for all of the functions contributing to the profitability of his group. These M-form organizations are more flexible and more decentralized than the old U-form structures that they have largely replaced in the contemporary world of giant corporations. They also are more responsible in the sense that each autonomous division is a profit center, a single group, performing all of the operating functions itself, and therefore directly responsible, itself, for the profitability of a particular product. Profit responsibility is built into the organization, replacing the organized irresponsibility of earlier corporate organizations. The financial performance of each of the multiple divisions or profit centers is monitored by a centralized corporate office, usually headed by the Chief Financial Officer of the parent corporation. The financial data gathering and number crunching at the corporate office greatly focuses and enhances the control of upper management over what now matters the most—the money. The General Motors Corporation pioneered in developing the new "M-form" organization during the period between the two world wars. It was only after World War II that other large corporations began following GM's lead.

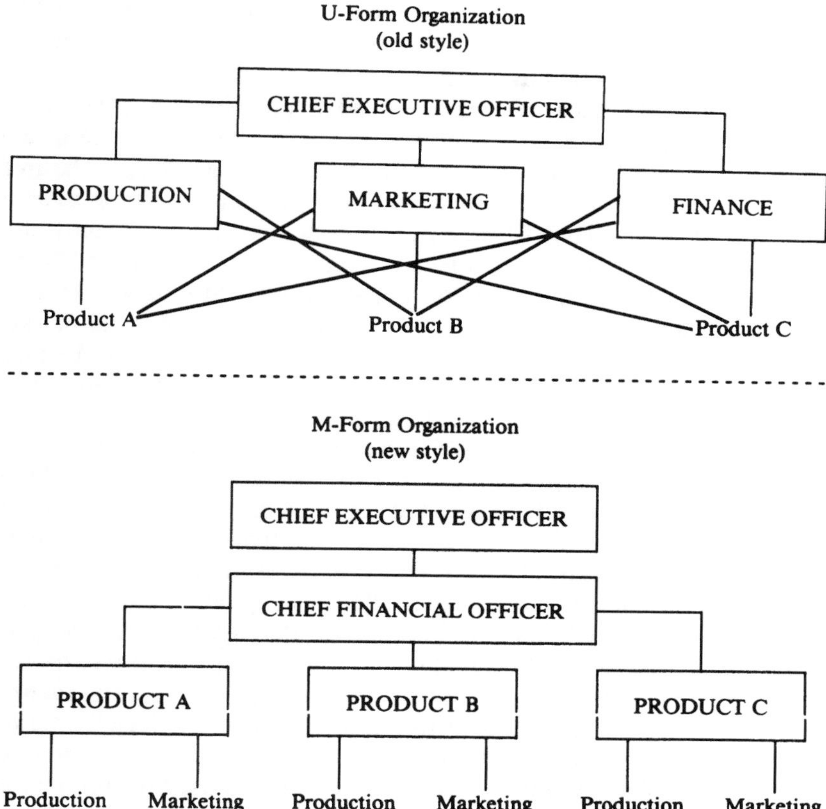

Figure 1: ***Organization Forms***

As Figure 1 illustrates, changing from the old U-form structure to the new M-form structure has greatly simplified the reporting responsibilities of managers at the product level (PRODUCT A, PRODUCT B, PRODUCT C in Figure 1). The change has made the product line managers directly responsible for the profits made by their product. Each product line manager in each of the multiple divisions now has direct control over the functions—production and marketing—that determine the profits earned in each product line. Furthermore, the new M-form structure centralizes the finance function into a new corporate head office, run by a powerful new corporate official—the Chief Financial Officer. The M-form can be expanded almost indefinitely to include additional product lines, as new products or new companies are added to the organization. The new M-form also maintains much tighter control over the financial flows within the organization.

The corporate offices of conglomerated corporations have become so powerful, they now serve as substitutes for the capital market of old. Most of the autonomous divisions of conglomerates used to be free-standing corporations with their own independent corporate officials and stockholders. They became divisions of a conglomerate only after they were taken over in a merger. As dependent subsidiaries of the acquiring conglomerate, they no longer pay out their surplus capital funds to shareholders who used to reinvest the funds in the financial market. Nor do they acquire new capital funds, when needed, from the financial market. Instead, the central corporate office of the conglomerate controls the funds of the dependent subsidiaries, who have been turned into operating divisions. The old independent corporations with excess funds used to pay out dividends to their shareholders. Then their shareholders used to reinvest the funds in the stock or bond market. The old independent corporation with a need for new funds used to acquire the new finance by issuing stocks or bonds to investors in the market. But now the new corporate head office allocates capital funds to the divisions it decides need them, and it appropriates capital funds from the divisions it decides should supply them. In this way, the new corporate office replaces with its own administrative decisions of central managers the old capital market with its supply and demand haggling of independent corporations and investors. In this way, the corporate head office also replaces the top layer of managers who used to run the formerly free-standing, independent corporations that have been merged into the conglomerate.

The very large corporation has adopted a more sophisticated structure that allows for decentralizing operational decisions and that allows for clarifying profit responsibilities, but the new structure creates a new kind of problem, similar to the problem encountered by large holding companies. (A holding company is a paper corporation, a hollow shell designed simply to own other corporations.) At their weakest, holding companies are unable to plan or coordinate the activities of their operating companies. The operating companies are little more than investments in a financial portfolio. Such holding companies are really not organizations at all. They are financial funnels and ownership depositories, the tools of nineteenth-century swashbucklers.[3] But the imperial conglomerate is the tool of the twenty-first century swashbuckler. It is a full-fledged, powerful organization that is managed as a whole.

It is more than the sum of its parts. The corporate office plans and coordinates the different divisions, forging them into a commercial empire capable of perpetually running any number of different industries of any size, anywhere on the earth or in the heavens. The essence of an imperial conglomerate is its lack of limits and its synergy. Being more than the sum of its parts, the limitations of any of its parts do not bind it. So its power is more than that of a commercial entity. It is more than a monopoly of any one market. It is an empire.

Herein lies the challenge of M-form conglomerate organizations, the dominate type of U.S. corporation today. To operate as a whole, to benefit from the synergy between the parts, the parts must be coordinated and the movement of the whole must be planned. The huge corporation has become so large that it has had to be broken down into its parts—hence the M-form structure composed of autonomous divisions. Breaking the organization down into parts, each one of which can be held accountable for its own operation as a profit center, has meant that corporations can now grow to unlimited, infinite size, and still be manageable. And yet, breaking the corporation down into its parts also threatens the synergy between the parts. Over-all coordination and long-term planning at the central corporate level are now more important than ever. They require far more information processing capacity than ever before, hence the proliferation of new information-based technologies and of new information-based jobs.

The corporate world is going through a true technological revolution. The technology involved, however, has little to do with the production of goods or services. It has to do with the organization and control of people. The technological revolution is in organization and information rather than in production and distribution.[4] The M-form structure is just the first stage of the organization-information revolution, but it is clearly forcing the corporate world into the next stage. Since corporations can live forever, they can—theoretically—grow forever as well. Until recently, however, their size was technologically limited by their primitive form of organization, the old U-form. However, the invention and spread of the new M-form lifted the limit on size; computer technology and communications advances helped lift the old size constraints as well. Nevertheless, with continued growth, new problems with size are being encountered. The operations of multiple, autonomous divisions can be planned by the corporate office, but plans must be implemented. The divisions must follow the general direction of the plan. They must not work at cross purposes, lest the synergy between them be lost. The divisions must pursue some common purpose, must hold some common values, must share some basic beliefs. In short, they must be united by something into a whole that is larger than the sum of the parts. They must develop a common corporate culture. The corporations that develop one, survive. The ones that do not, die.[5]

A corporate culture is a set of shared beliefs and values inculcated in the corporation's employees. The corporate culture reinforces and reshapes the employee's general desire to do well into a compulsion to get ahead, through loyalty to the corporation and through hard work for the corporation. Corporate culture is an internalization of corporate control. So it is a tool of social control. The huge and ever-growing corporate conglomerate needs a corporate culture to unify its autonomous divisions. In *The Reckoning,* David Halberstam shows that Nissan and several other Japanese corporations have already developed some excellent cultural models, ripe for export to the United States along with their cars.[6] William G. Ouchi, in his *Theory Z,* shows that leading U.S. corporations are borrowing and building their own unifying corporate cultures along Japanese and other lines.[7] Regardless of the source, U.S. corporations are acquiring the unifying cultural tool they need to continue growing while maintaining control over the employees of their far-flung empires.[8]

The leaders in corporate culture-building in the United States usually have been less diversified corporations, rather than imperial conglomerates. Among the better-known U.S. corporations to have developed strong cultures are Caterpillar Tractor, General Electric, DuPont, 3M, Digital Equipment Corporation, IBM, Dana, Procter and Gamble, Hewlett-Packard, Johnson and Johnson, Tandem Computer, and Continental Bank.[9] Only a few of them, like GE, DuPont, and 3M, are full-blown, imperial conglomerates. However, this is not to say that most full-blown conglomerates do not need strong corporate cultures. Quite the contrary; the imperial conglomerate's need for a strong culture is very pressing. In a recent *Fortune* article, business consultant Morty Lefkoe even claimed that most merger attempts that fail do so because of the lack of a common corporate culture.[10] Since most large conglomerates have grown through fairly recent takeovers of diverse, formerly free-standing corporations, many of which had cultures of their own, forging their diverse cultures into one common conglomerate culture has not been easy. Although the cultures of different U.S. corporations have many similarities, the personnel of captured corporations generally enter into their new conglomerate environment with considerable misgiving and even overt hostility, particularly in hostile takeovers. These attitudes make the inculcation of the new conglomerate's culture a slow and difficult process. So new conglomerates would be expected to have relatively weak cultures. On the other hand, GE, DuPont, and 3M are older imperial conglomerates who have had more time to inculcate the shared beliefs and values of their cultures into successive generations of managers. Although most new conglomerates do not yet have really strong cultures, if they follow the pioneers, they will soon enough.

Forging the new conglomerate corporation into an imperial conglomerate, into a unified whole, has become a growth industry. It has spawned the new high-tech, information economy. Furthermore, along with the investment bankers and corporate lawyers who have been arranging new mergers and restructurings as fast as possible, business consultants specializing in the problems of conglomerate management have been doing a very brisk business in the sale of advice.[11] The most influential pioneers in conglomerate consulting were in the Boston Consulting Group. They rose to prominence in the late 1970s with their so-called product portfolio approach to conglomerate management. In their approach, the corporate office of the conglomerate was advised to classify its subsidiary corporations or divisions into four basic types: (1) CASH COWS, these subsidiaries possessed a large market share of a stable or declining industry. Formerly powerful old industrial oligopolies made excellent cash cows. (2) STARS possessed a large market share of a growing industry. New high-tech, information-based service companies made excellent stars. (3) DOGS possessed a small market share of a stable or declining industry. (4) CATS or question marks possessed the potential for acquiring a large market share of a growing industry.

Once the corporate office determined the nature of its subsidiaries or divisions, it could then integrate them into an overall growth strategy for the conglomerate as a whole. With the help of its investment banker, the corporate office sold off the dogs for the best obtainable price. Such subsidiaries were of little use to the corporate office. Their weak market position offered little opportunity for a higher profit margin in the short run, and their stable or declining industry offered little growth opportunity for the long run.

After selling off its dogs, the corporate office tried to achieve an overall balance in its holdings of cows and stars. The cows, with their strong market positions, offered high profit margins in the short run. Also, since cows operated in stable or declining industries, they required little new investment in plant and equipment. Their large depreciation allowances were greater than their investment requirements, particularly if their existing plant and equipment were allowed to deteriorate. This left them with an accumulation of surplus funds for investing elsewhere. They were literally cash cows ready for vigorous milking. Cash cow subsidiaries provided the short-run funds for investing in the long-run growth of star subsidiaries. The stars, with their market power in growing industries, could grow very rapidly in output and in profit if they could acquire the large flow of funds they needed to expand their plant and equipment. So the conglomerate's corporate office matched the cash flow provided by its cash cows in the short run with the cash needs of its stars for expansion in the long run. It is no coincidence that most cash cows were manufacturing subsidiaries with high capital-output ratios because the higher the ratio of capital to output, the higher the depreciation allowances available for milking. Such manufacturing subsidiaries were located principally in the Midwest and were in stable or declining industries. Their vigorous milking by conglomerates speeded up or precipitated their declines and turned the old industrial heartland of the U.S. economy into the rustbelt. But their milking also provided the financing of conglomerate stars, who, also by no coincidence, are generally high tech companies located in the sunbelt or in low-wage, underdeveloped countries. Barry Bluestone and Bennett Harrison provide further discussion and empirical evidence in their *The Deindustrialization of America.*[12]

Conglomerate offices, once they had sold off their dogs and matched the need for funds of their stars with the flow of funds milked from their cows, had to decide which of its cats or question marks could be developed into new stars. Those that could were retained; the others were sold off, divested. Conglomerate divestiture of unwanted cats and dogs occurs quite frequently as a matter of course. Such divestitures do not represent a change in practice, just a house-cleaning. Conglomerates are not moving back to single-industry status. Census data show just the reverse—more instead of less diversification. Nevertheless, many financial analysts and business journalists continue to misinterpret conglomerate house-cleaning as a return to single-industry operation. Such interpretations simply are not supported by the broad empirical evidence.[13]

Another diagram will be useful here. Figure 2 illustrates how the financial flows, principally between stars and cows, are arranged before and after merger into a giant conglomerate. As Figure 2 shows, cats are gotten rid of as quickly as possible. If they cannot be turned into stars, they simply disappear from the conglomerate scene through divestiture. Dogs, on the other hand, remain in the conglomerate menagerie, but only long enough to be liquidated. The cows are milked vigorously, through disinvestment, to provide the cash flow needed to investment in stars. Figure 2 also shows the drastic reduction in the role played by shareholders and by the financial market. The powerful imperial conglomerate can largely dispense with the nuisance of shareholders and financial markets. They are dispensed with by simply bypassing them. Neither the pesky shareholders nor the risky financial market need be relied on for a regular flow of funds instead. The market does not really disappear, but its social control function does.

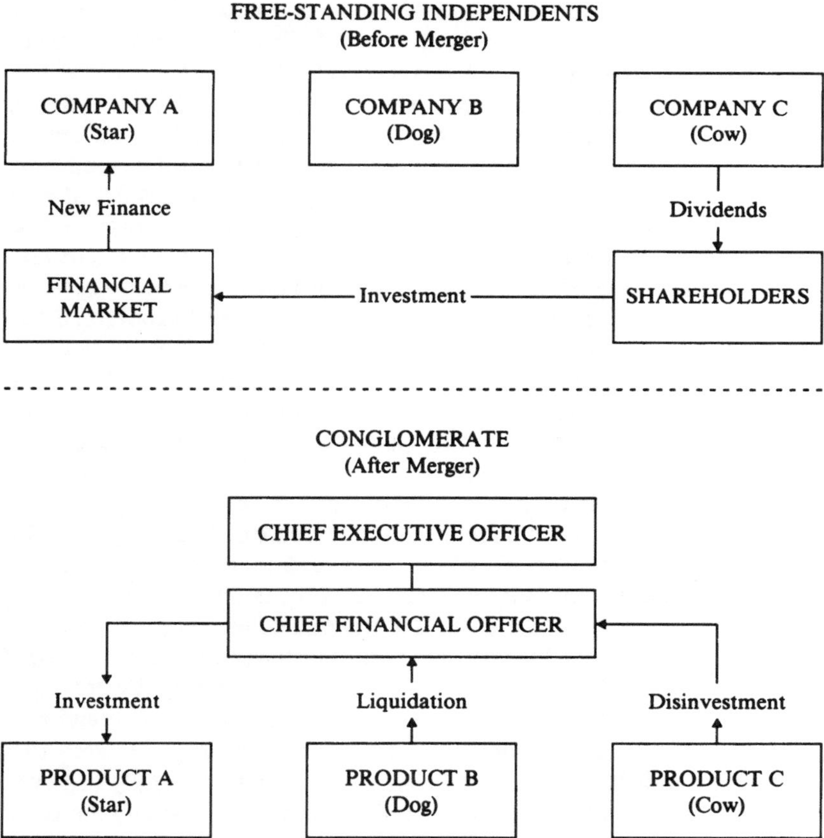

Figure 2: *Financial Flows*

The Boston Consulting Group's menagerie approach to managing the conglomerate did rationalize it into a kind of whole that was more than the mere sum of its parts. Nevertheless, the approach dealt only with the financial dimension of the conglomerate enterprise, creating a financial synergy between the parts, but nothing more. The Boston Consulting Group's approach was a halfway house on the road to full unification, a kind of financial expedient that kept the conglomerates of the 1970s going until the corporate culture of the 1980s developed.

Corporate culture unifies, not just the financial dimensions, but all the dimensions of conglomerate enterprise.[14] Over-emphasizing the financial results of subsidiaries or divisions to the exclusion of other performance dimensions can quickly lead to managerial neglect, at best, and to rampant opportunism, at worst. That is, subsidiary managers can meet their quantified financial objectives at the expense of their other, non-quantified duties. They can save expenses and make themselves look good financially by not performing costly functions in the short run, the slighting of which will not be felt until the long run. Of course, by the time the effect of this managerial neglect is felt, it will be the responsibility of someone else, the original perpetrator having been rewarded by a promotion to a larger division or to an important post at the corporate office, before his neglect finally affects the bottom line of his former division. By then, it is somebody else's problem. Such managerial neglect, under a system that over-emphasizes immediate financial results, naturally leads to rampant opportunism. Division heads learn to concentrate on meeting their own financial targets, at the expense of other objectives, and certainly at the expense of any non-quantified, non-rewarded objectives.

Opportunistic division heads quickly learned how to maximize the return to themselves from their corporate position. They began to do a bit of milking on their own behalf. They also became cynical opportunists who maximized their own salaries, perquisites, bonuses, and insider profits. They could do so at the expense of whoever was foolish or weak enough to bear the cost, be it another manager, another investor, the conglomerate, or the society at large. Even ignoring the personal and social costs of managerial opportunism, the costs to the conglomerate can become large. Under the circumstances, synergy between the different parts of the conglomerate whole becomes extremely difficult to create. A system of control far stronger than that devised by the Boston Consulting Group is required to teach the lower level managers to work together for the higher good. The continued growth in corporate size and diversification allowed for a rise in managerial slack, at the divisional level, that has to be taken up. A surprising majority of executives agree that more controls are necessary. In a fascinating survey of executives from thirteen representative U.S. corporations, Allan Cox learned:

> Most executives believe controls within the corporation are necessary. Fifty-one percent top executives and 56 percent middle agree such controls are needed to curb corruption—or at least indiscretion. Their thinking is that the size and complexity of their management structure is an invitation for unchecked indiscretions or outright dishonesty available to a random few.[15]

Learning to Work for the Higher Good

Corporations generally pay their managers well. The Administrative Management Society estimates that in 1984, U.S. managers in lower- to middle-level corporate positions were paid an average annual salary of $32,270, up 7.7 percent from 1983. These managers also received various packages of pension and insurance plans, profit sharing, and other fringe benefits. The lower- and middle-level positions covered by this average salary estimate ranged from accounting manager to general foreman.[16] Top management is paid much better, particularly in large corporations. The Dartnell Institute of Financial Research estimates that chief executive officers of large U.S. corporations (annual sales volume of $1–10 billion) received an average annual base salary of $138,000 in 1981 and an average total annual compensation of $221,000.[17] In that same year, 31.8 million Americans lived below the poverty level of income ($9,287 for a family of four).[18]

Relative to many millions of Americans, corporate managers are doing very well. Nevertheless, the corporate liberality toward its managerial class does not mean that the corporation exists for the good of its middle managers. It does not. Rather, the corporation exists for the good of its higher order—its CEOs and major stockholders. The potential opportunism and avarice of its middle managers (the lower good) runs counter to the higher good. Although middle managers are paid well, they are corporate employees, not autonomous agents free to trade for their own account. And the conscious purpose of corporate culture is to keep a tight reign on their pursuit of their own personal interests, particularly when those interests detract from the higher corporate interest. For no matter how well they are paid and no matter how closely they are watched, some middle managers can still misbehave; some can still pursue their own interest. Exploiting the corporation financially is the obvious misbehavior. But managers might also devote their energies to empire-building, to family matters, to friends, or to other superfluities. Corporate culture is designed to control such misbehavior.

Narrowly defined, corporate culture is the internalized control of managerial behavior. External control is applied, also. The M-form organizational structure is a major advance in the technology of external control; so too is the whole range of computer storage, processing, and monitoring technologies applied in the computerized office. But they are all insufficient because they are all external. Internal controls are also needed to stimulate and monitor managerial behavior. Up to now it has not been possible (legally) to physically insert the appropriate, computer-activated electrodes into the managerial brain. Although it cannot be done physically, at least not yet, it can be done culturally, particularly to those obsessed with career success.

How Values Change: Coercion and Career

The most secure and effective form of control over others is the power to alter their values. Control over others can be based on coercion—others can be forced to do as they are told. Such is the nature of the slave owner's control of the slave. But control based on coercion is tenuous. Slaves resist and revolt because control based on coercion creates resentment and duplicity in the coerced. Slaves learn to walk with a shuffle around their masters, even while burning with resentment. Slaves can be forced to give lip service to the master's values, but it is far more difficult to force the internal acceptance of those values. When the force is removed, so is the social control because it was not willingly accepted. Social control through coercion is temporary. More permanent social control is based on the ability to alter the internal values of others to gain their willing acceptance of the control. Then the control becomes legitimate. It is deemed right and good by those over whom it is exercised. It no longer requires the whip.

Ambition is a far more powerful social control mechanism than coercion. Based on fear, the power of coercion fades when the coercion is removed. But the power of ambition has its tap root sunk deeply into shared values and beliefs, into culture itself. Ambition is sunk particularly deep into the culture of the self-made man—into American culture, that is. In the nineteenth century that ambition manifested itself in the exuberance of the pioneer on the moving frontier. It bubbled over in the form of gold rushes and land booms. In the twentieth century, that ambition manifests itself in the rampant careerism of U.S. managerial strata and has become anchored even more deeply in the cultural reservoir of values and beliefs shared by the broad American middle class. Now it bubbles over in the form of dual career couples and suburban sprawl. But personal ambition is the same powerful motivator, whether pursued on the frontier or in the career.

Thorstein Veblen came to know American ambition and how it distorts values and beliefs better than any other social observer. So, cultural change and value distortion in the United States can be understood best by examining the four invaluation processes first sketched out by Veblen.[19] Those four processes are contamination, subordination, emulation, and mystification. All of them are intimately related to ambition and social control. Of course, numerous recent observers have studied the relations between ambition and social control. Their insights and evidence are also drawn upon here.

Invaluation Processes—Contamination

The first of the four invaluation processes of interest to us is contamination. The values of others can be altered and one's own values reinforced if their values can be contaminated with your own. Then their emotional attachment to their own, original value can be turned to your account. Contamination is a powerful way for those in positions of high status and authority to alter values into strings that can be pulled and buttons that can be pushed to get underlings to want to do what is wanted by the person or institution that is doing the manipulating. Most of us want to be good at what we do. We usually take pride in our workmanship, in the general serviceability of our skills. This pride of workmanship, when uncontaminated, makes most of us try to be craftsmen. Whether househusbands, typists, cleaning ladies, sculptors, truck drivers, or nuclear physicists, we value performing our craft well. But this value we place on a task well done, for its own sake, can be contaminated by another value. It can be turned into something else and used as a button by someone else. Then someone can push our button, for their sake. This is precisely what happens when technical craft becomes corporate career.

The value we place on our craft is a value that is inherent in the craft itself. We value our craft because we find it of intrinsic worth. As craftsmen, we are craft-directed and self-directed.[20] Nevertheless, through contamination, our craft becomes our career. Both craftspeople and careerists value the tasks they perform, but for very different reasons. The craftsperson's values are intrinsic and internal, while the careerist's values are extrinsic and external. The careerist is a contaminated craftsperson, a craftsperson on the make. The careerist performs tasks to advance his career, rather than to advance his craft. The careerist values a task performance because it gets him an external reward, because it gains the approval of others, particularly the approval of superiors rather than the approval of fellow craftspeople. The careerist and the craftsperson may perform the same task, but since the careerist does it to curry favor, the careerist can be manipulated far more readily than the craftsperson. From the point of view of the organization that needs to control its employees, the careerist is an asset. He comes to the organization fully equipped with buttons that can be pushed and string that can be pulled. He is useful. The craftsperson, on the other hand, is a problem to the organization. She lacks buttons and strings. She must have them installed before she is fully operational. Installation (contamination) can be time-consuming and expensive; better that it be done at school and at public expense than at work and at corporate expense. So the process of contamination usually begins in school where youthful explorers who learn for the fun of it are turned into obedient students who learn for the external rewards of grades. Regardless of where it is done and at whose expense, it is essential to the maintenance of organizational control. She must be taught career values to replace craft values. To get a handle on her performance, the internal and intrinsic must be contaminated with the external and extrinsic so that the emotional charge of the former (craft) can be activated by pulling on the strings of the latter (career). Michael Maccoby, author of *The Gamesman,* described how strongly the desire for success pulls on the managerial psyche, contaminating the craft of doing things with the career of getting ahead. Maccoby's psychological probings of corporate careerists show that the power of contamination is considerable.[21]

Invaluation Processes—Subordination

Closely related to contamination is a second way to alter or even implant values in those to be controlled. If their values resist contamination, the values of others can still be altered or at least overcome if their (lower) values can be subordinated to your (higher) values. A familiar illustration will help. As Commander-in-Chief, the President of the United States values young men as soldiers, sailors, and fliers. On the other hand, the women of the United States value the same young men as brothers, sons, and husbands. Military value conflicts with family value. If the military value is to prevail, then the President must be able to exercise power over the potential pacifists, over the potentially insubordinate women. He can do so by subordinating their "womanly" family values to higher, "manly" values. In large measure, the male-dominated culture has already done it for him. Just for good measure though, the women constantly should be taught the higher value of patriotism.

The subordination of others' values is never direct. An ambitious national leader, for example, never asks others to subordinate the value they place on their life to the value he places on defeating a rival national leader. Instead, such a leader calls upon some higher order of values such as national honor, as did Napoleon and Hitler. In economic conflicts, when subordinating community values to their own, corporate leaders never directly ask the community to give them more profit. Instead, corporate leaders refer indirectly to higher values or to natural laws. "Free enterprise" sells very well in the United States as a higher value and "the market" sells very well as a natural law. The high values afforded science and experts are also very effective. Never is a community directly asked to sacrifice clean air and clean water to corporate profit. Instead, "the market" needs deregulating and "free enterprise" needs defending. Furthermore, scientific experts, on corporate retainers, impress the community with cost-benefit ratios, statistical analysis, and other scientific talismans of great power. Corporations appear almost philanthropic in these matters, for they never argue to the public that regulation cuts their profits; though corporations will often point out that they may be forced to close their plants and lay off their workers because of the economic burdens imposed upon them by environmental controls.

Careerism and ambition play important roles in subordination as well as in contamination. As a manager learns to elevate his career to a higher-order value, he subordinates his other values to his career values. Male careerists are more prone to do so than female careerists, particularly when it comes to subordinating family to career. So from the point of view of the organization seeking to control the managerial worker, men are more useful because they are more willing to subordinate their family to their career than women. Men are the weaker sex because they are easier to subordinate to corporate career. Furthermore, men may more readily downgrade their family than women because men are more able to do so than women. Patriarchical family relations that raise the man above the woman make it possible for men to shirk their family duties by pushing them onto their wives. Jacqueline B. Stanfield shows that this is the general case even in dual-career families, where wives who take up a career frequently continue contributing far more time and effort to the family's welfare than their career husbands do. Many women in that situation are pushed into trying to be a superwoman, trying to perform two wholly-absorbing roles simultaneously and feeling guilty for not being able to do the impossible. Their husbands offer little help around the home, so, unable to subordinate one set of conflicting values to another, they are trapped.[22] Although men too are trapped by career values through subordination, most of them are able to subordinate their wives' values to their own. Career men have it easier because they usually can push their home duties off on their wife, leaving the men with a clear conscience when their family values are subordinated to their career values. Ralph Nader and William Taylor studied at length nine corporate leaders in the United States. In nearly all of those leaders, family and community values were subordinated to the values of corporate career.[23]

Invaluation Processes—Emulation

A third way to change the values of others is to get them to emulate you. Emulation is the most powerful invaluation process. It is the tap root of career and of conformity. At bottom, a careerist is an emulator, a mimic of those who are highly respected (envied) in their fields. Emulation occurs when people learn to envy (respect) the values of higher-status individuals and to mimic or duplicate them in a competition for personal status, for invidious distinction. Emulation is a complex form of personal attack on another person or persons to whom the attacker is actually attracted. It is based on attraction, not repulsion. It is an attempt to be like the other person or persons, only more so. It is raising one's standing in a group of status-ranked strivers, all of whom are constantly trying to inflate their own status while simultaneously deflating the status of their competitors.

Successful emulation requires constant self-aggrandizement through the conspicuous display of excellence in conventionally approved channels. It requires far more, however, than the ability to show off one's status. Merely showing off makes it too obvious that the show offs are not satisfied with their own status because it is lower than the status of their competitors. Merely showing off creates distinction, but the wrong kind. The right kind is invidious distinction, a distinction that creates envy in the minds of one's competitors but at the same time demonstrates complacency in the mind of the perpetrator. Successful emulators can become quite brutal towards those they have surpassed. In *Showing Off in America,* John Brooks described the qualities of the toughest top executives in the United States. "The qualities that distinguish these men are arrogance, gratuitous cruelty, self-centeredness, lack of consideration of others, pettiness, fickleness, schoolyard bullying—a catalogue of predatory-invidious traits."[24]

An emulator does not rock the boat. He does not want to destroy the values held by those whose status he attacks. He wants to possess them, but to a greater extent. This makes the emulator profoundly conventional, and it makes the process of emulation an extraordinarily powerful mechanism of social control. His study of emulation is Thorstein Veblen's major contribution to the study of values.[25] He showed how emulation transformed a potentially revolutionary situation in the United States into a very conservative era. The way Veblen saw it, by the close of the nineteenth century, American farmers and workers were clearly at odds with the growing power of big business. The frontier escape hatch had closed, so the traditional path to a better life in the United States had closed with it. It was in their purely rational, economic interest for the farmers and workers to throw the Robber Barons out of power. But the farmers and workers, Veblen's "common man," did not want to revolt against the Robber Barons. The common man wanted to become like the Robber Barons, only more so. According to Veblen, the power of emulation overcame the economic interest of the "common man," turning him into a highly conventional and conservative defender of the status quo rather than a revolutionary. As the frontier closed and as career ladders proliferated in the professional and managerial ranks of the growing corporate world, the man on the make eagerly tried his hand at the new game of corporate career. Pushing his way into the growing middle class of kept men, the "common man" became sucked into the petty rivalries and the invidious distinctions of middle-class life and of the white collar career.

Then within just a few decades, interrupted by a glorious but short revolt of the youth (the 1960s), the rivalries and invidious distinctions of the corporate career had so raised the acceptable standards of life that the "common man" had to be aided in the rat race by the "common woman." By the 1970s, one salary had become insufficient to finance the ever-rising level of conspicuous consumption. A house in the suburbs with two cars in the garage and two college-educated kids are impressively expensive, but no longer enough to keep up with the competition. The kids now need MBAs from prestigious private universities and to get those, the proper prep school is becoming almost mandatory. Furthermore, the level of living must not only be quite vast in quantity, but also quite refined in quality. All of this requires more money. Two or three cars are not enough. At least one of them must be a Mercedes or other suitably refined make. Summer vacations at a second home are also needed, but are not enough. Winter vacations, with tans to verify them, must be added. And so it has gone throughout the twentieth century, the relentless pressure of emulation has pushed the acceptable standard of living ever higher and has pushed down the self-esteem of those who do not keep up, ever lower. The pressure of emulation has placed the heavy hand of competitive conformity over everyone.

The emulative pressures of middle-class life and white collar corporate career in the United States have created the widespread insecurity required by corporate cultures. Make no mistake, the system is working. Their insecurity make managerial personnel highly susceptible to indoctrination into the values and beliefs of specific corporations. Most lower-level workers also come to the corporation ready-made for the deskilled and degraded tasks that need doing there. Their self-esteem properly lowered by emulative pressure, and their traditional jobs squeezed out by the fight against inflation, millions of unorganized or deorganized working class whites and dispirited minorities are grist for the corporate mill.

The force of emulation also explains why the egalitarian drives of the civil rights movement and of women's liberation are being lost. Despite the real successes of Reverend Jesse Jackson's Rainbow Coalition and Operation P.U.S.H., the flight of the black middle class from the urban ghetto and from black small business—following the earlier move of the white middle class into suburbia and white collar careerism—is depriving most blacks of the money and leadership that fueled their movement. The women's liberation movement also is being defanged. The old egalitarian drive of the sisterhood is being transformed by emulation into a drive for more career opportunity in the corporate world. Rather than trying to replace the emulation of careerism with a more egalitarian and humanitarian way of organizing work, the rage among women on the make is "networking." This "networking" merely replaces, or at least supplements, the old boy system of status-enhancement in the corporate world with an old girl system of status-enhancement in the corporate world. It is still emulative, inegalitarian, and careerist. That is, "networking" still involves status-seeking, self-aggrandizement, and the sacrifice of all other values to career values, whether or not the network of opportunists is male or female.[26]

A financial indication of the strength of emulation and conspicuous consumption is the distribution of financial and liquid asset holdings of American families. According to an authoritative study published in the *Federal Reserve Bulletin,* while only 10 percent of all families had been able to build up $50,000 or more in financial and liquid assets in 1983, fully 61 percent of all families held less than $5,000 in such assets.[27] This means that the vast majority of U.S. families have little slack in their budgets for building up a readily-available financial reserve. Even fairly affluent families, with annual incomes of $25,000–$29,999, had a median holding of only $5,147 in financial and liquid assets in 1983.[28]

Homeownership boosts the net worth of many affluent families, but the boost is largely illusory. If they sold their homes to get their net equity, they would have no place to live. Their equity would then be eaten up by rent payments, making their gain a temporary one. Furthermore, 40 percent of fairly affluent families (income from $20,000 to $29,999 a year) do not own their own homes in the first place.[29] Nevertheless, the net worth of affluent families (measured as the median net worth of families with incomes of $25,000 to $29,999) was only $28,876 in 1983.[30] That net worth includes the net equity in homes. Under the pressure of competitive spending for conspicuous consumption, even the fairly affluent are unable to build their net worth much above a mere pittance. In fact, half of all U.S. families had net worth of less than $25,000 in 1983.[31] This is a profound indication of the strength of emulation in a society originally based on Puritan frugality.

Emulation occurs not only in the realm of consumption spending, but in all dimensions of life where personal status plays a role, as it does in a career. Emulation is similar to subordination in that it also involves the lowering of the prestige or significance of one set of values and the raising of another set—conspicuous consumption over Puritan parsimony, for example. For another relevant example, consider the case of a young man raised in a tight-knit ethnic mill community who enters on a corporate career. Through emulating high-status corporate executives, he can be induced to denigrate the values and hopes of his boyhood friends and to elevate the values and career struggles of his corporate peers and corporate bosses. The former community member will then feel only slight pangs of conscience if, in his career climb, he finds it expedient to close the plant that provides employment for his former community, or if he finds it necessary to mount a decertification campaign against the union that represents his old buddies. Emulation is the most effective method of cooptation and is the process that has turned some of the radical yippies into the emasculated yuppies of the American pop scene.

Invaluation Processes—Mystification

A fourth way to change the values held by others is to mystify them, thereby confusing those whose values you oppose into supporting your values instead of theirs. Mystification requires the manipulation of valued symbols. If motherhood and apple pie, for example, can be mystified and confused with national honor and war, the values of nurturing within the family can be drawn upon for support by those who exercise power through the conquests of the state. Likewise, if workers value the right to earn a living, perhaps mystification can be used to induce them to value the right to work. Furthermore, values symbolized by "private property" and "individual initiative" can be manipulated to protect corporations from collective bargaining and from state regulation. Widely shared, communal values can be distorted or stretched to cover a multitude of actions, from polluting the air to exploiting the workforce, that run counter to those very communal values. Mystification is strongly akin to "newspeak." It allows the War Department to be the Defense Department, the MX Missile to be the Peacekeeper Missile, the economic surplus to be the cost of capital, and it allows conglomerate profit to be the higher good. Mystification involves the linking or confusing of different values. In the examples above, each negatively charged value is linked to or confused with a more positively charged value. This positive linkage reduces the repulsion felt by others to things that you value. So if you value war, multiple warheads, and surplus income (profit), while others do not, you should link them with things that others do value, such as defense, peace, and earned income. The importance of confusion in the shaping of human values cannot be over-estimated.

To serve one's employer, to pursue the higher corporate good, frequently requires managers and professionals to be absent from their families until late at night or to be away on distant assignments for extended periods. It also frequently requires the psyche's complete energy and attention, whether at home or on the road. From his extensive survey of U.S. executives, Allan Cox concluded, "While a good many executives may be appreciative of their families' needs and of their presence and support, some obviously view their homelife disdainfully. Many spend excessive hours at the office, and travel extensively even when they may not need to, in order to avoid a less than happy home."[32] Nevertheless, most corporate managers and professionals feel very negatively toward family neglect and toward emotional detachment from loved ones. If they neglected their families and emotionally detached from their loved ones, the guilt from doing so would be devastating. So, corporate managers do not neglect or detach. Instead of these negative things, they work hard into the night on their careers and they pursue challenging new opportunities out of town. This is not neglecting the family—a negatively charged value. This is advancing the career—a positively charged value. They do not bring their work home in their briefcases to remain detached from the family circle of emotions. Instead, they bring their work home in their briefcases to get a promotion. Or so they have learned to believe. So they feel pride, not guilt. But if their wives divorce them or their children rebel against them, they are mystified and feel betrayed. They did not neglect their families out of malice. They did not emotionally detach out of frigidity. Nevertheless, they still neglected their families, even if it was to get a promotion. They still emotionally detached from their loved ones, even if it was to pursue their career.

Corporate Culture

A culture is a set of shared values and beliefs. Spurred on by careerism, these four invaluation processes are changing pluralistic U.S. culture into hegemonic corporate culture. The values and beliefs of the corporate world are coming to replace the values and beliefs of the old frontier world. Just like success on the frontier required a certain set of values and beliefs, so too does success in the corporation. But a pluralistic culture's shared beliefs and values come from a number of independent institutions—church, state, family, school, union; while a hegemonic culture's shared beliefs and values come from a single dominant institution. Human character in a pluralistic culture is created by each person through a painful internal reconciliation and synthesis of conflicting values and beliefs. Human character in a hegemonic culture, on the other hand, is molded through an external inculcation of supporting values and beliefs. U.S. culture and U.S. character are already far more hegemonic than pluralistic, particularly among the corporate middle class. It is from this social strata that hegemony is evolving. Critical intellectuals seldom study the white collar middle-class world. As a result, most are being blindsided by the development of hegemony in the United States.[33]

Speeding Up the Managerial Class

The position of the managerial class is now a very precarious one. The working class in the United States is at least partially organized to defend its economic interests. But middle managers almost never organize into unions or into any collectivity to defend themselves. Instead, they pursue their own personal interests as individual careerists. Divided by their individualism and blinded by their careerism, middle managers are easy prey for the organized interest of big, conglomerated capital. Members of the working class feel solidarity with other workers. But a manager has no solidarity with other managers. So when a manager is fired or abused, his fellows do not come to his aid. Instead, they scramble for his job. He is on his own, and if he loses out in the career climb, then he alone is blamed for it and he alone must deal with it. His mates offer little solace—lest they become associated with a loser—and his wife frequently leaves him (as was the case with John DeLorean of General Motors).

The managerial careerist, although individualistic in his climb, does not serve his own interest with his corporate work. Instead, blinded by his careerism, he serves the interests of the controlling corporate ownership. He is as alienated as any member of the working class, but he does not know it. His values are so contaminated that when he works for someone else's profit, he never realizes that he is being manipulated. His buttons are pushed and his strings are pulled by someone else. He works for them, not himself. All the while, the managerial careerist remains unaware of his buttons and strings, and of the sacrifice he is making of himself. Unaware of being manipulated, the careerist sacrifices not only himself but also his family and friends to his career. Separated from family and friend, the managerial careerist emulates other, higher, managerial careerists who, in turn, emulate those of even higher status. The emulation and accompanying invidious distinction extend all the way up the ladder to the top rung. The top rung is occupied by big capital, by the controlling interest of the conglomerate that employs the careerists.

So although the managerial class is well-paid, its class position is precarious, even more so than its financial position. Denied an organized defense of its own interests by its careerism and impregnated with values from above, the managerial class is not really a class at all. The power exercised by managers is not their power. The corporate purpose that managers pursue is not their purpose. The wealth they manage is not their wealth. In truth, the managerial class is a dependent class, a kept class. It possesses no power, no status, no substantial wealth of its own. Even its culture is not of its own making.

Separation of Ownership from Control

Nevertheless, the managerial function is essential in our highly organized corporate world. Without managers, corporate organizations would collapse. Because they are essential, and because of what was once a separation of ownership from control, many observers have argued that managers comprise an independent class. From Adolf A. Berle and Gardiner C. Means through John Kenneth Galbraith, institutionalist students of the U.S. corporation have attributed independent motives to corporate managers.[34] These independent managerial motives are claimed to run counter to the profit motive of ownership. Berle and Means, in their pioneering study, *The Modern Corporation and Private Property,* argued that more and more mature corporations were controlled by the management rather than by the stockholders. As the original corporate owners died off, the ownership of stock was diffused; as the number of shareholders rose, no single shareholder owned enough stock to control the corporation. Stock ownership became a passive form of ownership. It became ownership without control, according to Berle and Means.

The separation of stock ownership from control and the continued growth of the corporation allowed for a broad range of managerial discretion relative to the stockholders. As long as the immediate profits flowing to stockholders were satisfactory, the management was free to pursue its own objectives. Those objectives could run along two very different lines: personal or organizational. If management used its discretion to pursue personal objectives, then instead of earning the maximum profit for the distant stockholders, managers could puff up their own salaries and perks, invent new incentive plans and retirement benefits, and grant themselves lucrative stock options. They could hire more and more subordinates to puff up their own status. They could farm out lucrative contracts to friends and relatives and waste stockholder resources on their own pet projects and grandiose schemes. Or, they could just take it easy and live the good life, playing golf, drinking scotch, and enjoying their secretaries.

But if management pursued objectives along a different line, they could do such things as sacrifice immediate stockholder profit for higher long-term corporate growth. They could even pursue technological advances (craft) instead of profit (career) by allocating resources to research and development instead of to dividends. They could, in general, take the long-run point of view for their organization and try to ensure its continued growth and prosperity, instead of constantly going after the short-run profits that look good to stockholders. Management could pursue these organizational objectives, as long as enough profits were earned to keep the distant shareholders satisfied. So not only was a running margin of managerial malfeasance opened up by the separation of ownership from control and by the continued growth in corporate size, but a margin of managerial statesmanship was also made possible by the lifting of the stockholder's obsession with short-run results. Exactly how management used its range of discretion depended on the circumstances of the case.

John Kenneth Galbraith, in his *New Industrial State,* argued that the opening up of the managerial range of discretion had a somewhat benign effect on corporate behavior. Corporate bureaucracies, originally organized for the single-minded pursuit of profit, evolved into "technostructures," according to Galbraith. Within these technostructures, the drive for more profit was softened to some extent by the goals of managerial "technocrats" (craftspeople). Galbraith saw corporate management as essentially technocratic rather than bureaucratic. That is, managers valued technological advance and expanding output for their division's organization rather than maximum profit for their conglomerate shareholder-employers. Whether or not the resulting behavior of organizations under this so-called managerial capitalism would be a single-minded pursuit of shareholder profits has been the focus of a long controversy.[35]

Nevertheless, in the 1980s the old, broad range of managerial discretion is being narrowed in three related ways. First, the conglomerate itself, with its new M-form organizational structure and its profit centers, is becoming a more effective system of external control of management performance. The sharp-penciled auditors and hard-nosed strategists of the conglomerate's corporate office are far more effective at forcing division heads to pursue the bottom line than the far-removed shareholders of the free-standing corporation of old. The information revolution has been crucial in improving corporate control over managerial performance. Conglomerate headquarters is now the center of a vast flow of timely and accurate information about the performance, particularly financial, of the conglomerate's far-flung empire. Second, the corporate culture itself is providing a growing system of internal, culture-based control to supplement the external, information-based control of the conglomerate's corporate office. Third, the growing threat of a hostile takeover, even of large corporations, keeps the managerial nose much closer to the proverbial grindstone. As a result, managers are being speeded up. Their short-lived discretion, originally opened up by the separation of ownership from control in the large corporation, is being taken away by the conglomerate, with its ability to take over even the largest corporations and to control even the most independent of CEOs. However, the conglomerate is eliminating not only the running margin of managerial malfeasance but also the longer-term objectives and the slight softening of the immediate profit motive experienced under independent managements.

In a recent study, Edward S. Herman of the Wharton School has thrown considerable doubt on the proposition that the profit motive was ever softened by the rise of a so-called managerial class, possessed of a wide margin of discretion. Herman concludes:

> In sum, the triumph of management control in many large corporations has not left them in the hands of neutral technocrats. . . . The frequently assumed decline in managerial interest in profits, which supposedly

should result from the decreased importance of direct owner control, has not, in fact, been proved.[36]

A closer control of managerial discretion is being achieved through new corporate culture, new organizational structure, new information technology, and through the growing threat of takeover. This tightening up will not lead to improvement in long-term corporate performance, however. Short-run profits may very well rise as a result of the tightening up, but long-run performance may very well deteriorate. Marc R. Tool explains: "The more complete and meticulous the control of subordinates, the *lower* one would expect the volume and quality of economic performance to be in the shop, the foundry, the office, the classroom, or even the board room."[37]

The U.S. managerial class is being sucked into the same vicious circle that sucked in the working class nearly eighty years earlier. That vicious circle is known, by labor radicals, as "the speed-up." The industrial workers of the United States, around the turn of this century, were subjected to Frederick Taylor's so-called "Scientific Management."[38] "Scientific Management" involved first finding the fastest way to perform each task in a particular manufacturing process. The fastest way was determined by managerial experts, by time and motion specialists, not by the workers themselves.

In the next step of the speed-up, all workers were held to the faster pace of work by an elaborate piecework system of payment. Higher output and profit were the results; so too, sometimes, was higher income for the workers. And frequent side-effects, of course, were worker alienation and industrial strife. But gradually a third step evolved in the speed up. This step was a response to the side-effects encountered in the second step. In the third step of the speed up, the recalcitrant workers were taught to like the speeded-up pace of work, or were at least taught to tolerate it. The "human relations management" movement, also known by a number of other names, involved showing the workers that the corporation really cared about them. A few dollars spent on bulletin boards, lunchrooms, bowling teams, better lights, personnel directors, newsletters, and the like, paid big dividends in reduced strife and easier worker cooptation.[39]

Of course, some workers were more difficult than others. Particular difficulty was encountered with workers who were organizing into industrial unions. The steelworkers and autoworkers took more than lunchrooms and bowling teams. Pensions, health insurance, large wage hikes, and more, were required in these more difficult cases. And even then, militant workers could never learn to like the speed-up. But they tolerated it, more or less.[40] Furthermore, even if some unions could not be coopted, they could be induced to shift the formal area of conflict away from the organization of the labor process. Collective bargaining dealt more and more with wages and fringe benefits, and less and less with how work was organized and managed. This more crucial question was left, increasingly, as a managerial prerogative. So, management was left free to continue the speed-up.

Continuing the speed up, however, required ever-closer control of the worker, and tighter control evoked more worker alienation and strife. These, in turn, called for tighter controls and more effective co-optation. But the more coopted and controlled the worker, the harder it was to speed her up, the harder to appeal to her sense of workmanship. A vicious circle had been entered of more control and more co-optation evoking less workmanship, which then called for even more control. The fundamental contradiction between managerial control and worker spontaneity greatly intensified the other contradictions of corporate enterprise because it slowed down or halted productivity improvement, making it harder and harder to get more profit out of the workers. So, more profit must come from the consumers and from the community at large. And now, at last, the hungry eye has also turned inward, looking for ways to squeeze more profit from the managers themselves. The temporary slack given them by the separation of ownership from control is being taken up.

The separation of ownership from control that occurred in many mature corporations gave management a large degree of control, but management quickly lost its control to the conglomerate. Management still controls daily operations and still makes the big policy decisions, but within a new, highly restrictive institutional framework—within a system of institutionalized greed. That institutionalized greed takes concrete form, not in the flimsy old conspiracies of a few wealthy capitalists, but in the powerful form of a new institution—the imperial conglomerate.

The Worm Turns, On Itself

The new conglomerate has gained control over the managers, as the managers earlier had gained control over the workers. But the managerial class, as it begins to speed itself up, has none of the defenses possessed by the working class. Managers feel no solidarity and have no unions to join. Nor would they join them if they existed.[41] Devotion to individual career success precludes any collective resistance, and the ambition of careerists also precludes any personal resistance. Ambitious members of the managerial class stand completely exposed and completely alone.

Speeding up the managers first involved the construction of M-form organizations composed of profit centers. Then the output of each profit center could be measured and the head of that profit center held responsible. Harold Geneen's management of ITT illustrates the point. Geneen's ITT was probably the most aggressive of the conglomerates to sweep over the corporate world in the 1960s, and Geneen was the driving force behind it. Every year, year after year, each and every one of his acquired subsidiaries was expected to increase its earnings by at least 10 percent. No matter what, the bottom line objective had to be met. When he took over a company,

> we would talk about our goal of at least 10 percent annual growth. It did not make any difference if times were good or bad. When they were good, we should be able to make our goal easily; when they were bad, we had to work harder. But we had to make our goal each and every year. That was the message. And the new company managements believed us, because they knew we meant what we were saying.[42]

This single-minded pursuit of short-run profit, this obsession with the immediate bottom line, described so frankly by Geneen, is by no means limited to him. It has become characteristic of American management. Geneen's single-mindedness is representative of the higher-level executives of conglomerated corporations. Not only is he representative, he is archetypal. He is the major shaper of post-war managerial practice in the United States. To see how different that practice has become from earlier managerial practice, contrast Geneen's post-war book *Managing* with Chester Barnard's pre-war classic *Functions of the Executive.*[43] Both of the men are experienced executives from major corporations; Geneen from ITT and Barnard from the Bell family of AT&T. Both are archetypes and both wrote their books out of their own experience. But while Barnard stressed the system-wide, cooperative behavior needed in large corporations, Geneen stresses the need to meet the immediate profit targets. The difference in emphasis between the two is indicative of a profound shift in how U.S. corporations are managed. That shift has involved a narrowing of focus, a shortening of horizon, and, paradoxically, also an intruding of corporate interest into other spheres of life.

As the focus has narrowed down to an obsession with profit, the time horizon has shortened down to short turn, annual, or even quarterly profit targets. (Geneen once absolutely forbid long-range planning at ITT.)[44] And, paradoxically, this narrowing and shortening of corporate purpose has necessitated a broadening of corporate control over the lives of corporate employees and over the general environment within which the tightly controlled employees attempt to meet the corporate purpose. (Geneen's ITT was accused of not only trying to bring down the elected government of Chile, but also of trying to tamper with the political and judicial processes of the United States.)[45]

In the U.S. corporation of the 1980s, the increased focus on purpose, on short-run profit, has placed nearly irresistible pressure on middle-level managers to use any means required to meet their assigned objectives. Geneen explains this Machiavellian management with characteristic candor in what he calls his mini-course on management:

> A THREE-SENTENCE COURSE OF BUSINESS MANAGEMENT: *You read a book from the beginning to end. You run a business the opposite way. You start with the end, and then you do everything you must to reach it.*[46]

In short, once you are given your end, it justifies whatever means you have to reach it. Geneen is remarkably candid about the general principles of management and should be commended for it. On the other hand, when it comes to particulars, he is silent. He says nothing about the difficulties encountered by ITT after his departure. After having to slash its dividend in 1984, in 1985, and into 1986, the once high-flying conglomerate is trying to fight off dissident stockholders with a massive, $1.7 billion divestiture program. Also, Geneen says nothing about the particulars of ITT's involvement in the ouster of Chile's elected government, and nothing about the interesting activities of Dita Beard, ITT's chief lobbyist during the most controversial part of Geneen's reign.[47] Although Geneen's account of his archetypal management may be self-serving in what it leaves out about specific means, his account does provide an excellent insight into conglomerate ends and into the dominance of ends over means in the conglomerate's world.

The M-form, profit center structure pioneered by GM, the cash cows, cats, dogs, and stars of the Boston Consulting Group, and the Harold Geneen style obsession with the bottom line have been adopted widely by conglomerates, who are now adding a new element to unify their organizations even further. The new element is the corporate culture, a set of shared beliefs and values that welds the conglomerate's disparate parts into a unified social whole, not just a financial whole. The creation and inculcation of this corporate culture—the brainwashing of the conglomerate's managerial cadres—is the most recent step in the speed-up of the managerial class. Corporate culture teaches middle-level managers to value being speeded up by the likes of Harold Geneen. Aided by their corporate culture, managers have learned to cheerfully work harder and faster and to work as a team for the higher good. Managers also gladly give their conglomerate employers their evening time and weekends. This surplus time is given with no overtime pay. After all, managers are career personnel, not mere hourly workers. Managers do not punch a clock. They do not have to, because they voluntarily exploit themselves for the higher good. They voluntarily intensify their efforts and extend their work days into the night and into the weekend.

Of course, this exploitation, this rich source of more profit, is not seen as such by the managerial class. Unlike the working class, which originally saw the speed up for what it really was, the managerial class is far more sophisticated.[48] Or so the managers think, when they have time. Their sophistication is a product of their culture—their corporate culture. So they never give a second thought to the institutionalized greed that they serve so tirelessly. Obviously, they have not read Marx, or Veblen.

Notes

1. Walter Adams and James W. Brock, *The Bigness Complex* (New York: Pantheon, 1986).
2. See Alfred D. Chandler, Jr., *The Visible Hand: The Managerial Revolution in American Business* (Cambridge: The Belknap Press of Harvard University Press, 1977); and his *Strategy and Structure: Chapters in the History of the American Industrial Enterprise* (Cambridge, Mass.: MIT Press, 1962).
3. Some holding companies and trusts are also vehicles for concentrating and controlling family wealth. The Christiana Securities Company and the Wilmington Trust Company, for examples, have held the Du Pont family's wealth together for many years.
4. See Peter E. Earl, *The Corporate Imagination* (Armonk, N.Y.: M. E. Sharpe, 1984). See also, Oliver E. Williamson, *Markets and Hierarchies* (New York: Free Press, 1975); and Oliver E. Williamson, "The Modern Corporation: Origins, Evolution, Attributes," *Journal of Economic Literature* 19 (December 1981): 1537–68. Contrast Williamson with Charles R. Spruill, *Conglomerates and the Evolution of Capitalism* (Carbondale, Ill.: Southern Illinois University Press, 1982) and with William M. Dugger, "The Transaction Cost Analysis of Oliver E. Williamson: A New Synthesis?" *Journal of Economic Issues* 17 (March 1983): 95–114.
5. See Morty Lefkoe, "Why So Many Mergers Fail," *Fortune* 20 July 1987.
6. David Halberstam, *The Reckoning* (New York: William Morrow, 1986).
7. William G. Ouchi, *Theory Z* (Reading, Mass.: Addison-Wesley, 1981).
8. Further discussion is in Thomas J. Peters and Robert H. Waterman, Jr., *In Search of Excellence* (New York: Harper & Row, 1982).

9. Terrence E. Deal and Allan A. Kennedy, *Corporate Cultures* (Reading, Mass.: Addison-Wesley, 1982), p. 7.
10. Lefkoe, "Why So Many Mergers Fail." See also Richard Pascale, "Fitting New Employees Into the Company Culture," *Fortune* 28 May 1984.
11. See Bruno Uttal, "The Corporate Culture Vultures," *Fortune* 17 October 1983.
12. Barry Bluestone and Bennett Harrison, *The Deindustrialization of America* (New York: Basic Books, 1982).
13. For a recent misinterpretation see Stewart Toy, "Splitting Up," *Business Week* 1 July 1985. For the empirical evidence, see William M. Dugger, "Centralization, Diversification, and Adminstrative Burden in U.S. Enterprises," *Journal of Economic Issues* 19 (September 1985): 687–701.
14. The need for organizational unity and the difficulty of achieving it in M-form corporations is referred to as the "indecomposability problem" in the technical literature. See Earl, *Corporate Imagination,* pp. 162–72.
15. Allan Cox, *The Cox Report on the American Corporation* (New York: Delacorte Press, 1982), p. 144.
16. Administrative Management Society, *Thirteenth Annual Guide to Management Compensation* (Willow Grove, Pa., 1985).
17. John P. Steinbrink and William B. Friedeman, *Executive Compensation: Dartnell's 14th Biennial Survey* (Chicago: Dartnell Press, 1982).
18. Bureau of the Census, *Statistical Abstract of the United States, 1984* (Washington, D.C.: U.S. Government Printing Office, 1983), p. 471.
19. Thorstein Veblen was the first to explore in depth the issues and processes involved in his *The Higher Learning in America* (New York: Augustus M. Kelley, 1965 [1918]). See also William M. Dugger, "Corporate Bureaucracy," *Journal of Economic Issues* 14 (June 1980): 399–409; "Power: An Institutional Framework of Analysis," *Journal of Economic Issues* 14 (December 1980): 897–907; and "The Continued Evolution of Corporate Power," *Review of Social Economy* 43 (April 1985): 1–13. Parts of this section were first presented in my paper, "Power and Values in Economics," at the March 1985 meetings of the Midwest Economics Association in Cincinnati. Stephen T. Worland made helpful comments.
20. In addition to his *Higher Learning in America,* see Thorstein Veblen, *The Instinct of Workmanship* (New York: Augustus M. Kelley, 1964 [1914]) and *Absentee Ownership* (New York: Augustus M. Kelley, 1964 [1923]). Michael Maccoby has also explored craftsmanship in his *The Gamesman* (New York: Bantam Books, 1978).
21. Maccoby, *The Gamesman,* pp. 98–123.
22. Further discussion of women in dual career families is in Jacqueline B. Stanfield, "Research on Wife/Mother Role Strain in Dual Career Families," *American Journal of Economics and Sociology* 44 (July 1985): 355–63.
23. Ralph Nader and William Taylor, *The Big Boys* (New York: Pantheon, 1986).
24. John Brooks, *Showing Off in America* (Boston: Little, Brown, 1979), p. 195.
25. Thorstein Veblen, *The Theory of the Leisure Class* (New York: Augustus M. Kelley, 1975 [1899]).
26. Although the article fails to draw the obvious conclusions, see the following description of a Chicago-based women's network: Grant Pick, "When Women Mean Business," *Chicago* (May 1985): 148–53; 186–89.

27. Robert B. Avery, Gregory E. Elliehausen, Glenn B. Canner, and Thomas A. Gustafson, "Survey of Consumer Finances, 1983," *Federal Reserve Bulletin* 70 (September 1984): 679–92, at p. 685. See also, by the same authors, "Survey of Consumer Finances, 1983: A Second Report," *Federal Reserve Bulletin* 70 (December 1984): 857–68.
28. Avery, Elliehausen, Canner, and Gustafson, "Survey of Consumer Finances, 1983," p. 686.
29. Ibid., p. 683.
30. Avery, Elliehausen, Canner, and Gustafson, "Survey of Consumer Finances, 1983: A Second Report," p. 863.
31. Ibid., p. 862.
32. Cox, *The Cox Report,* p. 271.
33. Strongly influenced by Veblen, C. Wright Mills was an exception to the myopia of U.S. intellectuals. See his *White Collar* (New York: Oxford University Press, 1951).
34. Adolf A. Berle and Gardiner C. Means, *The Modern Corporation and Private Property,* rev. ed. (New York: Harcourt, Brace and World, 1968); John Kenneth Galbraith, *The New Industrial State* (Boston: Houghton Mifflin, 1967).
35. See Robin Marris, *The Economic Theory of "Managerial Capitalism"* (New York: Basic Books, 1964) and Edith T. Penrose, *The Theory of the Growth of the Firm* (White Plains, N.Y.: M. E. Sharpe, 1980 [1959]).
36. Edward S. Herman, *Corporate Control, Corporate Power* (Cambridge: Cambridge Unversity Press, 1981), pp. 112–13.
37. Marc R. Tool, *The Discretionary Economy* (Santa Monica, Calif.: Goodyear, 1979), p. 143.
38. Frederick Winslow Taylor, *Scientific Management* (New York: Harper and Brothers, 1947 [1911]). Nothing here is to imply that Taylor and his followers were cruel men. For their human side see Frank B. Gilbreth, Jr. and Ernestine Gilbreth Carey, *Cheaper by the Dozen* (New York: Thomas Y. Crowell, 1948).
39. Elton Mayo, *The Social Problems of an Industrial Civilization* (Boston: Harvard University, 1945).
40. For more extensive treatments see Harry Braverman, *Labor and Monopoly Capital* (New York: Monthly Review Press, 1974) and Richard Edwards, *Contested Terrain* (New York: Basic Books, 1979).
41. This is not necessarily so for managers in the public sector.
42. Harold Geneen with Alvin Moscow, *Managing* (Garden City, N.Y.: Doubleday, 1984), p. 131.
43. Chester I. Barnard, *The Functions of the Executive* (Cambridge: Harvard University Press, 1968 [1938]).
44. Geneen, *Managing,* p. 47.
45. Anthony Sampson, *The Sovereign State of ITT* (New York: Stein and Day, 1973).
46. Geneen, *Managing,* p. 33, italics and capitalization in original.
47. Sampson, *The Sovereign State of ITT,* pp. 189–228.
48. But see Robert Tressell, *The Ragged Trousered Philanthropists* (New York: Monthly Review Press, 1962 [1914]).

11

Social Value Theory, Corporate Power, and Political Elites: Appraisals of Lindblom's *Politics and Markets*

Rick Tilman

> *For now we see through a glass, darkly; but then face to face: now I know in part; but then shall I know even as I also am known.*
>
> King James Version,
> I Corinthians, Chapter 13

Theories of social value (criteria of choice), perspectives of corporate power, and interpretations of political elites are closely linked in contemporary American political economy. Not surprisingly, much of the literature of the sociology of knowledge suggests such linkages and all the exhortations of positivist epistemology and its methodological derivatives are unlikely to weaken them.[1] Textual exegesis of leading theoretical works will also buttress this claim. However, the nature of the linkage between social value theory, corporate power, and political elites as the political spectrum is traversed from left to right is not self-evident. Thus, further inquiry must be made as to how adherence to particular social value theories affects the interpretation of corporate power and, in turn, relates to analysis of political elites. Specifically, I shall ask (1) which social value theory the theorist adheres to, (2) how this theory affects the theorist's perception of corporate power, and (3) how it affects his or her view of political elites. My central thesis is that the acceptance of a particular social value theory such as the utilitarian, Marxist, or instrumentalist fosters a mind set or ideological syndrome that results in a particular view of corporate power and political elites in the mind of the theorist. To support this claim I will analyze the reaction of critics—radical, liberal, conservative, and libertarian—to Charles Lindblom's recent *Politics and Markets*.

Several critics praised *Politics and Markets* when it was published in late 1977, and in giving it the Woodrow Wilson Book Award the American Political Science Association cited it as an important contribution to democratic theory and to the future of democracy itself. Yet, many reviewers were surprised by the book, for they thought that Lindblom and his one-time co-author Robert Dahl were still proponents of classical American pluralism. In their book *Politics, Economics, and Welfare* (1953), and in much of their subsequent writing, they had emphasized the dispersion and fragmentation of political power in America and its separation from class and social status. But in recent years Lindblom and Dahl, without many social scientists realizing it, had turned to the left and Lindblom, at least, now stresses the linkage of power-wealth-status relationships in the American polity and the incongruity of the present corporate structure with democratic theory.

Even before the publication of *Politics and Markets,* both Dahl and Lindblom clearly had begun a fundamental reappraisal of their own earlier work on power in America. They stated in the 1976 edition of *Politics, Economics, and Welfare* that when the book was originally published they had not been sufficiently sensitive toward inequalities of power and wealth in the American political economy. They also confessed to having been overly optimistic regarding the erection of successful planning mechanisms and the achievement of egalitarian social reform.[2] That *Politics and Markets* was no aberration in the evolution of Lindblom's thought is fully evident in his presidential address to the American Polital Science Association in 1981. After nearly four years of critical evaluation of his magnum opus, Lindblom unabashedly repeated most of its main themes in his speech and seems not to have changed his mind about any of its main points.[3] Indeed, he even challenged his listeners to pay more attention to radical political science.

As the central thesis in his book, Lindblom claims that the dominant economic and political entities in American and in other capitalist systems are the major industrial and financial corporations.[4] Although Lindblom's prescriptions for overcoming the deficiencies of the present system by aiding the corporations through government subsidies to serve the public interest are problematic, he certainly has located what critics on the left commonly regard as the "enemy": namely the upper class, with its powerful corporate linkages and its political and ideological potency. Nonetheless liberal-conservative critics in the center and libertarians on the right of the political spectrum have rejected much of Lindblom's analysis, viewing it as either exaggerated or simply wrong-headed, for they do not believe corporations have the political or economic power he attributes to them.

My concern, however, is not with the validity of Lindblom's thesis, although I am largely in agreement with it, but with the reaction of critics who reviewed the book or have dealt with it in scholarly articles, books, or debates. It is interesting to note that once the social value theory of a critic is known it can usually be predicted in advance how that critic will react to *Politics and Markets*. It may well be that several of the reviewers of *Politics and Markets* do not regard themselves as "radical," "liberal," "conservative," or "libertarian" as they are here labeled. Some critics believe these terms are too simplistic to encapsulate a particular social or political philosophy. Nevertheless, they are in common usage and it is impossible to engage in any rational dialogue about politics and political science without invoking them. If some of the reviewers of Lindblom's book are mislabeled, the point is to recognize that in spite of this the social value theory they employ predisposes them to interpret corporate power and political elites in certain largely preordained ways. Obviously, too, some of the interpretations of *Politics and Markets* do not adequately fit into any of the four categories because they are not ideologically evolved or philosophically explicit enough to be classified, or analyzed in this article.[5]

Libertarianism

Running through libertarian political economy like the proverbial scarlet thread is the utility theory of value. This particular social value theory has its own criteria of choice, for it claims that whatever subjective preferences economic actors display in the market must be given equal weight. Thus subjective preference equals value and value is measured by price. This is the position of both the moral agnostic and the equalistic relativist, who do not believe that there exist any criteria by which to measure value except those of individual preference, whatever they may be. In the words of Jeremy Bentham, that historically progressive but now archaic figure, "pushpin is as good as poetry," or conversely, it is no worse. Most libertarians and conservatives *qua* economists subscribe to the utility theory of value evident in the work of James Buchanan. He reviewed Lindblom's *Politics and Markets* in the *Journal of Economic Issues* and saw two flaws in it that illustrate my thesis. To paraphrase Buchanan, the first was Lindblom's claim that the interests of business necessarily take on primary importance in democracy. Buchanan denies the validity of this assertion because it is based on the assumption that business interests must come before those of all other groups since only "business" is in a position to do what government wants. Only the corporations can produce, innovate, employ, create capital, invest, distribute, and ensure economic growth. Hence, so the argument goes, corporations can, by threatening not to perform these vital functions adequately, gain acquiescence in their own demands from those allegedly controlling the government.[6] Buchanan asks rhetorically:

> But who or what is 'business'? The lie can be given to the argument quite easily by making the simple assumption that no 'business' exists at all. Suppose . . . that each and every industry were organized on ideally competitive principles, with literally thousands of small producers, employers, and investors in each product and service line. Precisely the same economic functions would need to be performed, and in order to ensure that these functions are performed with tolerable efficiency, precisely the same government policy set would be dictated.[7]

Buchanan's claim is that "business" really has no power other than that essential to the functioning of the capitalist system and, in any case, any market system would have to give the business community or its equivalent, whatever that might be, remarkably similar powers.

Buchanan then shifts his attention from the economic role of business in the market to what he claims is its impotence in the political and governmental spheres. "I am suggesting that public or governmental policy dictated by elementary efficiency considerations cannot, and should not, be attributed to the power of 'business interest.' Personally, I find it difficult to understand how anyone, viewing the political-economic setting of 1978, could argue that 'business interest' dominates much of anything."[8]

Buchanan thus denies that political elites are subservient to corporate enterprise. In fact, he apparently believes them to be largely autonomous from the corporate structure. Buchanan argues that corporate enterprise does not possess the economic power Lindblom attributes to it and that the business community has far less political power and governmental influence than Lindblom imagines. It follows that if competitive markets exist and remain substantially unfettered, market participants can pursue their utility maximizing quest as orthodox theory has long affirmed. Buchanan's deference to market phenomena is evident.

His adherence to the utility theory of value thus predisposes Buchanan to deny the economic power of corporations as well as the existence of powerful linkages between corporations and political elites. Mind-sets that focus on the subjective preference of individuals will not heed anything except those external restraints that impinge on the satisfaction of individual utility functions. Therefore anything that interferes with the expression and enjoyment of subjective tastes must be viewed as an unjustified encroachment on individual freedom. And from where are such encroachments likely to emanate? Mostly from the activity of government at all levels when backed by special interest groups. In theory, of course, private monopoly by corporations and smaller business enterprises could also restrain the free expression of subjective preference by individuals seeking maximum satisfaction of individual utility functions. In reality, however, libertarians believe the main threat comes from government and to a lesser extent from trade unions. Since "freedom" is defined as lack of external restraint and since restraint originates in the interventionist behavior of government and unions, the less visible constraining powers of the business community are largely ignored in the libertarian analysis; furthermore, the political elites that have attached themselves to the business community are assumed by libertarians to have an "entitlement" only so long as they do not demand intervention in the market by asking for more than protection of property rights and enforcement of contracts. With prior knowledge of Buchanan's commitment to utilitarian social value theory one would be able to predict how he would respond to Lindblom's claims regarding the magnitude of corporate power and its relationship to political elites.

Conservatism

Many conservatives *qua* economists agree with the utility theory of value but also find need for more enduring values to supplement it. In the tradition of Edmund Burke, who relied heavily on Adam Smith's economics, they add status, order, tradition, religion, and authority to utilitarian value theory. What emerges is an uneasy fusion of free market economics with an hierarchical view of society; the invisible hand joins incongrously with an organic view of the social order, thus maintaining Providence and the pursuit of self-interest in equilibrium in the same social and intellectual orbit. It is from this ideological perspective that Arthur Kemp attacked Lindblom:

> My chief differences with Lindblom are ideological and fundamentally irreconcilable. He seldom mentions religion or ethics, let alone God; just how many of the ten commandments he would accept, I cannot tell, but "Thou shalt not steal" is not one of them, for he places a very low value on private property rights. He also place a low value on individuality and spontaneity in the human processes. He favors a high degree of imposed equality of both income and wealth, yet his philosophy is essentially elitist. And he hates—the word is not too strong—what he calls "the privileged position of business," although there is no similar concern over the privileged position of professors who, it seems, are predestined to be the scientific elite among the future planners.[9]

Kemp then rises to the height of indignation when he claims that "basic differences in fundamental values are not only irreconcilable but can be settled, if at all, only by conflict. Lindblom is the epitome of the modern-day welfare statist or welfare socialist. . . . This book is . . . intended for those who are already willing and even anxious to *subject themselves* to the increasing power of the state."[10]

The ethically absolutist nature of Kemp's value position is evident. It is interesting to note that the inapplicability of ethically relative criteria (utility in all its versions) usually leads to a fall back on ethically absolute criteria—free enterprise, the ten commandments, etcetera.

James Q. Wilson, an eminent Harvard political scientist whose name is often associated with the "neoconservative" movement and who writes for its journal *The Public Interest*, reviewed *Politics and Markets* for the *Wall Street Journal.* He disagreed not only with Lindblom's assertion that the corporation is a locus of political privilege that distorts and even corrupts the democratic process, but also his claim that the possession of wealth ultimately translates into superior political power. "The fallacy of the Lindblom view is well known to every student of politics: One cannot assume that the disproportionate possession of certain resources leads to the disproportionate exercise of political power."[11]

Although he does not go so far as to claim that corporations are largely powerless, like the libertarian Buchanan, he does argue that Lindblom greatly exaggerates their economic and political power. Wilson rejects Lindblom's claim that the corporation is an authoritarian structure in which control is vested in those who own property rather than those who supply labor.

> The drift of public policy has been increasingly hostile to business. Public confidence in the corporation has fallen (indoctrination?), the national media are increasingly critical, capital formation is inhibited by taxes and inflationary policies, the profit margins of corporations have declined, social and economic regulations proliferate almost faster than the Federal

> Register can print them, anti-trust prosecution, though perhaps not as effective as one might desire, falls more heavily on firms here than elsewhere and the barriers to public control of traditionally private industries . . . are dropping rapidly.[12]

A similar analysis, although written in more muted tones, was that of Aaron Wildavsky, one of the most eminent American students of public policy, who wrote a lengthy analysis of *Politics and Markets* in the *Yale Law Journal.*[13] Although Wildavsky, like Wilson, is associated these days with the "neoconservative" movement, his reaction to Lindblom is not significantly different from that of other liberals and conservatives who are essentially political centrists occupying a position in the ideological spectrum slightly left or right of center. With regard to corporate political power, Wildavsky asks rhetorically: "Would Lindblom say, then, that business runs government? No, he is not a vulgar Marxist. He only says that business is uniquely and disproportionately privileged. But surely there are other important interests, such as agriculture and labor unions, that can compete with business for political power."[14]

Wildavsky attempts to counter Lindblom's view of the dominant role of corporate power in the American polity when he writes that "the blind spot in this book . . . is the converse proposition: the operation of markets (and therefore corporations) depends critically on the role of government in economic life. What corporations do to government, to reverse the flow of causality, may be dependent on what government does to (or for) them."[15] Wildavsky suggests that the dominant power position is held by government, and not by the corporation as Lindblom alleged. Wildavsky also questions the ability of the corporate structure to control and influence the production, dissemination, and acceptance of ideas that assure the continued dominance of corporate America. He comments that "if indoctrination is so successful, one wonders why business has to fight or how it ever loses."[16] In summation, then, Wildavsky believes that interest groups other than business are capable of strongly influencing, if not controlling, government; that government itself is a separate source of power and autonomy from the corporate structure; and that corporate America does not exercise ideological hegemony over mass society.

Liberalism

Liberal economists, like conservatives, approach the problem of social value theory (criteria of choice) in similar although modified form. Value is still subjective preference and is measured by price, but in the liberal paradigm negative externalities, market imperfections, and market failures arise on a significant scale. Liberals also give consideration to the social disorders that might arise if income disparities become too great. Nevertheless, liberals, *qua* economists, do not believe that the market mechanism fundamentally misallocates resources or fails to provide goods and services in accord with consumer tastes and preferences, except in unusual circumstances. They are somewhat less the intellectual captives of the utility theory of value than conservatives and libertarians but they are still utilitarians.

In the liberal scheme of things political elites are not viewed as lacking accountability to the public or as acting contrary to its interests but as the legitimate representatives of various interest groups interacting in a political sphere where power is dispersed and fragmented. Various types of interest groups are viewed as having access to the making of public policy and no particular set of interest groups is seen as dominant.

The philosophical parallels that exist between political pluralism and orthodox economics are important in understanding liberal views of the American political economy, since pluralists see the political process of rival and competing, usually economic, interest groups as the counterpart, if not a surrogate for, the competitive market process. Assumptions about human nature are mostly identical; wants and tastes are given, not examined or appraised. There is a deference to compromise and balance of power in the political process roughly comparable to the equilibrium tendencies of market processes.[17] All such positions are ethically relative although occasionally they shade into ethical absolutism with the retention of power becoming overriding. All are rooted in utility value and so reflect it.

The great diversity of opinion and analysis regarding *Politics and Markets* is well exemplified in comments made by L. L. Wade,[18] who appears to be close to the center of the political spectrum. Wade believes that the enthusiasm of many scholars on the left side of the political spectrum for Lindblom's work is indicative of the "intellectual disorder that now afflicts the academic community."[19] He contends that this uncritical reception of *Politics and Markets* indicates that the academic standards of many American political scientists are "sadly impaired," for Lindblom has written a "lamentable book."[20] Wade describes the book as consisting of "injudicious comparisons, question-begging, and poor scholarship. The result is that mere sentiment triumphs over fact and method . . . . The substitution of well-meaning wish-dreams for history, social science, and philosophical perspective can have, as in this case, dangerous and illiberal implications against which responsible scholars must carefully guard. Sympathy with a scholar's purpose cannot substitute for elementary rules of scholarly evidence."[21]

Wade strongly disagrees with all of Lindblom's main points about corporate power and political elites. First, he denies that corporations have the economic power Lindblom attributes to them. As evidence of this he points to the decline in corporate profit rates since 1950.[22] Second, Wade argues that corporations do not have the political power Lindblom alleges they have. To prove his point he cites the literature of campaign finance to show that Lindblom has greatly overestimated the dominant role of corporations in financing elections.[23] Third, Wade claims that corporations do not have the ideological power attributed to them by Lindblom, who focused in *Politics and Markets* on corporate ability to shape minds and foster values in mass society. As evidence of their lack of power in this area, Wade cites polls and studies of television programming that show corporate leaders as having little status, indeed.[24] Fourth, Wade claims that the U.S. government has been relatively effective at redistributing income, combating racism, improving medical care, etcetera.[25] By implication, it is sensitive to pressure from interest groups favoring these changes rather than dominated by pro-business political elites who might be expected to be indifferent or hostile to them.

One common complaint by liberals (and conservatives) is that Lindblom's emphasis on the economic power of the corporation is unwarranted because unions offset this power through collective bargaining. Indeed, a reviewer in that journal of English liberal orthodoxy, *The Economist*, wrote that Lindblom's emphasis on corporate power "strikes an odd note . . . some countries at any rate are preoccupied with the question of whether it is trade unions, rather than business, which effectively govern them."[26] Of course, it is but a short distance from the claim that Lindblom greatly exaggerates the power of corporations over the economy to the assertion that he overstates the "influence of business in political decision making."[27] The liberal case against Lindblom thus rests on the belief that corporations do not have the economic or political power he attributes to them and that business-oriented political elites have a relatively high degree of autonomy from the corporate sphere and are not dominant or pervasive in the political realm.

Another prime trait of the liberal intellectual posture is to claim to be "above the battle," thus preserving an alleged sphere of objectivity and value neutrality. One such reaction to Lindblom was that of Charles W. Anderson, who wrote a brief article on *Politics and Markets* for the *American Political Science Review* less than a year after its publication. Anderson apparently exempts himself from partisan bias when he cryptically writes that "inevitably too, much of what is said about this thesis that corporations have far too much power and that the corporation does not 'fit' with democratic theory . . . will simply reflect established partisan affinities. Lindblom is apt to be 'applauded' as an 'establishment liberal' who 'saw the light,' or condemned for a scurrilous attack on the business community."[28]

Anderson then tips his hand with the following comment:

> For those who hold no standing general brief either for or against the dominant institutions of modern capitalism the question of course is not where Lindblom stands but whether what he says makes sense. The issue is really whether the power of the corporation is as Lindblom represents it and whether it is unique. . . . It may be that modern industrial societies are no more convinced by one arcane formulation of the political economic problem than they are by another.[29]

It is the "observer as yet uncommitted to one of the standard orthodoxies" that Anderson admires, for it is himself to whom he refers.[30]

The liberal analysis often claims to center not on ideological misgivings about *Politics and Markets* but on its alleged technical, statistical, methodological, and communicative deficiencies. For example, we are told that the terms "capitalism" and "socialism" are archaic. Perhaps so, but it is unlikely that the values these ideologies encapsulate are. Apparently many liberal critics believe it no longer matters who owns the means of production, exchange, and distribution. This is clearly implied in several liberal reviews of Lindblom's book. Perhaps no adequate differentiation between conservative and liberal positions has yet been made. It should be remembered that both hover near the center of the political spectrum so there is no sharp line of demarcation between them. Liberals may be more inclined to attribute power to corporations and business-oriented political elites than conservatives but it is only a matter of degree and often the differences are insignificant. In any case *both* are the intellectual captives of utilitarian social value theory. Of course, as far as economics as a discipline is concerned, the prevailing neoclassical paradigm provides an ideological framework buttressed by a system of institutional pressures, rewards as well as sanctions, which makes it difficult for holistic economists to spread heterodox doctrine. The result is that the large majority of economists, when they engage in discourse regarding value, do so with both the jargon and norms of utilitarianism.

Radicalism

Michael Walzer, Robert Lekachman, Robert Solo, Robert Heilbroner, Barry Bluestone, and Daniel Fusfeld have all appraised Lindblom's magnum opus from a radical perspective.[31] All share "left" values of equality and community whether they approach political economy from a Marxist perspective, from the instrumentalist paradigm of Dewey-Ayres, or from the viewpoint of Western humanism. All see the major industrial and financial corporations as the center of the American power system and all believe political elites achieve their dominance from their relation to the system of corporate enterprise and the class structure it has produced in the United States. To illustrate, Fusfeld wrote a characteristically radical review of Lindblom's *Politics and Markets* for the *Journal of Economic Issues*. Fusfeld is a member of both the Association for Evolutionary Economics (neoinstitutionalist) and the Union for Radical Political Economy (Marxist), and thus has been influenced by Ayres-Dewey instrumentalism and the Marxian labor theory of value. His social value theory, then, appears to be a synthesis of Marxism and instrumentalism. In his view, corporate power looms large on the American economic landscape, and it is linked in a multitude of ways with the political elites who dominate the political arena. Both are seen by Fusfeld as instrumental in molding and shaping public opinion and controlling the larger process of socialization. Fusfeld agrees with Lindblom that big enterprise in modern industrial society plays a dominant role, that this negates popular control of government authority, and that the value system of the typical American is manipulated to accept this situation as desirable. Thus both agree that business interests have a disproportionately large influence in the determination of social choices. In Fusfeld's view, Lindblom is correct in believing that conflicts of interest among elite business groups center on secondary issues, since there is general agreement on such basic principles of the system as private property and business enterprise. Fusfeld also thinks that the one major point that should be added to Lindblom's discussion is the ability of business interests to get the rules of the game modified in their favor so they can amass an even greater amount of wealth and obtain an ever more powerful hold on politics.[32]

However, Fusfeld believes that Lindblom's unjustifiable separation of economics from politics creates still another problem, for he fails to explain why the corporation, which is an economic institution, dominates public policy, which is in the political realm. For neoinstitutionalists or Marxists, this is not an issue, since they hold that the political and the economic are characterized by an interlocking, interweaving, interpenetrating set of relationships. As Fusfeld puts it:

> Lindblom contrasts the political struggles of the authority relations with the harmonies of the pure exchange relation. Presumably nothing ever gets produced, for the economy seems to do nothing but exchange things. Defining economics as exchange, however, enables Lindblom to incorporate into his taxonomy the model of perfectly competitive general equilib-

> rium as of about 1950–1965. . . . This ideal type is qualified somewhat by the existence of monopoly (which is considered a quantitatively insignificant factor, again following pre-1965 conclusions), and not at all by such problems as externalities. Social choice is excluded from the exchange relations by the simple dictum that some of the things people need from others "will not willingly be provided and must be compelled." Thus, the "authority relation" and the "exchange relation" are separated from each other by assumption and obiter dicta, by the pure metaphysics of definition and taxonomy. But defining the two spheres as separate, in the tradition of Max Weber and Talcott Parsons, does not make them so.[33]

Fusfeld attacks Lindblom for his refusal to support transforming the economic base of society by socializing the means of production. Fusfeld also claims Lindblom believes that big business dominates political authority because it dominates economic power, for the greater its control over the forces of production, the greater will tend to be its political dominance. Lindblom is wrong in not drawing the conclusion inherent in his own argument, for if the masses are to gain political power, they must also control the economic base.[34]

Fusfeld's indignation regarding the corporate state seemingly originates in his commitment to John Dewey's self-adjusting value judgments as these relate to the promotion of human growth and development. Fusfeld also uses the Marxian labor theory of value to argue that the upper class extracts surplus value from the labor force. Thus, for Fusfeld, the instrumentalist approach and the labor theory of value forge links between extraction of surplus value and obstruction of means-ends adjustments that might otherwise facilitate human growth.[35]

It is only in the neoinstitutionalist and Marxist paradigms that the social value theory of neoclassical economics comes under a frontal assault and alternative theories of valuation are set forth. Subjective preference, the core of utilitarian theory, is no longer the locus of value. Instead, social value theory for neoinstitutionalists is the self-correcting valuation process made famous by John Dewey in his articulation of the means-ends continuum and philosophy of experimentalism. Its criteria of choice thus demands means-ends adjustments of an appropriate sort with human growth as the ends and institutional adjustments as the means. For Marxists, social value resides in human labor—that is, the unalienated labor process by which socially useful goods and services are produced. The criteria of choice implied is that which will reduce the current amount of alienation. This is, in principle, compatible with the Deweyan emphasis on growth and development. Consequently, it is primarily in the neoinstitutionalist and Marxist paradigms that greater sensitivity to corporate power, the potency of the upper class, and the role of business-oriented political elites exists; for underlying the rationale for proper means-ends adjustment and an end to alienated labor is a long-term commitment to human growth and development. The present system of corporate domination of the political economy is viewed by many neoinstitutionalists and most Marxists as thwarting proper fulfillment of human potential. Thus Dewey-Ayres instrumentalism converges with the Marxist view that proper human growth and development are unlikely in a system rooted in massive transfers of surplus value from one class to another, and where necessary means-ends adjustments are obstructed by corporate power.

Conclusion

This article has highlighted different, indeed often incompatible, social value theory positions by examining divergent responses to Lindblom as reflected in different views of linkages between corporate power and political elites. It has attempted to strengthen characterizations of the different value positions and demonstrated their implications for social science inquiry. One can now compare the linkages between social value theory and perceptions of corporate power and political elites in the analyses of contemporary political economists by suggesting that the more an economist subscribes to utilitarian social value theory the more probable it becomes that that scholar will disregard corporate power and corporate links with business-oriented political elites. Those libertarians who believe that value is subjective preference as measured by price pay little heed to corporate power and claim that political elites linked with the business community have little influence on public policy. On the other hand, those who adhere to Marxian or neoinstitutionalist social value theories are prone to see the corporation and the class that owns and controls it as the locus of economic power, and view political elites as subservient to the corporate structure. In between utilitarianism and the left are politically centrist elements, both liberal and conservative, whose social value theory is often eclectic, vague, or indecipherable. These centrist elements are on shifting ground regarding corporate power and political elites and occasionally adopt an "end to ideology" approach that permits them to avoid a politically focused stand on problems of political and economic power. However, in keeping with their doctrinal antiradicalism they also claim that Lindblom has greatly exaggerated the magnitude of corporate power and the political potency of business-oriented elites.

In any case, the more that the critic is the ideological captive of utilitarian theory, the more likely he or she will be to deny the dominance of corporate economic and political power. On the other hand the more the critic subscribes to the Marxian labor theory of value or the neoinstitutionalist instrumentalist theory of value, the more likely he or she will be to emphasize the political and economic potency of the corporation and business-oriented political elites. Although it would be difficult to delineate the exact perceptual and psychological processes by which this occurs, textual exegesis has shown that a linkage of the suggested sort does, indeed, exist. Are we back where we were fifteen years ago when dissident elements in the social sciences revolted because they recognized the impossibility and futility of a value-free social science? Certainly social scientists who believe in the ideal or the reality of a value-free "objective" social science can take little comfort from this analysis. Massive political cleavages exist within the social sciences and the amount of value assimilation, political compromise, or methodological convergence needed to change this is not going to materialize. There is no more chance of agreeing on the merits, empirical validity, and value judgments of Lindblom's *Politics and Markets* than there is of reaching agreement on Ronald Reagan's foreign and domestic policy.

I am not suggesting that the rules of evidence and the validity of empirical inquiry be ignored by social scientists in their work. Obviously these are and will continue to be of great importance in the future. However, as Richard Rorty has written:

> If we have a Deweyan conception of knowledge, as what we are justified in believing, then we will not imagine that there are enduring constraints on what can count as knowledge, since we will see 'justification' as a social phenomenon rather than a transaction between 'the knowing subject' and 'reality.' If we have a Wittgensteinian notion of language as tool rather than mirror we will not look for necessary conditions of the possibility of linguistic representation. If we have a Heideggerian conception of philosophy, we will see the attempt to make the nature of the knowing subject the source of necessary truth as one more self-deceptive attempt to substitute a 'technical' and determinant question for that openness to strangeness which initially tempted us to begin thinking.[36]

Obviously the methodologies employed by political economists as well as their epistemological assumptions are permeated with value judgments. Consequently, the conceptual apparatus employed by the scholar is structured by his or her cultural environment and is thus a cultural artifact. Also, the ideological and moral presuppositions of a society and the mores of the social studies do not have a merely casual or sporadic effect on a scholar's work. Instead, they have a pervasive, powerful, and penetrating effect. How else can we explain the utter inability of many prominent social scientists to agree on the claims and merits of an influential book written by an eminent author?

Notes

1. The literature of the sociology of knowledge will not be cited here since most social scientists, particularly neoinstitutionalists, will immediately recognize the relevance of Thorstein Veblen, Karl Marx and Frederick Engels, and more recently Karl Mannheim and C. Wright Mills.
2. See Robert Dahl and Charles Lindblom, *Politics, Economics, and Welfare* (Chicago and London: University of Chicago Press, 1976), pp. xxi–xxiv.
3. See Charles Lindblom, "Another State of Mind," *American Political Science Review* 76 (March 1982): 9–21.
4. Charles Lindblom, *Politics and Markets* (New York: Basic Books, 1977). Perhaps the most sophisticated and insightful critique of *Politics and Markets* is Joe A. Oppenheimer's "Small Steps Forward for Political Economy," *World Politics* 33 (October 1980): 121–51. Oppenheimer shows himself to be a man of the Left who prizes equality and is committed to the politics of redistribution. Paradoxically, he finds considerable merit in the work of both the conservative public choice theorists and the Marxists in the Union for Radical Political Economy. He chides Lindblom throughout his essay for neglecting the insights of both schools of thought. Unfortunately, he says so little about the degree of corporate power and the role of political elites in the American polity that it is impossible to place him within the parameters of this article.
5. This material is not cited here. As might be expected the bulk of the literature on *Politics and Markets* falls into the liberal/conservative politically centrist category, not into the radical or libertarian positions. Although the liberal/conservative contributions will not be cited again or analyzed individually, they form part of the data upon which this article is based. See Phillip H. Birnbaum, *Focus on Books* 22 (October 1979): 80–81; Anon., *Accounting Review* 54 (January 1979): 269; Royall Brandis, *Southern Economic Journal* 45 (January 1979): 962–64; George C. Lodge, *Harvard Business Review* 56 (March 1978); 172–173; Richard P. Nielsen, *The Journal of Consumer Affairs* 13 (Winter 1979): 415–17; Michael Mandelbaum, *Political Science Quarterly* 93 (Fall 1978): 507–508; R. L. Funk, *Newsletter on Intellectual Freedom* 27 (May 1978): 55; Ernest Erber, *American Planning Association Journal* 47 (January 1981): 102–103; Bernard Cunningham, *Business and Society Review* 27 (Fall 1978): 4–6, 77–78; Edward Ames, *Journal of Economic Literature* 16 (September 1978): 1027–28; Eugene Bardach, "Pluralism Reconsidered," *Commentary* 66 (August 1978): 68–70; Cedric Sandford, *Economica* 46 (August 1979): 319–21; Alastair Clayre, *Political Quarterly* 49 (October, 1978): 499–502. The last two authors cited are British, not American.
6. James Buchanan, *Journal of Economic Issues* 13 (March 1979): 215–17. Contemporary libertarianism differs considerably from important libertarian positions sometimes held by earlier economists like the late Henry Simons. A generation ago Simons, University of Chicago economist, friend and mentor of Milton Friedman, and forerunner of the present "Chicago School," argued for several policies ideologically consistent

with the main thrust of neoclassical economics in the sense that they oppose unearned gain obtained through possession of superior market power or inheritance. To illustrate: Simons, although opposed to many, perhaps most, New Deal regulatory and welfare measures, called for a highly graduated income tax, for stiff inheritance taxes, and for public ownership of monopolies. Today's prominent libertarians, with few exceptions, are strongly opposed to all of these policy positions. They dislike the progressive income tax and prefer proportional or even regressive taxes, wish to leave inheritances, even massive ones, largely untouched, and seem indifferent or even hostile toward efforts by the government to break up concentrated industries that administer prices. Thus those who seek to curb monopoly or reduce unearned gain invariably meet with denunciation from the present generation of libertarians, who claim that monopolies are caused by government anyway, so that mere withdrawal of government support will ameliorate the problem. In any case their dislike of egalitarianism is expressed in their belief that income legally obtained from market processes and "free exchange" relationships is deserved, so why tax some proportionately more than others? Consequently, the difference between most of today's libertarians and some earlier conservatives like Simons is indeed striking.

7. Ibid.
8. Ibid., p. 217.
9. Arthur Kemp, "Beyond Marx and Mao," *Modern Age* 23 (Winter 1979): 85–87.
10. Ibid.
11. James Q. Wilson, "Democracy and the Corporation," *Wall Street Journal*, 11 January 1978, p. 14. In another context, Wilson has recently written that "the constitutional system created by James Madison and the other Founding Fathers has worked brilliantly to insure that every interest would be accommodated but none would be allowed to dominate." James Q. Wilson, "The Riddle of the Middle Class," *The Public Interest* 29 (Spring 1975): 128.
12. Ibid.
13. Aaron Wildavsky, "Changing Forward Versus Changing Back," *Yale Law Journal* 88 (November 1978): 217–34. Also, see Rune Premfors, "Review Article: Charles Lindblom and Aaron Wildavsky," *British Journal of Political Science* 11 (April 1981): 201–25.
14. Ibid., p. 223.
15. Ibid., p. 221.
16. Ibid., p. 224.
17. The late John Livingston has perceptively written:

> From this point of view, the theory of compromise is an essentially conservative doctrine. It is so in the fundamental sense that, in insisting on the subjectivity and relativity of values and hence on the impossibility of a rationally meaningful concept of the public interest as anything other than what emerges out of the process of compromise, it has the following consequences: It makes any meaningful concept of progress impossible since, by definition, the results of a

> compromise cannot be held to be "better" than or "more valid" than the original interests in conflict, it denies the possibility of man's consciously and rationally examining and criticizing his institutions and the values which warrant them, and it therefore renders impossible the conscious direction of social change and mastery by man of his social environment; and finally, it deprives the ideals of freedom of thought and discussion of their most significant meaning as tools of truth-testing in the area of social choice and reduces them to instruments in the struggle for power.

John Livingston, "Liberalism, Conservatism, and the Role of Reason," *The Western Political Quarterly* 9 (September 1956): 652–53.

18. L. L. Wade, "Politics, Markets and Rationalistic Imbroglios," *The Review of Politics* 44 (April 1982): 187–213.
19. Ibid., p. 189.
20. Ibid., p. 188.
21. Ibid., pp. 188–89.
22. Ibid., p. 202.
23. Ibid., pp. 204–206.
24. Ibid., pp. 206–10.
25. Ibid., pp. 201–202. Also, see pp. 210–13.
26. Anonymous, "Two Sets of Villains," *The Economist* 66 (18 February 1978): 123.
27. D. E. Moggridge, *Journal of Economic History* 39 (June, 1979): 610.
28. Charles W. Anderson, "The Political Economy of Charles E. Lindblom," *American Political Science Review* 72 (September 1978): 114.
29. Ibid., p. 115.
30. Ibid.
31. See Michael Walzer, *New York Review of Books* 25 (20 July 1978): 40–42; Robert Lekachman, *New Republic* 177 (17 December 1977): 32–34; Daniel Fusfeld, *Journal of Economic Issues* 13 (March 1979): 209–15; Robert Heilbroner, *New York Times Book Review* (19 February 1978): 7, 37; Barry Bluestone, *Dissent* 26 (Spring 1979): 247–50; and Robert Solo, *Journal of Economic Issues* 13 (March 1979): 207–209. An interesting "Left" critique of *Politics and Markets* by an educationist is Irving J. Spitzberg, *Comparative Educational Review* 23 (June 1979): 326–27.
32. Daniel Fusfeld, *Journal of Economic Issues*, p. 214.
33. Ibid., p. 213.
34. Ibid., p. 215.
35. This analysis of Fusfeld's fusion of the social value theory of neoinstitutionalism and Marxism is based in part on his review of *Politics and Markets*, but more explicitly on his new text *Economics: Principles of Political Economy* (Glenview, Ill.: Scott-Foresman, 1982).
36. Richard Rorty, *Philosophy and The Mirror of Nature* (Princeton, N.J.: Princeton University Press, 1980), p. 9.

12

The Transfer of Control in Large Corporations: 1905-1919

David Bunting
and
Mark S. Mizruchi

In 1905, *Wall Street Journal* editor Sereno S. Pratt examined the control of large American corporations and found that, despite its republican form, "in practical operation, . . . the stock company is subject to autocratic or oligarchical control. The stockholders do not vote—they send proxies that are held by the powers that be. . . . It is not difficult for a small group of financiers to dominate properties worth billions of dollars, belonging to thousands of investors, who have really no voice in their management" [Pratt 1905, pp. 6704–5]. Twenty-five years later, A. A. Berle, Jr. and G. C. Means made a similar argument, but suggested that power "ultimately (lay) in the hands of management itself, a management capable of perpetuating its own position" [Berle and Means 1932, p. 124].

While both Pratt and Berle-Means believed that the inability of owners to effectively exercise ownership rights led to their usurpation by other, better organized forces, they disagreed as to who actually seized control. Berle and Means assumed that managers took control from shareholders. On the other hand, Pratt concluded that shareholders had long lost out to individuals who broadly can be described as "finance capitalists."[1] These views can be reconciled if, in the evolution of the control of large corporations, managers succeeded finance capitalists rather than owners. Once this is recognized, then the commonly accepted Berle-Means explanation for the separation of ownership from control becomes incomplete because it does not consider the process by which the control of large corporations shifted from finance capitalists to managers, and becomes misleading by failing to indicate that financial control of American industry preceded management control.

The possibility that control by finance capitalists was an integral step in the development of large corporations immediately raises an important issue: While the idea of management control is based on an analysis of the locus of control in particular companies, financial control is based on the location of control in the structure of intercorporate relations. By ignoring this structure, Berle and Means may have come to believe that a dispersal of corporate stock directly resulted in the rise of management control, when in fact, as Pratt indicated, it had already resulted in control by finance capitalists.

It is our view that between about 1900 and 1919 financial control of large American corporations became institutionalized as large firms established complicated relationships with most other large companies. These relationships were established by various individual finance capitalists who actively sought them. Near the end of the period these people came under heavy public attack because their influence on the policies of particular companies was thought to be nearly absolute. Congress enacted national legislation to curtail their activities while, coincidentally, many retired from active business or died. However, the control and the relationships established did not disappear. Instead, they were transferred to various subordinates, later identified as managers by Berle and Means. We contend that this institutionalization of financial control resulted in the establishment of enduring relationships among companies, and that the transfer of control from finance capitalists to managers merely resulted in many people doing what only a few did before. While the demonstration of the separation of ownership from control should not be depreciated, it seems to us that comprehension of the full process leading to it is as interesting and as potentially suggestive about the development of U.S. Big Business as the separation itself. Scholars have routinely assumed an owner-manager dichotomy; we maintain that this is incorrect, that different types of control are involved, and that the network of corporations in addition to single companies constitutes a basic unit for analysis.

Control

Control in any corporation has two distinct meanings. On the one hand, operating control entails daily supervision of the corporate asset. At this level, since input factors combine to produce goods and services, there is a close association between control and specific economic activities. On the other hand, policy control involves the ability to generally specify how the corporate asset will be utilized. At this level, general rules and procedures governing the physical corporation are formulated. Since policy control represents ultimate authority and operating control immediate authority, our study is concerned with the possession and transfer of the former, not the latter, in large corporations.[2]

Owners control corporations in a policy sense when they invoke their legal rights and select directors who choose managers to operate the company consistent with the owners' desires. Or, directors can control by selecting managers to operate the company in their interest and not necessarily that of the owners. This situation might arise for reasons such as those Pratt and Berle-Means indicated: owners are too numerous to combine or communicate, suffer indifference or deception, or possess trivial economic interest or divergent investment objectives. Finally, managers can control by selecting themselves or their alter egos as directors. This situation could occur when owners are unable to act as indicated above or when non-stockholding persons lack an outside basis such as control of credit or possession of information to compel their selection as directors.

These three methods of control have a common point—domination of the board of directors (see [Berle and Means 1932, p. 69]). Owners control through their ability to determine the board; directors control their office; managers control in their capacity as directors. Defining corporate control in this manner implies that physical control of the corporate asset does not determine control and that a listing of the board of directors is an enumeration of those individuals who actually control the corporation. It also implies that the rather common view that directors "do not direct" and are virtually powerless in corporate affairs is incorrect. M. L. Mace [1971] is the usual authority cited as supporting this view. In his study, Mace implied that directors functioned mostly as "corporate elders" who allow operating control wide discretion while providing advice and counsel as well as generally acting as the "corporate conscience" [Mace 1971, p. 206]. He also indicated that some directors served to ensure harmonious relations between companies, to retain existing business relations, and to signal the general business community that certain relationships exist

[Mace 1971, p. 201]. Thus, the claim that directors have no power is incorrect, even based on Mace's analysis. While it is likely that some directors have greater influence than others, it still remains that collectively they control their respective corporations.

However, it is very difficult to document the role of directors in the exercise of corporate control. Few directors have revealed their experiences, not only because the topic is extremely sensitive, but also because they are unwilling to expose their intimate business dealings to public scrutiny and possible condemnation. Nonetheless, a few examples have been found that provide a general indication of the uses of control at high levels in large corporations.

Perhaps one of the most vexing problems in oligopolistic markets is the avoidance of mutually destructive policies. An unfriendly act by one competitor invites retaliation by another, which invokes further acts and usually results in slight short-run gain to either. Resolution of such disputes often requires extraordinary steps to reaffirm mutually acceptable business tactics. For example, in 1901 a struggle over control of northwest railroads led to a corner in Northern Pacific stock that threatened the financial stability of the entire nation [Noyes 1909, pp. 294–309]. The leading financial capitalist of the era, J. P. Morgan, was questioned under oath about the dispute:

> QUESTION: Mr. Morgan, you know that the Union Pacific, of course, was a competing line with the Burlington. You know that it had attempted to wrest your property away from you; what was the object in putting their representatives on the board?
>
> J. P. MORGAN: Simply to show that there was nothing that the Northern Pacific management, or J. P. Morgan & Company, or anybody, which had bought the Burlington, to show that they were acting under what we know as a community of interest principle, and that we were not going to have that battle on Wall Street. There was not going to be people standing up there fighting each other [Peter Power v. Northern Pacific Railway Co. 1902, vol. 2, p. 179].

James J. Hill, who was associated with Morgan in the dispute, was also asked about the inclusion of these opposing interests on the Burlington board:

> J. J. HILL: I think Mr. Morgan said: Here, we will put Mr. Harriman on this board, and Mr. Schiff, too, to show them we are not afraid of them. . . . They feared we would swallow them or something. . . . I told them no; we were developing an entirely different section of the country. . . . I think that largely led to those people being put into the Burlington board that

> they might be witnesses; that there was nobody going to dig pitfalls, etcetera, for them in that country [Peter Power 1902, vol. 1, p. 157].

Directors in this situation served most of the functions Mace indicated. They represented an attempt to resolve a difficult dispute and an effort to reestablish mutually acceptable business strategies. They also represented fearlessness or acquiescence and provided information to preclude further treachery.

Morgan also demonstrated the information function of directors when he testified about the precise relationship between Northern Pacific and J. P. Morgan & Company:

> Q: I mean the daily conference between you and the members of your firm who were directors [of Northern Pacific], that was the way you got your advice as to the wishes of the board?
>
> A: They would tell me what the board wanted, but I did not deal with them as members of the board, I was not acting with them in that capacity.
>
> Q: I understood that, but I mean as channels of communication?
>
> A: Channels of communication, yes [Peter Power 1902, vol. 2, pp. 197–8].

Finally, Morgan directly asserted the role of directors in corporate affairs by denying that a majority of stock ownership gave corporate control:

> A: Adding their holdings of both stocks together, they had at that time a majority, but that did not give them control.
>
> Q: Well, what ordinarily controls a corporation besides a majority of stock?
>
> FRANCIS L. STETSON, Morgan's attorney, interjecting: The Board of Directors.
>
> MORGAN: The Board of Directors and the conditions under which the stock is issued.
>
> STETSON: So the Supreme Court has decided [Peter Power 1902, p. 202].

Examples of control and its uses from another perspective were reported by Henry Morgenthau.[3] Early in 1900 he formed the Central Realty Bond & Trust Company, the first large New York City real estate investment trust company. His board of directors was composed of "at least half a dozen of the greatest financial giants of the day—men who, as heads of enormous and often clashing interests, represented nearly every element in the epic struggle for the financial supremacy of America" [Morgenthau 1922, p. 64]. Morgenthau sought directors who could lend his company status, provide it with financial assistance, secure business for it, and facilitate amenable relations with potential financial competitors. He got James Stillman, "the leading bank president," Frederic P. Olcott, "the leading trust company president," A. D. Juilliard and James N. Jarvie, "the two best known and most influential [board] members of the Mutual Life Insurance Company, the largest investor in mortgages on New York City real estate," as well as Henry O. Havemeyer of the sugar trust, and James H. Hyde of Equitable Life Assurance [Morgenthau 1922, p. 58, 61, 65]. Although some of these directors were bitter business rivals—Jarvie and Havemeyer in sugar, Stillman and Olcott in banking, Juilliard and Hyde in insurance—they all sat together on the Central Realty board because of its extraordinary potential for themselves and their companies.

Morgenthau also explained how James Stillman, "a close second to Morgan," made National City Bank into one of the most powerful financial institutions in the country:

> He made it a leader in financing of industry by attracting to his Board of Directors the heads of the greatest enterprises in the country. These men brought to his bank not only money for deposit, but they brought what the subtle Stillman prized even more, and that was their knowledge and their brains. At his board meetings Stillman learned, at first hand, the inside facts about every business in the country, and this priceless information gave him the key to all the mysteries of financing that lay at the bottom of his success, and at these meetings Stillman had for the asking the advice and counsel of the shrewdest businessmen in the land [Morgenthan 1922, p. 77].

These examples of the uses of control illustrate the importance of the distinction between operating and policy control. Further, they demonstrate that those who controlled corporations used that control to mediate disputes, protect interests, acquire information, and facilitate personal endeavors. These directors also provided information, created respectability, and secured business for their companies. In conclusion, it seems clear that corporations were controlled by their boards of directors and that this control was used to enhance and protect a corporation's interests as circumstances dictated.

Transfer of Control

Although directors exercise policy control, their actual role in corporate governance is "largely advisory and not of a decision making nature," and serves mostly "to temper the inclinations of presidents with de facto control, and . . . contribute to the avoidance of excesses" [Mace 1971, pp. 197, 181]. Control of this type is largely negative and oriented toward steering a general rather than a specific course of action. However, in dealing with other corporations and in successfully surviving in a universe of hostile oligopolies, directors assume a much more positive role. As shown by the Northern Pacific episode and Morgenthau's experiences, directors must formulate agreements and understandings while resolving disputes and misunderstandings. In this capacity directors become corporate diplomats seeking accommodations with suppliers, customers, competitors, and lenders as well as with actual or potential friends and foes.

Perhaps the most positive form of corporate diplomacy is when a director of one company becomes a director of another company as well. This action, establishing a formal relationship between two otherwise independent entities, can have many possible consequences. As Mace indicated with reference to investment bankers, it might result in access to inside information, an identification of mutual interests, a declaration of good sponsorship, an indication of captive relationships, a signal to third parties, or a method for getting business [Mace 1971, pp. 128–53]. While it is difficult to determine the effects of any particular interlock, the overall effect of the activity is to establish a rather complicated network of formal relationships among the group of interlocked companies. Those in the network might be linked directly through an exchange of directors or indirectly through other members once, twice, or even three times removed. But whatever the degree of indirection, the relations that establish the network serve as a device for companies to negotiate on matters of mutual concern (for details, see [Mizruchi 1982]). In the following pages, we will consider this notion of a network in greater detail, under the assumption that changes in network relationships disclose changes in corporate relationships.

Previously we indicated that it is probable that only a subgroup of directors participate in corporate governance. For example, Berle-Means found that "approximately 2,000 men were directors of the 200 largest corporations in 1930. Since an important number of these are inactive, the ultimate control of nearly half of industry was actually in the hands of a few hundred men" [Berle and Means 1932, p. 46, fn. 34]. These active directors can be further subdivided into those whose interests concentrate on one corporation and those whom we will call "intercorporate leaders," whose interests transcend any particular company.[4] In effect, there was a hierarchy of directors, based on relative influence in general corporate affairs. At the lowest and least important level are many inactive directors; next in the hierarchy are active directors involved with a specific company; finally, at the highest level, are found intercorporate leaders involved with many corporations. It is our contention that these latter directors exercised the type of control observed by Pratt and ignored by Berle-Means.

While intercorporate leaders can be defined in a number of ways, we will identify them as interlocked directors because, as shown above, the interests of an interlocked director transcend those of any particular corporation. This definition is especially appropriate for the period of our study (1905–1919) in that lists of interlocked directors have been found, in fact, to contain nearly all of the major finance capitalists then known to be active [Bunting 1976, p. 15]. While this definition fails to identify intercorporate leaders formally affiliated with only one company, it is probable that other specifications will not be much more accurate. Sufficient information does not exist for company-by-company examinations, while financial press surveys suffer from insufficient coverage. Sometimes stock ownership is used to define controllers. Not only does this method fail to explain the control of mutual insurance companies like Mutual Life and New York Life, but also there are examples such as Equitable Life Assurance where absolute ownership could not control [Keller 1963, pp. 246–49]. In addition, as Pratt found, finance capitalists owned little stock in the companies they controlled. Sometimes, judgmental "circles of control" or "webs of influence" were used to identify active directors [Moody, 1904]. While superficially vague, this method is based largely on interlocking directorates and is therefore similar to ours. Finally, it is possible that directors holding multiple positions were, in fact, inactive. Based on biographical sources and historical accounts, we have been unable to identify any of the people on our lists as inactive. Instead, we found that our lists included most of the era's major finance capitalists, either by inclusion or by representation. Thus, we conclude that those who actually controlled large corporations can be identified by their interlocks. This group of intercorporate leaders were the finance capitalists that Pratt contended had financial control of American industry.

We are interested in how this control changed in the years between 1912 and 1919. These years, as well as 1905, selected for an earlier comparison, represent approximate dates in the shift from financial to management control of large corporations. Up through 1912 there was a clear tendency for a few intercorporate leaders to control increasing numbers of companies; however, by 1919 this trend had been reversed. Yet, while the type of control changed at the level of the individual firm, the network of intercorporate relations created in the years prior to 1912 continued with little modification. In effect, the dominance of individual finance capitalists declined, but their manager-successors continued existing policies with respect to other companies.

To examine this argument, for each of the years indicated we selected a sample of large companies that contained the largest 100 industrials, 25 railroads, 20 banks, and ten insurances as well as 12 large investment houses. For industrials and insurances, we measured size by assets; for rails and banks, we used capitalization (issued stock plus funded debt); we selected for investment houses after an extensive literature review because size data were not then disclosed. (A major source was [Carosso 1970] and the citations therein.) The names of all directors or partners and, in the case of industrials and railroads, top eight officers, were recorded and then processed to determine the extent of interlocking for each year. Specific data sources included *Moody's, Poor's, Manual of Statistics, Insurance Year Book, Banker's Directory and Collection Guide,* and *New York Stock Exchange Directory,* among others (for details, see [Bunting and Barbour 1971]). Overall, the companies in our sample represented a considerable fraction of the assets or capital in their respective economic sectors, ranging from about 30 percent for industrials and banks to more than 70 percent for insurances and railroads. Finally, it should be noted that since interlocks were determined on an exact name-match basis, any spelling or punctuation error would cause the match to fail. Thus, any measurement error would lead to an underestimation of the extent of interlocking.

Table 1 presents summary statistics on interlocking for the three years selected. (Director data could not be found for two 1905 industrials.) The total number of directors and positions increased steadily over time. On the other hand, the number of interlocked corporations remained almost

Table 1. ***Summary Statistics; Interlocking, 1905–1910***

Total:	*1905*	*1912*	*1919*
Corporations	165	167	167
Directors	1944	2110	2262
Positions	2542	2761	2834
Dir/Pos	76.5	76.4	79.8
Interlocked:			
Corporations	145	140	143
Directors	312	324	347
Positions	910	975	919
Dir/Pos	34.3	33.2	37.8

unchanged, the number of interlocked directors increased, and the number of interlocked positions rose and then fell. The decline in interlocked positions from 1912 to 1919 indicates that some change occured in interlocking practices during the period. Between 1905 and 1912, the ratio of directors (total or interlocked) to positions declined, indicating that fewer directors of either type held more positions of either type. However, by 1919 this trend reversed and the ratios began to rise, indicating that relatively more directors held fewer positions.

Greater detail on this shift can be seen by comparing the cumulative distributions of interlocked persons, companies, and positions for 1912 and 1919 as found in Tables 2 and 3, respectively. In 1912, 324 directors with 975 positions interlocked about the same number of companies as did 347 directors in 1919 with 919 positions. However, when we consider directors occupying more than two positions, it is apparent that a quantitative change in affiliating practices took place between the two years. In 1912, for example, nine directors, each with a least nine positions, linked a total of 57 companies, or about a third of the sample. In 1919 only two directors held nine positions and they linked less than half as many companies. Similar conclusions apply to the number of positions held. In 1912, 44 directors holding at least five directorships occupied 298 positions; by 1919, these figures were 24 and 150, respectively. Thus, a comparison of the two years reveals a clear pattern: while the number of interlocked companies remained virtually unchanged, the number of heavily interlocked directors sharply declined. We attribute this decline to the passing of individual finance capitalists as a dominant force in corporate control.

A dramatic indication of this decline is found in Table 4, which shows the number of positions occupied in 1919 by directors who held four or

Table 2. ***Cumulative Directors, Companies, and Positions Interlocked: 1912***

Cum. Pos. Held	*Cum. Num. Dirs*	*Cumulative Num.*			*Companies*			*Cumulative Num.*			*Positions*		
		Ind	*Tran*	*Ins*	*I.H.*	*Bank*	*Tot.*	*Ind*	*Tran*	*Ins*	*I.H.*	*Bank*	*Tot.*
2	324	78	25	7	11	19	140	370	241	54	29	281	975
3	134	59	25	5	9	19	117	211	168	28	19	169	595
4	71	54	25	5	6	19	109	135	116	17	13	125	406
5	44	43	24	4	5	18	94	94	88	11	11	94	298
6	27	38	22	4	3	15	82	75	65	8	6	59	213
7	17	33	20	4	2	14	74	54	45	7	5	42	153
8	12	29	19	4	2	14	68	45	34	5	4	30	118
9	9	26	16	4	1	10	57	39	26	5	2	22	94
10+	6	21	12	3	1	7	44	29	19	3	2	14	67

Table 3. ***Cumulative Directors, Companies, and Positions Interlocked: 1919***

Cum. Pos. Held	*Cum. Num. Dirs*	*Cumulative Num. Companies*						*Cumulative Num. Positions*					
		Ind	*Tran*	*Ins*	*I.H.*	*Bank*	*Tot.*	*Ind*	*Tran*	*Ins*	*I.H.*	Bank	*Tot.*
2	347	78	25	9	12	19	143	388	211	71	36	213	919
3	121	63	24	8	8	18	121	202	125	28	16	96	467
4	50	54	22	6	3	14	99	101	78	15	8	52	254
5	24	43	19	5	3	13	83	64	42	11	3	30	150
6	14	35	15	5	2	11	68	46	25	9	2	18	100
7	9	26	12	5	2	8	53	35	16	6	2	11	70
8	3	13	8	2	1	3	27	14	8	2	1	3	28
9	2	9	7	2	—	2	20	9	7	2	—	2	20
10+	2	9	7	2	—	2	20	9	7	2	—	2	20

more positions in 1912. The sharp reduction in holdings is obvious. By 1919, 22 (31 percent) of the original 71 intercorporate leaders were not interlocked while another 22 occupied three or fewer positions. For any other number of positions held except one, the 1919 figure is half or less than its 1912 equivalent. Essentially, two factors account for this decline. Beginning early in the twentieth century, financial control of large corporations came under repeated attack in the press and Congress (for example, see [La Follette 1908a and 1908b]). In 1905 a struggle over control of Equitable Life led to a New York State investigation whose disclosures greatly excited public opinion although its remedies had little lasting effect [Keller, 1963]. In 1912, the Pujo Committee investigated the control of money and credit and, while not "proving" control, found its potential existence through a "high degree of financial concentration in New York City. . . . It was centralization of financial power, the diverse, subtle, and personal nature of its influence, and the absence of any public control over it that worried the committee and disturbed so many Americans"[Carosso 1970, p. 153].

Out of this investigation came legislation prohibiting certain forms of industrial, railroad, and banking interlocking. Moreover, it appeared at the time that if these prohibitions were to fail, even more stringent ones would have been enacted. Hence, directors began reducing their directorships. At the same time, many of the people found by Pratt to constitute a financial oligarchy in 1905 had died or retired by 1913 and were not replaced by individuals of similar influence [Keys 1913, p. 400]. This trend, as Table 4 reveals, continued up to 1919. Thus, finance capitalists declined as a dominant force in the control of large corporations partly because of public harassment, partly because of actual or potential prohibitions, and partly as a consequence of death or retirement (for additional details, see [Mizruchi 1982, chap. 7]).

Table 4. ***Number of Positions Held by Directors with Four or More Positions in 1912***

Number Positions	*1912* *N*	*%*	*1919* *N*	*%*
0–1	—	—	22	31
2–3	—	—	22	31
4	27	38	9	13
5	17	24	7	10
6	10	14	4	6
7	5	7	5	7
8+	12	17	2	3
Total	71	100	71	100

While the relative influence of finance capitalists declined, the relationships they had established with other corporations remained, although somewhat altered in form. This can be shown by analyzing and comparing the network of corporate affiliations that resulted as intercorporate leaders sought to resolve oligopolistic disputes, form alliances, secure information, and generally seek accommodations in a universe of large companies. As opposed to a concentration on single economic units, the network approach seeks to examine corporate activities in relation to those of all other corporations. One of the major findings of this method is the suggestion that large corporations, at least within the twentieth century, do not exist as independent entities. Instead, they are all directly or indirectly linked through a series of formal relationships [Fennema and Schijf 1978].

As Table 5 shows, for each of the years considered the great majority of companies formed a single, continuous network. In 1905, 145 companies, or 88 percent, were members: in 1912, 137 (excluding three that formed their own separate group) or 82 percent belonged; in 1919, 143 or 86 percent were in the network.[5] Within this system, the maximum distance in successive interlocks from one company to another was six in 1905, declining to five in the following years. This diameter figure means that two companies were indirectly linked, at the extreme, through five others. A more precise measure of corporate affiliating tendencies is the average distance of one company to another. The figures in Table 6 indicate that in any year, any two companies were, on average, connected through two others.

Because any two companies can be interlocked by more than one director, ties rather than interlocks were used to determine the extent of cor-

Table 5. ***Summary Statistics, Networks: 1905–1919***

		1905		*1912*		*1919*	
Number Corporations		145		137		143	
Maximum Diameter		6		5		5	
Average Distance		2.57		2.33		2.50	
Ave. Ties per Corp.		371		316		355	
Ties:							
First Order	(%)	927	(9)	1048	(11)	780	(8)
Second Order	(%)	4167	(40)	4711	(51)	4400	(43)
Third Order	(%)	3956	(38)	3053	(33)	4111	(41)
Fourth Order	(%)	1390	(13)	504	(5)	862	(9)
Total	(100)	10440		9316		10153	

porate relationships. Formally, a first-order tie is a direct interlock; a second-order tie, an indirect interlock; a third-order tie, an interlock through two other companies, and so on. However, whereas a company can have any number of direct or indirect interlocks with any other company, it can have only one direct or indirect tie. In 1905, the number of ties—that is, the number of connections—required to link one company with all others in the network averaged 371. This figure declined in 1912, indicating that the network was becoming more dense, but increased thereafter as the connectivity among companies weakened. Table 5 includes the number and percentage of first- (or direct), second-, third-, and fourth- or more order ties for each year. From 1905, the time of Pratt's "financial oligarchy," to 1912, the percentage of first- and second-order ties increased, reflecting the efforts of intercorporate leaders to bring large companies under common control. On the other hand, from 1912 to 1919 the percentage of first- and second-order ties declined, reflecting the diminished influence of finance capitalists.

It is important to note that despite the decline in direct or near-direct affiliations, about the same number of companies continued to remain closely connected to one another. If the intercorporate relationships established up to 1912 by finance capitalists had been severed, then we would expect not only a sharp decline in low-order connections but also in connections of any order as well as in the absolute number of companies linked. This did not happen. Instead, as intercorporate leaders lost influence, their activities were continued by others who had assumed control of the companies involved. We have shown in Table 3 that the number of directors with many interlocks sharply declined by 1919; yet Table 5 shows that about the same number of companies remained connected, although more indirectly. The cause of this change in form but not substance was the replacement of a few intercorporate leaders, each holding a large number of positions, by a larger number of director-managers, each holding a small number of positions. In other words, while the control of individual companies passed from finance capitalists to managers, the relationships among these companies continued without significant alteration.

The effects of changes in corporate control can also be demonstrated by examining changes in the network relations of identical companies at different points in time. This method focuses directly on the connecting activities of directors by eliminating possible distortions in affiliating patterns caused by sample turnover or by unusually heavily interlocked directors in particular years. The 1905 and 1912 networks had 102 companies in common. The year-by-year order matrix of their connections is found in Table 6. If, between the two years, no changes occurred in the network these companies composed, then only the main diagonal would contain nonzero figures because a first-order link in the earlier year would be continued in the later one, a second would continue as a second, and so on. As can be seen, this did not happen. Instead, while most 1905 first-order links continued in 1912, some became second-, third-, or even fourth-order. Similarly, some second-order links later became first- or third-order. Overall, the upper off-diagonal triangle contains all of the increases in indirect affiliating order while the lower off-diagonal triangle contains all the decreases. From one year to the other, 63 percent of all the connections remained unchanged in order, 20 percent became more direct, and 16 percent less direct. Thus, between 1905 and 1912 there was a slight tendency for companies to become more closely affiliated. This is also shown by the row and column percentages, with the totals for the first- and second-order connections increasing from 60.8 percent in 1905 to 63.7 percent in 1912.

Table 6. ***Network Mobility: 1905–1912***

Year		*1912*					
	Order	*1*	*2*	*3*	*4+*	*Total*	*%*
	1	435	187	31	3	656	12.7
	2	177	1794	488	16	2475	48.1
1905	3	35	586	918	119	1658	32.2
	4+	3	63	182	114	362	7.0
Total		650	2630	1619	252	5151	100.0
%		12.6	51.1	31.4	4.9	100.0	

The year-by-year order matrix of the 1912 and 1919 networks, which had 104 companies in common, is found in Table 7. Compared to the previous table, this one shows a sharp tendency for the order of affiliating to become more indirect over time. For example, more direct 1912 links were broken in 1919 than maintained, while a large number of second-order connections became third-order. Overall, 58 percent of all connections remained unchanged in order, 11 percent became more direct, and 30 percent less direct. The row and column percentages also show this change. In 1912, 74.6 percent of all network affiliations were first- or second-order; by 1919, this figure had fallen to 61.4 percent. This pattern exactly parallels those previously discussed. Its importance is that although companies ceased to be as closely connected in 1919 as they were in prior years, they nonetheless remained connected. As intercorporate leaders, especially those holding at least four positions, declined in influence, they were replaced by directors who held fewer positions, which reduced the opportunities for direct links, thereby forcing more indirect second- and third-order connections. In other words, the intercorporate relationships established by a relatively few directors between 1905 and 1912 were continued by a much larger number in 1919 and thereafter (see [Mizruchi 1982]).

Table 7. ***Network Mobility: 1912–1919***

Year		*1919*					
	Order	*1*	*2*	*3*	*4+*	*Total*	*%*
	1	355	376	77	1	809	15.1
	2	170	1979	943	92	3184	59.5
1912	3	29	364	765	133	1219	24.1
	4+	1	10	36	25	72	1.3
Total		555	2729	1821	251	5356	100.0
%		10.4	51.0	34.0	4.7	100.0	

We have documented the process by which control of large corporations was transferred from a few finance capitalists to a larger number of corporate directors. The precise reasons for this transfer are many. Continued public hostility, opportunistic political harassment, prohibitory legislation, and threatened punitive actions all tended to restrict individual participation to a few companies. Bernard Baruch, whose financial career spanned both types of control, thought economic growth and complexity were the causal factors:

> Rather often I am asked why it is that we do not have any present-day equivalents to the financial giants who dominated Wall Street at the turn of the century. . . . I believe the main reason why Wall Street has lost that quality of dramatic personal adventure which was so marked in my youth will be found in the astonishing extension of the range and area of economic interests covered by the market's activities [Baruch 1957, p. 133].

Some intercorporate leaders sought to perpetuate their control through their sons, usually with little success. For example, James J. Hill designated his son James N. as his successor. However, the son did not seem to be cut from the same cloth as the father, nor did the father seem ready to actually relinquish control during his lifetime. The result was ambiguity and dissatisfaction, with Hill first considering another son and then non-family managers [Martin 1976, pp. 574–78]. There were numerous variations on this episode, all of which concluded with the son unable or unwilling to exercise control as his father did (for other examples, see [Burr 1927 and Sinclair 1981]).

Other finance capitalists were unable to find successors because they based their control on force of personality, an attribute that cannot be transmitted. The disintegration of the Harriman empire is a case in point:

> Where now is the kingdom of Harriman? All men know the authority of the one man who by his genius and courage created this greatest of all railroad systems is now split amongst a dozen men and delegated to officers in the four corners of the country, so that no man may boast that he controls the policy or dictates the destiny of the Union Pacific itself, less yet the other dozen great corporations that hung on the word Harriman [Keys 1913, p. 4078].

These problems of succession mostly were resolved by default. When some intercorporate leader died, retired, or failed, he was succeeded by his subordinates, all of whom were directly involved with the operation of distinct parts of his corporate network. Practically no other form of succession was possible because no other group was sufficiently familiar with the companies involved. However, whereas previously the separate parts of the network of companies were controlled by one person, now separate people controlled major parts. This result, which we showed led to a large number of directors continuing their established intercorporate relationships, also led Berle and Means to conclude that large corporations were manager-controlled. What they failed to realize was that by the time of their study in 1930, intercorporate relations had become institutionalized and were no longer an obvious factor in the control of large companies.

Conclusion

We have sought to show that both the notion and evolution of corporate control is more complicated than is commonly assumed. On the one hand, control can involve physical possession of the corporate asset or the more nebulous ability to dictate use of the asset. If control is thought to be based on possession, then it always leads to the owner-manager dichotomy because by definition, possessors who are not owners must be managers. Control based on the ability to dictate use is much more difficult to establish because there is no clear association between a company and those who dictate its activities. We have argued that directors had this power, although only a subset chose to exercise it. Identified as intercorporate leaders, this subset was defined by its extra-company activities, which, during the period we examined, consisted of interlocking directorates. We contended that large companies formed interlocks so they could amenably resolve disputes as well as protect their interests, signal rivals, and generally survive in a hostile environment.

Control in this sense of interlocked directors specifying overall policy implies that one cannot make precise distinctions between companies. If a director, or a group of directors, contributes to the formulation of policies governing two corporations, can these two economic units be considered independent of each other? Further, we showed that between 1905 and 1919 a large fraction of large American companies were connected together into a formal network. Can any company in this situation be assumed to function independently of any other? We would contend that they cannot, and that their network constitutes a practical solution to the theoretical problem of oligopolistic interdependence. Additionally, denial of the independence assumption implies that large companies should be analyzed collectively rather than separately. However, this methodological shift requires a theoretical foundation that does not now seem to exist.

On the other hand, the introduction of heavily interlocked directors as finance capitalists into the evolution of corporate control requires that some consideration be given to their influence on the development of large companies. We argued that this influence essentially involved establishing a series of formal relationships with other large companies to create a basis for harmony and commonality. We also examined the transfer of control of large companies from finance capitalists to managers. As finance capitalists suffered public attacks or restrictive legislation and as they died or retired, their influence in corporate affairs lessened. For a variety of reasons, they were rarely succeeded by other finance capitalists. Instead, control of their various companies passed, mostly by default, to subordinates who had been retained to manage particular companies. However, while financial control disintegrated into managerial control at the level of the individual firm, the intercorporate network established by the finance capitalists persisted. Thus, although the form of control changed, the structure of relations among large companies remained virtually unaltered, a situation that seems to have continued to this day.

Notes

1. Sullivan cautions that "the promoters and captains of industry were so varied in position and quality that one cannot speak of them as a group" [Sullivan 1927, p. 316]. Yet he failed to heed his own advice and followed the practice of every other historian of the period by adopting a label to identify the collection of men whose activities he was describing: "titans" [Sullivan 1927, p. 338]. Other writers used "interests," "bankers," "financiers," "magnates," "capitalists," and similar variations. Still others did not personify and used "Wall Street," "community of interest," "the System," "trusts," "finance," and so on [compare Sullivan 1927, pp. 326–29; Noyes 1909, pp. 284–354; and Youngman 1907]. We have adopted the phrase "finance capitalists" to emphasize that we are considering a special class of people within a capitalistic system. Since these people were involved in financial transactions that usually had great impact on the economy, we selected the adjective "finance" rather than "large," "big," "immense," or "humongous" to identify the particular capitalists of our interest. Later in the paper the phrase will be operationally defined.
2. For a modern discussion of control see D. M. Kotz [1978, pp. 14–22], whose analysis, from a slightly different perspective, is similar to ours.
3. "I have not heard of any man who had intimate business relations with the financial giants of that period, who has described, from his own experience, the intrigues and passions, the personalities and methods, of those men who dominated the financial structure of America" [Morgenthau 1922, p. 64]. "I propose to give the reader a picture of the way in which some financial deals were made in 'Wall Street,' and the control of corporations bandied about by a nod of the head, frequently given as a reward for a personal favor, or withheld as punishment for a personal slight" [Morgenthau 1922, p. 66].
4. The phrase "intercorporate leaders" is based on the "interorganizational leaders" concept of R. Perrucci and M. Pilisuk [1970].
5. A shortest path net work was calculated using R. W. Floyd's algorithm [Floyd 1962]. In a matrix w of k by k size where k = number of corporations, let element $w(i,j) = 1$ if corporations i and j are interlocked and $w(i,j) = 0$ if not interlocked. The kth iteration of w contains the shortest paths between any two elements if the elements are calculated by $w(k,i,j) = min(w(k-1,i,j), w(k-1,i,k) + w(k-1,k,j))$.

References

Baruch, B. M. 1957. *Baruch: My Own Story*. New York: Henry Holt.

Berle, A. A. Jr., and G. C. Means. 1932. *The Modern Corporation and Private Property*. New York: Macmillian.

Bunting, D. 1976. "Corporate Interlocking: Part I—The Money Trust." *Directors and Boards* 1 (Spring): 6–15.

Bunting, D., and Jeffrey Barbour. 1971. "Interlocking Directorates in Large

American Corporations, 1896–1964." *Business History Review* 45 (Autumn): 317–35.
Burr, A. R. 1927. *The Portrait of a Banker: James Stillman, 1850–1918.* New York: Duffield.
Carosso, V. P. 1970. *Investment Banking in America.* Cambridge, Mass.: Harvard University Press.
Fennema, M., and H. Schijf. 1979. "Analyzing Interlocking Directorates: Theory and Methods." *Social Networks* 1 (May): 297–332.
Floyd, R. W. 1962. "Algorithm 97: Shortest Path." *Communications of the Association for Computing Machinery* 5 (June): 345.
Keller, M. 1963. *The Life Insurance Enterprise, 1885–1910.* Cambridge, Mass.: Harvard University Press.
Keys, C. M. 1913. "The New Democracy of Business." *World's Work* 25 (February): 400–20.
Kotz, D. M. 1978. *Bank Control of Large Corporations in the United States.* Berkeley: University of California Press.
La Follette, R. M. 1908a. "Consolidation of Banking and 'Big Business.'" Congressional Record, 60th Congress, 1st Session, 42 (part 4): 3435–56.
La Follette, R. M. 1908b. "Critics Answered—Trust Control Analyzed." Congressional Record, 60th Congress, 1st session, 42 (part 4): 3793–805.
Mace, M. L. 1971. *Directors: Myth and Reality.* Boston: Division of Research, Graduate School of Business Administration, Harvard University.
Martin, A. 1976. *James J. Hill and the Opening of the Northwest.* New York: Oxford University Press.
Mizruchi, M. S. 1982. *The American Corporate Network: 1904–1974.* Beverly Hills: Sage Publications.
Moody, J. 1904. *The Truth About The Trusts.* New York: Moody.
Morgenthau, H. 1923. *All in a Life-time.* Garden City, N.Y.: Doubleday, Page.
Noyes, A. D. 1909. *Forty Years of American Finance.* New York: G. P. Putnam's Sons.
Perrucci, R., and M. Pilisuk. 1970. "Leaders and Ruling Elites: The Interorganizational Bases of Community Power." *American Sociological Review* 35 (December): 1040–56.
Peter Power v. Northern Pacific Railway Co. 1902. "Special Examiner's Transcript—Defendant's Testimony," U. S. Circuit Court, District of Minnesota, Equity Case 526.
Pratt, S. S. 1905. "Our Financial Oligarchy." *World's Work* 10 (October): 6704–14.
Sinclair, A. 1981. *Corsair: The Life of J. Pierpont Morgan.* Boston: Little, Brown.
Sullivan, M. 1927. *Our Times II: America Finding Herself.* New York: Charles Scribner's Sons.

13

Centralized Private Sector Planning: An Institutionalist's Perspective on the Contemporary U.S. Economy

John R. Munkirs

Introduction

Currently the typical economics textbook examines four types of market structures—Competitive Market Structures, Monopolistically Competitive Market Structures, Oligopolistically Competitive Market Structures, and Pure Monopoly. While these economic theories are still useful in describing and explaining the structure, conduct, and performance of some markets, the position advanced in this essay is that the theory of Centralized Private Sector Planning (CPSP) is a more accurate description and explanation of extant economic institutions. In other words, these four traditional economic theories are *special* cases, with the *general* case being Centralized Planning. The Centralized Planning proposition is a formidable one, namely, that the cumulative effect of changes in our economic institutions over the last half century or so have created a fundamentally different type of economic system. Indeed, it may well be that upon examining the arguments and data presented many will conclude, as I have concluded, that the term capitalism itself is no longer an appropriate label for describing the U.S. economy.

In short, the corporations and industries that are the foundation of U.S. industry (automobiles, energy, steel, computers, food processing, etcetera) have become, from both a structural and functional perspective, technologically, financially, and administratively interdependent. And they have developed a series of planning instruments that both allow and, indeed, to some extent, necessitate cooperation and coordination within, between, and among these key industries in their production and distribution activities. CPSP may be defined as *a process whereby the production and distribution activities of the economy's key corporations and industries are* organized and coordinated *so as to bind these corporations and industries together into a functionally integrated production and distribution system.*[1]

And, as a final introductory comment, the analytical frame of reference upon which the analysis is founded is the Veblenian dichotomy as presented by Thorstein Veblen in his book *The Theory of Business Enterprise*, and as applied by Veblen to the U.S. economy. For the uninitiated, the Veblenian dichotomy, in brief, may be summarized as follows: (1) The two major forces that dominate decision making in the production and distribution of goods and services in the U.S. economy are mechanical and/or technological imperatives (the machine process), and the pursuit of pecuniary gain (business enterprise). (2) Decisions based upon technological/instrumental reasoning are dynamic in character, and in large measure lead to a betterment in the economic welfare of the community; they may necessitate (from a purely technological perspective) a high degree of coordination and cooperation between and among industries. (3) Decisions based upon business enterprise/ceremonial reasoning are inhibitory to technological progress, at best permissive in the work of perfecting technological processes, and in the short run often lead to temporary breakdowns in the process of producing and distributing goods and services. (4) The pursuit of pecuniary gain will result in the cannibalization of businessmen by businessmen (behavior Veblen termed the "heroic role of the captains of industry"), a process that in turn results in an ever increasing concentration and consolidation of power within the hands of the few who survive. And finally, (5) the creative and dynamic nature of technological/instrumental reasoning, combined with the primarily static and past-binding nature of business enterprise/ceremonial reasoning, will eventually result in a vast dichotomy between the two decision making processes, a dichotomy that in turn will cause the "natural decay of business enterprise" and/or, perhaps, cause the cultural demise of the entire social system.[2]

The CPSP Model

The CPSP model consists of two basic parts: those industries that actually perform the production and distribution functions, and the Central Planning Core (CPC). For pedagogical reasons, explanation of the structural and functional characteristics of the CPC will follow the explanation of the structural and functional characteristics of the production and distribution component.

Production and Distribution Industries

In the CPSP there are two distinct yet interdependent types of planning instruments: (1) formal and/or legally binding planning instruments, and (2) informal and/or influential planning instruments. Within these two major groupings, there are several sub-categories, each of which will be discussed briefly. In the first category, there are three basic planning instruments: stocks, boards of directors, and debt.

Stocks. Stocks perform two distinct roles within CPSP: they are *one* of the important interstitial elements in forming an organizational *structure* conducive to centralized economic planning, and they may be used as a *functional* planning instrument conducive to organizing and coordinating the production and distribution activities within, between, and among corporations in various industries. Here the term *structure* refers to both the number of corporations *within* a given industry, as well as the various technological, financial, and administrative *intra*-locking ties that exist between and among these corporations. In addition, though, and perhaps even more important from a CPSP perspective, are the technological, financial and administrative *inter*-locking ties that also exist between and among various industries.

Table 1 illustrates how stocks are an important *structural* planning instrument. As presented in Table 1: Two corporations (General Electric and United Technologies) produce 90 to 95 percent of all commercial aircraft engines. They sell their engines to two other corporations (Boeing and McDonnell-Douglas) who, in turn, produce 90 to 95 percent of all commercial aircraft. McDonnell-Douglas and Boeing sell many of their jet aircraft to UAL, Inc., American Airlines, and Eastern Airlines, who, in turn, account for 30 to 40 percent of all commercial transportation.

Table 1. ***Illustration of Stock as an Important Intra-Interlocking Interstitial Element in Forming an Organization*** **Structure** ***Conducive to Economic Planning, for Selected Industries and Corporations, as of 1 January 1978.***

Industries and Corporations	*Concentration Ratios (%)*	*Minimum CPC Stock Holdings (%)*	*Cumulative Voting Required or Permitted*
I. Commercial Aircraft Engines	90–95		
General Electric Company		9.3	No
United Technologies Corp.		9.2	Yes
II. Commercial Aircraft	90–95		
The Boeing Company		10.4	Yes
McDonnell-Douglas Corp.		4.5	Yes
III. Commercial Air Transportation	30–40		
U.A.L., Inc.		13.5	Yes
American Airlines		10.5	No
Eastern Airlines		4.7	No
IV. Jet Aviation Fuel	60–70		
Exxon Corporation		10.4	No
Mobil Corporation		11.2	No
Standard Oil (California)		8.3	No
Standard Oil (Indiana)		16.6	Yes
Atlantic Richfield Company		13.0	Yes

SOURCE: Securities and Exchange Commission, Forms 13F.

Five corporations (Exxon, Mobil, Standard Oil of California, Standard Oil of Indiana, and Atlantic Richfield) account for 50 to 70 percent of all jet aviation fuel production. Of the twelve corporations mentioned, the CPC *controls* more than ten percent of the common stock in seven of these corporations and controls, at a minimum, 9.3, 9.2, 8.3, 4.7, and 4.5 percent of the common stock in the remaining five corporations. Six of the twelve corporations have cumulative voting procedures. The three key structural characteristics in Table 1 are: the small number of corporations in each industry, the fact that the four industries are both technologically and financially interdependent since they buy and sell from each other, and the fact that the CPC controls significant amounts of stock in each corporation in each industry.

These structural relationships seem to suggest a tremendous interdependency between and among the production activities of each industry.

On the one hand, there is a clear physical and/or technological interdependency, both from the standpoint of the actual quantities to be produced as well as the requisite integration requirements of size, weight, metallurgical specifications, etcetera. For example, engineers and technicians in the commercial aircraft engine industry must work closely with their counterparts in the commercial aircraft industry in developing and producing each new generation of transport aircraft. In turn, the types and amounts of aviation fuel produced depend directly on the various quantities and types of aircraft and aircraft engines manufactured. On the other hand, a very definite monetary interdependency also exists since the prices charged and the profits accumulated by each of the corporations in each industry are also interdependent. The commercial aircraft industry's profits, for instance, are partially determined by the *prices* they receive for their aircraft from the commercial air transportation industry. In addition, the size of their profits is also dependent on the *cost* they incur in purchasing aircraft engines.

A conscious recognition of these technological and financial interdependencies would seem sufficient, from a purely logical perspective, to indicate the economic benefits of coordinating the production and distribution activities within, between, and among the corporations in these four industries, if not their outright necessity. In short, then, what emerges is a form of vertical integration (aircraft engines, aircraft, air transportation, and jet aviation fuel) such as already exists, for example, in the petroleum industry, where the major companies own the oil fields, the pipelines, the refineries, and many of the gasoline distribution stations.

In addition to their role as a structural planning instrument, as mentioned above, stocks also play an important functional role. For example, the capacity to buy and sell large blocks of a corporation's stock places the CPC in a position of powerful influence over a corporation's administrative leaders, as both a carrot and a stick. As illustration, in order to persuade a recalcitrant management team to cooperate with a particular plan, the CPC could sell off the corporation's stock. One must keep in mind that "minority stock control" (five to ten percent) often means controlling shares of stock numbering in the tens of millions, with dollar values measured in the hundreds of millions—if not billions. Short of all-out economic warfare, a corporation's management is always sensitive to the economic results of even a limited sell-off of the corporation's stock by a large investor, for several very good reasons: (1) If a company's stock declines in price, the indication is that the company is not doing well. (2) This, in turn, has an adverse effect overall on the public relations of the company, which could adversely affect its business. (3) A decline in the value of the company's stock destroys the value of stock options held by the principal officers because it could cause the price of the corporation's stock to fall below the price at which the stock options were granted. (4) An adverse business climate could also make it much more difficult for the corporation to raise capital.[3]

On the other hand, as a carrot, the CPC could buy a corporation's stock, which would have the exact opposite effects of a sell-off; that is, the price of the corporation's stock would begin to rise, stock options would become more valuable, the public itself would begin to buy the corporation's stocks, and, as the corporation's image became more positive, the corporation's management would be able to raise even more capital through either borrowing and/or issuing more stock. This brings us to the *most* important tool: namely, the ability of a cohesive group, such as the CPC, to cause the general stock-buying public to sell and buy stock, which, in turn, can cause massive shifts of capital from this corporation to that corporation, from this industry to that industry, through the CPC's ability to enhance or depreciate a corporation's image by its own buying and selling maneuvers. In conclusion, the stock instrument is an important functional planning tool for achieving cooperation and compromise, and for achieving the necessary capital allocations to implement agreed-upon planning strategies.

Board of Directors. The "management" or leadership team in American corporations consists of the corporation's *board of directors* and the corporation's *officers.* In 1978, The Business Roundtable (one of America's most prestigious and authoritative business organizations) published a report concerning directorship responsibilities, stating, in part, that

> it is generally understood that a principal Board function is the selection of the Chief Executive Officer and his principal management associates. A corollary function is to replace managers, including Chief Executive Officers, who have not met their responsibility. . . . The Board does have a major role in, and a major accountability for, the financial performance of the enterprise; . . . The focus should be on a system assuring prior Board consideration of any major commitment of corporate resources over a period of time. Normally these corporate resource allocations decisions will be embodied in corporate "strategic plans" and Board consideration of such plans should be an integral part of the strategic planning process. Traditionally established procedures called for Board approval of significant capital investments—including plant and equipment construction or acquisition of land. . . . Moreover these investments budgets or plans must be reviewed in the context of a more comprehensive plan which takes into account projected cash flow and overall corporate financial capability . . . ; All of these considerations suggest the governing notion should be corporate resource allocation (strategic plan-

> ning); and, a Board should plan for its own continuity, succession for the retirement of directors, and the designation of new Board members.[4]

In essence, then, the executives and directors of many of America's Brobdingnagian corporations have provided a clear view as to what they consider their most important functions, namely: (1) to select the corporation's management team—its officers—and its directors; and (2) to establish the corporation's basic objectives and board policies and to "be an integral part of the strategic planning process."

After the board has formulated the corporation's strategic plans, the corporation's "operating" management—its officers—are responsible for conducting daily operations during the implementation process. Referring again to The Business Roundtable's report: "The role of the Board cannot be considered except in the context of the indispensable role played by operating management in the conduct of day-to-day corporate affairs. . . . However, despite its crucial role, operating management does not stand in an independent relationship. . . . Operating management derives its authority and legitimacy from the Board of Directors." Universally, a corporation's five or six highest ranking operating officers are also members of the corporation's board of directors. Having the operating officers actively participate in the corporation's "strategic planning" processes minimizes divisiveness and more nearly assures that the corporation's management will operate as a smoothly functioning team. A corporation's board, then, is usually composed of both "insiders"—members of the corporation's operating officer cadre—and "outsiders"—for the most part, business executives from other large corporations. The trend over the last several decades has been toward an ever-increasing percentage of director positions being held by "outsiders." In turn, as the number of outside directors increases, so does the number of board of director (BOD) interlocks between and among corporations and industries. This brings us to consideration of the BODs in light of CPSP.

Within the context of CPSP, boards of directors perform two distinct, yet interdependent, structural and functional roles. Just as with common stock, they are one of the important interstitial elements in forming an organizational *structure* conducive to CPSP, and they may also be viewed as a *functional* planning tool. As indicated in Table 2, from a structural standpoint, General Electric and United Technologies are indirectly *intra*-locked, since the corporations are in the same industry and both have directors who are also CPC directors. Specifically, seven members (35 percent) of General Electric's board and two members (including the Chief Executive Officer) of United Technologies' board are also CPC directors. Further, since two of Boeing's directors are also CPC directors,

Table 2. ***Illustration Depicting How Common Stocks and Boards of Directors are Important Interstitial Elements in Forming an Organizational Structure Conducive to Economic Planning, for Selected Industries and Corporations, as of 1 January 1978.***

	Concentration Ratios	*Minimum CPC Stock Holdings*	*Number and Percent of Direct BOD Interlocks with the CPC*		*Number of Indirect Directorship (IDI) and Indirect Institutional (III) Interlocks with CPC*
Industries and Corporations	*Percent*	*Percent*	*Number*[a]	*Percent*[b]	*IDI-III*[a]
I. Commercial Aircraft Engines	90–95				
General Electric Company		9.3	7	35	34–8
United Technologies Corp.		9.2	2*	14	20–4
II. Commercial Aircraft	90–95				
The Boeing Company		10.4	2	18	15–3
McDonnell-Douglas Corp.		4.5	0	0	3–1
III. Commercial Air Transportation	30–40				
U.A.L., Inc.		13.5	3*	18	27–6
American Airlines		10.5	3	18	49–7
Eastern Airlines		4.7	2	12	30–7

IV. Jet Aviation Fuel	60–70				
Exxon Corp.		10.4	7*	41	24–5
Mobil Corp.		11.2	4*	21	54–11
Standard Oil (California)		8.3	3*	21	21–4
Standard Oil (Indiana)		16.6	4*	22	20–4
Atlantic Richfield Company		13.0	5*	33	44–10

SOURCE: *Moody's Bank and Finance Manual* (New York: Moody's Investors Service, 1979), *Moody's Industrial Manual* 1979, *Moody's Transportation Manual* 1979, and Securities and Exchange Commission, Forms 13 F.

[a]These figures do not represent all of the personnel interlocks between the various corporations and the CPC. They represent *only* board of director interlocks.

[b]These figures represent the percentage of a corporation's board of directors that is directly interlocked with the CPC.

*Designates a corporation's Chief Executive Officer (CEO). In almost all cases, a corporation's CEO is also a member of its board of directors and quite often holds the board's chairmanship position. Thus, the CEO's of United Technologies and Boeing, as well as the CEO's for all five energy companies, are members of the CPC.

the two industries (Commercial Aircraft Engines and Commercial Aircraft) are indirectly *inter*locked. The term "Indirect BOD *Intra*lock," then, refers to companies *within* a specific industry that have indirect BOD linkages, while the term "Indirect BOD *Inter*lock" refers to companies in different industries that have indirect BOD linkages.

To illustrate, consider the following:

Commercial Aircraft Engines

G.E.—"X" is a director on G.E.'s board

U.T.—"Y" is a director on U.T.'s board

Citicorp—both "X" and "Y" are directors on Citicorp's board.

Therefore, G.E. and U.T. have an "indirect BOD *Intra*lock" via Citicorp.

Commercial Aircraft

Boeing—"N" is a director on Boeing's board

Commercial Air Transportation

U.A.L.—"O" is a director on U.A.L.'s board

Citicorp—both "N" and "O" are directors on Citicorp's board.

Therefore, Boeing and U.A.L. have an "Indirect BOD *Inter*lock" via Citicorp.

The existence of these types of indirect BOD intra- and interlocking ties is dependent upon *each* of the corporations having *direct* BOD interlocks with the CPC. For example, as indicated in Table 2, seven members of Exxon's board of directors are also CPC directors. All twelve corporations in Table 2, as a group, have forty-two "direct BOD interlocks" with the CPC. In addition to these three types of interlocking ties—Direct BOD Interlock, Indirect BOD Intralock, and Indirect BOD Interlock—there is a fourth type of interlocking tie—the Indirect *Directorship* Interlock (IDI). For example, assume that two members of General Electric's BOD were also directors for New York's electrical utility, Consolidated Edison (Con-Ed). In addition, assume that two directors from Citicorp were also on Consolidated Edison's board. This is termed an IDI between General Electric and Citicorp. In this particular example, a total of *four* directorships are interlocked—two from Citicorp and two from General Electric. Consider the following illustration:

Citicorp—"A" and "B" are directors on Citicorp's board

G.E.—"C" and "D" are directors on G.E.'s board

Con-Ed—"A," "B," "C," and "D" are directors on Con-Ed's board.

Therefore, Citicorp and G.E. have *four* Indirect Directorship Interlocks through Con-Ed.

In addition, these four IDI's occur through just *one* Indirect Institutional Interlock (III); that is, the four directorships are interlocked at one institution—Con-Ed. By knowing the absolute number of IDI's, coupled with the number of III's through which these IDI's take place, one can compute two important statistics. For instance, using General Electric as our example, and by knowing the number of III's as well as the fact that boards meet approximately twelve times yearly, we can compute from the data in Table 2 that directors from General Electric meet with CPC directors approximately ninety-six times per year (eight III's times twelve BOD meetings per year), just through III's. In addition, by dividing the absolute number of IDI's by the number of III's, we can compute that there are approximately 4.25 directorships involved per meeting (thirty-four DI's divided by eight III's). Thus, we also know that in each of these ninety-six meetings per year between General Electric and the CPC approximately 4.25 directorships interlock. The number of IDI's per meeting is indicative of both the variety and intensity of the information exchanged at any particular meeting, while the number of meetings per year is more indicative of both the variety and intensity of information shared over time.

Upon examining each of the five basic types of administrative ties—(1) direct BOD *inter*locks, (2) indirect BOD *intra*locks, (3) indirect BOD *inter*locks, (4) indirect *directorship* interlocks, and (5) indirect *institutional* interlocks—between and among the corporations and industries in Table 2, we find that all twelve institutions are, from an administrative viewpoint, *structurally interconnected*, quite solidly, via the CPC. As one example, just through IDI's, on the average, directors from each of the twelve companies in Table 2 meet approximately seventy-two times a year with CPC directors.

One final observation is in order concerning the specific data in Table 2. Whenever the symbol (*) appears, it signifies that the corporation's Chief Executive Officer (CEO) is also a CPC director. Seven of the CEO's of the twelve corporations illustrated, then, are also CPC directors.

In summary, from a purely *structural* point of view, we now have several industries, each dominated by a small number of corporations, that are technologically and financially interdependent in production, prices, and profits; and interlocked via the CPC through the CPC's control of large blocks of stocks and through an intricate system of intra- and interlocking administrative ties.

Before we examine the last of the Formal and/or Legally Binding

Planning Instruments (the Corporate Debt instrument), we will direct a few comments at the use of administrative intra- and interlocking ties at the board of director level as a *functional* planning tool.

To organize and coordinate the production and distribution of various corporations and industries in a complex industrial society requires a well-developed, stable, and effective information processing system. In this regard, the board of director planning instrument performs two distinct, yet interdependent, functions. First, the veritable labyrinth of intra- and interlocking board of director ties allows—or, more precisely, dictates—that an intensive and constant flow of information between and among the various corporations and industries be maintained. The word *dictate* is certainly not too forceful a term in this context, unless one assumes that corporations do not hold board meetings on a regular basis and, further, that when such meetings are held board members refrain from talking to one another about business matters. The more plausible and obvious assumption, particularly in light of the various structural interdependencies that exist between these corporate institutions, is that attitudes and habits of cooperation and collective decision making would, quite naturally, evolve as the most efficient, practical, and profitable mode of operation.

Second, since each of the industries are represented on the CPC, the CPC becomes a focal point of information concerning *all* industries. Being a director for, say, Exxon does not provide one with the variety and intensity and/or the kinds and types of information that one receives by virtue of being a CPC director. Being a CPC director gives one access to a broad range of data and information—data and information not available elsewhere. From a functional perspective, then, the intra- and interlocking administrative ties are structurally arranged so that the CPC becomes the focal point of the CPSP process.

Stated somewhat differently, a CPC director is uniquely situated so as to develop a holistic or macro perspective of the economy. In turn, the existence of a cohesive group with a macro economic perspective may function, for instance, so as to facilitate the planning involved in mergers and acquisitions undertaken in order to create the most technically efficient industry, both optimum plant size and in the optimum number of corporations. (This would be an example of intra-industry planning.) Such a cohesive group would also facilitate and plan for the sharing of technical information between industries that are technologically and financially interdependent in the quantity of products produced, prices, costs, and profits—that is, a sharing of technical information necessary to the production and integration of various component parts that, when joined together, constitute a final product, such as jet engines, jet aircraft, tires and tubes, jet fuel, etcetera. (This would be a typical example of inter-industry planning.)

Debt. Under law, a corporation has at its disposal two legal mechanisms for obtaining funds from sources other than retained earnings or profits. First, the corporation may sell stocks. Second, corporations may borrow money by issuing bonds. Borrowed monies, or bonds, are generally referred to as debt capital. A corporation's principal creditors may, under certain circumstances, also have a legal right to participate in the election of a corporation's management team, but are not legally entitled to share in the corporation's profits. Instead, creditors are paid an agreed-upon fixed interest rate for their investments in the corporation. When a corporation seeks monies by incurring a long-term debt, three separate legal contracts are generally involved—the bond itself, the bond indenture, and the trustee agreement. The bond certificate is the initial or primary contract between the corporation and the investor, or bondholder.

The bond indenture is an additional, or supplementary, contract (quite often several hundred pages in length) stating in specific detail the rights and responsibilities of the corporation and the bondholders. It is customary for a bond indenture to include the following: (1) a restatement of the general information contained in the bond certificate; (2) a detailed description of the corporation's property offered to guarantee or secure the loan; (3) a statement specifying the responsibilities of the corporation in maintaining the property offered as security for the loan, such as paying taxes, replacing obsolete equipment, making timely and necessary repairs, and maintaining adequate reserves necessary for depreciation requirements; (4) a statement specifying restrictive convenants, such as limiting the size of dividends to equity stockholders and/or requiring the maintenance of a specified amount of working capital, limiting the corporation's ability to make additional investments without prior creditor approval, limiting the corporation's ability to sell off assets without prior credit approval, and limiting the corporation's ability to incur further debt without prior creditor approval; (5) a statement specifying the rights of creditors representing a specific percentage (say, 60 percent) of the corporation's outstanding debt, in case the corporation defaults on its agreements, to declare the corporation's entire debt to be due and payable within a specified time period (say, thirty days), and to elect a certain percentage (say, 25 percent) of the corporation's board of directors at the next scheduled stockholders meeting; (6) a statement setting forth the exact duties and responsibilities of the "trustee," if the bonds are being sold to the public at large.

As with a stock, when bonds are sold to the public at large, the number of bondholders is quite numerous and geographically dispersed. In order to protect the legal rights of such bondholders, it is required by law that corporations offering public bond issues appoint a trustee to act on behalf of the bondholders. The trustee's role will be discussed more fully in the next section. It is mentioned here solely for the purpose of identifying the tripartite legal structure inherent to the issuance of Long-Term Debt—the bond, the bond indenture, and the trustee agreement.

The limitations and restrictions listed in points four and five above, while quite typical, nonetheless appear to infringe heavily upon decisions traditionally thought of as solely the prerogatives of management.

Before analyzing the role of corporate debt as a structural and functional planning instrument, we insert a brief note regarding the debt statistics used in this study. Corporations, as a general rule, are not required to report the sources of their loans in any systematic manner. Further, commercial loan creditors are likewise not required to systematically disclose information pertaining to their debtors—the major exception being that the Civil Aeronautics Board (CAB) does require air carriers to report annually the major holders of their indebtedness. Therefore, with the exception of the corporations in the commercial air transportation industry, the statistics on indebtedness are, for the most part, grossly underestimated and must be understood as such. Yet, without necessitating untoward extrapolations from the data obtained in CAB reports, as well as scattered data collected from various government studies, the statistics provided are nonetheless clearly noteworthy.

As indicated in Table 3, as of January 1, 1978, the CPC held 5.1 percent of the indebtedness of U.A.L., Inc., 70.1 percent of American Airlines' debt, and 42.2 percent of Eastern Airlines' debt. Also, the CPC held, at a minimum, 53.5 percent of the Boeing Company's debt and 24.9 percent of Atlantic Richfield's indebtedness. The logical presumption is that the figures would be similar for the other corporations in the table, were the data available. Concisely put, from the CPC's macro or holistic perspective, the debt instrument is also a very important interstitial element for structurally binding these corporations and industries together into a unified production and distribution system.

Of course, debt may also be used as a very important functional planning tool. A corporation's major creditor often has almost automatic access to the corporation's strategic planning documents. As already noted, such access to inside information is usually guaranteed to principal creditors by stipulations written into the bond indenture. In turn, having inside information concerning, for example, the discovery of new raw material (lead, zinc, petroleum, etcetera) deposits, the creation of a new wonder drug, or a technological breakthrough in a manufacturing process, can be quite useful for developing sound, long-run planning strategies that will coordinate the allocation of debt and equity capital in the economy, position key personnel in important policy positions, coordinate intra- and interindustry expansion or contraction plans, and encourage or discourage acquisition and/or mergers.

Considerable emphasis has been placed on the idea that habits of cooperation and coordination among the business elite in solving shared economic problems would be the most natural and evolutionary outcome to be derived from the economy's basic structural characteristic, that is, economic interdependency. Nonetheless, in any form of centralized economic planning, a certain amount of coercion may be necessary in order to create consensus or to create a unified approach to the solution of a particular problem. As the following quote illustrates, corporate debt may, at times, be used quite well as a coercive tool:

> A Senate hearing earlier this year was told that Mohawk Airlines was forced to merge with Allegheny because it was unable to increase the size of its credit. It was Chase Manhattan which told Mohawk it would call its loans unless the airline found new capital to buy replacement aircraft. The only place Mohawk could find the money was with Allegheny.
>
> While many marriages are made in Heaven, this one was made in the vaults of Chase Manhattan Bank, claimed Reuben B. Robertson, III, a consumer advocate on aviation issues. While the stockholders' interests were substantially diluted, Chase and the other participants emerged unscathed.[5]

The merger between Mohawk Airlines, Inc. and Allegheny Airlines, Inc. took place on April 12, 1972. Those in favor of the merger pointed to the increased efficiencies that often accompany larger-scale operations and that, in turn, might lead to a more effectively "competitive enterprise." For CPSP, though, the crucial point was not whether the merger was economically sound, but, rather, that the merger came about because of the leverage creditors were able to exert on their debtors. In short, the corporate debt instrument, within the context of the CPSP, is a key functional component and is quite often used as such.

When one simultaneously focuses on all of the structural and functional characteristics of the model presented in Table 3 (that is, the small number of firms in each industry; the financial interdependencies of cost, prices, and profits; the physical interdependencies of both technological interfusion and quantities produced; and the many intra- and interlocking interdependencies in stock, debt, and boards of directors created via the CPC), Adam Smith's invisible hand and impersonal market forces may

Table 3. ***Illustration Depicting How Common Stocks, Boards of Directors, and Corporate Debt are Important Interstitial Elements in Forming an Organizational Structure Conducive to CPSP, for Selected Industries and Corporations, as of 1 January 1978.***

Industries and Corporations	Concentration Ratios	Minimum CPC Stock Holdings	Number Direct BOD, Indirect Directorship (IDI), and Indirect Institutional (III) Interlocks with CPC		Minimum[a] of Outstanding Debt Held by CPC
			Number		
	Percent	Percent	Direct	IDI-III	Percent
I. Commercial Aircraft Engines	90–95				
General Electric Company		9.3	7	34–8	11.6
United Technologies Corp.		9.2	2*	20–4	6.4
II. Commercial Aircraft	90–95				
The Boeing Company		10.4	2	15–3	53.5
McDonnell-Douglas Corp.		4.5	0	3–1	6.7
III. Commercial Air Transportation	30–40				
U.A.L., Inc.		13.5	3*	27–6	51.1
American Airlines		10.5	3	49–7	70.1
Eastern Airlines		4.7	2	30–7	42.4

IV. Jet Aviation Fuel	60–70				
Exxon Corp.		10.4	7*	24–5	5.0
Mobil Corp.		11.2	4*	54–11	14.2
Standard Oil (California)		8.3	3*	21–4	6.5
Standard Oil (Indiana)		16.6	4*	20–4	1.0
Atlantic Richfield		13.0	5*	44–10	24.9

SOURCE: *Moody's*, various 1979 Security and Exchange Commission Forms 13 F, and the Civil Aeronautics Board's "Air Carrier Indebtedness (Long- and Short-Term Debt) By Major Holder as of December 31, 1977."

[a]Corporations, as a general rule, are not required to report the sources of their loans. The major exception is that the Civil Aeronautics Board (CAB) does require air carriers to report annually the major holders of their indebtedness. Therefore, with the exception of the corporations in the commercial air transportation industry, the figures on indebtedness are, for the most part, grossly underestimated.

appear to some to have undergone a rather dramatic metamorphosis. In any event, this brings us to a consideration of the Informal and/or Influential Planning Instruments.

To explain all of the Informal Planning Instruments would itself require a monumental study—they run into the hundreds.[6] Herein only three—the trustee, the transfer agent, and the stock registrar—are presented. These three were chosen primarily because the statistical data were readily available for comparison, and because of the stock exchange and/or legal requirements surrounding the performance of these particular functions. The trustee's role is, by far, the most specifically relevant to the actual planning process.

Trustee

Each time a corporation undertakes a bond issue, wherein the bonds are sold to the public at large, it must submit the review. The SEC will not approve a bond issue unless the bond indenture specifically provides for a trustee. The trustee may be an individual, another corporation, or a commercial bank's trust department. This procedure is mandated by law through the Trust Indenture Act of 1939. Each bond indenture must state specifically the duties and responsibilities of the trustee. Such duties would normally include: furnishing individual bondholders with annual reports explaining the status of the loan agreement; notifying bondholders in case of default and representing their interest in any foreclosure proceedings; arbitrating any disputes between individual bondholders; certifying that each bond certificate issued is covered by the bond indentures; and generally making sure that the corporation issuing the bonds abides by the provisions in the bond indenture by promptly taking the steps to rectify any irregularities, including notifying bondholders of such irregularities. In short, a trustee is charged with the overall responsibility of protecting and enforcing individual bondholders' rights (for perhaps tens of thousands of individual bondholders) by acting as if the trustee were the sole owner of the entire bond issue. In order to fulfill these responsibilities, a trustee must have a sound working knowledge of the debtor corporation's economic conditions. This, in turn, requires that the bond indenture be written so as to provide the trustee with adequate rights and powers vis-a-vis the debtor corporation. While the trustee is the bondholder's legal representative, the debtor corporation appoints and pays the trustee. A trustee must be assigned for each individual bond issue. As indicated in Table 4, General Electric had eight bond issues outstanding as of January 1, 1978, and the CPC acted as trustee for seven of the eight issues. United

Table 4. ***Illustration Depicting How the Trustee, Transfer Agent, and Registrar are Important Interstitial Elements in Forming an Organizational Structure Conducive to Economic Planning, for Selected Industries and Corporations, as of 1 January 1978.***

	Trustees (TR)		*Transfer Agents (TA)*		*Registrars (R)*	
Industries and Corporations	*Total No. of Bond Issues*	*CPC as (TR)*	*Total Number*	*CPC as (TA)*	*Total Number*	*CPC as (R)*
I. Commercial Aircraft Engines						
General Electric Company	8	7	2	0	2	1
United Technologies Corp.	5	5	2	1	1	1
II. Commercial Aircraft						
The Boeing Company	NA[a]		1	0	1	0
McDonnell Douglas Corp.	2	2	2	1	2	1
III. Commercial Air Transportation						
U.A.L., Inc.	4	3	3	2	3	0
American Airlines	5	2	2	0	2	0
Eastern Airlines	3	1	1	1	1	1
IV. Jet Aviation Fuel						
Exxon Corp.	2	2	4	2	4	2
Mobil Corp.	3	2	4	2	4	2
Standard Oil (California)	4	0	CO[b]		1	0
Standard Oil (Indiana)	8	7	3	2	3	2
Atlantic Richfield Co.	10	6	3	1	3	1

SOURCE: *Moody's* various 1979.

[a]NA = Not available.

[b]CO = Standard Oil (California) acts as its own transfer agent.

Technologies, on the other hand, had five bond issues outstanding; the CPC acted as trustee for all five. As a group, the twelve corporations listed in Table 4 had fifty-four bond issues outstanding, and the CPC acted as trustee thirty-five times.

By acting as "the" major trustee for the corporation world's debt obligations, the CPC gains another valuable information processing system—a system that is intra- and interindustry in structure, thus further strengthening structural ties—and another valuable functional tool, a tool that adds still greater flexibility to the CPC's organizing and coordinating capabilities.

Transfer Agents and Registrars

The CPC, as also indicated in Table 4, is quite active as both a transfer agent and a registrar. Literally tens of millions of shares of corporate stock are bought and sold each day on the New York Stock Exchange. Any corporation listing its stock with the Exchange is required (by the Exchange) to maintain both a transfer agent and a stock registrar. The transfer agent may be the corporation itself but is normally the trust department of a large commercial bank. The exchange also requires that both the transfer agent and the registrar reside in New York's financial district. The basic responsibilities of a transfer agent are: to maintain an up-to-date record of a corporation's current stockholders and registered bond owners—names, addresses, social security numbers, and the number of stock or bond certificates held; to cancel a previous owner's stock or bond certificates and to issue new certificates to the new owner; to serve as a disbursing agent for dividends and interest payments; and to distribute annual reports, proxy solicitations, and notifications for shareholder meetings. The basic responsibilities of a stock registrar are: for new stock issues, to certify that the number of shares issued does not exceed the amount of shares authorized, by comparing the number of shares authorized with the number of shares represented by stock certificates, and by registering, recording, and signing each new stock certificate; and for corporate stock already outstanding, to check the work of the transfer agent when stock is bought and sold, by certifying that each stock certificate issued by a transfer agent to a buyer is accompanied by a certificate representing a like number of cancelled stock certificates, and by countersigning all stock certificates issued by the transfer agent.

The stock registrar, then, provides a check on the transfer agent's work. On the one hand, the transfer agent and registrar's work may be viewed solely as a routine processing procedure. On the other hand, one may take notice of the fact that the transfer agent knows, before any other person or corporate entity, who actually owns a corporation at any given moment. The transfer agent obtains this information even before the corporation whose stock is being bought and sold knows who its new stockholders are. In essence, the transfer agent occupies the most favorable position for obtaining information on possible corporate take-over attempts. When a corporation begins to buy and sell large blocks of stock, the transfer agent is the first to know who the major participants are.

Nevertheless, the importance of these services for informal and/or influential planning instruments is not that the CPC performs any individual service for corporations. The CPC performs literally scores of such services in addition to the three highlighted in this discussion. What is important is the impact of these services in their totality and in light of the formal and/or legally binding planning instruments that also exist.

The Central Planning Core (CPC)

The CPC consists of seven banks, four insurance companies, and one diversified financial institution (see Table 5). As of January, 1978, the CPC accounted for approximately $410 billion in assets, $230 billion in deposits-premiums, and the trust departments of the seven banks controlled approximately $100 billion in trust assets. Nine of the institutions are headquartered in New York City, one in Newark, and two in Chicago. Among all U.S. banks, Citicorp ranked second in assets, Chase was third, Manufacturers Hanover was fourth, J.P. Morgan was fifth, Chemical was sixth, Continental Illinois was seventh, and First Chicago was ninth. Among U.S. insurance companies, Prudential, Metropolitan, Equitable, and New York Life ranked first, second, third, and fourth in assets. Last, Continental Corporation ranked tenth in assets among U.S. diversified financial institutions. The interstitial elements that bond these institutions into a cohesive and solid structural and functional unit will now be considered.

Direct Board of Director (BOD) Intra-Core Interlocks

The *direct* BOD and non-BOD intra-Core interlocks between and among the CPC institutions are depicted in Table 6. An example of a typical non-BOD institutional interlock would be where a member of one Core institution's BOD has a relative who is a member of another Core institution's senior operating management. This would certainly constitute an important intra-Core institutional interlock between the two insti-

Table 5. ***The Industry, Corporate Name, Rank, Assets (Deposits - Premiums), Trust Assets, Headquarters, and Number of Employees as of 1 January 1978.***

Industries and Corporations	*Rank*[a]	*Assets (000)*	*Deposits/ Premiums (000)*	*Trust Assets (000)*	*Headquarters/ City*	*Employment*
A. BANKING						
1. Citicorp	2	77,112,434	55,651,250	24,542,985	New York	47,200
2. Chase Manhattan Corp.	3	53,180,295	43,508,258	14,473,907	New York	30,760
3. Manufacturers Hanover Corp.	4	35,787,568	29,782,691	10,892,233	New York	18,809
4. J.P. Morgan and Company	5	31,663,815	23,831,026	24,236,011	New York	9,932
5. Chemical New York Corp.	6	30,705,933	23,296,823	8,506,434	New York	16,285
6. Continental Illinois Corp.	7	25,800,280	18,753,785	7,312,683	Chicago	10,132
7. First Chicago Corp.	9	22,613,959	17,054,104	8,813,377	Chicago	8,586
B. INSURANCE						
8. Prudential Insurance Co.	1	46,423,607	6,742,457		Newark	61,863
9. Metropolitan Life	2	39,575,922	5,521,311		New York	52,300
10. Equitable Life Assurance	3	24,798,678	3,850,290		New York	23,856
11. New York Life	4	15,848,213	2,194,734		New York	19,744
12. Continental Corp.	10[b]	6,410,950	2,772,928		New York	23,096
TOTALS		409,921,654	232,959,657	98,777,630		322,563

SOURCE: *Fortune*, July 1979.

[a]Ranked by assets and by industry. For example, Citicorp is the second largest bank in the country while Metropolitan Life is the second largest insurance company.

[b]Continental Corporation is usually classified as a diversified financial institution and not as an insurance company.

tutions even though it is not a BOD interlock. Another typical example would be where the *same individual* was a BOD member for one of the Core institutions while simultaneously serving on another Core institution's—say, for illustrational purposes—International Advisory Committee.

On the average, each Core corporation has five direct intra-Core interlocks (BOD and non-BOD combined) and four direct BOD intra-Core interlocks with the other Core institutions. As illustration, New York Life has one director who is also a director for Citicorp, three directors who are also directors for Manufacturers Hanover (Manny-Hanny), one director who is a director for J.P. Morgan, and finally, two directors who are also directors for Chemical Bank. In addition, one of the three BOD interlocks with Manny-Hanny is Manny-Hanny's Chief Executive Officer, while New York Life's Chief Executive Officer is a director for J.P. Morgan. In other words, whenever New York Life has a BOD meeting, directors from Chemical, J.P. Morgan, Manny-Hanny, and Citicorp are present. In all, seven directors from four banks are on New York Life's BOD. Conversely, whenever J.P. Morgan has a BOD meeting, Prudential, Metropolitan Life, New York Life, and Continental Corporation each have one director present. In essence, then, the banks have *intra*locked the insurance companies, while the insurance companies have *intra*locked the banks. It is noteworthy that seven of the twelve companies have senior operating officers who are BOD members for other Core institutions. For instance, both Metropolitan Life's and New York Life's Chief Executive officers are on Chase Manhattan's BOD.

A careful examination of Table 6 will reveal many different patterns of intralocking relationships among the Core institutions.

Indirect Directorship Interlocks

As important as these direct *intra-Core* interlocks may be in illustrating one of the CPC's primary structural characteristics, the *indirect directorship interlocks* (IDI) between and among the CPC institutions within the corporate boardrooms of other non-Core institutions are, especially within the CPSP context, of much greater significance. It is important for purposes of clarity to maintain a distinction between the two concepts—direct BOD intralocks and indirect directorship interlocks. The former signifies a connection involving only CPC institutions, while the latter connotes an interlock that involves two or more CPC institutions, each of which has one or more of its directors sitting on the board of a third, non-Core corporation. As illustration of the IDI, consider the following:

Table 6. *Total and Individual Core Institutional Breakdown of the* Intracore, *Direct BOD Interlocks and the Direct Non-BOD Institutional Interlocks (II) between and among the Twelve Core Financial Institutions, as of January, 1978.*

Interlocks	*Total Interlocks*	*Direct (BOD and Non-BOD) Interlocks Between Each of the Core Institutions*												*Total Interlocks*
Industries and Corporations	*II and BOD*[a]	*CIT*	*CMB*	*MH*	*JP*	*CB*	*CIC*	*FC*	*PL*	*ML*	*EL*	*NYL*	*CC*	*BOD*[b]
A. BANKING														
1. Citicorp	4									D,F	D	D		4
2. Chase Manhattan Corp.	8					2A	A			D	2D		2D	5
3. Manufacturers Hanover Corp.	7*											2,D*	3D,O	7*
4. J.P. Morgan and Company	4								D	D		D	D	4
5. Chemical New York Corp.	8		2A						A	2D	A	2D		4
6. Continental Illinois Corp.	3		A							A	D			1
7. First Chicago Corp.	0													0

B. INSURANCE								
8. Prudential Insurance Co.	2				D	A		1
9. Metropolitan Life	7*	O,F	*		D	2D	A	6*
10. Equitable Life Assurance	5*	D	D,*			A	D	4*
11. New York Life	7*	D		3D	*	2D		7*
12. Continental Corp.	7*		2D	3D,*	D			7*

SOURCE: Moody's *Financial Manual*, 1979.

[a] The number of interlocks in the column "Total Interlocks II and BOD" may differ from the number in "Total Interlocks BOD" column since the former column includes both BOD and Non-BOD interlocks. For example, an individual may be a BOD member for one Core institution and also be on another Core institution's international advisory committee. This would constitute an institutional interlock (II) but not an interlock between the two institutions' boards of directors. Another example would be where a member of one Core institution's board had a relative who was a member of another Core institution's senior operating management but was not on its board of directors.

[b] See a above.

SYMBOLS: D=Board of Directors; O=Officer and board member; *=Chief Executive Officer and board member; A=Institutional interlock, but not a BOD interlock (see Footnote A); F=Family BOD interlock—for example, a father and son each sitting on the board of different Core institutions. When a number appears before a symbol, such as "3D," "2A," etc., it signifies the actual number of whatever type of interlock is indicated.

CAUTION: To interpret symbols correctly, read from left to right and then up. For example, Metropolitan Life's * (Chief Executive Officer) is a member of Chase's board.

Chase Manhattan Bank — "X" and "Y" are on Chase's BOD
J.P. Morgan — "M," "N," and "D" are on Morgan's BOD
General Motors — "X," "Y," "M," "N," and "D" are on G.M.'s BOD

Since this example is factually accurate, when General Motors (G.M.) has a BOD meeting, Chase and J.P. Morgan have five directorships indirectly interlocked. It is significant to note that these five directorship interlocks occur in just *one* indirect institutional interlock (III). As is indicated in Table 7, Chase and J.P. Morgan have nine additional III's. Also, since each of the ten corporations in which these III's occur have around twelve BOD meetings annually, directors from Chase and J.P Morgan are in meetings with each other approximately 120 times per year—just through III's. Clearly, then, the data presented in Table 7 are indicative of both the volume and the variety of information and responsibilities shared by the directors of Chase and J.P. Morgan.[7]

The data in Table 7 also allow one to compute the average number of CPC directorships interlocked per each III. For example, Citicorp has a total of 134 IDI's with the other eleven CPC institutions. In turn, these 134 IDI's occur in twenty-nine III's. Therefore, on the average (134 divided by 29), there are 4.6 CPC directorships interlocked in each III.[8] In short, just through III's, Citicorp's directors are in approximately 348 meetings annually with other CPC directors, with approximately 4.6 CPC directors present. Clearly, the data in Tables 6 and 7 suggest that the 263 CPC directors are in *almost constant—that is, daily contact*. In any event, let us now turn our attention to the stock, debt, trustee, etcetera, *intra*-Core interlocks, which also exist in considerable abundance.

Stock, Debt, Trustee (Etcetera) Intra-Core Interlocks

The data presented in Table 8 illustrate that CPC institutions control significant amounts of each other's stock, as well as performing the functions of trustee, transfer agent, and registrar for each other. For the reader who has mastered the ideas and concepts developed in this and the preceding section, the meaning and significance of the data in Table 8 will be largely self-explanatory. A close examination of this information, however, will reveal several peculiarities and important comparative relationships that may prove helpful. First, the four insurance companies are "mutual" companies, and, as such, have no capital stock outstanding. Having no stock to be issued or to be bought and sold on the exchange, these companies have no need for the services of a registrar or transfer

Table 7. *Total and Individual Institutional Breakdowns of the Indirect Directorship Interlocks (IDI) and Indirect Institutional Interlocks (III) Occurring Between and Among the Twelve Core Institutions—Within the Corporate Boardrooms of the Non-Core Institutions, as of January, 1978.*[a]

Industries and Corporations	*Total Interlocks*												
	IDI-III	*CIT*	*CMB*	*MH*	*JP*	*CB*	*CIC*	*FC*	*PL*	*ML*	*EL*	*NYL*	*CC*
A. BANKING													
1. Citicorp	134–29		11	11	14	14	4	3	8	5	2	2	4
2. Chase Manhattan Corp.	129–30	11		13	10	10	6	6	4	6	1	7	4
3. Manufacturers Hanover Corp.	123–25	11	13		14	10	3	2	4	8	3	6	6
4. J.P. Morgan and Company	105–26	14	10	14		11	3	1	2	4	5	3	3
5. Chemical New York Corp.	121–26	14	10	10	11		4	3	4	3	7	2	5
6. Continental Illinois Corp.	74–16	4	6	3	3	4		10	1	3	1	0	2
7. First Chicago Corp.	84–19	3	6	2	1	3	10		2	4	0	1	2
B. INSURANCE													
8. Prudential Insurance Co.	57–12	8	4	4	2	4	1	2		3	2	0	3
9. Metropolitan Life	90–22	5	6	8	4	3	3	4	3		3	7	4
10. Equitable Life Assurance	51–12	2	1	3	5	7	1	0	2	3		3	3
11. New York Life	65–17	2	7	6	3	2	0	1	0	7	3		5
12. Continental Corp.	69–14	4	4	6	3	5	2	2	3	4	3	5	

SOURCE: Moody's *Bank and Financial Manual*, 1979; Moody's *Industrial Manual*, 1979; and Standard and Poor, *Million Dollar Directory*, 1979.

[a] The numbers represent indirect directorship interlocks among the Core institutions that are accounted for solely through interlocks with the other non-Core institutions.

Table 8. ***Total Number of Indirect Directorship Interlocks (IDI), Indirect Institutional Interlocks (III), Direct BOD* Intra-*core Interlocks, the Percentage of Each Core Institution's (1) BOD's Intralocked, (2) Stock and Debt Intralocked and/or Controlled by Other Core Institutions; and the Trustee, Transfer Agent, and Registrar* Intra-core *Interlocks, as of 1 January 1978.***

	IDI's, III's, Direct BOD Intra-Core Interlocks; Numerical Size of Each Institution's BOD; and Percent Intralocked				*Minimum Stock and Debt Holdings Intralocked*		*Trustee (TR)*		*Transfer Agent (TA)*		*Registrar (R)*	
Industries and Corporations	*IDI-III*	*Direct BOD*	*Number on Board*	*BOD's Intralocked (Percent)*	*Stock (Percent)*	*Debt[d] (Percent)*	*Number of Bond Issues*	*CPC as (TR)*	*Total Number*	*CPC as (TA)*	*Total Number*	*CPC as (R)*
BANKING												
1. Citicorp	134–29	4	29	14	14.2	4.4[d]	7	0	3	0	2	1
2. Chase	129–30	5	27	19	6.1	1.0	4	4	1	0	Co.[c]	
3. Manny-Hanny	123–25	7*	20	35*	16.9	1.0	6	2	2	1	2	2
4. J.P. Morgan	105–26	4	22	18	14.7	6.2	4	2	1	1	Co.[c]	
5. Chemical	121–26	4	23	17	8.4	14.4	6	6	1	0	Co.[c]	
6. Continental Ill.	74–16	1	20	5	12.1	4.7	3	0	2	1	1	1
7. First Chicago	84–19	0	24	0	21.3	4.3	3	0	2	1	1	1
INSURANCE												
8. Prudential Life	57–12	1	24	4	NA[b]	NA[b]	NA[b]		NA[b]		NA[b]	
9. Metropolitan Life	90–22	6*	25	24*	NA	NA	NA		NA		NA	
10. Equitable Life	51–12	4*	32	12*	NA	NA	NA		NA		NA	
11. New York Life	65–17	7*	24	29*	NA	NA	NA		NA		NA	
12. Continental Corp.	69–14	7*	18	39*	11.3	1.5	0	0	3	2	3	1

SOURCE: Moody's *Bank and Finance Manual*, 1979; and Securities and Exchange Commission forms 13F.

[b]NA = Not applicable.

[c]These companies act as their own registrar.

[d]Debt statistics are limited to the debt held by the insurance companies and were taken from each company's annual *Schedule of Investments.*

agent. Second, the debt statistics would appear to indicate that the debt instrument is not used as a significant intra-Core interlocking tie. This may be an erroneous conclusion, however, since the data presented do not include any debt held by the banks. The insurance companies annually publish a detailed investment portfolio, showing every government and private institution to which they have loaned monies, including the amount, rate of interest, and due date. On the other hand, no information on bank loans was obtainable. The debt statistics, therefore, are incomplete and must be viewed as such. The trustee data, though, may be viewed tentatively as criteria indicating the closeness between and among the banks in their debtor relationships. Chemical Bank, for example, has six debt instruments outstanding, and, in all six instances, other Core banks act as the trustee for Chemical's bond indenture.

Third, one Core institution, First Chicago, does not have any direct BOD intra-Core interlocks. But, it is also the only bank in which the Core institutions, as a group, control more than 20 percent of the common stock. This points up the relevance of (1) viewing each of the interstitial elements individually, and then (2) doing a comparative analysis. In other words, while each of the interstitial elements—from a structural standpoint—are important bonding agents, *each* specific corporation and industry must be analyzed to determine which particular interstitial element is the most significant for that particular corporation or industry.

Finally, the statistics on stock holdings must also be viewed tentatively. As with bonds, the insurance companies publish an annual, detailed investment portfolio showing every institution in which they hold stock, including the number of shares and their market value. Likewise, banks that belong to the Federal Reserve System are required at the end of each year to submit to the Securities and Exchange Commission a list detailing every institution in which the bank's trust department has stock holdings, including the number of shares and their market value. The data on stock presented in Table 8 were computed primarily from these two sources and, as such, do *not* include, for the most part: (1) stock that individual BOD members within the Core may own personally or control through foundations; (2) stock held by the banks in custodial or corporate trust accounts over which the banks normally do not exercise any investment or voting authority; (3) convertible subordinated debentures that may readily be converted to common stocks; or, finally, (4) stocks that non-Core corporations own in other non-Core corporations. In addition, many members of the country's wealthier families and/or financial elite are also CPC board members, and the combined total of their personal stock holdings is undoubtedly quite significant in and of itself.

Nonetheless, there is no systematic procedure for finding this information. The limited data presented on Core family stock holdings were obtained largely from newspaper articles and business-type publications that occasionally mention such facts. As a case in point, in Table 9, there is a partial listing of stock owned by the Rockefeller family that was published in a 1974 *New York Times* article. For instance, the Rockefeller family

Table 9. ***Amount and Percent of Shares Outstanding of Stock Held by the Rockefeller Family, in Selected Corporations within the Master Planning Model, as of 1974.***

Company	*Amount of Stock Held (In Shares)*	*Percent of Shares Outstanding*
1. Chase Manhattan Corporation	429,959	1.3
2. Eastern Airlines	925,000	4.7
3. Mobil Corporation	1,762,206	1.74
4. Standard Oil of California	3,410,148	2.0
5. Allis Chalmers	430,000	3.45
6. Aluminum Company of America	405,783	1.2
7. Exxon	2,288,171	1.02
8. Merck & Company, Inc.	455,100	.61
9. Monsanto Company	213,273	.64
10. Texas Instruments	203,900	.90
11. Eastman Kodak	535,973	.49
12. International Business Machines (IBM)	384,042	.26
13. General Electric	509,952	.29
14. Minnesota Mining and Manufacturing	221,700	.20
15. Kresge	336,800	.28

SOURCE: *New York Times*, 4 December 1974, p. 29.

owns more than two percent of the common stock of Eastern Airlines, Standard Oil Company (California), and Allis-Chalmers, and between one and two percent of the common stock of Exxon, Aluminum Company of America, Mobil Corporation, and the Chase Manhattan Corporation. The CPC consists of 263 individuals, many of whose names (Rockefeller, Goelet, Grace, DuPont, Hewlett, Ingersoll, Milliken, Hillman, Prince, Hatfield, Houghton, McCormick, etcetera) are synonymous for American industry. The stocks owned by these individuals and their families (often held by bank trust departments in custodial accounts) must be taken into consideration when one tries to determine the percentage of stock actually controlled by the CPC. Indeed, to say that the CPC's stockholdings as presented in this study are probably less than half of their actual stockholdings is no doubt a very conservative estimate. As illustration, if just forty people owned one-fourth of one percent of the common stock of a corporation, they would, as a group, control ten percent of the corporation's stock.

Yet, it is most important to understand that vast personal wealth and/ or stock ownership is not as significant a factor in the importance of stock as a structural and functional planning instrument as is being a CPC member. Just within the trust departments of the six Core banks, CPC members control approximately $100 billion in stockholdings (see Table 5).

When one carefully examines the entire web of direct and indirect *intra*locks (director, stock, debt, trustee, etcetera) among the Core institutions, a very clear structural reality emerges. Indeed, a conscious recognition of these structural interdependencies and shared responsibilities would necessitate a high degree of cooperation by the participants. Both logically and practically, for CPC members to act as if these interdependencies did not exist would be highly irrational.

In turn, a conscious awareness of these interdependencies would almost automatically contribute to a great deal of intra- and inter-industry coordination and cooperation, that is, to CPSP. The argument in brief is that structure begets behavior, that the particular structure in question begets coordination and cooperation, and lastly that when coordination and cooperation reach a certain level, it is perhaps more accurate to describe and explain the economy as CPSP as opposed to its more traditional conception as a competitive market system.

Some Final Observations

Within the Veblenian frame of reference, CPSP in the United States may appropriately be viewed as the provisional end result of an evolutionary process. As advances in the industrial system's technologically based production processes made it possible to concentrate administrative control over the country's key industries in fewer and fewer hands, corporate leaders simply adapted traditional ideas and concepts of business enterprise to create a centralized management process. In a very real sense, the CPC's planning instruments are simply modifications of traditional business devices (boards of directors, stocks, bonds, etcetera)—modifications made in such a way as to *simulate*, from an administrative perspective, the concentration, or consolidation, that technological advances made possible in the country's production processes. After all, in a society that has enshrined the values of laissez-faire, self-interest, and profit maximization, one would quite naturally expect corporate leaders to take full advantage of the entire spectrum of administrative and technological possibilities available for maximizing their personal power and prerogatives. Stated somewhat differently, CPSP may be viewed as the evolutionary end result of entrepreneurs creating, *albeit unconsciously*, the most centralized administrative and production system possible, given existing technology, because of their entirely *conscious, logical, and rational* pursuit of monetary gain, or profit.

Nonetheless, to say that the use of *some* modern technologies in an efficient manner necessitates, is conducive to, or merely permits a form of centralized economic planning does *not* prejudge what specific form or type of planning process per se a society will, or should, adopt—or indeed, into whose hands the planning process should be entrusted. For example, President Franklin D. Roosevelt once commented on economic planning within business enterprise as follows:

> The liberty of a democracy is not safe if the people tolerate the growth of private power to a point where it becomes stronger than their democratic state itself. . . . The power of a few to manage the economic life of the Nation must be diffused among the many or be transferred to the public and its democratically responsible government. If prices are to be managed and administered, if the Nation's business is to be allotted by plan and not by competition, that power should *not* be vested in any private group or cartel, however benevolent.[9]

Unfortunately, in America, the real choices made possible by our technological knowledge have been circumscribed by, or encapsulated within, our capitalistic ideology and, in particular, by the values of self-interest, profit maximization, and laissez faire.

Quite frequently, authors (especially if their work has an iconoclastic bent) are reminded by their peers of the widely accepted belief in the author's responsibility to provide the community with possible solutions or courses of action for dealing with the problems and concerns addressed in their writings. The simple fact is that, given the dichotomy between our current beliefs and ideas about economics and power, and the realities of economics and power in our society, there is no viable solution to our economic problems. Existing economic theories (neo-classical, Keynesian, Marxist, or the so-called and currently fashionable Supply-Side Economics) concerning the causes of inflation, unemployment, pollution, a carcinogenic food supply, maldistribution of income, inadequate health care for the poor, retarded economic growth, etcetera, are woefully devoid of adequate insight or understanding of the economy's dominant structural and functional characteristics. Of course, theories based on false assumptions, however rational or logical, cannot provide a foundation for effective and responsible private or public decision making. Let there be no mistake. Orthodox economic theories and beliefs, whether of the left or of the right, have become part of the problem, rather than helping organize our thoughts and discussions so as to provide realistic, workable solutions to our problems.

If I am correct in asserting that we must eliminate the dichotomy between our currently held economic beliefs and economic reality as a *necessary precondition* to finding solutions to our increasingly serious economic maladies, then the starting point for developing such solutions is quite clear. In brief, it is long past time for our country's leaders to stop all the self-serving ideological prattle about the Welfare State, Socialism, and Capitalism and, instead, take a long hard look at the economy's dominant structural and functional characteristics. If we do not do this, the nation's economic problems will, no doubt, increasingly disrupt society's basic social fabric. Fundamental reforms are now absolutely essential. Fundamental reforms that are not soundly based on the economy's structural and functional realities, however, no matter how well intentioned the reformers may be, will simply not work. Therefore, *the only* starting point that makes any sense at all is for the United States Congress to commission a comprehensive and detailed study of the economy's structural and functional characteristics. Obviously such a study must be completely nonpartisan. Also, those conducting the study must be granted the legal powers to gain access to all the relevant materials.

Penultimately, it is the firm and unequivocal belief of this writer that three of the most fundamental lessons to be learned from history are: that evolutionary economic reform predicated on real world, concrete technological realities and based upon sound technological/instrumental reasoning have in the past and can in the future lead to a better world for all; that reforms predicated on ideological world views inevitably lead to either a leftist or rightist authoritarian or totalitarian society; and that a society that clings to outmoded political and religious forms as well as to a nonrational conservatism will not long endure as a vibrant and dynamic society. The creation of the CPSP theory is a modest attempt to provide the community with an alternative, more accurate description and explanation of the economic system's dominant structural and functional characteristics. The lack of an alternative explanation of the market system or competitive capitalism mirage is a major—if not the primary—impediment to fashioning an *effective* rational debate (as opposed to mere sophistry) on the nation's social, political, and economic problems. As long as the economic community continues to adhere to the notion that a competitive market system actually exists, *effective* rational debate and solutions to the country's increasingly disruptive economic problems will not be forthcoming. It is hoped that the CPSP theory will be of some benefit to the economic community in beginning a debate on the economy's structural and functional realities. As stated earlier in this essay, Thorstein Veblen once noted that "history records more frequent and more spectacular instances of the triumph of imbecile institutions over life and culture than of peoples who have by force of instinctive insight saved themselves alive out of a desperately precarious institutional situation."[10]

Notes

1. In my forthcoming book, *The Transformation of American Capitalism: From Competitive Market Structure to Centralized Private Sector Planning*, I present a central planning tableau that includes 138 corporations segregated into thirty-two industries. The industries included, in addition to those presented in this paper are: Motor Vehicles, Heavy Industrial Machinery and Farm Equipment, Tires and Tubes, Iron and Steel, Aluminum, Copper Metal Containers, Soft Drinks (Syrups), Canned Soups, Dairy Products, Breakfast Cereal Preparation, Soaps and Detergents, Cigarettes, Drugs (Ethical), Film and Photo Finishing Supplies, Hospital Medical Supplies & Equipment, Computers, Mini Computers & Electronic Calculators, Photocopying, Industrial Chemicals, Heavy Electrical Equipment, Television Broadcasting, Telecommunication Equipment & Service, and Electric Utilities.
2. As a purely prophylactic exercise, it may be beneficial to state the quintuplet schematic of Veblen's dichotomy in Veblen's own words:

> The material framework of modern civilization is the industrial system, and the directing force which animates this framework is business enterprise. Its characteristic features, and at the same time the forces by virtue of which it dominates modern culture, are the machine process and investment for a profit.
>
> * * *
>
> In order to achieve an efficient working of this industrial process at large, the various constituent sub-processes must work in due coordination throughout the whole. . . . The higher the degree of development reached by a given industrial community . . . and the more fully a given industry has taken on the character of a mechanical process, and the more extensively and closely it is correlated in its work with other industries that precede or follow it in the sequence of elaboration, the more urgent, other things being equal, is the need of maintaining the proper working relations with these other industries. . . . This mechanical concatenation of industrial processes makes for

solidarity in the administration of any group of related industries, and more remotely it makes for solidarity in the management of the entire industrial traffic of the community.

* * *

The economic welfare of the community at large is best served by a facile and uninterrupted interplay of the various processes which make up the industrial system at large; but the pecuniary interests of the business men in whose hands lies the discretion in the matter are not necessarily best served by an unbroken maintenance of the industrial balance. . . . Great and many are the items of service to be set down to the business man's account in connection with the organization of the industrial system, but when all is said, it is still to be kept in mind that his work in the correlation of industrial processes is chiefly of a permissive kind. His furtherance of industry is at the second remove, and is chiefly of a negative character. In his capacity as business man he does not go creatively into the work of perfecting mechanical processes and turning the means at hand to new or larger uses. That is the work of the men who have in hand the devising and oversight of mechanical processes. The men in industry must first create the mechanical possibility of such new and more efficient methods and correlations, before the business man sees the chance, makes the necessary business arrangements, and gives general directions that the contemplated industrial advance shall go into effect. The period between the time of earliest practicability and the effectual completion of a given consolidation in industry marks the interval by which the business man retards the advance of industry.

* * *

So long as related industrial units are under different business managements, they are, by the nature of the case, at cross-purposes, and business consolidation remedies this untoward feature of the industrial system by eliminating the pecuniary element from the interstices of the system as far as may be. The interstitial adjustments of the industrial system at large are in this way withdrawn from the discretion of rival business men, and the work of pecuniary management previously involved is in large part dispensed with, with the result that there is a saving of work and an avoidance of that systematic mutual hindrance that characterizes the competitive management of industry. To the community at large the work of pecuniary management, it appears, is less serviceable the more there is of it. The heroic role of the captain of industry is that of a deliverer from an excess of business management. It is a casting out of business men by the chief of business men.

* * *

But the discipline of the machine process cuts away the spiritual, institutional foundations of business enterprise; the machinery industry is incompatible with its continued growth; it cannot, in the long run, get along with the machine process. In their struggle against the

> cultural effects of the machine process, therefore, business principles cannot win in the long run; since an effectual mutilation or inhibition of the machine system would gradually push business enterprise to the wall; whereas with a free growth of the machine system business principles would presently fall into abeyance.

These quotes are from Veblen's *The Theory of Business Enterprise* (New York: Charles Scribner & Sons, 1904; reprint ed.: Clifton, N.J.: Augustus N. Kelley, 1975), pp. 1, 16–17; 27–45, 48–49, 374.

3. See U.S. Congress, House, Staff Report for the Subcommittee on Domestic Finance, Committee on Banking and Currency, *Commercial Banks and Their Trust Activities*, H. Dept., 90th Congress, 2d Session, 8 July 1968, p. 2.
4. See *The Role and Composition of the Board of Directors of the Large Publicly Owned Corporations* (New York: The Business Roundtable, January 1978), pp. 9–11.
5. "Rockefeller Family Holdings Touch Every Economic Sphere," *The Washington Post*, 13 September 1974, p. A5.
6. A partial listing of the services that wholesale banks provide corporations reveals a veritable collage of informational conduits—informational conduits that, provided over a long period of time, further strengthen and add an additional dimension to the planning process. David Leinsdorf and Donald Etra, in their book *Citibank* (New York: Grossman, 1973), supply the following list of services that most wholesale banks routinely provide to corporations:

> equity financing advice; arranges for the presentation and clearance of drafts by collecting checks, drafts with securities attached, acceptances, coupons for bills, dividend warrants, documentary and clean drafts, etcetera; purchases commercial paper and banker's acceptances for clients; acts as agent for the exchange of securities in reorganizations and mergers; collects bond coupons on called and due bonds; gives out credit information; transfers funds by mail, wire, and telephone; works with freight forwarders to assist clients in collecting from their customers; acts as escrow agent; does old-line factoring and accounts receivables financing; purchases conditional sales contracts, chattel mortgages, and leases; processes and collects freight bills; collects customers' interest and principal on bonds issued by corporations; maintains bondholders' ledgers; audits and countersigns stock certificates as registrar; provides vault space; documents, prepares, and delivers stock certificates; maintains shareholders' lists and ledgers; prepares and mails cash and stock dividends; prepares meetings and mails proxies; assists at shareholders' meetings and mails reports to shareholders; prepares, issues, and forwards subscription warrants to shareholders; buys and lends against receivables; advises on the money markets and issues certificates of deposit; acts as trustee for corporate securities; transfers and delivers share certificates; acts as a depository of public money by receiving from corporations manufacturers' excise taxes and employees' with-

holding taxes; issues commercial and travelers letters of credit; advises on foreign trade and banking; receives deposits and makes loans through overseas branches; quotes exchange rates on foreign currencies; provides complete payroll services; acts as a clearinghouse for capital investors and merger-minded companies; conducts cash flow studies; and finally, provides corporations with overall financial planning advice and introductions to additional sources of capital. (Pp. 77–78.)

By providing a corporation with all these services, one would undoubtedly develop an in-depth understanding of the corporation. It is also just as apparent that, over several decades, these additional working relationships would further strengthen the strong ties that already exist as a result of the presence of BOD, stock, and debt intra- and interlocking ties.

7. The twelve CPC institutions, as a group, have 263 BOD members. On the average, each director holds four directorship positions within the 138 corporations included in the Planning Tableau presented in my forthcoming book (see note 2). This would indicate that each individual was responsible for attending approximately fifty BOD meetings per year.
8. A word of caution is in order concerning the interpretation of the data in Table 8. The III's between, say, Citicorp and each of the other eleven institutions will *not* produce the same total that appears in the "Total III" column. Summing these data would amount to double counting. Assume, for instance, that Citicorp, Chase, Manny-Hanny, and Prudential each have *one* direct BOD interlock with G.M. On the one hand, Citicorp and Chase have an III at G.M., Citicorp and Manny-Hanny have an III at G.M., and Citicorp and Prudential have an III at G.M. On the other hand, G.M. counts as only *one* III between Citicorp and the other CPC institutions, *not three*.
9. U.S. Congress, Temporary National Economic Committee, *Investigation of Concentration of Economic Power*, Part I: "Economic Prologue" (Washington, D.C.: U.S. Government Printing Office, 1939), pp. 85–90.
10. Thorstein Veblen, *The Instincts of Workmanship* (New York: The Macmillan Company, 1914; reprint ed.: New York: The Viking Press, 1946), p. 25.

14

Political and Policy Implications of Centralized Private Sector Planning

John Munkirs and Michael Ayers

You have to start with a realization that the country is principally run by big business for the rich. Maybe you have to live in Washington to know that and maybe everyone in the country knows it intuitively, I don't know, but a government of the people, by the people, and for the people, has become, I think, a government of the people, certainly, but by the corporations and for the rich.[1]

Nicholas Johnson, former
commissioner, Federal
Communications Commission

Many government officials who clamor for economic deregulation and the softening of antitrust law enforcement do not, by and large, consciously believe themselves to be acting as corporate agents. Instead, they sincerely believe that their position logically follows from their commitment to the *economic principle* of laissez faire and free private enterprise. In turn, those who believe in laissez faire *cannot* be expected to use the policing power of government as a countervailing force against corporate interest on behalf of the general public.[2] This inability of government officials to envision government institutions as a countervailing force in the public interest may quite appropriately be labeled Ideological Self-Encapsulation.

This encapsulation is viewed by those in power in the private sector as a trait to be sought in those who seek public office and are to receive campaign support. Using this characteristic as a selection criterion whenever possible ensures the choice of government officials who have (1) a strong commitment to the free enterprise mythology, and (2) a strong sensitivity to the working environment desired by business enterprise interests. This "encapsulated mentality" is important to the corporate interest, not only in the executive branches of government, but in the so-called "fourth branch of government" (regulatory commissions) as well. These regulatory commissions and departments within the government's executive branch have primary responsibility for carrying out and enforcing the laws passed by the legislative branch. In turn, regulatory commissioners and executive branch department secretaries are themselves never required to stand for election before the people.

Periodically in our country's history, "grass roots" pressures have given rise to the passage of legislation that, if enforced, would have made it impossible for an institutional arrangement such as the Central Planning Core (CPC) (identified in the article by John Munkirs, above) to exist. It would not be unduly harsh, however, to argue that the government's enforcement efforts regarding such legislation, especially in relationship to the Centralized Private Sector Planning (CPSP) corporate institutions, have been little more than an elaborate charade. Certainly, one should not expect department secretaries and regulatory commissioners who are strongly committed either to a laissez faire philosophy or to the notion that the best decisions are those made in the private sector to vigorously enforce laws and regulations that would hurt the interests of business enterprise. Nor should it be doubted that the corporate community has been successful—especially since the 1890s—in ensuring that these positions are staffed with individuals with strong laissez faire convictions.

The corporate community, primarily under the leadership of CPC members, has pursued its governmental policy influence-peddling through the establishment of private organizations that operate (1) as organizational vehicles for creating a consensus among the country's political, intellectual, and business elite over major public policy issues; (2) as informational conduits for relating such decisions to the proper private and governmental bodies and, if deemed appropriate, to the general public; and (3) as screening mechanisms for potential candidates for public office on the one hand and as a means of having themselves appointed to the more important government advisory committees on the other. The "private" organizations they engendered may be categorized as Private-Public

Policy Formulating Committees on International Affairs and as Private-Public Formulating Committees on Domestic Affairs.

Political Implications of Centralized Private Sector Planning

Private-Public Policy Formulating Committees on International Affairs

There are two major committees that have significant shaping influence on the government's policies in international affairs—the Council on Foreign Relations (CFR) and the Trilateral Commission (TC). Much work has historically been done on the influence of the CFR.[3] Hence, the focus of this paper is on the constitution and activities of the TC.

David Rockefeller, a CPC member, founded this particular commission in 1973 and appointed Zbigniew Brzezinski as its first director. Rockefeller's principal purpose in establishing this committee was to create an organization that would bring together more than 200 distinguished "citizens" from the democratic industrialized nations—North America, Western Europe and Japan. These leaders develop policies that address the political and economic problems facing the industrial democracies. As stated in a Trilateral Commission pamphlet:

> The Trilateral Commission is a policy-oriented organization. Based on analysis of major issues facing North America, Western Europe, and Japan, the Commission has sought to develop practicable proposals for joint action. . . . The renovation of the international system is . . . a task of global as well as trilateral dimensions, and the work of the Commission, as evidenced in its meetings and reports, has moved accordingly. . . . The renovation of the international system will be a very prolonged process. The system shaped after World War II was created through an act of will and human initiative in a relatively restricted period of time. One power had overwhelming might and influence, and others were closely associated with it. In contrast, a renovated international system will now require a process of creation—much longer and more complex—in which prolonged negotiations will have to be initiated and developed. In nurturing habits and practices of working together among the trilateral regions, the Commission should help set the context for these necessary efforts.[4]

In essence, during the post-World War II period, the economies of these three regions had become so interdependent that many CPC members became convinced that coordination of policies, among and between the regions, was necessary. The Commission conducts a portion of its affairs through plenary meetings every nine months, at which it considers reports from Commission task forces.

> Task force work is at the center of the Policy Program of the Commission. At the core of each task force are rapporteurs from each of the three regions. In the course of their work the rapporteurs are likely to draw on a wide range of consultants, including Commission members and others. The final stage for each task force, before publication of its report, is discussion of the report by the full Commission or its Executive Committee. The Commission or Executive Committee may then use the reports in issuing recommendations of its own, as has been done on a number of occasions.[5]

In 1973, the Commission issued a task force report entitled "Towards a Renovated World Monetary System (1973)." The TC's North American rapporteur on the task force that wrote this report was Yale University Professor of Economics Richard N. Cooper. Subsequently, Cooper became U.S. Under Secretary of State for Economic Affairs. One recommendation in this particular report was to coordinate the sale of government-held gold to private markets, with the profits to be used for assisting underdeveloped countries. This was "partially realized" when the International Monetary Fund, in mid-1977, instituted such a policy.

The work of these rapporteurs has been buttressed within the formal structure of the U.S. government by CPC members' work on critical advisory committees. For example, during this same year, the U.S. Department of the Treasury's Advisory Committee on Reform of the International Monetary System went to work. This committee had nineteen members, five from the CPC and a sixth from a firm heavily tied to the Core. During this same period, the U.S. Department Advisory Committee for Multilateral Trade Negotiations met. Of the twenty-two members of that committee, six were CPC members. Four others were from companies heavily tied to the core. These ten members represented fifteen institutional ties (see Table 1).

In 1976, the Commission issued a task force report that was to dovetail with the above-mentioned work, entitled "The Reform of International Institutions." C. Fred Bergston, then a senior fellow at the Brookings Institution, was the North American rapporteur for this particular report. Subsequently, Mr. Bergston was appointed Assistant Secretary of the Treasury for International Affairs.

"The Crisis of International Cooperation" was a task force report issued in 1974 by the Commission. This report "sought to clarify the present historical situation, and supplies an underlying rationale for trilateral cooperation. . . . In broad strokes, the Trilateral Political Task Force

Table 1. ***CPC Representation on Two Foreign Affairs Advisory Committees, 1977.***

Advisory Committee/ Core Member's Name	*Institution(s) Represented*	*Committee Size*	*Core Ties*	
			Directorship	*Institution*
Dept. of Treasury: *Advisory Committee on Reform of the International Monetary System*		19	6	7
David Rockefeller	CMB			
Gaylord Freeman	FC			
Walter Wriston	CIT			
Reginald Jones (CEO, Chrmn.)	GE			
Gabriel Hauge	MH, NYL			
Elmore Patterson	JP			
Dept. of Commerce: *Industry Policy Advisory Committee for Multilateral Trade Negotiations*		22	6	15
William Verity, Jr.	ARMCO Steel, CMB			
Walter Fallon	Eastman Kodak, JP			
Charles Pillird, Jr.	Goodyear Tire & Rubber, MH			
James Binger	Honeywell, CMB			
Brooks McCormick	International Harvester, FC			
William Sneath	Union Carbide, ML			
W. H. Krome George (CEO, Chrmn.)	ALCOA			
Jack Parker (Vice Chrmn., Ex. Ofcr.)	GE			
David Packard (Chrmn.)	Hewlett Packard			
William Allen	Boeing			

SOURCE: U.S. Senate, Subcommittee on Energy, Nuclear Proliferation, and Federal Services of the Committee on Governmental Affairs: *Federal Advisory Committees*, Washington, D.C. 95th Cong., 2d Session, 1978.

sketched the main political, economic, and social trends effecting a transformation of the postwar international system."[6]

The Task Force recommended the institutionalization of periodic "International Summit Meetings" between the heads of state of the various trilateral countries. Consequently, some summits were held. At the London Summit of 1977, the third such "summit meeting" between the trilateral countries' heads of state, Henry D. Owen, Director of Foreign Policy Studies at the Brookings Institution, member of the Trilateral Commission's executive committee, and the North American rapporteur for the report on the summit, was chosen to be the coordinator of the U.S. government's preparations for the meeting as well as the government's coordinator for post summit follow-ups. In commenting on the goals of the London Summit, Owen made the following remarks:

> I think the goals of the American Administration at the London Summit were the same as the purposes of most of the other governments present. I did not detect any marked difference in the purposes with which most of the seven national governments approached the Summit. They were anxious to try to concert their policies in areas where this made sense: first, domestic economic policy; second, the international balance of payments situation, international indebtedness, and related issues; third, the Tokyo Round Table trade negotiations; fourth, energy, both conventional and nuclear; and fifth, North-South relations. The participating governments felt that in these five areas it was useful to try to reach agreement on common policies or, at least, to concert their national policies.[7]

Here, then, are three rather straightforward examples where committees developed public policy positions and, subsequently, placed members in government positions directly related to the implementation of such policies and, also, where the TC coordinated its activities with formal Public Policy Advisory Committees within the Departments of Commerce and the Treasury.

In Table 2, there is a list of some of the Trilateral Commission's members who occupied significant policy making positions in the federal government during the Carter presidency. In 1973, Jimmy Carter was introduced to the Commission by J. Paul Austin; subsequently he became a TC member. Austin was also a member of J. P. Morgan and Company's Board of Directors and was Coca Cola's Chief Executive Officer. Need one be reminded that Coca Cola headquarters is in Atlanta, Georgia? When Carter was elected president, it was only natural and eminently reasonable that he turn to the Commission for many of his cabinet appointments. As stated by President Carter, "Membership on this Commission has provided me with a splendid learning opportunity, and many of the other members have helped me in my study of foreign affairs."[8] Quite simply, the President chose his appointees from a group of distinguished citizens whom he respected and with whom he had worked. He knew these individuals to be well acquainted with their business, intellectual, and political counter-

Table 2. ***Partial Listing of Trilateral Commission Members Who Occupied Significant Policy Making Positions in Government During the Carter Presidency.***

Name	*Government Position*
Jimmy Carter	President of the United States
Walter F. Mondale	Vice President of the United States
Harold Brown	Secretary of Defense
W. Michael Blumenthal	Secretary of Treasury
Anthony M. Solomon	Under Secretary of the Treasury for Monetary Affairs
Zbigniew Brzezinski	Assistant to President for National Security Affairs
Paul A. Volcker	Chairman, Federal Reserve Board
Cyrus R. Vance	Secretary of State
Warren Christopher	Deputy Secretary of State
Richard N. Cooper	Under Secretary of State for Economic Affairs
Richard Holbrooke	Assistant Secretary of State for East Asian and Pacific Affairs
Lucy Wilson Benson	Under Secretary of State for Security Assistance
Richard N. Gardner	Ambassador to Italy
Andrew Young	Ambassador to the United Nations
Paul C. Warnke	Director, Arms Control & Disarmament Agency; Chief Disarmament Negotiator
Gerard C. Smith	Ambassador at Large for Non-Proliferation Matters
Eliott L. Richardson	Ambassador at Large with Responsibility for U.N. Law of the Sea Conference
Robert R. Bowie	Deputy Director of Intelligence for National Estimates
Jean-Luc Pepin	Co-Chairman, Task Force on Canadian Unity
Sol Linowitz	Chief Negotiator, Panama Canal Treaty and Presidential Envoy to the Middle East

SOURCE: A Trilateral Commission membership list entitled "The Trilateral Commission," dated 31 December 1977. The Commission will send its membership list and a list of its various publications upon request.

parts among our international allies. These individuals also shared some of his own understandings of the world's growing and increasingly complex political and economic problems.

The Trilateral Commission's *raison d'etre* is perhaps best described by its founder and North American chairman, David Rockefeller, in a speech delivered to the Los Angeles World Affairs Council entitled "In Pursuit of a Consistent Foreign Policy": "In such an uncertain and turbulent climate . . . we must . . . work together *to help frame a foreign policy that best reflects the courage and commitment that are the cornerstones of this great nation*" (emphasis added).[9] In essence, Trilateral Commission members see their role as one of creating consensus among the international allies on commonly shared economic and political problems, taking public positions in their respective governments so as to participate in the policy implementation process, and developing political leaders for the U.S. government. The number of CPC representatives on both the CFR and the TC is presented in Table 3.

Private-Public Policy Formulating Committees on Domestic Affairs

In addition to their international affairs organizations, the country's corporate leaders have also created several policy formulating committees on domestic affairs. The most prominent of these are the Business Roundtable, the Conference Board, the Business Council, and the Committee for Economic Development. A discussion of each would take considerably more space than is feasible in this article; thus we will discuss only the Business Roundtable.

The Rountable was founded in 1972 and, by the close of the decade, had emerged as the most powerful, articulate, and informed business lobby in America. Membership in the Roundtable is limited to the chief executive officers of only 180 of the very largest corporate institutions. As stated in a Roundtable brochure entitled "The Business Roundtable":

> A principal strength of the Roundtable is the extent of participation by the chief executive officers of the member firms. Working in task forces on specific issues, they direct research, supervise preparation of position papers, recommend policy, and speak out on the issues. In this process, the Roundtable draws on the staffs of member companies for talent and expertise. Activities of the task force are reviewed by the Roundtable Policy Committee. *Position papers approved by that committee are circulated to members and to the government* and are made available for use in the public discussion of issues.[10] (Emphasis added.)

In 1977, Irving S. Shapiro, then chairman of the Roundtable's Policy Committee, E. I. DuPont's Chief Executive Officer, and a member of I.B.M.'s and Citicorp's Board of Directors, made the following comments in a Roundtable position paper:

> It was decided that one way business could be a more constructive force, and have more impact on government policymaking was to bring the chief executives directly into the picture. The Roundtable therefore was formed with two major goals:
> —to enable chief executives from different corporations to work together to analyze specific issues affecting the economy and business, and
> —to present government and the public with knowledgeable, timely

Table 3. ***Central Planning Core (CPC) Inter- and Intralocking Ties with Selected Private-Public Policy Formulating Committees on International Affairs, as of 1978.***

International Affairs Committees	*CPC Institutions*[1]												*Total Intralocks*	
	CIT	*CMB*	*MH*	*JP*	*CB*	*CIC*	*FC*	*PL*	*ML*	*EL*	*NYL*	*CC*	*Institutional*	*Individual*
Council on Foreign Relations	12	10	4	6	8	2	4	0	5	7	5	2	65	63[2]
Trilateral Commission	0	2	1	1	1	2	2	0	0	0	0	0	9	9

SOURCE: See Master Planning Model.

[1]CIT — Citicorp
CMB — Chase Manhattan Corporation
MH — Manufacturers Hanover
JP — J. P. Morgan and Company
CB — Chemical New York Corporation
CIC — Continental Illinois Corporation
FC — First Chicago Corporation
PL — Prudential Life
ML — Metropolitan Life
EL — Equitable Life
NYL — New York Life
CC — Continental Corporation

[2]On the Council on Foreign Relations, the 12 Core institutions have 63 individuals representing 65 Core directorships; that is, G. Hauge sits on the boards of directors of both Manufacturers Hanover and Metropolitan Life, while J. Holland sits on the boards of both Manufacturers Hanover and Continental Corporation.

> information, and with practical, positive suggestions for action ... *My own judgment is that the Roundtable is a success. It is doing what it was created to do. It has had a visible and direct effect on public policy and legislation in a number of cases.* . . . Leaders there have had a chance to test the information we have brought to them and they have found it credible and useful. Through the task force approach, the Roundtable has found a way to move rapidly when events call for fast action.[11] (Emphasis added.)

Others have also noticed the Roundtable's "visible and direct effect on public policy and legislation in a number of cases." As stated in the June 30, 1980 issue of *Fortune*:

> The Roundtable helped win a signal victory by defeating a bill for a consumer protection agency—in retrospect, a watershed in the history of consumerism.
>
> Then labor's efforts to occupy higher ground were beaten back. A bill that would have permitted a single striking union to picket an entire construction site, and another that would have made it easier for labor to organize non-union corporations, were both defeated. *The urging of the Roundtable and other groups also led to the rejection of central planning for the national economy*, put forward in an early version of the Humphrey-Hawkins bill (and now resurfacing in some proposals to re-industrialize America).[12] (Emphasis added.)

In 1978, the Business Roundtable's Policy Committee consisted of forty-five members, four of whom were designated as officers. As indicated in Table 4, twenty-five members, or 55.5 percent, of the Policy Committee's membership were also CPC members. As illustration, Citicorp had eight, Chase Manhattan, four, and J. P. Morgan and Company, six interlocks with the Roundtable's Policy Committee. CPC connections with each of the four major policy formulating committees are presented in Table 4.

Stated straightforwardly, after examining both the foreign affairs and domestic policy formulating committees, one is warranted in saying that Commissioner Nicholas Johnson's view, that is, a "government of the people, certainly, but by the corporation," is reality. Just as assuredly, as long as this remains true, the government itself will continue to play a key role in perpetuating the free enterprise mythology. Penultimately, and perhaps most importantly, as long as the general public continues to believe in and to elect and support the appointment of public officials who profess to believe in the *actual existence* of a market system economy, government institutions will continue to play a key role in perpetuating the mythology of markets.

Table 4. ***Central Planning Core (CPC) Inter- and Intralocks with Selected Private-Public Formulating Committees on Domestic Affairs, as of 1978.***

Domestic Affairs Committees	*CPC Institutions*[1]														*Total and Percent of Leadership Committee Intralocks with the CPC*	
	CIT	*CMB*	*MH*	*JP*	*CB*	*CIC*	*FC*	*PL*	*ML*	*EL*	*NYL*	*CC*	*Institutional*	*Individuals*	*Total Committee*	*Percent Interlocked*
Business Rountable	8	4	1	6	2	1	0	1	3	0	0	0	26	25	45	55.5
Business Council	6	0	1	0	1	1	0	1	0	0	0	0	10	10	19	52.6
Conference Board	5	2	1	1	0	1	1	1	2	0	0	1	15	14[2]	31	45.2
Committee for Economic Development	6	5	6	6	4	1	6	2	6	2	2	4	50	44[2]	207	21.2

SOURCE: See Central Planning Tableau

[1]CIT — Citicorp
CMB — Chase Manhattan Bank
MH — Manufacturers Hanover
JP — J.P. Morgan and Company
CB — Chemical New York Corporation
CIC — Continental Illinois Corporation
FC — First Chicago Corporation
PL — Prudential Life
ML — Metropolitan Life
EL — Equitable Life
NYL — New York Life
CC — Continental Corporation

[2]The Business Roundtable has one dual directorship interlock with the CPC; that is, R. C. Adams is on both J. P. Morgan's and Metropolitan Life's board of directors. The Committee for Economic Development has three such dual directorship interlocks.

Finally, and perhaps it should be stated explicitly, *both* the Republican and Democrat parties draw heavily from the Private-Public Policy Formulating Committees to staff key government positions. Review the examples given in Table 2 for the Carter presidency, and compare that data with the staffing choices of President Reagan, shown in Table 5.

Up to this point in the discussion we have attempted to show how the CPC, through public policy formulating committees, thwarts public policies and enhances private power by formulating the national agendas and setting the tone for national policy debates. We turn now to some specific assertions regarding the ability of the CPC to likewise lessen the effectiveness of stabilizing policies for the nation's economy and, in fact, thwart the use of traditional Keynesian policies as a countervailing force against private power.

Monetary and Fiscal Policy

At a time when oligopolistically competitive market structures had already become the dominant form of market structure in the economy, John Maynard Keynes constructed a macroeconomic analysis that provided government policy makers with both a theoretical justification and a set of practical tools for eliminating depressions, while simultaneously assuring stable and steady economic growth. Government policies based on traditional macroeconomic theories, however, no longer work. Just as Adam Smith's competitive market structures gave way to oligopolistically competitive market structures, oligopoly markets have given way to CPSP. Stated quite simply, theories predicated on a structural economic reality that, in fact, does not exist, *will not* work. For example, from a monetary policy perspective, in order to eliminate inflation by attempting to slow economic growth within the economy's CPSP sphere, the Federal Reserve Board would need to drive interest rates so tremendously high, or so severely constrict the money supply, or both, that many of the country's middle-sized businesses would literally be destroyed while unemployment would rise to the double digit level. How high, for instance, would the cost of capital (the interest rate) need to go to stop the CPC from *allocating* funds to, say, A.T. & T.? Consider the following: (1) Thirty-seven percent of A.T. & T.'s board members are CPC members; in addition, there are 102 IDI's and 200 III's. (2) The CPC has acted as the trustees for twenty-one of A.T. & T.'s twenty-three outstanding bond indentures, etcetera, etcetera. A.T. & T.'s present debt obligations are approximately $30 billion. In other words, while the cost of capital may be quite meaningful when a typical middle-sized business borrows money, it

Table 5. ***Partial List of Individuals from Prominent Private-Public Policy Formulating Committees on both Domestic and International Affairs, Appointed to Significant Policy Making Positions with the Government by President Reagan.***

Individual	*Government Position*	*Private-Public Formulating Committee**
George Bush	Vice President of U.S.	CFR and TC
Alexander Haig	Secretary of State (1980-82)	CFR
George P. Shultz	Secretary of State (1982)	BR, CFR and CED
Lawrence Eagleberger	Assistant Secretary of State for European Affairs	CFR
Myer Rashish	Assistant Secretary of State for Economic and Business Affairs	CFR
Philip C. Habib	Special Middle East Peace Envoy	CFR
Walter J. Stoessel	Under Secretary of State for Political Affairs	CFR
Caspar Weinberger	Secretary of Defense	TC
Frank Carlucci	Deputy Secretary of Defense	CFR
Fred C. Ikle	Under Secretary of Defense for Policy	CFR
John R. Lehman	Secretary of the Navy	CFR
Donald Regan	Secretary of Treasury	CFR, BR and CED
Malcolm Baldridge	Secretary of Commerce	CFR and BC
William Casey	Director, Central Intelligence Agency	CFR
A. W. Clausen**	Director, World Bank	BR, BC and CB
Murray Weidenbaum	Chairman, Council of Economic Advisors (1980-82)	CFR
Eugene V. Rostow	Director, Arms Control and Disarmament Agency	CFR
Bill Brock	Presidential Envoy, International Trade	TC and CFR
Arthur Burns	Ambassador to West Germany	CFR
Maxwell Rabb	Ambassador to Italy	CFR

*TC = Trilateral Commission; CFR = Council on Foreign Relations; BC = Business Council; BR= Business Roundtable; CB = Conference Board; CED = Council for Economic Development.

**Clausen was actually appointed by President Carter after the 1980 general elections with President-elect Reagan's consent and approval.

may not be so important from the point of view of the CPC allocating capital among non-Core corporations.

In other words, in many instances, the function of debt itself has evolved from being an instrument for "loaning money with the expectation of making a profit" to being an instrument for the "allocation of funds between institutions" administratively and financially tied to one another.

This, of course, diminishes the role of the interest rate as an allocation mechanism, which in turn diminishes the power of the Federal Reserve Board to use the cost of capital as a mechanism for fine tuning the economy. Therefore, increasingly high interest rates during this period did not directly reduce production, but rather, rates became so abnormally high as to decrease consumer credit purchases, which, in turn, decreased industrial production, with an excessive number of bankruptcies being the end result.

In turn, from a fiscal policy perspective two factors are noteworthy. First, the existence of the CPSP makes Gardiner Means's notion of administered prices more pertinent than most economists seem willing to admit.[13] In other words, corporate leaders, within the economy's CPSP sphere, interact and cooperate so closely that they can manipulate industry-wide supply in response to demand decreases within a given industry. Hence, prices may be either raised or maintained as demand decreases. Second, and perhaps most important, the centralization of vast sums of money within the structurally cohesive core financial group described above, has allowed the major industrial and retail sectors of the economy to create credit mechanisms (Visa, Mastercard, increased pay-back periods for loans, and check overdraft privileges) that tend to negate the effectiveness of combating inflation by cutting spending and manipulating tax rates.

In short, the CPC's ability to amass, control, and allocate vast sums of money, *for all practical purposes*, simply places the economy's CPSP sphere outside the purview of the traditional Keynesian analysis and tends to mute the possible effects of policies when endeavored. This is *not* to say, however, that monetary and fiscal policies have no effect on the economy, but rather, that as currently conceived and practiced such policies are insufficient as tools for bringing about full employment and a stable price level.

Concluding Observations

While the purpose in writing this article was *not* to set forth an elaborate and detailed set of policy recommendations, a few general observations will be offered. The primary generalized policy implication emanating from the CPSP analysis is the absolute necessity of developing a two-tiered approach in the formulation and application of governmental public policies: one tier is the CPSP sphere; the other tier is the non-CPSP sphere. Regardless of the specific area under consideration (environmental, foreign trade, price accountability, employment, and monetary or fiscal policy), following a two-tiered approach is imperative. Consider the following: the country has approximately 325,000 manufacturing concerns; the country's 500 largest manufacturers account for approximately 80 percent of all manufacturing sales, employ only 15 percent of the workforce, account for almost all of the significant price increases that make up the inflation index, and finally, are either members of or are significantly influenced by the economy's CPSP sphere.

To solve the stagflation dilemma, for example, within a two-tiered framework, the following policies are recommended: In regards to the economy's CPSP sphere, our government institutions should establish a Price Accountability Program while also pursuing deflationary monetary and fiscal policies; and in regards to the economy's non-CPSP sphere, our government institutions should pursue expansionary monetary and fiscal policies.

The specific content of any public policy enactment is, of course, as much a political matter as economic—as it should be. Nonetheless, if governmental public policies are to be effective in providing a climate wherein freedom of choice, economic efficiency, and economic justice remain relevant goals, economic reality must be our guide. And, CPSP, at this point in time, is the economy's dominant characteristic. Other specific recommendations could be made. However, until the dichotomy between our economic theories and our economic realities is widely recognized and made the basis for fresh analysis, all such recommendations based thereon may well be stillborn for lack of popular support.

Notes

1. ABC-TV, "Dick Cavett Show," 25 August 1969.
2. Government officials can generally be placed into one of three categories: (1) those who believe that government has a sizable and legitimate role in the political and economic affairs of a dynamic and democratic nation; (2) those who *believe* in traditional notions of laissez faire, free-enterprise and truly wish to see the role of government minimized and indeed eliminated in certain spheres of life; and (3) those who simply believe that all decisions should be made by those who hold power in the private sector rather than those in the public sector. Historically the justification for laissez faire and free enterprize has been closely associated with the acceptance of the notion of competitive market structures. While many in government have used laissez faire as a justification for arguing that decisions should be made in the private sector, the actual number of those falling into category (2) or (3) above is currently unascertainable in the

absence of an empirical examination. We know of no such current study that addresses this.

3. For an excellent study detailing the development of foreign policy within the Council on Foreign Relations and the subsequent adoption of these policies by our governmental foreign policy organizations, see: Laurence H. Shoup, "Shaping the Postwar World: The Council on Foreign Relations and United States War Aims During World War II," *The Insurgent Sociologist* 5 (Spring 1975): 9–52. Also see G. William Domhoff's *The Higher Circles* (New York: Vintage Books, 1971), pp. 112–55.
4. The Trilateral Commission, "The Industrialized Democratic Regions in a Changing International System" (New York: The Trilateral Commission, no date).
5. Ibid.
6. Ibid.
7. The Trilateral Commission, "Trialogue" (New York: The Trilateral Commission, N.A.), Winter 1977–78, no. 16, p. 1.
8. Jerry Flint, "What's a Trilateral Commission?" *Forbes*, 24 November 1980, p. 46.
9. David Rockefeller, "In Pursuit of a Consistent Foreign Policy" (speech before the Los Angeles World Affairs Council, Los Angeles, California, 10 April 1980).
10. "The Business Rountable," a brochure published by the Business Roundtable (200 Park Avenue, New York, N.Y. 10017), June 1979.
11. Irving S. Shapiro, "What is the Business Roundtable?" Roundtable position paper, 1977, pp. 2–4.
12. Walter Guzzardi, Jr., "A New Public Face for Business," *Fortune*, 30 June 1980, p. 49.
13. For an excellent and contemporary coverage of Gardiner Means's notion of administered prices, see *Administered Prices: A Compendium on Public Policy, U.S. Senate*, 88th Congress, 1st Session; also see John Blair, *Economic Concentration* (New York: Harcourt Brace Jovanovich, 1972).

15

Oligopolistic Cooperation: Conceptual and Empirical Evidence of Market Structure Evolution

John R. Munkirs
and
James I. Sturgeon

In this article we introduce the concept of oligopolistic cooperation based on structural intradependence, and propose it as a more accurate description of the industries that comprise the industrial core of the U.S. economy. Many economists agree that oligopoly is the most prevalent market structure in the United States and other industrialized countries.[1] This is especially true in finance, mining, and manufacturing. Even though the chief characteristics of oligopoly are "few" firms and psychological interdependence among these firms, it is usual to characterize their behavior as competitive, although not always via price. This characterization of their behavior suggests the name "oligopolistic competition."

Here we distinguish between oligopolistic competition and what we call oligopolistic cooperation.[2] Specifically, cooperation is intended to signify behavior that goes beyond coordination or "unconscious parallelism." And, while cooperation is similar to coordination in some respects, there are fundamental differences. The primary difference is that in oligopolistically cooperative industries specific, legally binding, quasi-permanent organizational structures exist. In turn this type of organizational structure provides not only the means but the necessity for cooperative behavior. Cooperative behavior, in turn, has profound implications for the *relevance* of micro and macro economic theory as well as public policy.

Oligopolistic Competition: The Standard View

Leading oligopoly theorists such as Fritz Machlup and E. H. Chamberlain have argued that as a result of mutual interdependence the basic problem facing oligopolists involves the reaction of competitors to each others' price, quality, production, and capacity decisions. Fewness creates a psychological awareness and intense rivalry absent in other market structures. More than thirty years ago Machlup made the point as follows:

> In no type of seller's attitude is the feeling of rivalry and competitiveness as prevalent as in some forms of oligopoly. Under perfect polypoly the feeling of rivalry is completely absent from the attitudes of the 'pure competitors.' Under imperfect polypoly a seller may be aware of the fact that he has competitors but, although he may watch them, he is not self-conscious about his own actions, because he has not the feeling of being watched by them. Since he is sure his actions cannot hurt any one of them and no one of them would ever 'come back' at him for anything he might do, he will not have any particular 'rival' or 'rivals.'
>
> This is different under certain forms of oligopoly. The oligopolist usually thinks of certain firms as his rivals: he knows they are watching him or, at least, will notice his 'competitive' actions; he believes he can hurt them or make them angry or cause them to take action they would not take but for what he has done. And all this means that he will be very conscious of being in competition, actively or potentially.[3]

Chamberlain, twenty years before Machlup, noted:

> When a move by one seller evidently forces the other to make a counter move, he is very stupidly refusing to look further than his nose if he proceeds on the assumption that it will not. As already argued, the assumption of independence cannot be construed as requiring the sellers to compete as though their fortunes were independent, for this is to belie the very problem of oligopoly itself.[4]

And after describing how, in an oligopoly market structure, an equilibrium price may be established above the minimum average cost that would obtain in a competitive market structure, and also be accompanied by excess capacity, Chamberlain added:

> The outcome described involves no combination—not even a tacit agreement—among the sellers. It is the result of each seeking independently his 'ordinary' profit. The idea of conspiring (even 'tacitly') with his

rivals may not enter the head of the man who takes it as a matter of course that he deals with his own customers and charges enough to make a good profit. But it is fortified in actuality by formal or tacit agreements, open price associations, trade association activities in building up an *esprit de corps*, 'price maintenance,' the imposition of uniform prices on dealers by manufacturers, and excessive differentiation of product in the attempt to turn attention away from price.[5]

Both Machlup and Chamberlain argue that oligopoly is distinguished from other market structures because awareness leads to psychological interdependence. The vast literature dealing with oligopolistic behavior is in large measure derived directly from Machlup and Chamberlain's idea of structural *independence,* psychological interdependence, and rivalry.[6]

Psychological interdependence and intense rivalry, as concepts, are logical, intuitively appealing to many, and, while disagreement does exist, seem to have widespread adherence among orthodox economists. But, it should be remembered, both are based on the assumptions of (1) fewness of sellers and (2) structural independence among sellers. And, while fewness of sellers in many markets is a difficult concept to reject, a passing familiarity with economic reality confirms that the concept of structural independence is open to question.

Oligopolistic Cooperation: A New View

The basic characteristic underlying the theory of oligopolistic cooperation is structural *intradependence* as opposed to *independence.* Many types of structural intradependencies among firms have evolved in the last several decades; however, this analysis will examine three: (1) administrative intradependence, (2) ownership intradependence, and (3) stock control intradependence. In this study then, structure refers primarily to various types of organizational ties—administrative, ownership, and stock control. Nonetheless, we do recognize the traditional structural characteristics of absolute size and concentration. Finally, for illustrative purposes, in the area of financial markets we examine both banking and insurance, while in the industrial arena the analysis is limited primarily to the petroleum industry.

Our view is that oligopolistic competition, based on psychological interdependence, has evolved into and been replaced by oligopolistic cooperation, based on structural intradependence. The data we marshall represent significant evidence that the banking, insurance, and petroleum industries have evolved almost completely into cooperative oligopolies. We assert that this new market structure is now, or soon will be, more typical of most of the key industries that comprise the heart of the U.S. economy. A point vital to this analysis is that a qualitatively different "rational" course of administrative action emerges when day-to-day interaction among corporate employees replaces the more or less psychological guessing game created by mutual interdependence. Interaction places corporate decision makers (employees in both top and middle management as well as those carrying out the work required by the decisions) in circumstances where the corporate identity becomes less important than the successful completion of the task at hand. And, the longer these direct and indirect associations remain in place the more the market structure moves toward oligopolistic cooperation.

Banking and Insurance

For this study the nation's ten largest banks and five largest insurance companies were selected for examination. This examination produced sufficient evidence to designate seven banks, four insurance companies, and one diversified financial enterprise as having administratively and financially evolved into oligopolistically cooperative market structures.[7]

As of January 1984, these organizations accounted for approximately $678 billion in assets and $330 billion in deposits-premiums, and the trust departments of the seven banks controlled about $124 billion in trust assets (see Table 1). Nine are headquartered in New York City, one in Newark, and two in Chicago. In the banking industry—ranked by assets—the group included the first, second, third, fifth, sixth, eighth, and eleventh largest banks, while the insurance companies, ranked by assets, were first, second, third, and fifth. Continental Corporation ranked eighteenth among diversified financial institutions. In absolute size and concentration, the banking and insurance organizations, nationally, accounted for 23 percent and 32 percent of the total assets within their respective industries. For purposes of constructing meaningful concentration ratios, while it is admittedly difficult to define relevant market areas since these firms operate at the local, regional, national, and international levels, at the local and regional levels these industries are typically characterized as having either "loose" or "tight" oligopolistically competitive market structures.[8]

Administrative Intradependence

The direct administrative intralocks among these organizations are shown in Table 2. As illustration, New York Life has one director that is also a director at Citicorp, two that are also directors at Chemical Bank,

Table 1. ***The Industry, Corporate Name, Rank, Assets (Deposits-Premiums), Trust Assets, Headquarters, and Number of Employees for Selected Banks and Insurance Companies, as of 1 January 1984.***

Industries and Corporations	*Rank*[a]	*Assets (000)*	*Deposits/ Premiums (000)*	*Trust*[b] *Assets (000)*	*Headquarters/ City*	*Employment*
A. BANKING						
1. Citicorp	1	134,655,000	79,794,000	21,435,623	New York	65,700
2. The Chase Manhattan Corporation	3	81,921,449	56,299,557	9,633,506	New York	37,230
3. Manufacturers Hanover Corporation	4	64,332,306	42,284,115	21,531,623	New York	28,250
4. J.P. Morgan and Company, Incorporated	5	58,023,000	38,070,000	39,117,769	New York	12,965
5. Chemical New York Corporation	6	51,164,860	32,452,401	12,008,457	New York	19,464
6. Continental Illinois Corporation	8	42,097,371	29,431,468	12,456,422	Chicago	12,189
7. First Chicago Corporation	11	36,323,324	27,680,040	7,486,358	Chicago	11,154
B. INSURANCE						
8. The Prudential Insurance Company	1	72,248,810	9,514,847		Newark	59,847
9. Metropolitan Life Insurance Company	2	60,598,562	5,947,671		New York	40,000
10. Equitable Life Assurance Society of the U.S.	3	43,305,559	1,102,684		New York	22,836
11. New York Life Company	5	24,228,095	3,554,362		New York	19,320
12. Continental Corporation[c]	18	9,278,499	3,946,566		New York	18,250
TOTALS		678,176,835	330,077,711	123,669,216		347,205

SOURCE: *Fortune*, July 1984.

[a] Ranked by assets and by industry. For example, Citicorp is the largest bank in the country while Prudential is the largest insurance company.

[b] Trust Assets data are for first quarter, 1983.

[c] Continental Corporation is usually classified as a diversified financial institution and not as an insurance company.

Table 2. ***Total and Individual Institutional Breakdown of the Direct BOD Intralocks and the Direct Non-BOD Institutional Intralocks (II) Between and Among Selected Financial Institutions, as of 1 January 1984.***

Row / *Col.*	*Total Intralocks*	*Direct (BOD and Non-BOD) Intralocks Between Selected Financial Institutions*												*Total Intralocks*
Industries and Corps.	*II*[a]	*CIT*	*CMB*	*MH*	*JP*	*CB*	*CIC*	*FC*	*PL*	*ML*	*EL*	*NYL*	*CC*	*BOD*[b]
A. BANKING														
1. Citicorp	4				FD					D, FD		D		2
2. Chase Manhattan	2									2D				2
3. Mfgrs. Hanover	4											D	2D*	4
4. J.P. Morgan	5	FD							D	2D		D		4
5. Chemical-N.Y.	3										D	2D		3
6. Cont. Illinois	1										D			1
7. First Chicago	1		A											0
B. INSURANCE														
8. Prudential	1				D									1
9. Metropolitan	6	D, FD	2D		2D									5
10. Equitable	2					D	D							2
11. New York Life	5	D		D	D	2D								5
12. Continental Corp.	3			2D*										3

SOURCE: *Moody's Financial Manual*, 1984.

[a] The number of intralocks in the column "Total Intralocks II" may differ from the number in "Total Intralocks BOD" column since the former column includes both BOD and Non-BOD intralocks. For example, an individual may be a BOD member for one institution and also be on another institution's international advisory committee. This would constitute an institutional intralock (II) but not an intralock between the two institutions' boards of directors. Another example would be where a member of one institution's board had a relative who was a member of another institution's senior operating management but was not on its board of directors.

[b] See *a* above.

SYMBOLS: D = Board of Directors: O = Officer and board member; * = Chief Executive office and board member; A = Institutional intralock, but not a BOD intralock (see Footnote A); F = Family BOD intralock—for example, a father and son each sitting on the board of different institutions. When a number appears before a symbol, such as "3D," "2A," etc., it signifies the actual number of whatever type of interlock is indicated.

CAUTION: To interpret symbols correctly, read from left to right. For example, Continental Corporation's Chief Executive Officer, i.e.*, is a member of Manufacturers Hanover's Board of Directors.

one that is a director at J. P. Morgan, and finally one that is also at Manufacturers Hanover. Therefore, when New York Life has a Board of Directors (BOD) meeting directors from Chemical, J. P. Morgan, Manufacturers Hanover, and Citicorp are present. Conversely, when J. P. Morgan has a BOD meeting, Prudential, Metropolitan Life, and New York Life each have one or more directors present. In essence, then, the companies *within* the insurance industry are *intra*locked via the banks, while the companies *within* the banking industry are *intra*locked via the insurance companies.

While these *intra-industry* administrative ties may be of some importance, the *indirect directorship administrative intralocks* (IDI) among these organizations within the corporate boardrooms of other economic enterprises are the key element in creating a *structural administrative intradependence* within the industry. It is important, for purposes of clarity, to maintain a distinction between the two concepts—direct BOD *intra*locks and indirect directorship intralocks. The former signifies a connection involving only the twelve financial organizations, while the latter connotes an intralock involving two or more financial organizations, each of which has one or more of its directors sitting on the board of a third, non-financial enterprise. As illustration of the IDI, consider the following:

CITICORP—X and Y are on Citicorp's BOD
J. P. MORGAN—M and Y are on Morgan's BOD
METROPOLITAN LIFE—A and P are on Metropolitan's BOD
CHASE MANHATTAN—Q is on Chase's BOD
GENERAL MOTORS (GM)—X,Y,M,N,O,P,Q are on GM's BOD

Since, as of January 1984, this example is factually accurate, when GM has a BOD meeting, Chase, J. P. Morgan, Citicorp, and Metropolitan Life have seven directorships indirectly intralocked. It is significant to note that these seven occur at just *one* indirect institutional interlock (III). As indicated in Table 3, Citicorp and J. P. Morgan have thirteen more III's. And, since each of the fourteen corporations in which these III's occur have around twelve BOD meetings annually, directors from Citicorp and J. P. Morgan are in meetings with each other approximately 168 times per year, more than three times weekly, just through III's. The data presented in Table 3 give an indication of both the volume and variety of information and responsibilities shared by J. P. Morgan and Citicorp's administration.[9]

The data in Table 3 also allow the computation of the average number of directorships intralocked per each III. For example, Citicorp has a

Table 3. ***Total and Individual Institutional Breakdown of the Indirect Directorship Intralocks (IDI) and Indirect Institutional Intralocks (III) that Take Place Between and Among Selected Financial Institutions—Within the Corporate Boardrooms of Other Selected Corporations as of 1 January 1984.****

	Total Intralocks	*Indirect Institutional Intralocks*											
Industries and Corps.	*IDI - III*	*CIT*	*CMB*	*MH*	*JP*	*CB*	*CIC*	*FC*	*PL*	*ML*	*EL*	*NYL*	*OC*
A. BANKING													
1. Citicorp	168 - 40		18	12	14	7	6	4	5	13	2	5	6
2. Chase Manhattan	127 - 28	18		9	13	8	3	0	4	7	0	7	5
3. Mfgrs. Hanover Corp.	99 - 22	12	9		13	5	4	2	1	5	2	5	2
4. J.P. Morgan and Co.	136 - 33	14	13	13		11	2	1	1	6	5	7	3
5. Chemical N.Y. Corp.	102 - 21	7	8	5	11		3	2	1	5	3	6	4
6. Cont. Illinois Corp.	61 - 14	6	3	4	2	3		6	1	2	1	2	2
7. First Chicago Corp.	47 - 12	4	0	2	1	2	6		1	2	0	1	3
B. INSURANCE													
8. Prudential	34 - 9	5	4	1	1	1	1	1		4	2	1	0
9. Metropolitan	104 - 24	13	7	5	6	5	2	2	4		2	6	5
10. Equitable	35 - 8	2	0	2	5	3	1	0	2	2		2	1
11. New York Life	78 - 18	5	7	5	7	6	2	1	1	6	2		3
12. Continental Corp.	61 - 13	6	5	2	3	4	2	3	0	5	1	3	

SOURCE: *Moody's Bank and Financial Manual*, 1984, *Moody's Industrial Manual*, 1984, and Standard and Poor *Million Dollar Directory*, 1984.

*A word of caution is in order concerning the interpretation of the data in Table 3. Totalling the III's between, say, Citicorp and each of the other eleven institutions will *not* produce the same number that appears in the "Total III" column. Summing these data would amount to double counting. Assume, for instance, that Citicorp, Chase, Manny-Hanny, and Prudential each have *one* direct BOD intralock with G.M. On the one hand Citicorp and Chase have an III at G.M., Citicorp and Manny-Hanny have an III at G.M., and Citicorp and Prudential have an III at G.M. On the other hand, G.M. counts as only *one* III between Citicorp and the other selected institutions, *not three.*

total of 168 IDI's with the other eleven financial organizations. In turn, these IDI's occur in forty III's. Therefore, on average, there are about four directorships intralocked in each III. Just through III's, Citicorp's directors are in about 480 meetings per year with directors from the other eleven companies where approximately four financial directorships are intralocked. The data in Table 2 and 3 clearly suggest that top level administrators of the organizations are in *almost constant (daily) contact.* We now turn briefly to another structural tie—stocks.

Stock Control Intradependence

The data in Table 4 illustrate that the twelve financial organizations control significant amounts of each other's stock. For example, 14.2, 16.9,

Table 4. ***Total Number of Indirect Directorship Intralocks (IDI), Indirect Institutional Intralocks (III), Direct BOD Intralocks, the Percentage of Each Institution's (1) BOD's Intralocked, and (2) Stock Intralocked, as of 1 January 1984.***

	IDI's, III's, Direct BOD Intralocks; Numerical Size of Each Institution's BOD; and Percent Intralocked				*Minimum Stock Holdings Intralocked*
Industries and Corporations	*IDI-III*	*Direct BOD*	*No. on Board*	*BOD's Intralocked (Percent)*	*Stock* (Percent)*
A. BANKING					
1. Citicorp	168-40	2	23	9	14.2
2. Chase Manhattan	127-28	2	25	8	6.1
3. Manny-Hanny	99-22	4	18	22	16.9
4. J. P. Morgan	136-33	4	23	17	14.7
5. Chemical	102-21	3	26	12	8.4
6. Continental Ill.	61-14	1	16	6	12.1
7. First Chicago	47-12	0	20	0	21.3
B. INSURANCE					
8. Prudential Life	34- 9	1	17	6	NA[a]
9. Metropolitan Life	104-24	5	21	24	NA
10. Equitable Life	35- 8	2	23	9	NA
11. New York Life	78-18	5	22	23	NA
12. Continental Corp.	61-13	3	16	19	11.3

SOURCE: *Moody's Bank and Finance Manual*, 1984, *Moody's Industrial Manual*, 1984, and Security and Exchange Commission forms 13F.

NA[a]: Not Applicable, are mutual enterprises.

*All Stock Control data from the 13F reports are for first quarter, *1978*.

14.7, 12.1, and 21.3 percent of Citicorp, Manufacturers Hanover, J. P. Morgan, Continental Illinois, and First Chicago's outstanding stock, respectively, is held within the group.[10]

Stock being an important structural characteristic, it is most important to note that within the trust departments of the six banks, there are about $124 billion in stockholdings (see Table 1).

When carefully examined, this web of direct and indirect administrative intralocks, as well as the joint stock control that exists among these organizations, reveals a very clear structural reality. Indeed, a conscious recognition of these structural intradependencies and shared responsibilities would necessitate a high degree of cooperation by the participants. For these members to act as if these intradependencies did not exist would be both logically and practically indicative of irrational tendencies. The administrative and financial ties are so numerous as to present a cohesive structural edifice; the basic assumption is that structure begets behavior.

More specifically, fewness of sellers, structural independence, and psychological *interdependence* lead to intense rivalry in traditional oligopoly theories; fewness of sellers, structural *intradependence*, and personal/psychological interplay between decision makers lead to cooperation.

Petroleum

Table 5 lists seventy-two brands or names of corporations that sell gasoline in the United States. During 1976 an advertisement appearing in several leading magazines displayed these names along with each company's brightly colored logo. The text of the advertisement, in part, read as follows:

> You're looking at some of the brands and names of companies that sell gasoline. Some people say oil companies are a monopoly. If so, it's the world's most inept 'monopoly.'
>
> This 'monopoly' is so inept that it offers the world's richest country some of the world's most inexpensive gasoline.
>
> This 'monopoly' is so inept that it lets everybody and his brother horn in on the action. Did you know that of the thousands of oil companies, none has larger than an 8.5% share of the national gasoline market?
>
> In fact, this 'monopoly' is so inept that you probably wouldn't recognize that it is a monopoly because it looks so much like a competitive marketing system.
>
> People who call us a monopoly obviously don't know what they're talking about.[11]

Table 5. ***List of 72 Brand Names and/or Names of Corporations that Sell Gasoline in the United States, as of 1976.***

List of 72 Brand Names and/or Names of Corporations that Sell Gasoline in the United States, as of 1976

1. Lion	37. Pennzoil
2. Kerr McGee	38. Ashland
3. Marathon	39. Billups
4. Gulf	40. Power Test
5. Thrifty	41. Sohio
6. Tesoro	42. Colonial (Minuteman)
7. Time	43. Total
8. Clark	44. FS
9. Mohawk	45. Certified
10. Texaco	46. Amoco
11. Lerner	47. Getty
12. Conoco	48. Tresler Comet
13. Crown	49. Chevron
14. Crystal	50. Texgas
15. Quaker State	51. Wood River
16. MFA Oil	52. Union
17. Malco	53. COOP
18. Martin	54. Tenneco
19. Western	55. Shell
20. Fina	56. APCO
21. ARCO	57. Southland
22. Sunoco	58. Shamrock
23. Colonial	59. Mobil
24. Exxon	60. Midland
25. Checker	61. Zephyr
26. Vickers	62. Dixie
27. Terrible Herbst	63. FCX
28. Powerline	64. ETNA
29. Derby	65. Phillips 66
30. Beacon	66. UCO
31. SPUR	67. CITGO
32. Star Gas	68. Husky
33. Midwest	69. Champlin
34. Cenex	70. Keystone
35. Hess	71. Sunland
36. USA	72. SOC

SOURCE: *Sports Illustrated*, 21 June 1976. s.v. "What a way to run a monopoly!"

The creators of this advertisement were *technically* correct in pointing out (1) that the oil industry is not a monopoly (one company accounting for all of an industry's output), and (2) that the industry, as it is portrayed in the advertisement, "looks . . . much like a competitive marketing system." Just as obviously, however, the statistics presented in this advertisement, while technically correct, are almost a total distortion of economic reality: Ten of the seventy-two companies listed (see Table 6) account for 70-75 percent of the production and refining of petroleum products consumed in the United States. The same ten companies average 5.5 III's among themselves, wherein they average approximately sixty-six administrative meetings per year. The retail prices many of the smaller companies must charge their customers are partially determined by the larger, fully integrated companies since many of the smaller companies must (1) buy substantial amounts of their crude petroleum from the larger "fully integrated" companies,[12] and (2) transport their crude oil and refined product through pipelines owned by these larger companies. Some of the companies listed have percentages of their stock owned by other petroleum companies: for example, Royal Dutch Shell owns 69 percent of the Shell Oil Company (Shell), and British Petroleum owns more than 50 percent of Standard Oil of Ohio (Sohio).[13] And finally, many of the companies listed are currently partners with each other in many of their petroleum operations through a contractual (and sometimes organizational) arrangement called a joint venture.

Administrative Intradependence

The data in Table 6 illustrate that administrators from the ten petroleum companies examined in this study attend formal meetings with each other almost weekly.[14] For example, when J. P. Morgan and Company holds a BOD meeting, directors from Mobil, Tenneco, and Atlantic Richfield attend; when Metropolitan Life holds a BOD meeting, directors from Mobil, Exxon, Standard of Ohio, and Atlantic Richfield attend, etcetera. Stated somewhat differently: administrators from Mobil, Exxon, Texaco, and Atlantic Richfield meet with administrators from within this ten-company petroleum group 156, ninety-six, eighty-four, and sixty times per year, respectively. Nonetheless, Board of Director intralocks are not the only means of facilitating frequent interaction for sharing information and decision making responsibility in this industry.

Joint Venture Intradependence

A joint venture is a form of enterprise in which companies create partnerships with other companies, governments, or organizations.[15] Traditional oligopoly theories do not explain the behavior of firms within a

Table 6. ***Total and Individual Institutional Breakdowns of the Indirect Directorship Intralocks (IDI) and Indirect Institutional Intralocks (III) that Take Place Between and Among 10 Petroleum Corporations—Within the Corporate Boardrooms of Other Corporations as of 1 January 1984.*****

	Total Intralocks	*Indirect Institutional Intralocks*									
*Petroleum Corporations**	*IDI-III*	*EXX*	*MOB*	*TEX*	*STD*	*CHV*	*ARC*	*OCC*	*SUN*	*TEN*	*UNO*
1. Exxon	21- 8		3	3	1	1	2		2		
2. Mobil	37-13	3		3	2	2	6		1	3	
3. Texaco	21- 8	3	3			2	2		1	1	
4. Standard (IN)	13- 5	1	2					1			1
5. Chevron	12- 4	1	2	2							
6. Atlantic Richfield	21- 7	2	6	2						2	
7. Occidental	2- 1				1						
8. Sun Oil	9- 4	2	1	1						1	
9. Tenneco	11- 4		3	1			2		1		
10. Unocal	5- 1				1						

SOURCE: *Moody's Industrial Manual*, 1984.

*These 10 corporations account for approximately 70 to 75 percent of the production and refining of petroleum products *consumed* in the United States, but *not* necessarily produced and/or refined in the United States.

**A word of caution is in order concerning the interpretation of the data above. Totalling the III's between, say, Exxon and each of the other nine institutions will *not* produce the same number that appears in the "Total III" column. Summing these data would amount to double counting. Assume for instance that Exxon, Texaco, and Chevron each have one direct BOD interlock with GM. On the one hand, Exxon and Texaco have an III at GM, Texaco and Chevron have an III at GM, and Chevron and Texaco have an III at GM. On the other hand, this is counted (in the total column) as only one III between Exxon and the other three institutions, *not three*.

given industry in which the major firms jointly own the means of production. In the petroleum industry these arrangements cover every phase of activity from bidding on leases or concessions to marketing the end product.

A tally of the joint venture activities of nine petroleum companies (Exxon, Mobil, Texaco, Standard of California [now Chevron], Gulf [now merged with Chevron], Atlantic Richfield, Continental [now owned by Dupont], Cities Service [now owned by Occidental], and Standard of Indiana) is given in Table 7. These nine companies have 594 joint venture activities among them outside the United States. A few examples of joint ventures, chosen from those tallied in Table 7, illustrate the variety of joint associations in the industry.

Perhaps the most important joint venture, just because of its sheer size and impact on the industry, is the Arabian American Oil Company (Aramco). Aramco has four participants—Exxon, Mobil, Standard of California (now Chevron), and Texaco (see Table 8). It is a Delaware corporation, and is now the sole partner of the Saudi Arabian government in the production of petroleum in that country. Since it operates as a collective unit it would seem logical that the partners would be able to negotiate from a stronger position than as individual bargainers. This would be true not only for operations in Saudi Arabia, but in all aspects of their worldwide petroleum operations. The main point is that the four owners of Aramco, otherwise thought to be oligopolistic competitors, actually cooperate and interact as joint owners of the world's largest oil producing company. (Since the end of World War II Aramco has, on a yearly basis, produced 20 to 25 percent of the petroleum and 25 to 30 percent of total world reserves outside the Communist Block countries).

A somewhat more complex joint venture is illustrated in Figure 1. This is a joint venture in Venezuela involving Gulf/Chevron, Mobil, Royal Dutch Shell, Texaco, and Exxon. In one part of this venture Gulf (50 percent), Exxon (25 percent), and Shell (25 percent) have a contractual agreement involving a concession and a producing operation. The second part of the venture involves a refining operation called Venezuelan Gulf Refining Company. Gulf/Chevron, via a subsidiary, owns two-thirds and Texaco one-third. Since Gulf/Chevron is involved in both the production and refining aspects of this joint venture it is engaged in direct day-to-day association with Shell, Exxon, and Texaco. Through Gulf/Chevron, Texaco is involved with Shell and Exxon.[16]

The joint venture tabulations provided in Table 7 are not, however, a complete accounting; specifically, there are significant amounts of joint bidding and production on the Outer Continental Shelf (OCS) of the

Table 7. ***Joint Ventures Among Selected Companies in Exploration and Drilling, Production, Pipelines, and Refining, Outside the United States.***

	Exxon	*Mobil*	*Texaco*	*SoCal*	*Gulf*	*Arco*	*Conoco*	*Cit Srv*	*SoInd*	*Total*[a]
Exxon		59	32	19	21	20	12	5	10	178
Mobil	59		31	31	14	12	7	2	3	159
Texaco	32	31		10	23	15	12	2	8	133
SoCal	19	31	10		15	19	11	1	6	112
Gulf	21	14	23	15		10	26	1	7	117
Arco	20	12	15	19	10		10	6	112	204
Conoco	12	7	12	11	26	10		16	4	98
Cit Srv	5	2	2	1	1	6	16		2	35
SoInd	10	3	8	6	7	112	4	2		152
Total[b]	178	100	70	52	44	128	20	2	0	594

[a]The total in this column (the horizontal total) is the number of joint ventures participated in by each firm, not the total number of joint ventures.

[b]The total in this column (the vertical total) is the total number of joint ventures. To arrive at this total only the numbers below the main diagonal are included. The number in the last cell (594) is the sum of these numbers.

The numbers in the cells on both sides of the main diagonal are duplicates. The duplication is only for ease of reading the data for a particular company.

SOURCE: Calculated from data in "Joint Ventures in the International Petroleum Industry: Exploration and Drilling" (Ph.D. diss., University of Oklahoma, 1974), by James I. Sturgeon, pp. 175-76.

Table 8. ***Ownership of the Major Petroleum Producing Operation in Saudi Arabia, as of 1 January 1980.***

Country, Company Ownership, and Fields	*Percent Ownership*	*Production (b/d)*
ARABIAN AMERICAN OIL COMPANY		9,200,000
Standard Oil Company, California	28.3	
Standard Oil Company, New Jersey (Exxon)	28.3	
Texaco Inc.	28.3	
Mobil Oil Corporation	15.0	
Fields: Khurais, Manifa, Ghawar, Abqaiq, Berri, Abu Sa'Fah, Abu Hadriya, Safaniya, Qatif, Khursaniyah, Fadhili, Dammam, Shaybah		

SOURCE: James C. Tanner, "Mobil to Expand Stake in ARAMCO to 15% by 1979," *The Wall Street Journal*, 10 April 1975, p. 3; and John R. Munkirs, "Joint Ventures in the International Petroleum Industry: Production and Pipelines" (Ph.D. diss., University of Oklahoma, 1973), p. 125.

United States.[17] The data in Table 9 give an idea of the magnitude of the OCS joint venture interaction by these nine companies. These data indicate that as of 1975 they had submitted some 2,040 joint bids for offshore leases.

The most important fact concerning joint ventures is not their numerical magnitude. While significant, it is more important to realize that these companies have become structurally intradependent via joint ownership arrangements throughout most of the world. Further, they are intraconnected in all phases of their operations—land acquisition (leases and concessions), exploration, drilling, production, transportation, refining, and marketing. The industry-wide magnitude of joint activity leads to the conclusion that the means of production are, in large degree, jointly owned and controlled.

These formal, legally binding arrangements do not encourage competitive behavior. On the contrary, joint ownership results in structural intradependencies that drive the participants to more and more cooperative behavior. Joint ventures heighten the necessity to interact, share information and technical skills, and make joint decisions; the success of one partner has become inextricably bound to that of the others.[18] One would be, in Chamberlain's terms, "stupidly refusing to look further than his nose" not to understand this. But Machlup and Chamberlain's ephemeral and *psychological interdependence* has been replaced by structural intrade-

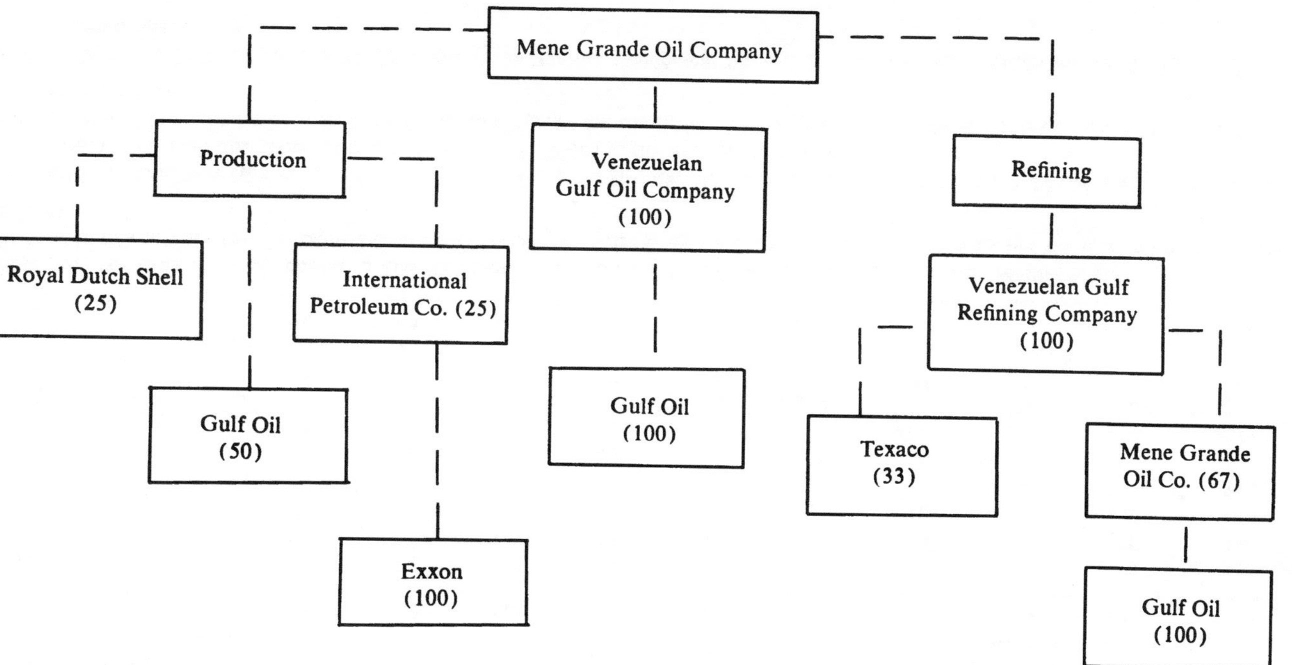

Figure 1. ***Joint Venture Producing and Refining Operations of Mene Grande Oil Company in Venezuela.***

SOURCE: Revised from James I. Sturgeon, "Joint Ventures in the International Petroleum Industry: Exploration and Drilling" (Ph.D. diss., University of Oklahoma, 1974), p. 167.

Table 9. ***Number of Joint Ventures Among Selected Companies On the U.S. Outer Continental Shelf, 1954-1975.***[a]

	Exxon	*Mobil*	*Texaco*	*SoCal*	*Gulf*	*Arco*	*Conoco*	*Cit Srv*	*SoInd*	*Total*[b]
Exxon		20	8	63	35	22	0	0	0	148
Mobil	20		61	75	78	38	4	12	86	374
Texaco	8	61		0	51	20	0	0	150	290
SoCal	63	75	0		46	45	0	0	127	356
Gulf	35	78	51	46		14	0	0	31	255
Arco	22	38	20	45	14		604	255	76	1074
Conoco	0	4	0	0	0	604		91	4	703
Cit Srv	0	12	0	0	0	255	91		24	382
SoInd	0	86	150	127	31	76	4	24		498
Total[c]	148	354	221	218	45	935	95	24	0	2040

[a]These joint ventures included successful and unsuccessful bids for tracts in lease sales on the Outer Continental Shelf.

[b]The total in this column (the horizontal total) is the number of joint ventures participated in by each firm, not the total number of joint ventures.

[c]The total in this column (the vertical total) is the total number of joint ventures. To arrive at this total only the numbers below the main diagonal are included. The number in the last cell (2040) is the sum of these numbers.
The numbers in the cells on both sides of the main diagonal are duplicates. The duplication is only for ease of reading the data for a particular company.

SOURCE: Compiled from data in U.S. Department of the Interior, Geological Survey, LPR 5 and LPR 10 data sets of the Outer Continental Shelf.

pendence among these allies, partners, and project co-operators. A joint venture agreement forces cooperation in the daily affairs of the participants and does not, in the final analysis, provide a motivation for competition or intense rivalry; in short, oligopolistic competition has evolved into oligopolistic cooperation.

While we have chosen the petroleum industry to illustrate the joint venture concept, we do not want to leave the impression that it is the only industry that utilizes joint ventures, or other structual intradependencies leading to coperation. Other industries such as iron ore mining and steel manufacturing also utilize, abundantly, joint ventures.[19] In addition, recently, companies in the automobile industry have initiated formal joint operations.[20] Chrysler Corporation has entered joint venture arrangements with both German and Japanese automobile companies, while General Motors and Toyota have built a jointly owned production facility that is currently in operation. These arrangements are also likely to result in the elimination of independence and in the institution of structural intradependence in the automobile industry. And, of course, every major industry in the United States has become structurally intradependent through numerous administrative IDI's and III's.[21]

Economic and Public Policy Implications

Oligopolistic cooperation leads inexorably to questions of public policy. A policy of *laissez faire* is usually held to be appropriate under purely competitive conditions, and some of a more conservative bent hold it to be appropriate under conditions of oligopolistic competition. However, advocacy of a *laissez faire* policy is open to considerable question under conditions of oligopolistic cooperation. In turn, the more customary policy prescription for oligopolistic competition—vigilance, and if necessary, prosecution by antitrust agencies—is also questionable. We think it is clear that the "cop on the beat" approach has not been successful in preventing the petroleum industry from becoming oligopolistically cooperative.[22] Those who advocate a *laissez faire* policy assume that competition or oligopolistic competition are sufficient to regulate most business activity. They also assume that competition is superior to cooperation in the general run of production activities.

However, under a system of oligopolistic cooperation new forms of direct public action may be superior to *laissez faire* and antitrust. Such new forms may require (1) changing the elements of structural intradependence so they cannot serve as a basis for cooperation or (2) that the public take a more direct role in the affairs of business enterprises while leaving the existing elements of intradependence largely intact. The latter approach depends upon the *recognition and demonstration* that cooperation is superior to competition in *some* areas of production and hence that direct action is better than *laissez faire* or antitrust. Cooperation, left in place by a *laissez faire* policy, will have the ill effects on society that economists have for two hundred years attributed to such combinations. In other words, cooperation may or may not be desirable, but it *cannot* be left unattended or attended only by private interests.

Oligopolistic cooperation also has implications for economic literature. Current *textual* literature usually treats oligopoly as being characterized by completion and "unconscious parallelism," but not cooperation. In this regard we think it is incomplete, in that it does not sufficiently consider the changing structure of industries. This literature needs to be recast to account for the evolution of industrial structure and in particular, so we would argue, oligopolistic cooperation.

Additionally, most current and past *empirically* based literature on industrial structure has been confined to characteristics such as the number of firms, concentration, and firm size. However, industrial organization studies should also examine structural intradependencies such as joint ownership and joint venture activity as well as administrative and stock intradependencies—in point of fact, these are more important than the traditional structural characteristics. Studies that do not include an examination of these types of intradependencies are, quite simply, incomplete.

As Adam Smith noted more than two centuries ago: "People of the same trade seldom meet together, even for merriment and diversion, but the conversation ends in a conspiracy against the public, or in some contrivance to raise prices."[23] And,

> The cruellest of our revenue laws, I will venture to affirm, are mild and gentle, in comparison of some of those which the clamour of our merchants and manufacturers has extorted from the legislature, for the support of their own absurd and oppressive monopolies. Like the laws of Draco, these laws may be said to be all written in blood.[24]

And finally,

> I mean not, however, by anything which I have here said, to throw any odious imputation upon the general character of the servants of the East India Company, and much less upon that of any particular persons. It is the system . . . the situation in which they are placed, that I mean to censure; not the character of those who have acted in it. They have acted as

their situation naturally directed, and they who have clamoured the loudest against them would, probably, not have acted better themselves.[25]

The policy implications of oligopolistic cooperation—oligopolistic cooperation being "the system . . . the situation in which most" industries "are placed"—are complex and controversial, but one thing is clear: the present industrial policy, based on an out-of-date view of real world market structures, is deficient.

Conclusion

In this article we have advanced the position that the present view of oligopoly is incomplete and inadequate. The primary sources of this inadequacy are a result of market structures having evolved from oligopolistic competition to oligopolistic cooperation, resulting, in turn, from structural independence having evolved into structural intradependence. The evidence presented in this article is primarily from the banking, insurance, and petroleum industries and for three structural elements: joint administrative control, joint stock control, and joint ownership of the means of production. However, our view is that evidence for other industries can be marshalled and that this work would benefit from a consideration of oligopolistic cooperation as a dominant structure in those industries. The structures providing a basis for cooperation in the petroleum and financial industries are known to be present in varying degree in most of the country's industrial enterprises. And finally, the existence of oligopolistic cooperation demands a thorough reexamination of government's current public policy formulations—both statutory and regulatory, as well as, perhaps, in some instances, ownership.

Notes

1. Standard industrial organization textbooks analyze the structure, conduct, and performance characteristics of four basic market structures: pure competition, monopolistic competition, oligopolistic competition, and monopoly. And, while there are many variants of the oligopoly model, including those with elements of monopolistic competition, there are no variants of the oligopoly model that are based on structural *intradependence*; that is, existing oligopoly theories all assume structural *independence* among the various competitors.
2. In earlier works we have advanced the Centralized Private Sector Planning (CPSP) thesis as being a more realistic *macro* descriptive explanation of the U.S. economy. See for example, John R. Munkirs, *The Transformation of American Capitalism* (Armonk, N.Y.: M. E. Sharpe, 1985);

John R. Munkirs, "Centralized Private Sector Planning: An Institutionalist's Perspective on the Contemporary U.S. Economy," *Journal of Economic Issues* 17 (December 1983): 931-68, and James I. Sturgeon, "Micro Macro Literature and the Implications of Centralized Private Sector Planning," *Journal of Economic Issues* 17 (December 1983): 969-84. In this present article attention is directed toward the main characteristics of the micro sub-structure of the CPSP thesis.

3. Fritz Machlup, "The Characteristics and Classifications of Oligopoly," *Kyklos* 5 (1951/1952).
4. Edward H. Chamberlain, *The Theory of Monopolistic Competition*, 8th ed. (Cambridge: Harvard University Press, 1965), pp. 46-47.
5. Ibid., p. 106.
6. Two excellent texts that cover this material and also review much of the literature are F. M. Scherer, *Industrial Market Structure and Economic Performance* (Chicago: Rand McNally College Publishing, 1980), esp. pp. 67-68; and William G. Shepherd, *The Economics of Industrial Organization* (Englewood Cliffs, N.J.: Prentice-Hall, 1979).
7. The seven banks are Citicorp, The Chase Manhattan Corporation, Manufacturers Hanover Corporation, J. P. Morgan and Company, Chemical New York Corporation, Continental Illinois Corporation, and First Chicago Corporation. The four insurance companies are Prudential Insurance Company of America, Metropolitan Life Insurance Company, Equitable Life Assurance Society of the United States, and New York Life Insurance Company. The diversified financial corporation is Continental Corporation. Continental Corporation was not among the original fifteen organizations studied, but was added to the group because of the magnitude of its interlocking ties with the other banks and insurance companies.
8. See, for example, Shepherd, *The Economics of Industrial Organization*, pp. 146-56.
9. The twelve financial organizations, as a group, have 250 members. On average, each director holds four directorship positions with non-financial enterprises. This would indicate that each individual is responsible for attending around sixty BOD meetings per year.
10. For a detailed and exhaustive analysis of the evolution and present relationship between (1) stock ownership versus stock control, (2) management versus ownership control, and (3) the concentration of stock control, see Munkirs, *The Transformation*, esp. chaps. 3 and 5.
11. "What a Way to Run a Monopoly!" *Sports Illustrated*, 21 June 1976.
12. A fully integrated company is one that operates in all four phases of the industry's production and distribution processes: production, oil fields; transportation, pipelines and tankers; manufacturing, refineries; and marketing, service stations. The fully integrated companies are able to control retail gasoline prices by controlling the prices the smaller, non-integrated companies must pay when buying crude oil from them or when transporting oil or refined product through their pipeline.
13. Royal Dutch Shell and British Petroleum, along with Exxon, Mobil Gulf, Texaco, and Standard Oil of California, are known as the International

Majors. This group has dominated the world oil industry since the early 1920s.

14. The ten companies are Exxon, Mobil, Texaco, Chevron (Standard Oil of California), Atlantic Richfield (ARCO), Standard of Indiana (Amoco), Standard Oil of Ohio (Sohio), Sun Oil Company (Sunoco), Union Oil Company, and Tenneco.
15. Other forms of association in the industry include exchange agreements, unitization and prorationing, trade associations, etcetera.
16. We do not here examine the indirect connections resulting from joint ventures. For a brief treatment of this see James I. Sturgeon, "Joint Ventures in the International Petroleum Industry: Exploration and Drilling," 1974, and John R. Munkirs, "Joint Ventures in the International Petroleum Industry: Production and Pipelines," 1973, both unpublished Ph.D. dissertations at the University of Oklahoma.
17. These joint ventures include both successful and unsuccessful lease bids and the production operations that follow joint bids. Not included are joint pipelines from the OCS, or joint terminal and storage facilities.
18. The reasons usually given by the various petroleum firms for entering joint ventures include: (1) to lessen both financial and political risks, (2) to bring order to the market, (3) to allow the "parent" firms to more easily conform to the many and varied political and social environments that exist around the world, and (4) to allow firms to share costs. An examination of these reasons is beyond the scope of this article. A discussion of this may be found in Sturgeon and Munkirs, "Joint Ventures."
19. See Daniel R. Fusfeld, "Joint Subsidiaries in the Iron and Steel Industry," *American Economic Review* 48 (May 1958): 578-87.
20. It should be noted that the automobile has a history of cooperation, primarily through patent pools, parts sharing, etcetera. However, these ties are less formal and less binding than joint ventures or board of director intralocks.
21. See Munkirs, *The Transformation.*
22. For example, the Federal Trade Commission has dropped its 1972 case against eight petroleum corporations. There were several reasons for this, but one was that the industry, and thus litigation, was too complex to be adjudicated. This does not mean the case was without merit from an antitrust point of view.
23. Adam Smith, *An Inquiry Into the Nature and Causes of the Wealth of Nations* (New York: The Modern Library, 1937), p. 128.
24. Ibid., p. 612.
25. Ibid., pp. 605-606.

16

Idealism and Realism: An Institutionalist View of Corporate Power in the Regulated Utilities

David S. Schwartz

I wish to share with you my experience of more than thirty years as an academic and practitioner as it relates to the regulated public utilities. While my primary emphasis will concern the regulation of the electric power and gas industries, I will in addition address a number of generic pricing policies and market structure issues that affect utility performance and consumer equity.

Before narrowing the focus of the article, it may be helpful to indicate the underpinnings of my institutionalist perspective, which, I believe, was acquired honestly, if not intuitively. This is easily explained by the fact that as an undergraduate I studied under Allan Gruchy at Maryland, and that I did my graduate work at Wisconsin under Martin Glaeser, a student of John R. Commons. Both as teachers, in the fullest sense of the word, and as seminal thinkers, they sharpened my awareness of the economic system as a dynamic process, stressing the importance of the indigeous customs, traditions, attitudes, and values implicit in the existing and evolving institutional arrangements.

In my perception the most basic and critical distinction in the study of the regulated public utilities is that emphasized by both Thorstein Veblen and J. M. Clark in their contrasting of market values and social values.[1] This is particularly true in the field of public utilities, where we are dealing with industries that are "affected with the public interest." In other words, adequacy and availability of service, consumer protection from exorbitant prices, and protection against price discrimination in inelastic residential markets are key concerns in industries that deal with basic necessities and that are essential in a modern society. In this respect, the regulator, as a principal representative of government, should serve as a protector of those social values affecting the environment as well as low-income consumers, and act as a shield in neutralizing the negative effects of the use of market power by the regulated utilities.

I would like to make one last point before addressing the substantive issues of market power in the regulated energy utilities. After serving many years both as a staff member on regulatory commissions and as a public interest economic consultant before numerous state and federal regulatory commissions, I realize that a careful distinction must be drawn between scientific inquiry and social advocacy. This differentiation ties directly to the social scientist's need for realism and objectivity in inquiry. Nonetheless, it should not impede the efforts of the public interest advocate to delineate a programmatic approach for regulatory reform.

Regulaton in the Electric Power Industry

In a recent article in the JEI, Harry Trebing discusses the development of public utility regulation and traces its historical progression, which he divides into five phases. The first phase, covering the period from 1877-1920, he captions Populist/Progressive Reform. He then discusses the nature of regulation in the interim periods leading up to the current phase, 1969 to the present, which he captions Rising Costs, Destabilizing Technological Advance, and Growing Disenchantment with Regulation.[2] It is this latter period upon which my analysis centers.

The traditional view of economic regulation of public utilities is that it exists to achieve direct control of prices and earnings of monopolistic or oligopolistic firms. In addition, in order to achieve economies of scale and adequacy of service, commissions have authority over the entry and exit of firms in the regulated markets. For those visionaries who perceive of regulation as a form of social control with objectives that transcend the financial stability of the firm, economic regulation is a vehicle for achieving economic and social justice.

Despite this broad authority placed in the hands of regulators at both the state and federal level to permit effective economic regulation, since the early 1970s regulation has been under intense attack. The marked and continually escalating price increases for electricity and gas have led to criticism of the regulators and the regulatory process by the regulated, consumer groups, and environmentalists, as well as from political and academic circles. The remedies prescribed have varied from utilities advocating maintenance of the structural *status quo* but with more generosity in regulatory application, on the one hand, to total deregulation on the other. Somewhere between these extremes a small band of consumer advocates, practitioners, regulators, and academics have formulated specific programs, policies, and structural changes for regulatory reform that would improve and broaden public control.

This debate over improving and broadening public control versus decontrol and reliance upon market solutions is clearly underlined when one considers the position of the neoclassical and Chicago School economists with respect to the role of government intervention in the marketplace. The differences between institutional economists and the neoclassical and Chicago School economists are cogently discussed in a 1976 article in the JEI by Trebing, from which I quote as follows:

> Thus Friedman had introduced a major change in the Chicago solution to the public utility problem. Private monopoly, subject to the eroding forces of change, was superior to government regulation of public ownership. This shift appears to have had a significant effect on other adherents to the Chicago School, and more detailed arguments were soon offered to demonstrate that unregulated private ownership was superior, that private monopoly could be reconciled with competitive levels of profits without regulation, and that publicly owned utilities would follow pricing policies that maximize voter support rather than efficiency.[3]

Trebing continues as follows:

> The position of the Chicago School differs in significant respects from that of the others studying the adequacy and effectiveness of regulation. The view of the former is uncompromising regarding the inability of government regulation to promote efficient resource allocation. In contrast, those making industry case studies may argue that deregulation is appropriate for one industry because it is workably competitive, but may argue that continued regulation is necessary for another industry because it displays monopolistic characteristics. Similarly, those studying regulatory behavior usually accept some form of government regulation or control as desirable and focus on the adequacy of existing practices, methods to improve the performance of the commission system, or the desirability of transferring regulatory functions to other agencies or branches of government. Consumer advocates and environmentalists tend to be pragmatic regarding the contribution of regulation and as a result draw criticism from adherents to the Chicago position.[7]

It is not my primary task to respond to the neoclassical and Chicago School economists' oversimplification, bias, and naïveté with respect to adequacy of markets in checking monopoly power in the regulated energy utilities. My concern is with the criticism of regulation, and with the failure of government intervention, which has provided its critics the ammunition for such damaging impact. In order to approach this objective, one must be aware of the pricing procedure generally utilized by regulatory commissions. So-called cost-of-service rate-base regulation depends upon determining the operating expenses for a representative period (usually termed a test year), ascertaining the rate base, and fixing a return on investment (rate base) that services equity and debt; all are combined to reflect the revenue requirement that must be covered by rates set by the commission for various classes of customers of a utility.

This rather neutral ratemaking masks the controversy. In fact, the areas in dispute, which can involve millions of dollars in some instances, and hundreds of millions in others, cover what should be included in operating expenses (for example, appropriate depreciation rates, general and administrative expenses when a utility is diversified), what should be included in a rate base upon which a return is applied (for example, plant still under construction or only plant providing service), what is the appropriate rate of return, particularly for diversified utilities, and whether a projected or historical test year should be used in determining operating expenses and rate base.

Of major concern once the revenue required is determined, based on the cost of service, is how it will be allocated among residential, commercial, and industrial customers. This is particularly true in any industry where joint costs are predominant. In this regard, I will refer you to an article in the JEI, September 1978, by Edythe Miller which explores fully the controversy in rate structure reform, the issues of marginal cost vs. average cost pricing, and allocative efficiency and equity.[5]

Time does not permit a full exploration of the rate design issues and the debate surrounding peak vs. off-peak pricing, or in a broader theoretical context, average cost vs. marginal cost (or some variant such as time-of-day) pricing. In the context of market power alternatives it would appear that a utility could use the rationale of marginal cost pricing to shift cost to the inelastic residential market because the latter has less flexibility to move off-peak than do the industrial users. As to the resource efficiency and conservation argument, one must realize that this is a period of excess capacity, and that peak vs. off-peak pricing is more of a blackboard consideration than a choice of resource commitment in the real sense in the near future. More importantly, it would appear that once the plant is built and we are dealing with sunk costs, the major concern is equity and not allocative efficiency.

This discussion of the ratemaking process and the procedures reflected in the cost of service, rate base, revenue requirements, and rate design may seem arcane to those without a background in public utility economics. Nonetheless, as the future discussion will illustrate, it is the implementation of these ratemaking procedures that is to a large extent responsible for increasing electric and gas prices.

For example, the electric utility currently is faced with excess capacity, serious cost overruns, and plant abandonment. The underlying technological and economic factors that gave rise to these destabilizing conditions that began in the late 1960s are grounded in the fact that after several decades of declining real prices the electric industry was then faced with increasing real and monetary costs never previously experienced. The industry was then confronted with the exhaustion of scale economies, rising capital costs, rising fuel costs (particularly after the Arab embargo in 1973), increasing costs legislated for pollution abatement and safety equipment, and the general effects of inflation on the cost of other factors of production.

At the same time long-term trends in the increase in real per capita income moderated dramatically. Faced with rising prices and stagnating incomes, consumers drastically reduced their demand for electric power. As a result, utility systems are significantly overbuilt in comparison to current demand levels. Nonetheless, utilities insisted on including this excess capacity in rate base, earning a return on this investment, and reflecting the operating expenses associated with redundant plant in electric rates.

In this period of escalating costs, the earnings level of the electric utilities began to erode, and the commissions experienced unprecedented rate increase filings running into billions of dollars annually. This period provided the real test for the regulatory commissions as social control agencies. The critical question is, How did the commissions respond to the pressure by the electric utilities for rates escalating at more than twice the rate of inflation? Most commissions accommodated significantly to the demands of the electric utilities to modify the traditional cost-of-service rate-base regulation.

The radical departure from traditional regulatory policies is reflected in the decision by many commissions to use such procedures as the automatic flow-through of fuel costs in fuel adjustment clauses, the use of a projected test year (which built inflation into rates), an allowance for an inflation factor in rate base, and the allowance of construction work in progress in rate base (usually referred to as CWIP). I will further expand on the implications of the approval of CWIP in rate base shortly. The obvious result of these new commission procedures was to shift the financial and operating risk from the regulated firm to the ratepayer. In addition, the signal sent to the utilities was just the opposite of the constraints required, that is, the commissions sent a message that they were ready to adopt the policies necessary to protect earnings and insulate the utilities from risk. Finally, in a period of rapidly declining load growth (demand), adoption of these procedures by the regulators removed any incentive for utility management to reconsider projects about to be built, or to postpone projects under construction.

Allowing CWIP in rate base appears to be the most serious violation of an equitable balance between utility stability and consumer protection. It undermines a long established regulatory principle that any investment by a utility should not earn a return before it provides service and is considered "used and useful." In addition, by permitting CWIP in rate base, commissions are placing in jeopardy their ability to question the prudency of investment in plant under construction, because placing the plant in rate base makes an implicit prejudgment of prudency, making it difficult, if not impossible, to disallow the plant for ratemaking.

The latest Annual Report of the National Association of Regulatory Utility Commissioners (NARUC) reveals that the Federal Energy Regulatory Commission (FERC) and forty-one state commissions permit total or partial allowance for plant under construction to be included in rate base for electric utilities. In addition, the report indicates that nearly all state commissions allow the use of a fuel adjustment clause, and that twenty-one state commissions and the FERC permit a full or partially projected test year.[6]

The fundamental problem facing regulators and the electric industry today is that utility systems are overbuilt with respect to current demand. By the end of the 1970s utility reserve margins (that is, the relationship of demonstrated generating capacity to the peak demand for power) were significantly above the level that had been justified historically for purposes of reliability. The September 1984 issue of *Electrical World*, a trade publication, indicates that for the summer of 1984 the reserve margins were 35.7 percent. This is about twice the reserve margin considered necessary, usually recommended to be 15-20 percent.

The problems of excess cost and abandoned plant can be directly traced to the construction of nuclear facilities. Recent studies of the cost of nuclear plant show costs ranging as high as $4,900 per kilowatt capacity, in contrast to coal-fired generation of similar size capacity that runs $1,500-$2,000 per kilowatt.[7]

A recent study by the Environmental Action Foundation (EAF) entitled *Rate Shock: Confronting the Cost of Nuclear Power* concludes that more than 35 million families, about one-third of U.S. households, will pay an additional $200 billion dollars in utility charges reflecting the cost of newly completed nuclear plants. The EAF study found that nuclear costs will exceed lifetime fuel savings for every plant under construction. The report states that "the national nuclear damage bill will be approximately $200 billion (in constant dollars from the dates of commercial operation), using conservative estimates of future nuclear costs." It goes on to say that "residential ratepayers of a dozen electric utilities will experience annual increases of more than $400 when the new plants come on line, compared to costs of continued reliance on existing coal, oil, and gas-fired power plants."[8]

Finally, as an indication of the type of power used by the utilities to maintain the *status quo*, the following quote, from an article in *The Washington Post* entitled "Utility Lobbies Keep Power Turned On In Annapolis," is instructive:

> Only a cadre of utility company lobbyists occupied the public gallery of the House Environmental Matters Committee room one day last week when Torrey Brown, the panel's chairman and vote-broker, began to pull the session's consumer-oriented utility bills from a stack on his desk.
>
> 'Does anybody want to vote for this?' Brown would ask in a tone betraying his own lack of interest in the issue as he held up each bill file for the committee to see. In every case, hearing little argument, the chairman would put the bill folder aside and mumble: 'Okay, next bill.'
>
> Within 30 minutes, six of those consumer bills had been erased in a legislative massacre that has become an annual event in this stately, high-ceilinged committee chamber.
>
> Over the past five years, Maryland legislators have proposed scores of new laws and limits for the state's utility companies in an effort to retard an unprecedented inflation in the costs consumers pay for their electricity, their heat, and their telephones.
>
> But every year, in the House Environmental Matters Committee and the Senate's Economic Affairs Committee and on the floors of both houses, the vast majority of the bills has been killed at the urging of the utility companies, which last year alone spent at least $185,000 lobbying in Annapolis.
>
> A study by *The Washington Post* showed that 215 bills were introduced

in the four legislative sessions between 1976 and 1979 to limit utility rates, improve services, or help consumers pay their bills. Of those, 182—or 85 percent—were voted down by the legislature or vetoed by the governor.

Of the 33 bills that were enacted, only two are commonly identified as significant pieces of legislation.[9]

The preceding discussion highlights the current dilemma of regulation at the state and federal level. I will discuss the potential remedies for a number of these structural and functional maladies subsequently. The framework for addressing these major institutional distortions in the regulated utilities must be centered in an understanding of the use of power in fulfilling the objectives of the vested interests. In this regard an article by Wallace Peterson, in a December 1980 issue of the JEI, is particularly relevant, and makes the following point:

> The problem of power and the economy is largely neglected in conventional economic analysis, the reason being that the classical heritage abstracts power from the picture. When competition reigns, power appears as an occasional aberration, not something worthy of serious and prolonged study.[10]

Natural Gas Regulation

The natural gas industry can be divided into three functional sectors—that is, wellhead production, transmission, and distribution. In many instances a firm will be totally integrated and perform all functions, in other cases it may perform just one function (for example, distribution of gas exclusively or as an independent producer of gas). In the case of the major oil and gas producers, such as Exxon, Texaco, Mobil Oil, etcetera, all have pipeline transmission facilities, and are also major producers of gas. Approximately 75-80 percent of the final delivered price to consumers reflects transmission and wellhead production costs. The remaining 20-25 percent are distribution costs of the local utility, which are under state commission regulation. The cost of transmission and wellhead production are under the regulation of the Federal Energy Regulatory Commission. I have provided this information to present the total framework of natural gas regulation. In fact, the major policy issues and public controversy relate to the question of the continued regulation or decontrol of wellhead prices of gas. Central to this issue is the nature of the market structure in the natural gas producing industry.

I have written and testified many times before various congressional committees on the oligopolistic market structure of the natural gas producer industry. The specific anticompetitive characteristics of the natural gas producing industry, to which a great deal of testimony was addressed in proceedings before the Federal Power Commission (predecessor to the Federal Energy Regulatory Commission) and the Congress, are as follows: (1) significant concentration over "new" gas supplies; (2) interlocking relationships among major producers and between major producers and smaller independent companies; (3) interlocking relationships between producers and purchasing major interstate pipeline companies, all of which are also producers; (4) the existence of major bidding combinations of major oil and gas companies in offshore lease purchases; (5) individual and bank director interlocks between major petroleum companies as well as between petroleum companies and interstate pipelines; (6) the dual role of major oil and gas companies as intrastate purchasers of gas for their own pipeline systems and also as sellers of gas in the interstate market; and (7) the backward integration of distribution companies to the production function.[11]

In testimony before a House committee I concluded that this extensive web of interlocking relationships and joint ventures precludes the possibility of competition:

> The evidence presented on both the buying side and the selling side of the natural gas producer market reflects serious market imperfections that are so all-pervasive that they render competition unworkable. The various institutional arrangements reflecting interdependence and commonality of interests preclude rivalry and competitive interplay. The implications for competition and new entry, as well as for reasonable prices, are clear in that the public interest cannot be served by deregulation in a market manifesting these oligopolistic characteristics.[12]

The Nation, in a May 21, 1983 article by Fred J. Cook, entitled "Big Oil's Stake in Deregulation," quoted from a brief of a number of consumer and public interest groups to provide some specifics relative to the natural gas producer market:

> Such majors as Exxon (Monterey Pipeline), Continental Oil, Texaco, and Phillips Petroleum have major intrastate pipeline networks. One of the practices used by the major producers during the 1970s was to bid up prices in the intrastate market for the purchases for their intrastate pipeline system, then use these prices as evidence before the FPC (Federal Power Commission) of going price levels in the intrastate market that had to be met to attract gas for emergency sales in the interstate market.

The article goes on to discuss the interties between producers and pipeline companies in offshore operations: "In almost every case the oil company was a partner of one or more of the major pipeline companies. For example, Atlantic-Richfield held ninety-four leases in partnership with major oil firms and two pipeline companies, Tenneco and El Paso."

Finally, with respect to interlocks with large banks, the article points out that more than eighty directors of banks served as directors of two or more oil companies and provides the following information:

> On Exxon's board, there were members from Chase Manhattan, Citibank, and the First National Bank of Chicago. On Mobil's board, there were members from Citibank (also Exxon), First National Bank of Boston and Bankers Trust. Standard of Indiana (Amoco) had members on its board from Chase Manhattan (also Exxon), First National Bank of Chicago, Continental Illinois, Harris Trust, and American National Bank (Chicago).

Unfortunately, during the 1970s Congress and the public at large did not pose the issue of continued regulation or deregulation of gas prices on market structure issues, or on the broad long-range interests of the country. Instead, the narrower focus of the immediate dislocations associated with serious curtailments of gas supply during most of the 1970s, and the industry's contention that gas was underpriced in the regulated interstate market, became the basis for public policy debate. This linkage of gas shortages with the regulated interstate price of gas was the premise for many decontrol bills, full, partial, and many variations thereof, during the Nixon and Ford administrations. It was the same rationale for the Natural Gas Policy Act passed by the Carter administration in 1978.

Despite the fact that evidence that producers were withholding gas and constraining supplies was introduced into Congressional hearings and before the Federal Power Commission, the neoclassical arguments won the day. Supply-price elasticity studies filled the Congressional hearing rooms, and the only possible benefit of these efforts was that they provided a number of academics with supplemental income.

If anything, the supply-price relationships indicated negative elasticity. This is not surprising in a situation that promises significant gains from speculative expectations. As I told a reporter for the *St. Louis Post-Dispatch*, in rather inelegant language, when a decontrol bill was before the Congress in 1974, "When these guys can anticipate a threefold increase in price it pays them to hold out. You've got to be out of your mind to contract to sell for 50 cents when you can get $1.50."[13]

A report by the Energy Policy Task Force of the Consumer Federation of America, issued in June 1977 in hopes of forestalling the passage of the Carter bill, made this same point:

> President Carter's proposed legislation for natural gas pricing as with oil is premised on the assumption that higher prices will encourage producers to increase production. Historical experience dramatically contradicts this assumption and indicates, on the contrary, that higher and higher prices have resulted in decreased production. For example, despite a price increase of 445 percent for new natural gas between 1972 and 1976, of 126 percent in the weighted average price between 1972 and 1976, gas production decreased 12 percent and reserves declined 19 percent.[14]

With respect to the underpricing of gas, the relevant facts on this matter were contained in an article in the March 1984 *Atlantic*, by David Osborne:

> In 1975, the last time the Federal Power Commission tried to estimate the total exploration, production, and development costs for gas, it came up with a figure of 67 to 80 cents per thousand cubic feet, which allowed for a 15 percent rate of return on investment. (This estimate primarily reflected the cost of shallow gas, since the production of deep gas was rare in 1975.) Today inflation has probably raised the figure to $1.50.
>
> In 1983, the federal Energy Information Administration made a similar study. In a working draft, the EIA concluded that the vast majority of new gas in the nation could be produced for under $3.00 per mcf, allowing for a 15 percent profit. Even gas from most fields at 17,500 feet, the deepest the EIA analyzed, fell under the $3.00 mark. The study did not include exploration costs, but this omission was offset by the fact that its base year was 1981.[15]

Finally, on the question of supply constraint, an article in *The Washington Post* on April 7, 1980 points to an ironic twist that will benefit Texaco, Inc. despite its illegal diversion of gas from the interstate market to the intrastate market:

> Texaco, Inc. is reaping a harvest of an estimated $373 million as an ironic consequence of a 1977 U.S. government ruling that it knowingly violated federal law for 11 years by diverting a vast amount of natural gas from public lands to its own use.
>
> As a result of the ruling, Texaco agreed to "pay back" 208 billion cubic feet of gas—enough to supply 1.7 million homes for a year. The company, which illegally kept the gas from interstate pipelines, consented to sell the pipelines an equal quantity of fuel—from nonfederal lands—over 10 years.
>
> Experts who asked not to be named said the settlement will increase Texaco's gross by at least $373 million because the prices it is allowed to charge for the replacement gas are several times higher than the prices that prevailed during the diversion period, 1967 to 1977.[16]

It may be helpful to provide a brief historical background before addressing the specific aspects of the current statute governing the wellhead pricing of natural gas—that is, the Natural Gas Policy Act (NGPA), which was passed midway through the Carter administration. The passage of the original Natural Gas Act in 1938 was prompted by a Federal Trade Commission Report issued in 1935 that concluded there was significant concentration in both distribution and production of natural gas. Because the Federal Power Commission made no effort to regulate wellhead prices, natural gas producers did not pursue any legislative efforts to exempt themselves from regulation until 1947. In that year both the D.C. Court of Appeals and subsequently the Supreme Court in a new famous case, *Interstate Natural Gas* vs. *FPC*, ruled that the FPC had the authority to order substantial reduction in the sales of natural gas in certain fields in Louisiana. The producers now realized that the FPC's jurisdiction over interstate sales of gas could extend to wellhead prices. A number of bills (for example, the Kerr Bill, vetoed by President Truman in 1950) were introduced seeking exemption from regulation prior to the *Phillips* decision in 1954 that explicitly gave the FPC authority to regulate wellhead prices of gas sold in interstate commerce.

After the *Phillips* decision the gas producing industry intensified its efforts to obtain exemption from regulation. It appeared that success was at hand when the Harris-Fulbright bill was pushed through the Congress in 1956. This anticipated success was fueled by the public relations efforts of the firm of Hill and Knowlton, which were funded by nearly $2 million worth of producer contributions. In addition, the favorable disposition of Congress and President Eisenhower convinced the gas producers that they would win the battle for decontrol once and for all.

With victory in their grasp, the forces of fate manifest in the form of excessive greed ultimately defeated the Harris-Fulbright bill. On February 3, 1956, Senator Francis Case (Republican) told the Senate that he was offered, but refused, a $2,500 bribe from a representative of the Superior Oil Company. A special Senate Committee was established to investigate the proposed contribution; it found the attempted bribe "improper but not illegal." A federal grand jury did not agree and returned indictments against Superior and the two attorneys involved. They all pleaded guilty, and Superior paid a fine of $10,000 and the attorneys $2,500 each.

Despite the scandal, Congress passed the bill, but President Eisenhower refused to sign it, saying, "A body of evidence has accumulated indicating that private persons, apparently representing only a very small segment of a great and vital industry, have been seeking to further their own interests by highly questionable activities."[17]

What Republican administrations could not accomplish, the Carter administration achieved in part. The Natural Gas Policy Act, introduced in April 1977 and signed into law in November 1978, is a price decontrol bill. It is characterized as follows by the Citizen/Labor Energy Coalition:

> The proposed Natural Gas Policy Act of 1978 (H.R. 5289) is no more and no less than a deregulation bill. It is supported (either actively or passively) by most of the major oil companies and is the culmination of their 30-year effort to force Congress to remove the consumer-protection standards of the Natural Gas Act as well as procedures to set wellhead prices on a 'just and reasonable' basis. This bill is opposed by consumer groups, labor unions, farm organizations, state utility commissions, a number of large industrial users and others—all of whom recognize the widespread economic damage this bill would cause.[18]

Under previous Republican administrations the Democrats, particularly in the House, were able to stymie any decontrol legislation. With a Democrat in the White House former opponents of decontrol either capitulated or remained silent and inactive. The type of wheeling and dealing used by the Carter administration to finally achieve partial decontrol of gas prices at the wellhead is typified in the following *Washington Post* article, dated September 7, 1978, entitled "Political Dealings Prompt Big Steel's Flip-Flop on Gas Bill," by Robert G. Kaiser and J. P. Smith:

> Until August 23, America's major steel companies were virtually unanimous—some vehement—in their opposition to the compromise natural gas legislation that the Carter administration so avidly championed. On August 24 all that changed.
>
> Big steel's flip-flop—brought on by tantalizing hints of federal aid and tax relief—was one modest victory for the White House in its continuing and intense campaign to win the support of key interest groups for the gas legislation. It is an example of the administration's willingness to engage in old-fashioned political dealing even as President Carter defends the gas bill in patriotic terms as a measure of 'the national will.'
>
> Big steel changed its mind—or at least changed its tune—after a meeting at the White House on August 23 involving senior steel executives, Vice-President Mondale, special trade negotiator Robert S. Strauss, and Federal Reserve Board Chairman G. William Miller.
>
> The meeting culminated a series of sessions between steel executives and government officials, including officials in the Treasury Department who have been dealing with the steel industry's pleas for tax relief, protection against imports, and other aid.

Another article in *The Washington Post*, dated July 30, 1978, discusses the price concessions made by the Carter administration, and the impact on residential users versus industrial users:

> When Carter announced his energy plan, the regulated interstate price for new gas was an average of $1.42, up from 52 cents in 1976. The president first proposed $1.75. The argument moved upward to $1.93. The compromise bill envisions a final price by 1985 in the neighborhood of $2.60 per thousand cubic feet. . . .
>
> In the simplest terms, the measure will authorize a substantial transfer of income within American society—at least $28.5 billion over the next six years—from all the consumers of natural gas to all the companies that produce it. Some critics claim that the transfer will be much larger, closer to $50 billion, but at the very least the gas industry should derive an increase of 17 percent in its expected revenue. . . .
>
> When President Carter first proposed his national energy plan, one principle was clear: The nation's dwindling pool of natural gas would be saved for the homeowners of America. Industry would be coaxed or driven, by taxes and regulatory rules, to shift to other less-precious fuels.
>
> Now, 15 months later, that priority has been reversed.
>
> Carter's compromise natural gas bill, scheduled this week or next for an up-or-down climax vote in the Senate, is skewed in the other direction —big industry is supposed to get more natural gas in the future, a lot more, while homeowners and businesses are expected to get along on less.
>
> The reason for this is simple, according to C. William Fischer, deputy administrator of the Department of Energy's quasi-independent analytical section. The final prices set for homeowners are much higher in the compromise measure than they were in the original plan—high enough to drive residential and commercial users away from gas, not toward it.

The Natural Gas Policy Act establishes four key provisions: (1) maximum lawful prices that fall into three categories—old gas, new gas, and decontrolled gas produced from below 15,000 feet; (2) a formulary basis for pricing (base price and inflation and other adjustment) as well as removing wellhead prices from a cost of production regulatory framework; (3) a path toward total decontrol by prescribing that "new" gas will be deregulated on January 1, 1985 (that is, gas committed to contract from April 1977, the date the act was introduced); (4) for the first time in this interim period it placed intrastate gas under this regulatory scheme.

Ann Lower, in an article in the June 1983 issue of the JEI, points out that if old gas were to be deregulated the major oil and gas producers would benefit most: "Under an immediate decontrol scenario the top twenty natural gas producers will reap a $68.3 billion windfall from their sales of old gas to the fifteen largest pipelines for the period 1983-1990."[19]

The effects of the NGPA over the past five years have been controversial. In the above-mentioned article, Ann Lower characterizes the benefits: "What was established as long-term gas policy under the NGPA was, then, a carefully crafted mix of 'right' price relationships, which, despite the current need for adjustments consistent with the Act, have worked remarkably well."

In the last Congress, The Citizen/Labor Energy Coalition, in a major legislative effort, tried unsuccessfully to roll back the prices resulting from the NGPA and to establish a price freeze or postpone the decontrol of new gas. The Coalition criticizes the NGPA in its *National Gas Factbook*:

> Natural gas prices have risen to unreasonable and unaffordable levels, despite a surplus of gas supply.
>
> Residential gas consumers have seen their gas bills increase by 124 percent over the last six years.
>
> Senior citizens and low-income families have been hardest hit; hundreds of thousands have already lost their gas heat because they could not pay their bills.
>
> Financially strapped family farmers have faced heating cost increases, as well as large operating and fertilizing cost increases caused by rising gas prices.
>
> Nearly two-thirds of urban school districts plan to lay off personnel in order to finance their rising fuel bills.
>
> Unless Congress acts soon to correct this situation, it is likely to grow far worse.
>
> Roughly half of the nation's natural gas supply is scheduled to be decontrolled on January 1, 1985.
>
> Wellhead gas prices are expected to rise another 20 percent and residential bills an additional 14 percent in 1985.[20]

The Citizen/Labor Energy Coalition's estimate of the amount of gas to be decontrolled on January 1, 1985 was based on data collected in early 1984. A report issued in July 1984 by the Energy Information Administration, entitled "Drilling and Production Under Title I of the Natural Gas Policy Act," estimated that 66 percent of production will be decontrolled in 1985.

This significanct increase in the amount of gas to be decontrolled could have been predicted by anyone familiar with the report issued by the Subcommittee on Oversight and Investigations released in November 1983.

This report, in which Milton Lower had a major hand, indicates the dilatory attitude of the Reagan regulators at the FERC. The report states:

> One recurring result of the analysis in the second section of this report is that old gas increased in price and affected overall wellhead costs more than was expected. The third part of the report, which summarizes the results, to date, of a continuing oversight project of the Subcommittee, suggests a possible explanation. The Federal Energy Regulatory Commission (FERC), through lack of interest or sheer incompetence due to primitive data collection and methods, may simply have failed to enforce NGPA ceiling prices for older vintages of old gas.[21]

To put it simply, the FERC has permitted gas formerly classified as "old" gas to be reclassified as "new" gas and subject to decontrol in 1985.

The NGPA has had a devastating effect on interstate pipelines and distribution companies. The pricing procedures have caused instability and financial distress because of market erosion in these industry sectors. More importantly, it has resulted in serious hardship for residential consumers in general, and in termination of gas service to the poor, resulting in a number of deaths.

The fact that it has enriched the major oil and gas companies is clear from the following facts. In 1978 the average wellhead price of gas was 91 cents per thousand cubic feet. By the end of the five-year period 1979-1983, the average wellhead price had risen to $2.59. The marketed production of gas in 1978 was 19.9 trillion cubic feet (Tcf), but by 1983 it had fallen to 16.8 trillion cubic feet. The revenues received from the sale of 19.1 Tcf in 1978 was $18.1 billion. The revenue received from the sale of 16.8 Tcf in 1983 was $43.6 billion. If the same quantity of gas had been sold in 1983 as in 1978, that is, 19.9 Tcf, producers would have received $51.3 billion.[22]

These figures indicate the magnitude of the income transfer from consumers to natural gas producers. The nature of the inequity of this income transfer should not be measured just in dollars, but in human suffering and despair.

Conclusion

The essential questions therefore are what is to be done, and what is the role of government regulation in the future. As Allan Gruchy pointed out in a June 1974 article in the JEI, "The social control of business in the U.S. economy is a long-standing problem that has continued to engage the attention of economists since the fourth quarter of the nineteenth century."

In postulating the need for national planning Gruchy points out that

> neoinstitutionalists believe . . . there can be no satisfactory control of business until the government is freed from the powerful influences of those who manage the large financial and industrial enterprises. If the basic issue in the social control of business is who controls the state, it is important to investigate what may be done to neutralize the economic and political power of big business.[23]

Gruchy makes clear that institutionalists and neoinstitutionalists have differed in their approach to the social control of business, and in their choice of the economic system to promote the public welfare:

> Different responses to this problem have been made by institutionalists and neoinstitutionalists. Thorstein Veblen recommended the abolition of the capitalist system and its replacement by a socialist one. In his program for the reconstruction of the economic system the problem of the power exercised by all private business would be taken care of by eliminating all private business. The institutionalists who followed Veblen, such as John M. Clark, Wesley C. Mitchell, and Rexford G. Tugwell, proposed to domesticate private business by establishing a national planning program, or what Clark described as 'social-liberal planning.' Big business then would be placed in an institutional framework in which all sectional interests, including private business, would be subordinated to the national interest, although not to the exclusion of sectional and local interest.[24]

In posing the institutionalist objectives, Gruchy points out that "effective social control of business must take account of the efficiency, the power, and the value aspects of the problem of how to fit private business into the advanced industrial society if the issue is to be dealt with adequately."

The wellspring of this institutional theory of dynamic change goes back to Veblen's *The Place of Science in Modern Civilization*:

> Like all human culture this material civilization is a scheme of human institutions—institutional fabric and institutional growth. But institutions are an outgrowth of habit. The growth of culture is a cumulative sequence of habituation, and the ways and means of it are the habitual response of human nature to exigencies that vary incontinently, cumulatively, but with something of a consistent sequence in the cumulative variations that so go forward.[25]

In addition, Clarence Ayres reemphasized and extended Veblen's theory of institutional adjustments in the *Theory of Economic Progress.* Ayres emphasizes that the driving force of the mental processes that generate ideas become the point of departure for changes in structural institutions.[26]

Finally, as Gruchy points out, in the previously cited article, the extension of these institutional dynamics resulted in developments in the industrial sector that are but part of the overall movement toward an integrated and collective society. Therefore, to offset the effects of corporate concentration institutionalists in the 1930s turned to national planning as the appropriate framework for both antitrust action and public utility regulation.[27]

The most vital institutional change required to bring about structural and substantive reform in the regulated public utilities was postulated by Horace Gray in a 1976 article entitled "The Sharing of Economic Power in Public Utility Industries." His proposals for improving the public control of regulated utilities stressed the need to reassert government's primacy in policy formulation. In other words, regulators, as protectors of social values, would establish the parameters within which the the regulated utilities would operate, and not the other way around.[28]

In this context, in a 1976 article in the *Indiana Law Journal* entitled "The Deregulation of Industry: A Built-in Bias," I concluded, "Rather than posing the choices in terms of continuing the status quo (ineffective regulation) or total reliance upon market forces (deregulation) in my view it is preferable to continue but drastically to restructure regulation. . . . This requires the formulation of public interest standards with clear and unambiguous differentiation from the objectives of the regulated form."[29]

Rodney Stevenson, in an article entitled "Institutional Objectives, Structural Barriers, and Deregulation in the Electric Industry," provides a short answer to those critics who seek a simple solution to the many deficiencies of current regulation by advocating deregulation:

> In the case of the electric utility industry, many of the proposals for deregulation are simple solutions that favor one group (generally the dominant utility) at the expense of others without substantial improvement in institutional quality. Enlightened reform of the current regulatory system will require a much more careful institutional crafting that builds on potentials for diversity without summarily rejecting consumer safeguards and mechanisms for rational economic coordination.[30]

Finally, Harry Trebing in a 1974 article entitled "Realism and Relevance in Public Utility Regulation," discusses various market structure issues, particularly oligopolistic coordination by electric utilities to promote their common interests, as major impediments to improving social control and promoting performance in the public interest:

> The existing commission system is ill-equipped to meet the types of problems posed by these market-structure considerations. But the task of reformed regulation is even broader, for it must integrate structure and structure-related variables within a conceptual and decision-making framework that also includes matters of motivation (incentives and penalties), equity and fairness in the treatment of parties, the prevention of monopolist earnings, the establishment of pricing guidelines, and the forecasting of future requirements and available resources. At present the commissions assume an essentially passive posture, emphasizing a review audit rather than a forward planning perspective. The role is hardly conducive to an exploration of this range of issues, whether in a rule-making or in an adjudicatory proceeding.[31]

Trebing and other institutional economists working in the regulatory arena have profoundly documented the need to redefine and broaden the parameters of economic regulation. While recognizing that market power persists and that the control of such power remains a primary task of regulation, these economists have not fully comprehended or articulated the need to utilize power to promote the public interest. If we are to reverse the current procedures and policies of regulators shifting the risk forward to consumers and insulating the firm, then an understanding of how power is used is essential. If we are to assure the preservation of essential services, then an understanding of power politics is critical. I am suggesting that without political, economic, and moral pressure at the local, state, and federal levels revitalized regulation in the public interest will not become a reality.

I do not accept the dichotomy posed by advocates of private power vs. public power, or *vice versa*, as the panacea assuring efficient and lower cost service. With publicly owned utilities following the same path as private utilities toward nuclear power and opting for power supply at the expense of the environment, the choice is not as clear as it was in the heady days of the New Deal. Probably, a diversity of ownership would best serve the public interest. More importantly, only a coalition of informed and active consumers, environmentalists, and public interest advocates will achieve the regulatory and social reforms previously discussed.

Legislation is required to prohibit joint ventures, interties, and interlocks among the major oil and gas companies. In addition, to inject some degree of arms-length bargaining and rivalry, further legislation should impose a functional separation, so that a firm would have to choose either production, transmission, or distribution as its singular line of business. Finally, in industries as basic to the economy as oil and gas, we should emulate many of the Western European democracies, such as Norway, England, and Holland, and form a government corporation to explore, develop, and produce oil and natural gas on public lands. This is the only meaningful countervailing force to check the oligopolistic power of the petroleum industry. Here again diversity of ownership is the appropriate public policy choice.

What should be evident from this discussion is that the only way to translate the public interest policy alternatives into regulatory reform is to integrate completely the issues, policies and procedures, and structural changes. If we are to be successful in pragmatically implementing and broadening the regulatory framework for social control, then we must gain access to the centers of power.

Notes

1. Thorstein Veblen, "Why Is Economics Not an Evolutionary Science?" reprinted in *The Place of Science in Modern Civilization* (New York: B. W. Huebsch, 1919), pp. 173-79. John M. Clark, "Toward a Concept of Social Value," in *Preface to Social Economics* (New York: Farrar and Rinehart, 1936), p. 49.
2. Harry M. Trebing, "Public Utility Regulation: A Case Study in the Debate over Effectiveness of Economic Regulation," *Journal of Economic Issues* 18 (March 1984): 223-50.
3. Harry M. Trebing, "The Chicago School versus Public Utility Regulation," *Journal of Economic Issues* 10 (March 1976): 97-126.
4. Ibid., p. 98.
5. Edythe S. Miller, "Rate Structure Reform: A Review of the Current Debate," *Journal of Economic Issues* 12 (September 1978): 609-26.
6. *1983 NARUC Annual Report on Utility and Carrier Regulation*, National Association of Regulatory Utility Commissioners, December 1984.
7. Salomon Brothers, "Nuclear Power Plant Under Construction—Quantifying Risk," December 7, 1983.
8. "Study Predicts $200 Billion Rate Shock," *Power Line*, September/October 1984.
9. Jackson Diehl, "Utility Lobbies Keep Power Turned On in Annapolis," *The Washington Post*, 30 March 1980.
10. Wallace C. Peterson, "Power and Economic Performance," *Journal of Economic Issues* 14 (December 1980): 827-69.
11. See David S. Schwartz, "Recent Developments in the Natural Gas Industry—A New Perspective," in *Public Utility Regulation*, ed. Weiner Sichel and Thomas G. Gies (Lexington, Mass.: Lexington Books, 1975).
12. David S. Schwartz, "The Market Structure of the Gas Producing Indus-

try and the Implications for Deregulation of Wellhead Prices," Subcommittee on Energy and Power of the House Interstate and Foreign Commerce Committee, March 21, 1975.

13. William K. Wyant, Jr., "Natural Gas Legislation: Visions of Sugarplums," *St. Louis Post-Dispatch*, December 1974.
14. "President Carter's National Energy Plan—Paradise for Producers and Purgatory for the Public," Energy Policy Task Force, Consumers Federation of America, June 27, 1977.
15. David Osborne, "America's Plentiful Resources," *The Atlantic* 253 (March 1984): 86-98.
16. Morton Mintz, "Texaco to Reap $373 Million in Gas 'Pay Back,'" *The Washington Post*, 7 April 1980.
17. *Natural Gas Factbook*, Energy Action Committee, American Public Gas Association, Energy Policy Task Force—Consumers Federation of America, p. 37.
18. Citizen/Labor Energy Coalition, *Factbook on the Proposed Natural Gas Bill*, September 25, 1978.
19. Ann K. Lower, "Natural Gas Pricing: Market Outcome or Industrial Policy," *Journal of Economic Issues* 17 (June 1983): 423-32.
20. Citizen/Labor Energy Coalition, *The Natural Gas Factbook*, August 1984, p. 1.
21. "Natural Gas Pricing," Staff Report, Subcommittee on Oversight and Investigations, Committee on Energy and Commerce, November 1983, p. iv.
22. Gordon W. Koelling and Charles L. Readling, "Natural Gas Production and Wellhead Price, 1983," *Preliminary Data Report*, Energy Information Administration, Washington, D.C., November 14, 1984.
23. Allan G. Gruchy, "Government Intervention and the Social Control of Business: The Neoinstitutionalist Position," *Journal of Economic Issues* 8 (June 1974): 235-49.
24. Ibid., p. 242.
25. Veblen, *The Place of Science*, p. 241.
26. Clarence E. Ayres, *The Theory of Economic Progress* (Chapel Hill: University of North Carolina Press, 1944), p. 298.
27. Gruchy, "Government Intervention and Social Control," pp. 238-45.
28. Horace M. Gray, "The Sharing of Economic Power in Public Utility Industries," *Salvaging Public Utility Regulation*, ed. Werner Sichel (Lexington, Mass.: Lexington Books, 1976), p. 18.
29. David S. Schwartz, "The Deregulation of Industry: A Built-in Bias," *Indiana Law Journal* (Spring 1976): 720-33.
30. Rodney E. Stevenson, "Institutional Objectives, Structural Barriers, and Deregulation in the Electric Utility Industry," *Journal of Economic Issues* 17 (June 1983): 443-52.
31. Harry M. Trebing, "Realism and Relevance in Public Utility Regulation," *Journal of Economic Issues* 8 (June 1974): 209-33.

14. "Analysis of Carter's National Energy Plan—Benefits for Producers and Disaster for the Public," Energy Policy Task Force, Consumer Federation of America, June 22, 1977.

15. David Osborne, "America's Natural Gas Problem," *The Atlantic* 253 (March 1984): 66.

16. [illegible] Allen, "Lessons to [illegible] 1973 Mistake in Gas Pay Back," *The Washington Post*, [illegible] 1981.

18. Citizen/Labor Energy Coalition, "A Guide to the Proposed Natural Gas Bill," April 27, 1978.

19. [illegible] "[illegible] Outcome of [illegible] Energy [illegible]," *Economic Inquiry* 17 (June 1983): 4[illegible].

23. Mark O. Gyllick, "Government Intervention and the Social Control of Business: The Natural Gas [illegible] Coalition," *Journal of [illegible]* 4 (June 1979): 156–92.

1984, p. 27.

25. Osborne, "The Natural Gas Problem," p. 275.

27. Gyllick, "Government Intervention and Social Control," pp. 156–65.

29. David S. Schwartz, "The Organization of Industry: A Built In Bias?," *[illegible] Law Journal* 56 (1981): 730–[illegible].

30. Andrew S. Carron, "Incentives and Objectives: Structural Barriers and [illegible] in the Electric Utility Industry," *Journal of Economic Issues* 17 (June 1983): 469–82.

17

Corporate Power and Economic Sabotage

Walter Adams
and
James W. Brock

Some forty years ago, Professor Henry C. Simons of the University of Chicago pictured economic giantism (and the unique power flowing therefrom) as posing perhaps the gravest threat to a democratic, competitive market society. He observed that, in a highly-developed economy with an intricate division of labor and functional interdependence, "every large organized group is in a position at any time to disrupt or to stop the whole flow of social income," and that "the system must soon break down if groups persist in exercising that power or if they must continuously be bribed to forgo its disastrous exercise." Government, Simons warned, "must not concede to any functional group the power ('right') to withold its contribution to an elaborate production process or to exact tribute by threat of such collective action." The most important means for protecting society from such economic sabotage, he concluded, was to guard against disproportionate economic size, including corporate giantism: "There is simply no excuse . . . for allowing corporations to hold stock in other corporations—and no reasonable excuse (the utilities apart) for hundred-million-dollar corporations, no matter what form their property may take. Even if the much-advertised economies of gigantic financial combinations were real"—a possibility that Simons doubted, and that subsequent empirical evidence soundly refutes—"sound policy would wisely sacrifice these economics to preservation of more economic freedom and equality."[1]

These insights did not impress the mainstream of modern economists. As the newly-installed president of the American Economic Association told his colleagues in 1973, the profession's greatest fault was its persistent failure to factor economic power into its hyper-sophisticated analyses and policy prescriptions. The most commonplace features of economic orthodoxy, he observed, "are the assumptions by which power . . . is removed from the subject." This exclusion of power from our discipline, he said, destroys the relation of economics to "the real world," and condemns economists "to the social sidelines where they either call no plays or urge the wrong ones."[2]

Theorists and practitioners of the dismal science were not noticeably moved. In their world, it is still *de rigeur* to dismiss power as irrelevant. They may lampoon government policies for benefiting a privileged few at society's expense (such as protecting domestic industries from foreign competition, bailing out bankrupt giants like Lockheed, Chrysler, and Continental Illinois, or creating tax loopholes for particular firms and industries). At the same time, however, economists (on both the left and the right of the political spectrum) find it fashionable to glorify the giant corporation as the handmaiden of production efficiency, technological advance, and international competitiveness in the "new" global economy. And it is a precept of virtually all orthodoxies today to vilify structural antitrust policy—especially with respect to megamergers—as an intellectually embarrassing anachronism in a "modern" age.

That deficient or counterproductive government policies might reflect the exercise of private economic power; that the capacity to undermine and to subvert rational public policy might be a nontrivial consequence of corporate Bigness; that encouragement of megamergers and giantism might render resolution of structurally embedded economic problems more intractable—these possibilities are ignored.

In this article we propose to raise some central but neglected questions about the political economy of power and public policy: Is economic giantism relevant to an understanding of the shape and practical consequences of government policies? Does the power of gigantic economic organizations—corporations in conjunction with their labor unions—include the capacity to compound, frustrate, and subvert rational public policy? Does it include the capacity to elicit counterproductive and anti-social government intervention? To what extent are the failures of public policy attributable to disproportionate size and its capacity to practice economic sabotage (in Simons's terms, "to disrupt or to stop the whole flow of social income")? And what does the power of giantism portend for the design and implementation of public policy—and for the relevance of economics—in the resolution of overarching social problems?

We shall pose these questions for analysis in three important fields. First, we shall examine the impact of corporate giantism on regulatory policy in the automobile industry. Next, we shall explore the consequences of Bigness for international trade policy in steel. Then we shall assess the significance of economic giantism for macro-economic stabilization policy. In our conclusion, we shall highlight some general public policy implications.

Regulatory Policy: A Case Study in Automobiles

In a surfeit of scholarly treatises, economists in recent years have advocated a reform of government regulation of industry.[3] In particular, they have criticized traditional regulation for its crude reliance on centralized, bureaucratic "command-and-control" methods comprising direct orders to industry to desist from acting in anti-social ways. As a more elegant alternative, the *nouvelle vague* has devoted considerable intellectual effort to the design and promotion of more sophisticated and theoretically satisfying regulatory systems relying on price- and market-based incentives to alter corporate conduct.

William J. Baumol and Wallace E. Oates have explained the essence of the incentives-based approach to regulation in the following terms:

> Suppose we decide that the oil industry is currently paying the right total amount in taxes, but that it is also desirable to encourage the removal of lead from fuels. For this purpose one could *reduce* the tax on unleaded gasoline, and *increase* it on leaded gasolines. This would give the industry the opportunity to behave in a manner consistent with social goals with no loss to itself. Nor need this procedure constitute either a drain on the public budget or a subsidy to industry. Given the efficiency with which private enterprise pursues its profits, the speed of the resulting change-over to lead-free fuels would, no doubt, be impressive . . . [B]y offering virtue its just (financial) reward, we change the rules of the game to induce industry . . . to alter their behavior to promote an environmental objective.[4]

Proceeding from this premise, Herculean efforts have been devoted to designing economically optimal incentive-based systems for social control and regulation. An impressive list of criteria against which to evaluate the economic efficacy of incentive-based regulation has been elaborated, including dependability, permanence, adaptability to economic growth, equity, economy, and inducement to maximum effort.[5] Problems of defining with precise exactitude the behavior to be altered have been discussed. The kinds of incentives to impose ("fees," "tradeable permits," auctions of "property rights") have been dissected in detail, and the theoretically correct magnitude of the incentives to be applied have been subjected to intricate scholarly disquisition. Alternative mechanisms for implementing such regulatory systems have been promulgated. Questions of the proper legislative and administrative bodies to oversee these systems have been raised and explored, and fine points regarding the disposition of the proceeds collected under such systems (that is, should the proceeds be earmarked for some general purpose? Devoted to research? Rebated? Added to general government revenues?) have been investigated.[6]

These elegant analytical exercises, of course, make no allowance for the possibility that corporate power might be mobilized to sabotage even the most finely tuned incentive-based regulatory policy. This omission of power is unfortunate, however. Efforts to regulate fuel economy in the U.S. automobile industry are a dramatic case in point.

The U.S. auto oligopoly's lackluster performance in the field of fuel economy is familiar to students of the industry. The Big Three producers—General Motors, Ford, and Chrysler—traditionally considered neither the fuel inefficiency of their products, nor limited petroleum supplies, to be matters of any particular concern. They ignored warnings of the inevitability of limited petroleum supplies, even when voiced by responsible officials within the industry itself. They seemed casually indifferent to innovations (including alternative powerplants) capable of enhancing fuel economy. And, not surprisingly, the fuel inefficiency of U.S. automobiles steadily worsened over the post-World War II era.[7]

Of course, the full social ramifications of the industry's delinquent performance appeared with a vengeance in the 1970s, when the nation was convulsed by oil shortages, gasoline crises, miles-long service station lines, and a torrent of small fuel-efficient cars imported from abroad.

In the midst of the fuel crisis, observing that automobiles accounted for forty percent of all petroleum products consumed in the United States, and sensibly concluding that better automotive fuel economy could significantly reduce the United States' dependence on foreign energy supplies, Congress enacted legislation in 1975 to prod the domestic industry to increase the fuel economy of its cars.[8] Doubtless influenced by eminent economic discourse, Congress elected to use an incentives-based approach to the problem which, on the basis of orthodox theory, seemed to be the epitome of economic wisdom: Standards were specified requiring that the overall average fuel efficiency of each producer's annual new car sales reach eighteen miles per gallon by 1978, and increase each year thereafter until 1985, when the standard would reach (and remain at) 27.5 miles per gallon. Failure by a producer to achieve these mileage standards would simply result in the imposition of a noncompliance fee of $5 for each tenth of a mile per gallon by which the firm's overall fleet average fell below the specified standard, multiplied by the number of new cars sold by the firm in the year in which it failed to attain the standard.[9]

Economists applauded this enlightened approach. Thomas C. Schelling called it a "regulatory innovation" because the "manufacturer is not given a mileage standard that every car must meet, or a schedule of mileages for cars of different weight, engine size, or price, or quotas by number or sales value of cars in alternative mileage categories. Rather, the manufacturer is given a mileage figure that all cars produced during the year must together meet on the average. . . .By 1985 the average . . . will be 27.5 miles per gallon. A manufacturer will be within the requirements if every car meets that figure. He will also be within the requirements if half the cars achieve 30 m.p.g. and the other half at least 25. If two-thirds achieve 30, the remaining third can be as low as 22.5. Cars can get as few as 10 or 15 m.p.g. as long as there are compensatory sales of cars that keep the average up."[10]

Lawrence J. White also praised Congress's use of incentives. As he evaluated them, the "fuel economy standards . . . embody two nice properties. First, they employ the sale-weighted average principle, allowing the manufacturer to trade off more expensive ways of achieving the required fuel economy against less expensive ways. They even allow a one-year carry-forward, carry-back feature, so that a manufacturer's achievements beyond the required standards can be used to offset shortfalls one year earlier or one year later. Second, they contain a noncompliance fee, rather than the 'achieve-it-or-else-we-will-close-you-down' provisions."[11]

The response of the industry's giants, however, proved that this praise was somewhat premature. General Motors and Ford soon demonstrated the futility of economic theorizing that ignores the capacity of corporate giants to engage in social economic sabotage. GM and Ford did *not* change their behavior to conform to "incentive-based" regulation. Instead, in 1985, when the fuel economy standards began to bind, they blatantly pressured government to loosen the mileage standards and permit them to continue to act as they pleased.

In a variation of the "national catastrophe" ploy that successfully obtained a federal bailout for Chrysler, General Motors and Ford raised the specter of plant closings, shutdowns, and layoffs, and unemployment on a massive scale in a critical sector of the economy should the mileage standards not be relaxed. Unless the requirements were reduced, a General Motors vice president warned Congress in May 1985, "full-line manufacturers [that is, GM and Ford] face the prospect of restricting product availability."[12] This, she noted for the benefit of a Congress facing upcoming elections, "translates into plant closings, job losses, and lower economic growth."[13] Failure to accede to GM's demands, she repeated, "would mean inevitably fewer sales, closing some plants, putting people out of work, slowing down the economy."[14] To drive home the point, GM submitted an extensive list of eighty-eight plants—with the city and state location of each conveniently specified —that could be adversely affected should the government refuse to act.[15] The consequences of resisting the Big Two's demands, a Ford vice president echoed, might well entail "the job dislocations of closing down plants."[16] (The industry asserted these claims despite the fact, as even the industry-oriented National Highway Traffic Safety Administration admits, that car companies "influence demand [for large fuel-inefficient cars] through their marketing and pricing strategies"; and despite the fact that an easing of the mileage standard could well *cost* U.S. jobs by leaving the domestic firms free to pursue their plans to import more small cars from abroad.)[17]

Orthodox economic theory thus seemed embarrassingly irrelevant when, in late 1985, the government lowered automotive fuel economy standards in accordance with the wishes of GM and Ford—firms whose absolute size empowers them to engage in economic extortion on a grand scale, and to leave an otherwise theoretically more satisfying "incentives-based" regulatory policy in tatters. A spokesman later explained that the government relaxed the mileage requirements on the basis of "adverse economic consequences, including job losses in the tens of thousands in the auto industry, if the standard was not lowered."[18]

Thus, in the field of regulatory policy, the central public policy questions arise: Is it realistic to assume that government would impose penalties, fines, or "fees" if to do so would jeopardize the financial viability of corporate leviathans? Would the government ever seriously consider the shut-down of major plants if their corporate masters should refuse to meet regulatory standards? In the face of Bigness and its capacity to engage in social sabotage, is the government not forced to grant delays, extensions, exemptions, and so forth, almost regardless of the public harm concomitant therewith? Can social regulation really be effective under these conditions? Orthodox economics fails to raise—much less seeks to answer—these critical questions. The cost of this omission, it seems, is to render economics largely irrelevant in a world of political economy.[19]

International Trade Policy: A Case Study in Steel

It is a fundamental tenet in economics that protection of domestic industries from foreign competition is harmful to society. International trade and international competition promote the economic welfare of trading partners by keeping prices of goods low (including the costs of inputs for domestic producers who, in turn, compete in world markets), expanding buyers' choices, enhancing production levels through specialization and the gains from comparative advantage, and raising material standards of living. Conversely, protectionism is harmful because it undermines economic well-being in all the foregoing respects.

So powerful is this belief in the virtues of international competition that some ("neo-liberal") economists are prepared to abolish the antitrust laws and to abandon efforts to maintain competitively structured domestic industries. They argue, on the one hand, that foreign competition provides all the protection that U.S. consumers need against exploitation by domestic oligopolies and, on the other hand, that U.S. firms must be allowed to merge (without antitrust restraint) to achieve "world class" dimension and thus to become competitive in global markets. Lester Thurow states the new policy with unalloyed bluntness: "America should abolish its antitrust laws" because "the techniques of the 19th century are not applicable in getting ready for the 21st."[20] This view is echoed by top officials in the Reagan Administration, led by Secretary of Commerce Malcolm Baldridge, who have just submitted a package of proposed antitrust revisions to Congress that would, in effect, condemn the anti-merger proscriptions of the Clayton Act to legislative euthanasia.[21]

Apart from the dubious assumption that corporate giantism and megamergers promote good economic performance (an assumption on which empirical evidence casts considerable doubt), this "new learning" is flawed by its failure to consider the political economy of merger-induced giantism and its impact on government policy.[22] Economic power is not inert. Nor is it merely a decorative status symbol. Corporate giants do not submit passively to the rigors and penalties of the global market. They do not shun the use of political power to immunize themselves from competition—whether foreign or domestic. In the real world, corporate giants—typically in tacit vertical collusion with organized labor—will reach out, whenever they find it necessary, to manipulate the state in order to *alter* the rules of the global market game. They will not hesitate to use their political power to escape the consequences of their delinquent performance by shifting the costs of private failure to society at large. They will not be reluctant to try to neutralize foreign competition through tariffs, quotas, orderly marketing agreements, et cetera, and thus to subvert the global market which Thurow, Baldridge, et al. picture as an omnipotent control mechanism.

The U.S. steel industry provides an apt case in point. Here is an industry wherein oligopoloid giantism has been almost exclusively the product of an ongoing (and virtually unmolested) merger and consolidation movement since the turn of the century.[23] Here is an industry that has been congenitally afflicted with the predictable maladies of elephantine size and noncompetitive industry structure: innovation has been lethargic, hampered by the dry-rot of bureaucracy; the dominant integrated firms have long been shackled with bloated costs and the disabilities of exaggerated size; and price policy has been directed at uniformity and rigidity, except in an upward direction, and anything but competitively determined. (We shall return to the importance of this pattern in the next section.)[24] Moreover, it is an industry where a powerful labor union (the United Steelworkers) has until very recent years demanded, and obtained, wages far outstripping productivity gains—wages that the oligopoly traditionally passed on to buyers in a virulent pattern of price-wage-price escalation.

When imports grew sufficiently large in the late-1950s to begin to threaten this well-ordered preserve, the industry acted. But rather than meeting foreign competition in the global marketplace, the Bigness complex in steel mobilized a massive, permanent counteroffensive in the halls of government.[25]

Beginning as early as 1967, a succession of proposed bills surfaced in Congress calling for statutory limits on steel imports. Shortly thereafter, the Congressional Steel Caucus was organized to receive and to promote Big Steel's complaints against foreign competition. The industry's efforts were not in vain, and, in 1968, the State Department persuaded major steel exporting nations—Japan and members of the European Community—to enter into a Voluntary Restraint Agreement (VRA). Under the Agreement, steel imports from Japan were limited to 5.8 million tons annually and from the European Community to 5.8 million tons annually (approximately a twenty percent reduction in imports from these sources).

Within three years, however, the domestic steel oligopoly found the

VRA unsatisfactory.[26] Responding to the industry's demands, the White House announced a three-year extension of the VRA in 1972, set specific tonnage limitations on three categories of specialty steels, and set the quotas at less than their 1971 level. In addition, fabricated and structural steel and cold finished bars were added to the agreement. Exporting countries further agreed to freeze their product mixes and geographic distribution patterns.

The industry again grew disenchanted, and demanded that additional and far more extensive restraints be placed on imports. In response, the government instituted a Trigger Price Mechanism (TPM) beginning in 1978—a thinly-veiled price floor for virtually all imported steel products. Initially, the Bigness complex was quite pleased with this arrangement. So, too, were foreign producers—and for obvious reasons. M. Jacques Ferry, head of the Common Market's steel group, explained: "We don't have any problems" with the trigger price mechanism. "It has raised steel prices all around the world."

Within two years, the steel oligopoly found TPM inadequate, and —in an election year—it mounted a renewed offensive in the International Trade Commission and the Congress. In 1982 alone, the industry swamped government agencies with more than two hundred anti-import complaints[27] (which, in a number of cases, were substantively groundless), and then deployed these complaints as a lever for forcing European and Japanese producers to "voluntarily" restrain carbon steel imports to the United States.

As the 1984 election drew nigh, the industry continued its political fusillade against foreign competition. Producers and steelworkers lobbied both houses of Congress. In the House, the "Fair Trade in Steel Act" of 1984 was introduced which, if enacted, would have established highly product-specific quotas across forty-four steel product categories, with the overall objective of fixing at fifteen percent the share of all imports in the U.S. market. Significantly, the bill proposed to dispense with any considerations of "fair" or "unfair" competition. In the midst of his re-election campaign, and beset by industry pressure, President Reagan directed his Special Trade Representative to negotiate comprehensive "voluntary" restraint agreements with all nations exporting steel to the United States. To lend urgency to the negotiations, the White House indicated it would block access to the U.S. market to any country refusing to participate. This threat was not without effect. By November 1985, "voluntary" restraint agreements involving fourteen nations and covering ninety percent of U.S. steel imports were in place, potentially limiting total imports to 18.5 percent of the U.S. market, down from 25 percent in 1984.

The burden on the economy of Big Steel's political machinations has not been insignificant. Estimates of the annual cost burden of VRA range from $386 million to $1 billion.[28] For the year 1979 alone, the total cost of the TPM to consumers has been placed at $1 billion, and possibly as high as $6 billion.[29] Steel-using U.S. producers, who must compete in world markets, have also been significantly handicapped by having to pay steel prices as much as twenty percent higher than those paid by their rivals abroad.[30]

Nor, it is important to recognize, is steel unique. When Chrysler, then the nation's tenth largest industrial concern, confronted imminent bankruptcy in 1978–79, owing to a succession of bad management decisions and poor product and production strategies, the firm—joined by the United Auto Workers, as well as by suppliers, dealers, Congresspeople, and mayors and governors across the country—brought pressure to bear on government and obtained a federal bailout. Two years later, in 1981, when, as a result of having ignored market trends for decades, the auto oligopoly faced growing inroads by innovative, fuel-efficient Japanese cars, the Bigness complex in autos—companies and the union—successfully obtained a bailout of the entire industry from global competition through governmentally-negotiated "voluntary" Japanese export restraints—at a cumulative estimated cost since 1981 of as much as $15 billion to U.S. car buyers.[31]

Clearly counterproductive and seemingly irrational government trade policies do not materialize out of thin air. Nor are they the handiwork of untutored, bumbling bureaucrats. In a representative democracy, the attacks on free trade and the clamor for protectionism can be understood only in the context of political economy—the power of giant oligopolists acting in collusion with powerful labor unions to manipulate government. Abolishing antitrust and facilitating the consummation of megamergers will not ameliorate our "trade problem"; the creation of Brobdingnagian power structures will only exacerbate it.[32]

Macroeconomic Stabilization Policy

In the macroeconomic field, the challenge is to formulate fiscal and monetary policies capable of promoting full employment and economic growth, subduing inflation, and mitigating cyclical fluctuations in the economy. Macroeconomists passionately debate the kinds of policies best able to achieve these objectives. Keynesians and neo-Keynesians assert the imperative of government management of aggregate demand and the importance of "fine-tuning" macro-policy to counteract shifts and shocks to the economy. Monetarists insist upon the primacy of the money stock, inveigh against what they perceive to be the evils of discretionary policy, and debate fine points in the theoretically proper fixed rate of growth that should be maintained in the money supply (if agreement could be reached as to precisely what "money" is). For the cynically inclined, "rational expectationists" offer the assurance that no macro-policy is viable because economic agents fully anticipate, and act to counteract, any policy moves the government might make. "Supply-siders" propagandize tax cuts and "Laffer curves" as the cure-all for the nation's macroeconomic ills.

For all of these orthodoxies, consideration of structurally rooted economic power is passé. Their proponents recommend monetary and fiscal stabilization measures *as if* the economy approximated a state of "perfect" competition; *as if* economic power is inconsequential; and *as if* structural concentration of power in the economy is incapable of exacerbating macroeconomic instability and compounding, distorting, or neutralizing macro-policy stabilization measures. Disproportionate economic size, noncompetitive industry structures, and the political economy of power—these are, by convention, omitted from the discourse.

In reality, however, experience shows that Bigness and concentrated power pose at least three important problems in the performance and stability of the macroeconomy: First, oligopoloid and monopoloid corporate giants, typically in collusion with monopolists in the labor market, force up prices and wages at less than full employment levels of production, even in the face of substantial unemployment and declines in demand. Second, concentrated power in key sectors of the economy (such as steel and autos) thus aggravates cyclical instability. This is especially the case during cyclical recessions and downturns, when prices in important sectors are held rigid or are raised, thereby magnifying the severity of declines in demand, sales, production, and unemployment. Third, as a result of the foregoing, the task of devising rational macro-policy is nullified or counterproductive, as inflation arises at less than full employment, as anti-inflation policies produce price *increases* (not declines) in key sectors, and as the potency (and, hence, the risks) of monetary and fiscal policies to counteract cyclical fluctuations must be increased in strength.

The Steel Industry

Here again, the U.S. steel industry provides a case in point. As we have seen, it is an industry characterized by oligopoloid giantism in the product market, and by monopoly in the labor market. Moreover, steel, of course, is an important basic input in the manufacture of many products throughout the economy, including automobiles, consumer appliances and other consumer durable goods, and in the construction of factories, plants, and equipment. For these reasons, pricing behavior in steel affects costs, competitiveness, and prices across the economy.

The actual pattern of pricing in steel is highly significant, characterized by price rigidity and perverse price increases in the face of sales declines—a pattern that significantly exacerbates cyclical instability in steel, and in the economy at large.

From 1947 to the end of the 1950s, steel prices were steadily increased at regular intervals regardless of costs or demand. Between December 1955 and August 1957, for example, the price index on cold-rolled sheets rose 20 points, whereas the production index dropped 80 points; on cold-rolled strip, the price index advanced 23.8 points, whereas the production index slumped 45.6 points; on hot-rolled sheets, the price index rose 30.4 points, whereas the production index fell 58.6 points. Similar trends occurred in hot-rolled bars, pipe and tube, rails, plates, and other steel products.[33] Steel prices increased when demand fell in 1949, in 1954, and in 1957. The untoward consequences for macroeconomic performance were noted by President Johnson's Council of Economic Advisors in a 1965 report:

> Steel prices played an important role in the general price increases of the 1950s. Between 1947 and 1951, the average increase in the price of basic steel products was 9 percent per year, twice the average increase of all wholesale prices. The unique behavior of steel prices was most pronounced in the mid-1950s. While the wholesale price index was falling an average of 0.9 percent annually from 1951 to 1955, the price index for steel was rising an average of 4.8 percent per year. From 1955 to 1958, steel prices were increasing 7.1 percent annually, or almost three times as fast as wholesale prices generally. No other major sector shows a similar record.[34]

With only occasional exceptions due to the temporary impact of foreign competition, this perverse, recession-magnifying pattern of pricing has persisted. Professor Zolton Acs explains: "In the two recessions during the 1970s, steel prices *rose* 6.4 percent in 1970 and 26.8 percent in 1974, while output fell. During the 1980 recession, steel production fell by 18 percent and steel prices increased by 6.8 percent."[35] Then, in 1982–83, with steel demand at its lowest level since the Great Depression, and with nearly one-half the nation's steelworkers laid off, the steel oligopoly pushed through price increases averaging 6 percent on sheet and strip steel products widely used throughout the industry.[36] It was, *Business Week* observed, a clear demonstration of "steel pricing that ignores the market."[37]

The steelworkers—at least those who remained employed—shared in Big Steel's price escalation game. Over the years 1964 to 1980, average hourly compensation far outstripped productivity gains, unit labor costs approximately doubled, and the gap between hourly employment costs in steel relative to all U.S. manufacturing rose from twenty-five percent in the mid-1970s to sixty percent by 1980.[38]

Thus, economic giantism and power in steel have significantly contributed to price-cost-price push inflation in the economy, and militated to even greater declines in demand, production and employment during recessions—in steel, as well as in the broad range of manufacturing industries that consume this important basic product.

The Automobile Industry

The automobile exerts an even greater impact on the U.S. economy. In recent years, as many as one-fifth of all U.S. manufacturing workers have been employed in jobs either directly or indirectly tied to automobile production.[39] The auto industry is one of the nation's largest consumers of a broad array of industrial products: it purchases six percent of the total U.S. plastics production; twelve percent of the nation's aluminum; nineteen percent of all steel produced in the United States; twenty percent of the machine tools manufactured; fifty percent of the lead produced; and sixty-seven percent of the nation's rubber output.[40] It accounts for a sizeable share of manufacturing employment, not just in Detroit and Michigan, but in major metropolitan areas and states across the country.[41] And automobile purchases account for approximately one-fifth of the total national retail sales of all goods and services.[42] As summarized by former UAW president Douglas Fraser, "Auto is pivotal, in terms of employment, technology, and links to other industries."[43]

In autos, as in steel, however, oligopoloid giantism in the product market has coalesced with monopoly in the labor market to fuel secular inflation, to exacerbate macroeconomic instability, and, especially, to aggravate the severity of cyclical recessions in the economy.

The record of long-run inflation in automobile prices is evident in Table 1. Over the years 1967 to 1984, the rate of increase in U.S. new car prices has exceeded the rate of increase in consumer prices generally (and, indeed, has significantly contributed to inflation economy-wide) by seventeen percent.[44] In recent years, the gap between auto price increases and general consumer price inflation has widened, with average new car prices rising forty-four percent between 1977 and 1983—a rate more than two and one-half times greater than the rise recorded in the consumer price index during the same period.[45] (Of course, protection of the industry from foreign competition has contributed significantly to recent new-car price inflation.)[46]

Table 1 ***Average U.S. New Car Selling Prices***

Year	*Average New Car Price*	*Index of New Car Price (1967=100)*
1967	$ 3,200	100.0
1968	3,240	101.3
1969	3,400	106.3
1970	3,430	107.3
1971	3,730	116.6
1972	3,690	115.3
1973	3,930	122.8
1974	4,390	137.2
1975	4,750	148.4
1976	5,470	170.9
1977	6,120	191.3
1978	6,470	202.2
1979	6,950	217.2
1980	7,340	235.3
1981	8,850	276.6
1982	9,910	309.7
1983	10,725	335.2
1984	11,100	346.9

SOURCE: Automotive News, *Market Date Book Issue,* 1985.

The shorter-run pattern of auto prices over the course of the business cycle, is, as Figure 1 shows, one in which prices not only fail to decline in response to sizable declines in demand and sales (which would cushion production declines by sustaining demand), but in which prices are persistently—and significantly—*raised* in the face of sales declines (thereby inducing an even greater falloff in production and employment). This pattern of perverse pricing was especially pronounced in the early-1980s.[47] In 1980, on the eve of what would soon prove to be the worst national recession since the Great Depression, with an unemployment rate of twenty-six percent in the motor vehicle industry, and with another 350,000 to 650,000 layoffs in auto-related industries, the domestic oligopoly announced price increases that the *Wall Street Journal* incredulously described as "rivaling anything in modern Detroit history."[48] Another round of price increases engineered by the industry shortly thereafter prompted one exasperated dealer to exclaim the auto companies "don't know what's going on in the market. They defy the law of supply and demand," he said with rueful insight.[49] As the recession deepened through 1981, and as auto sales continued their free-fall, "General Motors Corp. slapped an exceptionally steep price boost on its 1982 models"—a price hike matched by Ford and Chrysler.[50] That this display of market power in action was less than macroeconomically desirable was obvious. "After pushing through a stiff 6% price increase last fall on 1982 models, GM spent much of the year suffering through the deepest sales plunge of the three-year-old auto-industry recession," the *Wall Street Journal* later observed.[51]

Figure 1

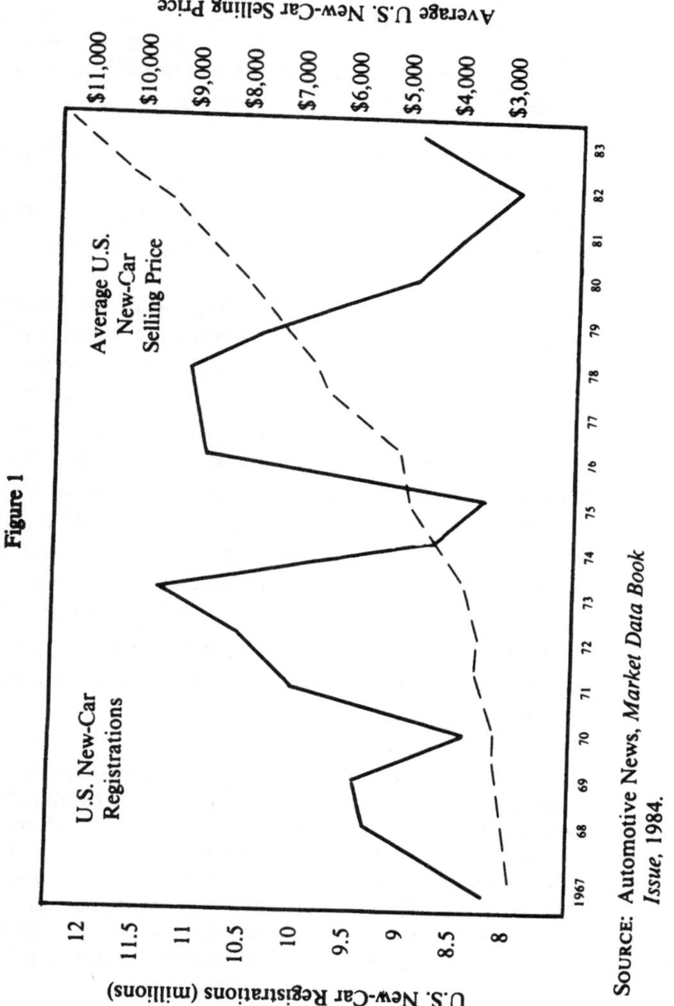

SOURCE: Automotive News, *Market Data Book Issue*, 1984.

Organized labor—at least the workers who remained employed—shared in the fruits of administered inflation in autos. Average hourly compensation in autos rose 214 percent over the years 1967 to 1980 (far greater than labor productivity growth of thirty-five percent over the same period).[52] Charles L. Schultze has evaluated wage inflation in the industry in the follow terms:

> In the mid-1960s hourly employment costs (wages and fringe benefits) in the major auto companies were about 20% above the average for manufacturing industries. Every three years since, the labor contract negotiated between industry and the union has widened the gap. . . . Finally, in 1979—faced with mounting interest rates, an incipient recession, sharply higher gasoline prices, growing resistance to large American cars and increased imports from Japan—what did the industry do? It negotiated a contract that by 1980 put auto wages and fringes about 60% above the manufacturing average.[53]

The industry's most recent contract, negotiated between Chrysler and the UAW in late-1985, continues the tradition of price-cost-price inflation—a burden that Paul A. London points out is ultimately borne by "the people who would like to work in an expanding industrial America."[54]

The steel and automobile industries are prototypical of the problems posed for macroeconomic stabilization by economic giantism and power.[55] In the field of macro stabilization policy, power compounds the problems of rational public policy-making. It presents the almost intractable dilemma of combatting inflation with restrictive fiscal or monetary policies before full employment levels are reached (thereby tolerating high unemployment) or, alternatively, choosing to aim for low unemployment at the cost of high inflation. The exercise of economic power obviously frustrates and neutralizes anti-inflationary macro policies when oligopoloid and monopoloid corporate giants *raise*—rather than reduce—prices in response to policy-induced deflationary macroeconomic conditions. Indeed, as Simons pointed out in 1944, the existence of concentrated economic power calls into question the very viability of *any* macroeconomic policy:

> No amount of monetary or fiscal stimulation will give us adequate employment or investment if strategically situated unions and enterpriser monopolists insist upon utilizing improved demand conditions to increase their wages and prices rather than to increase employment, investment, and output—or to hold up prices where improved technology is markedly reducing costs. And there is no reason why organized producer groups, holding adequate organizational and political power, should, acting in their separate interests, forego the opportunity to improve their rel-

> ative position in such circumstances. They may, to be sure, injure themselves along with the community, all or most of them being worse off by virtue of their restrictive measures than if none had practiced them. But each group may be better off than if it alone has behaved less monopolistically.[56]

Short of "dictatorship at one extreme and real competition at the other," he pointed out, "there would appear to be no means for getting co-ordinated or co-operative action from such groups as a whole."[57] Regrettably for the relevance of economics, Simons's point is lost amid today's macro-theoretical din of "Laffer curves," "fixed money growth rules," and "rational expectations."[58]

Conclusion

In *The Titan,* a classic tale of public utility corruption in Chicago at the turn of the century, Theodore Dreiser wrote that novitiates introduced into that city's fashionable society were "remote not so much from a serious as from an accurate conception of life."[59] In our article we have inquired into the neglected relationship between economic giantism, economic power, and the formulation, implementation and efficacy of public policy. In the fields of regulatory policy, international trade policy, and macroeconomic stabilization policy, we find that size and the power attached thereto are relevant, and that they are not the trivia that regnant economic dogmas presume them to be. Instead, economic giantism in product and labor markets acts to frustrate, compound, undermine, and subvert intelligent public policy. To ignore the reality of the economic power problem as is currently the fashion, we submit, is tantamount to professionally inculcated delusion; it is to suffer (in Dreiser's words) not so much from a serious as from an inaccurate conception of life.

In the light of this, the most important implications of our study are three-fold:

First, our findings suggest that if relevance is not taboo, then the time has come for economists to explicitly recognize the political economy of disproportionate size, noncompetitive industry structure, and the economic power flowing therefrom. Failure to do so condemns economics to what Kenneth Boulding has called the misguided search for the celestial mechanics of a non-existent universe.

Second, an important first step requires an appreciation of the fact that economic power comprises considerably more than the mere (and altogether innocuous) capacity to influence price in an isolated market. As we have seen, economic giantism includes the far more potent ability to manipulate the state, to elicit anti-social government interventions, and to undermine the rational resolution of major economic problems.

Third, recognition of reality in this regard requires considerably more emphasis on antitrust policy, particularly its structural orientation. It suggests that the social benefits of structural antitrust policy against monopoly, oligopoly, and megamergers are not limited to the economic gains from competitive industry structures alone. Perhaps even more importantly, vigilance on the structural antitrust front may be an essential prerequisite for sound public policy across a broad range by freeing society from being held hostage to Bigness and its capacity for economic extortion and social sabotage. At a minimum, recognizing the reality and consequences of economic power counsels considerable skepticism with respect to current proposals for the euthanasia of antitrust and the promotion of economic giantism as a matter of national policy.

Notes

1. See Walter Adams and James W. Brock, *The Bigness Complex* (New York: Pantheon Books, 1986). Henry C. Simons, *Economic Policy For A Free Society* (Chicago: University of Chicago Press, 1948), pp. 52, 122, 218. Thomas Jefferson touched upon the problem much earlier, when he warned his countrymen of "the aristocracy of our monied corporations which dare already to challenge our government to a trial of strength, and bid defiance to the laws of our country." Quoted in Lawrence Goodwyn, *Democratic Promise: The Populist Moment* (New York: Oxford University Press, 1976), p. 1.
2. John Kenneth Galbraith, "Power and the Useful Economist," *American Economics Review*, 63 (March 1973): 1–11.
3. See, for example, Stephen Breyer, *Regulation and Its Reform* (Cambridge, Mass.: Harvard University Press, 1982); Robert E. Litan and William D. Nordhaus, *Reforming Federal Regulation* (New Haven, Conn.: Yale University Press, 1983); LeRoy Graymer and Frederick Thompson, *Reforming Social Regulation* (Beverly Hills, Calif.: Sage Publications, 1982); Lawrence J. White, *Reforming Regulation* (New York: Prentice-Hall, 1981); *Social Regulation: Strategies for Reform* ed. Eugene Bardach and Robert A. Kagan (San Francisco: Institute for Contemporary Studies, 1982).
4. William J. Baumol and Wallace E. Oates, *Economics, Environmental Policy, and the Quality of Life* (Englewood Cliffs, N.J.: Prentice-Hall, 1979), pp. 231–32.
5. Ibid., pp. 232–42.
6. See Thomas C. Schelling, "Prices as Regulatory Instruments," in *Incentives for Environmental Protection* ed. Thomas C. Schelling (Cambridge, Mass.: MIT Press, 1983); Breyer, *Regulation and its Reform*, pp. 271–84; Charles L. Schultze, *The Public Use of the Private Interest* (Washington, D.C.: Brookings Institution, 1977); Baumol and Oates, *Economics, Enviromen-*

tal Policy, and the Quality of Life, pp. 246–54; Lawrence J. White, *The Regulation of Air Pollutant Emissions from Motor Vehicles* (Washington, D.C.: American Enterprise Institute, 1982), pp. 92–107.

7. For a more detailed analysis, as well as complete documentation, see Walter Adams and James W. Brock, "Bigness and Social Efficiency: A Case Study of the U.S. Auto Industry," in *Corporations and Society*, ed. Arthur S. Miller and Warren Samuels (Westport, Conn.: Greenwood Press, 1986).
8. U.S. Congress, H.R. Rep. No. 340, 94th Cong., 1st sess., 1975, p. 86.
9. Energy Policy and Conservation Act, P.L. 94–163, 89 Stat. 871, 502 (1975).
10. Schelling. "Prices as Regulatory Instruments," p. 37.
11. White, *Reforming Regulation*, p. 120.
12. U.S. Congress, Senate, Subcommittee on Energy Regulation and Conservation, *Automobile Fuel Economy Standards, Hearings*, 99th Cong., 1st sess., 1985, p. 57.
13. Ibid.
14. Ibid., p. 81.
15. Ibid., pp. 284–88.
16. Ibid., p. 71.
17. Ibid., pp. 27, 41.
18. *New York Times*, 2 October 1985, p. 11. The auto companies have honed the leverage of size to a fine art in demanding government favors, privileges, and dispensations. This is especially the case with General Motors. For example, in their recent book, Ralph Nader and William Taylor report that for its Poletown plant in Detroit, GM obtained federal, state and local government subsidies of approximately $220 million, which were used "to acquire the area, relocate the residents, demolish the structures, build roads and rail facilities, and for other site preparations. A twelve-year, 50 percent property-tax abatement brought a total subsidy package to General Motors of $350 million." See Ralph Nader and William Taylor, *The Big Boys: Power and Position in American Business* (New York: Pantheon Book, 1986), pp. 121–22.

    In Missouri, GM successfully lobbied the city council of Kansas City to close a municipal airport and offer the land to GM. Then the race for additional subsidies began in earnest: GM applied for low-interest bonds; the state established an enterprise zone on the airport site, thereby exempting GM from sales, use, property, and *ad valorem* taxes; and the city agreed to issue $775 million in economic-development revenue bonds for the project. See Nader and Taylor, *The Big Boys*, p. 129.

    In Michigan, GM has demanded unprecedented reductions in its property taxes, even in localities like Genessee Township where the firm already enjoys a twelve-year, 50 percent tax abatement on the value of its plant and property. "In effect," the traditionally sympathetic *Flint Journal* concludes, "GM is saying it can take its payroll elsewhere if local jurisdictions don't cry 'uncle'." See Nader and Taylor, *The Big Boys*, p. 131. Indeed, according to a high ranking official of the corporation, GM intends to expand its efforts at tax privileges across the country: "Now we are trying to go to the communities, one by one, and say to them, 'We don't intend to bring you to your knees, we can do a phase-in.'" See Nader and Taylor, *The Big Boys*, p. 132.

    And most recently, GM capped its efforts with the lure of its "Saturn" small-car project: "Twenty-seven governors, as well as the economic development officials of nine other states, journeyed to Detroit to plead for the project. They carried promises of free land, cheap electricity, low-interest loans, tax holidays, taxpayer-financed job training." In this case, GM orchestrated what some have called "the most extensive and expensive bidding war over an industrial project in American history." See Nader and Taylor, *The Big Boys*, p. 115.

19. It is a tribute to the resilience of convention that, having witnessed the demise of the government's fuel economy program, economists should now propose extending the same approach to other areas of automotive regulation. See Robert W. Crandall et al., *Regulating the Automobile* (Washington, D.C.: Brookings Institution, 1986), p. 102.
20. Lester C. Thurow, "Let's Abolish the Antitrust Laws," *New York Times*, 19 October 1980. See also Lester C. Thurow, *The Zero-Sum Society* (New York: Basic Books, 1980), p. 146.
21. Malcolm Baldridge, "Rx for Export Woes: Antitrust Relief," *Wall Street Journal*, 15 October 1985, p. 30; and "How to Ruin an Entire Industry," *New York Times*, 11 March 1984, sec. 3, p. 2.
22. See Adams and Brock, *The Bigness Complex* and the evidence and sources cited therein.
23. See U.S. Congress, House. Select Committee on Small Business. *Steel—Acquisitions, Mergers, and Expansion of 12 Major Companies, 1900 to 1950. Hearings*, 81st Cong., 2nd sess., 1950. See also Federal Trade Commission, *Report on the Merger Movement* (Washington, D.C.: 1948), Appendix 1.
24. See Walter Adams and Hans Mueller, "The Steel Industry," in *The Structure of American Industry*, 7th ed., ed. Walter Adams (New York: Macmillan, 1986).
25. Except where indicated otherwise, the following account is drawn from Adams and Brock, *The Bigness Complex*, chap. 20.
26. For example, the fact that the VRA was expressed in physical tonnage terms meant that Japanese and European Community producers could expand their shipments of stainless steel and other high-value products to the U.S. market. Moreover, both the Japanese and the Europeans claimed that fabricated structural steel and cold-finished bars were not included in the VRA limitations.
27. See Stephen L. Lande and Craig VanGrasstek, *The Trade and Tariff Act of 1984* (Lexington, Mass.: Lexington Books, 1986), p. 144.
28. Adams and Mueller, "The Steel Industry," p. 113.
29. Walter Adams and James W. Brock, "Countervailing or Coalescing Power? The Problem of Labor/Management Coalitions," *Journal of Post-Keynesian Economics*, 6 (Winter 1983/84): 180–97.
30. According to the *Wall Street Journal*, "Just a 7% rise in steel prices could add more than $30 million in annual expense for Caterpillar Tractor Co. . . . which faces fierce foreign competition of its own." *Wall Street Journal*, 7 January 1985, p. 19.

    It is also important to note that foreign producers do *not* necessarily suffer from steel import restraints, as importers raise their prices to match artificially inflated U.S. levels: "Asked whether overseas producers will benefit from the trade restraints, Myungsik Chung, executive vice president at Korea's largest steelmakers, Pohang Iron & Steel Co., smiles, then replies, 'It is very bad for the U.S. consumer.' " Ibid.

31. See Walter Adams and James W. Brock, "The Automobile Industry." in *The Structure of American Industry.* U.S. International Trade Commission, *A Review of Recent Developments in the U.S. Automobile Industry, Including An Assessment of the Japanese Voluntary Restraint Agreements,* pub. no. 1648 (Washington, D.C.: U.S. International Trade Commission, February 1985), p. ix; Robert W. Crandall, "Import Quotas and the Automobile Industry: The Costs of Protectionism," *Brookings Review* 2 (Summer 1984): 8–16.
32. Although Thurow senses that a key problem of protectionism "is not the trade laws themselves, but the political power of troubled industries like steel," he fails to recognize that the political power problem he decries would expand and become even more intractable were mergers, consolidations, and corporate giantism to be encouraged, as he advocates. Thurow, quoted in *Dun's Review,* February 1981, p. 73.
33. U.S. Congress. Senate. Subcommittee on Antitrust and Monopoly. *Administered Prices in Steel. Report,* 85th Cong., 2nd sess., 1958, pp. 17–26.
34. Council of Economic Advisors, *Report to the President on Steel Prices,* (Washington, D.C.: April 1965), pp. 8–9.
35. Zolton J. Acs, *The Changing Structure of the U.S. Economy: Lessons from the Steel Industry* (New York: Praeger, 1984), p. 93 (emphasis added).
36. *New York Times,* 28 December 1982, p. D3; 21 January 1983, p. 36.
37. *Business Week,* 2 February 1981, p. 26.
38. See "Tacit Vertical Collusion and the Labor-Industrial Complex," *Nebraska Law Review* 62 (Fall 1983): 621–707, p. 705.
39. U.S. Department of Transportation, *The U.S. Automobile Industry: 1980* (Washington, D.C.: 1981), p. 84.
40. U.S. Congress. House. Subcommittee on Economic Stabilization. *To Determine the Impact of Foreign Sourcing on Industry and Communities, Hearing,* 97th Cong., 1st sess., 1981, p. 17.
41. U.S. Department of Transportation, *The U.S. Automobile Industry: 1980,* p. 87.
42. U.S. Congress. Senate. Subcommittee on International Trade. *Issues Relating to the Domestic Auto Industry, Hearing,* part 2, 97th Cong., 1st sess., 1981, p. 204.
43. U.S. Congress, House, Subcommittee on Trade, *Fair Practices in Automotive Products Act, Hearings,* 97th Cong., 2nd sess., 1982, p. 151.
44. Consumer price information taken from Council of Economic Advisers, *Economic Report to the President* (Washington, D.C.: 1986), Table B–55, p. 315.
45. New car prices have also risen faster than consumer wages and incomes, with the result that new cars have become relatively more expensive and less affordable commodities. The *Wall Street Journal* reported in 1983 that "the purchase of a new car requires an average of 36.6 weeks of salary . . . In 1979, it took 31.2 weeks. The figure has been steadily rising from a 1973 low of 27.9 weeks." *Wall Street Journal,* 3 August 1983, p. 13.

The rapid rise in new car prices *cannot* be attributed primarily to costs of government regulation of automotive safety and pollution. According to the Bureau of Labor Statistics, costs incurred by auto companies to comply with government regulations in these areas accounted for less than 12 percent of the total increase in auto prices between 1975 and 1979. U.S. Congress. House. Subcommittee on Economic Stabilization. *The Chrysler*

Corporation Financial Situation, Hearings, part 1A, 96th Cong., 1st sess., 1979, p. 557.

46. "The Quotas raised the general level of automobile prices in this country so that today those prices are very high," one financial analyst points out. "It's a common theme for the auto makers to talk about how they've lowered their break-even point, but they didn't pass the break on to the consumer." *New York Times,* 8 April 1984, sec. 3, p. 1.
47. For detailed documentation of similar pricing patterns in the industry during the 1950s, see U.S. Congress. Senate. Subcommittee on Antitrust and Monopoly. *Administered Prices: Automobiles, Report,* 85th Cong., 2nd sess., 1958.
48. *Wall Street Journal,* 3 October 1980, p. 1; U.S. Department of Transportation, *The U.S. Automobile Industry: 1980,* pp. 83–85.
49. *Wall Street Journal,* 5 January 1981, p. 5.
50. *Wall Street Journal,* 10 August 1981, p. 2; 1 September 1981, p. 2.
51. *Wall Street Journal,* 29 June 1982, p. 2.
52. "Tacit Vertical Collusion and the Labor-Industrial Complex," *Nebraska Law Review* 62 (Fall 1983): 621–707, pp. 701–702.
53. *Wall Street Journal*, 20 March 1981, p. 24.
54. Paul A. London, "Car Bomb," *The New Republic,* 25 November 1985, pp. 14–15.
55. For a painstakingly extensive documentation of the perverse behavior of prices in concentrated industries, as well as their cyclically de-stabilizing impact on the economy, see John M. Blair, *Economic Concentration* (New York: Harcourt Brace, 1972), pp. 405–66; idem, "Market Power and Inflation: A Short-Run Target Return Model," *Journal of Economic Issues* 8 (June 1974): 453–78.
56. Simons, *Economic Policy for a Free Society,* p. 115.
57. Ibid.
58. Mancur Olson is a notable exception. "The most important macroeconomic policy implication" he draws from his exhaustive examination of stagflation, unemployment, and business cycles "is that the best macroeconomic policy is a good microeconomic policy. . . . If combinations dominate markets throughout the economy and the government is always intervening on behalf of special interests, there is no macroeconomic policy that can put things right." Mancur Olson, *The Rise and Decline of Nations* (New Haven, Conn.: Yale University Press, 1982), p. 233.
59. Theodore Dreiser, *The Titan* (New York: John Lane Co., 1915; reprint ed., New York: World Publishing, 1946), p. 36.

18

Corporate Size and the Bailout Factor

Walter Adams
and
James W. Brock

The role of the giant corporation has been a topic of perennial debate among economists. Yet, almost without exception the dispute has been cramped within the confines of two narrow issues: the relationship between corporate size and efficiency in production, and the relationship between corporate size and technological progress. Defenders of bigness contend that the giant firm fosters efficiency in production at lowest unit costs; that it is able to assemble and administer the vast funds needed for technical experimentation and advance; and that corporate giantism thus promotes good economic performance. Critics, on the other hand, argue that corporate bigness undermines operating efficiency, militates against innovation, and subverts economic performance. Each side has amassed empirical evidence to support its position. Each attacks the validity of the other's evidence, as well as the appropriate public policies to be fashioned therefrom.

It is all the more curious, then, and ironic, that the one area where the advantages of corporate bigness are clearest and most unequivocal should be omitted from discourse. That is, the capacity of the giant corporation to demand—and to obtain—government bailouts. "Roughly speaking," John Kenneth Galbraith observes, "if you are in trouble and big enough, you will be rescued and recapitalized in one way or another by the government."[1] A cursory review of such episodes as those involving Penn-Central and Lockheed in the 1970s and Chrysler and Continental Illinois in the 1980s, appears to affirm the point.

Theoretically, the source of this advantage of bigness seems obvious: by virtue of *disproportionate* size, the giant corporation vitally affects the fortunes of broad segments of society—buyers, suppliers, subcontractors, employees, trade unions, stock and bondholders, financial markets, communities, cities, and states—and exerts a profound impact on the economic fate of society. Once a corporation attains the size of a Lockheed, a Chrysler, or a Continental Illinois, its fortunes reverberate throughout the economy. Once firms assume gigantic proportions, they come to be perceived as too big and too important to be allowed to fail. Acting through government, society then feels compelled to guarantee the survival of corporate giants almost regardless of how inefficient, unprogressive, or mismanaged they may be. Then government is in the position of the bank so deeply committed to a borrower that it cannot permit the client to default for fear of jeopardizing the solvency of the bank itself. In short, society becomes a hostage to bigness.

In this article we shall examine corporate size and the bailout factor. In the following section we shall analyze *direct* government bailouts, such as those involving Lockheed and Chrysler. Next, however, we shall show that bailouts of giant firms occur in a variety of other indirect, but equally potent ways, including protection from foreign competition, regulatory delays and dispensations, privileged government procurement practices, state-sponsored promotion, tax favors, and exemption from prosecution for illegal acts and practices. We shall conclude our analysis by highlighting some implications of our findings.

Direct Government Bailouts

Direct government bailouts of bigness occur when government rescues failing corporate giants through direct cash infusions or financial credit and loan guarantees. The scenario is familiar enough: through misfeasance, malfeasance or nonfeasance, a giant firm confronts imminent bankruptcy. Platoons of lobbyists and emissaries of affected interests are then dispatched to Washington to plead the corporation's case for government support. They approach top officials in the executive branch (that is, the Secretary of the Treasury, the Secretary of Commerce, the Secretary of Labor). They persuade Congress to stage emergency hearings where the catastrophic consequences of the firm's demise are portrayed in lengthy, bleak terms. On the other side, a corporal's guard of economists will testify passionately to the *materia medica* of the market, the folly of government rescue, and the principles of free enterprise. In the end, however, bigness is bailed out.

The Chrysler case is prototypical.[2] In October, 1979, company officials announced a record quarterly loss of $460 million, bringing total losses for the year to date to a staggering $721 million. Chrysler, it seemed, was on the verge of going "belly up" unless it could obtain outside assistance to continue operations.

Chrysler attributed its plight largely to three key factors over which it had no control. These included: (1) federal regulatory requirements in the areas of pollution control, safety, and fuel economy, which were claimed to put a "small" company like Chrysler at a competitive disadvantage; (2) gasoline shortages, which cut severely into the market for Chrysler's most profitable vehicles—large cars, vans, and light trucks; and (3) economic recession accompanied by a relatively large decline in car and truck sales across the board. However, at a congressional hearing, the chairman of the corporation admitted that Chrysler's problems to a large degree stemmed from a record of poor management decisions. These included (1) the company's expansion into often doubtful overseas operations in the 1960s, which became a financial drain in the 1970s; (2) the decision to redesign its large cars in the early 1970s and delay the development of smaller cars; and (3) a persistent pattern of delays in production and in the introduction of new models.[3]

In the course of protracted hearings, Congress heard a succession of bailout proponents describe the economic catastrophe they foresaw if Chrysler went bankrupt. Treasury Secretary G. William Miller provided a clinical assessment. "Chrysler is the tenth largest industrial corporation in the United States. Its 1978 revenues were $13.6 billion, generated almost entirely from the sale of 1.2 million cars and 490,000 trucks. Its employment at the beginning of this year was 131,000 and today approximates 113,000. Approximately a quarter of a million others are employed by Chrysler dealers and principal suppliers."[4] He then delineated the economic ramifications of a Chrysler failure. A "Chrysler bankruptcy could cost the federal government more than $1.5 billion in 1980 and 1981 alone. We estimate the federal cost for those years at a total of at least $2.75 billion, an amount that includes loss of revenues, unemployment claims, welfare costs, and other incidental costs. Furthermore, there would be a substantial cost to the state and local governments. Moreover, this does not take account of any cost to the Pension Benefit Guarantee Corporation on Chrysler's unfunded vested pension liabilities of approximately $1.1 billion, which would ultimately be borne by other pension fund sponsors."[5]

He cited "the need to maintain a competitive domestic auto industry.

Without Chrysler, the two remaining major domestic producers would represent a very narrow competitive base. This would be especially troublesome given current concerns about the strength of the competitive process and the high barriers to entry. Chrysler has exercised an important competitive role in challenging General Motors, Ford, and others throughout the market, despite its current lack of profitability. Its recent success in the subcompact market is indicative of its competitive importance."[6]

He also pointed to the "potential loss of Chrysler's current and planned increases in capacity in the small-car market, at a time when the amount of small-car, domestic capacity is critical for trade, environmental, and other reasons."[7]

There would, Miller said, be important "negative effects on the U.S. balance of payments because Chrysler's production would be displaced by substantial foreign imports. The negative impact could be up to $1 billion per year through 1981 from increased imports, largely of subcompacts but also of other models."[8]

Douglas Fraser, president of the United Auto Workers, testified: "I am more concerned with the 600,000 workers in the United States threatened with short- and long-term unemployment should Chrysler fail than I am with the hand-wringing of those worried about protecting the 'free enterprise system.'" With government loan guarantees, he said, "Chrysler can meet its short-term capital needs and return to health by producing the kind of small, fuel-efficient, non-polluting, safe, and attractive cars the American consumer wants to buy."[9]

William G. Milliken, then governor of Michigan, a state suffering from the most virulent recession since the 1930s, supported the bailout. "Chrysler paid $2.4 billion in wages in Michigan in 1978, and paid an additional $2.4 billion to Michigan-based suppliers," he explained. "The initial shock to the Michigan economy of a Chrysler bankruptcy would throw 165,000 individuals out of work either from Chrysler or from suppliers. . . . It would cost the state more than $200 million in revenue annually. At the same time, the two-year period following a bankruptcy would see welfare costs in Michigan [rise] some $460 million with roughly half paid by the State and half by the Federal Government."[10]

Coleman A. Young, mayor of Detroit, explained that "Chrysler employs approximately 37,000 Detroiters, providing some 7 percent of the city's total employment." He estimated that "the loss of these jobs could effectively double Detroit's unemployment rate which, as of September 1979, stands at 10 percent." He stressed the obvious—namely, the "impact of a Chrysler shutdown on the City of Detroit's budget would be severe." Mayor Young added that Detroit was not alone and that a Chrysler bankruptcy would have a devastating impact in Wilmington, Newark, Syracuse, St. Louis, and Huntsville, Alabama, among other cities.[11]

Wendell Miller, Dodge dealer and first vice president of the National Automobile Dealers Association, straightforwardly warned Congress "the real story is that 4,700 [Chrysler dealers] in every congressional district in this country will be out of business in a very short period if Chrysler is not given the cash-flow assistance it needs to carry it over the one-year transition period between energy, economic, and management problems to a period of viability and profitability."[12]

Benjamin L. Hooks, executive director of the National Association for the Advancement of Colored People, emphasized that the "Chrysler Corporation has a higher employment rate of blacks than the average industrial corporation and a higher number of black employees in urban areas where the majority of blacks reside and the unemployment figures of blacks are excessively high." Therefore, on behalf of the NAACP, he called upon "the executive and legislative branches of government to provide a program of federal financial assistance to the Chrysler Corporation."[13]

Taking all this into account, Chrysler's charismatic chairman, Lee Iacocca, summarized what he and others saw as the choice confronting the country. "If government wants to do something about unemployment," he said; "if it wants to keep the nation's urban areas and cities alive; if it wants to prevent increased welfare dependency and government spending; if it wants to offset an $8 billion imbalance of automotive trade with Japan, let it approve Chrysler's legitimate and amply precedented request for temporary assistance."[14]

And so, after lengthy hearings and negotiations, Congress passed the Chrysler bailout bill by comfortable margins in both the House and the Senate. The overwhelming lobbying pressure from diverse interest groups—labor and management, state and municipalities, dealers, suppliers, and creditors, Democrats and Republicans—carried the day. The fact that leading economists of different ideological and philosophical persuasions—ranging from Milton Friedman and Alan Greenspan to James Tobin, John K. Galbraith, and Robert Eisner—vigorously opposed the rescue mission obviously made little difference.

But the Chrysler bailout is not unique. The story in the case of Lockheed and, more recently, the cases of Continental Illinois and the government bailout of big banks with sour Third-World loans is substantively similar. For example, in 1984, when Continental Illinois—the nation's eighth largest bank holding company—experienced a run of withdrawals by depositors and investors disillusioned with the bank's risky growth strategy, the firm was bailed out with more than $8 billion in credit transfusions and was accorded unlimited access to government monies. (This is in sharp contrast to the treatment received by scores of failing smaller banks, which are permitted to disappear ignominiously, and whose depositors are compensated only up to statutory limits.) An official of the avowedly "free market" Reagan administration justified this preferential treatment on the grounds that a large bank's failure would have vastly greater consequences than would the collapse of small banks. Indeed, the Comptroller of the Currency testified that the government realistically could not permit any of the nation's eleven largest banks to fail—prompting Congressman Stewart B. McKinney to remark: "We have a new kind of bank. It is called too big to fail, TBTF, and it is a wonderful bank."[15]

Import Protection

Government protection of large corporations from foreign competition constitutes a second genus of bailouts for bigness.

Foreign competition, of course, is a challenge to firms that must struggle for profits and growth in a competitive market. It forces them to innovate and to produce efficiently. It is a disruptive force that undermines monopoloid market control and cartel-like pricing schemes. It threatens corporate giants luxuriating in delinquent performance behind formidable barriers to new competition.

In recent years, government restraints on foreign competition have become an important means for bailing out noncompetitive domestic giants. The American steel industry affords an apt case in point.

For decades, the steel industry in the United States has been afflicted by the typical maladies of bigness and oligopoly. Innovation has been lethargic, hampered by the dry rot that tends to accompany corporate giantism and noncompetitive industry structure. Bigness has shackled the dominant integrated firms with bloated, uncompetitive costs. Price policy in the industry has been uniform and inflexible, except when prices rise; and though leadership has rotated among the big-steel oligopolists, the level of product prices has been anything but market-determined.[16]

When a rising tide of imports intruded on this well-ordered preserve, U.S. steel makers organized for a counteroffensive. As an alternative to meeting foreign competition in the market place, Big Steel sought a bailout through government protection.

After initial defeats before the U.S. Tariff Commission (now the U.S.

International Trade Commission), the domestic industry (backed by the State Department and Congressional pressure) succeeded in persuading Japan and the European Economic Community to enter into a Voluntary Restraint Agreement (VRA). The agreement, which went into effect in 1969, and was extended for three years in 1972, set quantitative limits on steel imports into the United States by these major steel exporters. Under VRA, the composite steel price index rose at an annual rate fourteen times greater than in the nine prior years of relatively free trade in steel. According to one reliable estimate, domestic steel prices would, in the absence of VRA, have been 13 to 15 percent lower. VRA's cost to American steel consumers between 1969 and 1974 has been estimated at a minimum of $1.97 billion and possibly as much as $6.5 billion. [17]

Starting in 1978 and ending in 1982, the domestic steel industry was protected under a new bailout formula—the Trigger Price Mechanism (TPM)—which put a thinly veiled price floor under steel imports. In the first year of its operation, the government raised trigger prices by 10.6 percent. Steel buyers, however, reported that the prices they had to pay were actually 15 percent higher because, as the *Wall Street Journal* noted, "last fall's widespread discounting has evaporated."[18] TPM's cost to American consumers, between 1978 and 1982, has been estimated at $4.35 billion.[19]

After less than two years, however, Big Steel grew disenchanted with TPM and, as the 1984 election drew nigh, steel producers and the steel workers lobbied both houses of Congress to obtain yet a different protectionist bailout. In the House, the Fair Trade in Steel Act of 1984 was introduced, which aimed to establish specific quotas for forty-four steel product groups, with the objective of restricting imports to fifteen percent of the U.S. market (with no discomfitting questions of whether foreign competition was "fair" or "unfair"). Then, in the midst of his re-election campaign, President Reagan directed his special trade representative to negotiate comprehensive "voluntary" restraint agreements with all countries exporting steel to the United States market. The resulting agreements, starting in 1984 and covering more than a dozen countries, aim at holding total steel imports to 18.5 percent of the U.S. market (down from about 25 percent in 1984). They cover imports of all finished steel products, and are scheduled to remain operative for five years. By 1985, these "voluntary" agreements covered 90 percent of all American steel imports. According to Federal Trade Commission estimates, this bailout alone will cost the American economy as much as $18 billion in higher prices and welfare losses. [20]

In this fashion, then, government restraints on foreign competition have bailed out Big Steel from the consequences of noncompetitive size, conduct, and performance. Nor is steel unique. Protectionism has played the same role in automobiles, where restraints on Japanese producers have bailed out the U.S. oligopoly, and where the decisive impact of bigness has unmistakably been in evidence. Thus, in arguing for limits on small, innovative and fuel-efficient Japanese cars in 1981, a Ford vice president instructed Congress: "Some 2,100 domestic dealerships have closed their doors; some 140 domestic supplier plants have closed as well, auto employment remains at unacceptable levels—185,000 auto production workers are on permanent layoff status; and import levels for 1980 were a record high—a 26.5 percent share versus 15 percent in the mid-1970s." But he went on to stress: "A lot more is at stake than the health of auto companies alone. Autos account for one out of twelve U.S. manufacturing jobs, a quarter of U.S. steel production and over half of U.S. rubber production. This industry is such a vital part of the U.S. economy," he said in clinching the bigness argument, "it should be clear that we can't have a healthy U.S. economy without a healthy U.S. auto industry."[21]

Regulatory Delays and Dispensations

A third advantage of bigness in obtaining bailouts arises in the field of regulation. Owing to its disproportionate size, the giant corporation can argue, first, that meeting government regulations, such as those involving air and water pollution, or product safety, would adversely affect the firm and, second, that these difficulties would therefore have grave effects on the economy at large. As a result, corporate giants can obtain bailouts in the form of regulatory delays and dispensations.

The automobile industry illustrates this aspect of bigness and the bailout factor. The Big Three auto companies—particularly GM and Ford—rank, of course, as the very largest industrial firms in the United States. Their size, they have discovered, provides a potent instrument for extracting regulatory bailouts.

In the field of automotive smog regulation, for example, a recent Brookings Institution treatise observes that the auto companies "can easily argue that their inability [or unwillingness] to meet a deadline will force them to abandon production altogether. Such a threat catches the attention of politicians; hence [smog control] delays were granted in 1973, 1974, and 1977. . . . Announcements by the major domestic manufacturers that they could not [or would not] comply have at times forced changes in the law, most recently in the 1977 Clean Air Act Amendments." In this way, U.S. auto giants "have found they can obtain [smog control] waivers, postponements, or changes."[22]

In the area of automotive fuel economy, GM and Ford provided a graphic demonstration of bigness in action in their successful machinations in 1985 to force government to relax its mileage standards. In a variant of the "national catastrophe" theme that produced a bailout for Chrysler five years earlier, GM and Ford threatened plant closings, shutdowns, and layoffs, and unemployment on an epic scale in a critical sector of the economy should their demands for special dispensation on the fuel economy front be refused. Unless the standards were lowered, a GM vice president warned Congress in May 1985, "full-line manufacturers [that is, GM and Ford] face the prospect of restricting product availability." This, she pointedly noted for the benefit of a Congress facing an upcoming election year, "translates into plant closings, job losses, and lower economic growth." Failure of government to accede to GM's demands, she threatened, "would lead to potentially serious economic upheavals, including massive layoffs." To drive home the point, GM submitted an extensive list of 88 plants—specifying the city and state location for each—which could be adversely affected should the government refuse to act. The consequences of resisting the Big Two's demands, a Ford vice president echoed, could well entail "the job dislocations of closing down plants."[23] Thus confronted, the government subsequently relaxed automotive fuel economy standards in accordance with the wishes of GM and Ford. A government spokesman explained that this was done out of fear of "adverse economic consequences, including job losses in the tens of thousands in the auto industry, if the standard was not lowered."[24]

Privileges in Procurement

A fourth bailout advantage of size arises from privileges in the procurement of goods and services accorded giantism by government.

The defense industry illustrates this dimension of bigness and the bailout factor. Major weapons producers, depicted in Table 1, dominate the field. The twenty-five largest defense contractors collectively account for slightly more than half of the more than $70 billion annually spent by government in recent years in the procurement of weaponry; the hundred largest together account for 70 percent.[25] The largest of these are weapons "conglomerates" dominating the supply of several major weapons systems. General Dynamics, for example, produces F-16 and F-111 fighter aircraft, nuclear submarines, Tomahawk and Stinger missile systems, and the M-1 tank. McDonnell Douglas produces F-18 and F-15 fighter aircraft, the AV-8 Harrier and KC-10 aircraft, and the Harpoon missile system.[26] Moreover, the biggest contractors also rank among the largest industrial firms in the nation, with plants, facilities, suppliers and subcontractors located across the country.

These giants enjoy a myriad of unique privileges in the procurement of weaponry:

First, defense expert James R. Kurth concludes that major contracts, rather than being awarded on the basis of competitive merit, are frequently designed to ensure a full menu of business for the largest defense producers. He characterizes this as the "follow-on imperative," by which giant contractors are treated as favored instruments. The dynamic of this process is reinforced, Kurth points out, "by the imperatives of the political system. Six of the production lines are located in states that loom large in the electoral college: California (Lockheed-Missiles and Space, Rockwell, and Douglas division of McDonnell-Douglas), Texas (General Dynamics and Vought), and New York (Grumman)."[27]

Table 1. ***The Ten Largest U.S. Defense Contractors, Fiscal Year 1985***

Company	*Prime Defense Contract Awards ($ billions)*	*Fortune 500 Rank*
McDonnell Douglas	8.8	29
General Dynamics	7.4	42
Rockwell	6.2	30
General Electric	5.8	10
Boeing	5.4	21
Lockheed	5.1	36
United Technologies	3.9	16
Hughes/GM	3.5	1
Ratheon	3.0	60
Grumman	2.7	131

SOURCES: *The Economist,* May 3, 1986, p. 25; *Fortune,* April 28, 1986

Second, colossal cost overruns by big contractors not only are tolerated, but have become an accepted feature of the weapons acquisition landscape. Lockheed's C-5A military transport jet provides a classic—but by no means unique—example.[28] When Lockheed was selected to produce the C-5A in 1965, the firm contracted to supply 120 planes for $3.4 billion. Within four months, the C-5A program began to exhibit signs of cost overruns; by midsummer of 1966, costs of key components and work in progress were running 27.30 percent over budget. In 1968, the program was running $2.2 *billion* over budget, and the projected costs per plane had escalated from $28 million to $60 million. Lockheed's chairman informed Defense Department officials that because of these overruns, the firm was unable to complete the C-5A as originally contracted. Because Defense considered the plane essential, it renegotiated Lockheed's contract, including full reimbursement of costs in order to minimize the firm's losses. The C-5A continued to exhibit a number of what the Comptroller General characterized as "significant deficiencies." Perhaps most disturbing among these was the rather alarming refusal of the plane's wings to remain attached to the fuselage. Thus, in 1975, Lockheed received a billion-dollar contract to strengthen the C-5A's wing structure—this *in addition* to other multi-billion-dollar cost overruns on the craft! "In a $1.6 billion program still going on at the Lockheed-Georgia plant, and paid for by the U.S.," the *Wall Street Journal* reported in 1983, "the company is rebuilding the entire section of the fuselage on each C-5A in the fleet and attaching stronger wings—merely to bring the planes up to original specifications."[29]

Third, weapons giants enjoy procurement privileges in the form of contrived tests, relaxed performance standards, and (in some cases) freedom from testing altogether when they supply deficient or defective weapons systems. For example, the staff of one Congressional committee assigned to investigate a key "test" of McDonnell Douglas' $40 billion F-18 fighter found:

> either the contractor or the Navy, aware of the aircraft's range deficiencies, attempted to structure [the test] to provide the aircraft with extra advantage. This conclusion is based on the following: (1) the mission was flown by a contractor's employee rather than a navy test pilot (as directed by the Secretary of the Navy); (2) the F/A-18 was "towed" into takeoff position for engine start on the runway to conserve fuel; (3) the interdiction profile was not conducted and attack was made on the target at "idle" power setting on the aircraft, which also conserves fuel; and (4) the approach into Patuxent River was made in the "minimum fuel condition."[30]

When the F-18 failed to meet contracted acceleration standards, the staff reported, the "Navy could choose one of two alternatives; (1) fix the airplane, or (2) 'fix' the specification. . . . The Navy's solution . . . was simply to adjust the contractual acceptance level to [that] where the aircraft performs best."[31] In some cases, testing is dispensed with altogether: when prototypes of Ford Motor Company's DIVAD air-defense gun appeared unlikely to meet performance requirments, tests of the vehicle's reliability, availability, maintainability, and durability were cancelled, and an additional $2 billion expended on the project.[32] In other cases, such as Lockheed's C-5A and McDonnell Douglas's F-15 fighter, weapons produced by giant contractors are accepted despite significant deficiencies and defects.[33]

Finally, giant defense contractors like General Dynamics, Lockheed, and Rockwell International benefit from the gifts of billions of dollars in plants and facilities initially constructed by the government at public expense. "The Defense Department estimates that it has turned over facilities worth more than $100 billion to private firms in this matter since World War II," analysts James Coates and Michael Kilian report. *"Nearly all of these free factories are in the hands of the top two dozen defense contractors."* These magnanimous gifts bail out defense giants from the threat of potential competition, Coates and Kilian conclude, by ensuring "that no aggressive new companies . . . will be able to wrest contracts away from the old establishment, because the newcomers can't afford the front-end costs of building the kind of factories that the defense industry establishment got for nothing."[34]

Government Promotionalism

Bailouts also occur in the form of promotionalism by the state. Indeed, as the U.S. nuclear electric power industry's experience demonstrates, government promotionalism may render bailouts endemic and virtually inevitable—at enormous cost to the public.[35]

At the close of World War II, and after having developed nuclear technology in utmost secrecy for its atom bomb program, government chose to make its technology available for commercial exploration as a potential method for economically generating electricity. But government did not restrict its role merely to transferring its technology to private interests for purposes of experimentation. Instead, it took the vastly more significant step of striving to *actively promote* nuclear electric power. Prodded in important part by such corporate giants as General Electric and Westinghouse, the government (through the Atomic Energy Acts of 1946 and, especially, 1954) committed itself to encouraging peaceful uses of atomic energy. This was done in the belief, expressed at the time by the Joint Congressional Committee on Atomic Energy, that "teamwork between government and industry . . . [was] the key to optimum progress, efficiency, and economy in this area of atomic endeavor."[36]

From the outset, government promoted nuclear electric power by subsidizing the research, development, production, and sales of civilian reactors. It also subsidized the production and enrichment of the uranium isotopes needed to fuel nuclear power reactors. The beneficiaries of the program eventually came to include some of the country's very largest corporations:

> Just four companies—Westinghouse, General Electric, Combustion Engineering, and the Babcock and Wilcox subsidiary of McDermott—have supplied virtually every nuclear reactor ever purchased by U.S. electrical utilities. The same four, plus Exxon, completely control the market for ready-to-use nuclear fuel. Three giant construction firms—Bechtel, Stone and Webster, and the United Engineers and Constructors division of Raytheon—have built more than 75 percent of America's nuclear power plants. Five companies, including oil companies Gulf, Kerr-McGee, and the Conoco subsidiary of du Pont, own almost half of the nation's uranium reserves. Nearly 70 percent of U.S. uranium-milling capacity belongs to Exxon, Atlantic Richfield, Kerr-McGee, the [former] Utah International subsidiary of General Electric, and United Nuclear.[37]

Behind these giants stand some of the nation's largest banks and financial houses—J.P. Morgan, Manufacturers Hanover, Citicorp, Chase Manhattan, Prudential Life—which have sizable investment stakes both in producers of nuclear power equipment and material, and in electric power generating utilities.[38]

Having thus chosen the path of promotion, and having thereby called into being vast vested interests, government subsequently became committed to acting in a variety of ways as a perpetual bailout agency once the industry began to confront economic failure:

First, the federal government has poured ever-larger sums into reactor research and development in striving toward the continually receding mirage of commercially viable nuclear power. At the state and local government level, compliant utility regulatory commissions tolerated (until only very recently) nuclear powerplant cost overruns of epic proportions.[39]

Second, government has bailed out the industry and its corporate giants by assuming ultimate responsibility for the disposal of nuclear wastes—which remain toxic for 250,000 years or longer, which are accumulating at the rate of thousands of tons per year, and for which no safe, permanent method of disposal has yet been demonstrated.[40]

Third, government traditionally has bailed out industry from unsafe reactor design and operation by minimizing, suppressing, distorting, or ignoring safety hazards and threats. In the case of reactors featuring containment systems similar to that of the ill-fated Chernobyl reactor, for example, an Atomic Energy Commission staff expert's recommendation in the early 1970s to ban the design as unsafe was overidden on the grounds that to do so "would make unlicensable the GE and Westinghouse ice condensor plants now in review" and "could well be the end of nuclear power."[41] Other examples abound.[42]

Fourth, when insurance companies refused to insure nuclear reactor manufacturers and utilities, government bailed out the industry (through the Price-Anderson Act) by assuming, and by limiting, liability for damages in the event of reactor accidents, malfunctions, or meltdowns. As a General Electric official candidly confessed to Congress in 1956, the industry could not be viable without this kind of protection.

Fifth, government has facilitated bailouts of the industry by permitting nuclear power advocates and former employees of the industry to hold important offices in government agencies charged with regulating the field. In recent years, these have included, among others, the Secretary of Energy, as well as the Chairman of the Nuclear Regulatory Commission.[43]

Finally, and perhaps most significantly, by devoting the lion's share of federal research and development funds to nuclear power, while according benign neglect to other alternative energies (for example, solar power, biomass), government has rendered the bailout factor in nuclear power an almost self-perpetuating phenomenon. It has artificially constricted the range of energy options available to the nation. It thus has strengthened the industry's leverage in demanding further bailouts. As articulated in 1979 by Robert Kirby, then chief executive officer of Westinghouse: "The public must be told that it will have to choose . . . between nuclear energy and some tough alternatives. Alternatives like inflation, higher unemployment, no economic growth, and national insecurity."[44]

Tax Favors and Loopholes

Taxation provides a further, fertile field of advantage for corporate giantism. Clearly, the tax statutes, and changes in those statutes, can serve as bailouts by enhancing giant corporations' cash flow and income, by reducing their tax payments or by providing them tax refunds and payments from government.

The advantage of bigness in influencing tax policy at the federal level has been succinctly described by Charls Walker, considered to be one of the most powerful tax lobbyists in Washington, and whose clientele features fourteen of the largest corporations in the country (including Alcoa, AT&T, DuPont, Ford Motor Co., IBM, Goodyear, and Procter & Gamble, among others).[45] Asked about his remarkable record of success in influencing federal tax legislation, Walker explains that members of Congress "will listen to me, let me in, when I am coming to talk about jobs, payrolls, economic growth in their districts. Because that is issue number one." In this, he suggests, large corporate size affords a decisive advantage: "If you [represent] twelve major multinational corporations and you look over the country, you have got operations, employment, in most of the states and many of the congressional districts . . . And so you have a coalition to begin with."[46]

In fact, Walker played a key role in engineering just such a federal tax bailout for bigness in the early 1980s, in the form of "Safe-Harbor" leasing provisions contained in the Economic Recovery Tax Act of 1981.[47] These provisions (which were subsequently abolished) enabled firms to transform their losses into revenues, and to slash their federal tax bill (and even obtain refunds from government), by allowing companies, in effect, to trade tax credits and depreciation deductions with one another. "Safe-Harbor" thus was tantamount to corporate welfare. It rewarded poor management. It provided (in the words of the *Wall Street Journal*) "a new lease for losers."[48] It was estimated to potentially cost the Treasury in excess of $40 billion in lost tax revenues.[49] And, most notably, its benefits flowed primarily to the nation's very largest corporations. For example, by procuring deductions, General Electric, with pre-tax earnings of $26.6 billion in 1981, was able to cut its tax bill to zero—and, indeed, to obtain tax *refunds* amounting to $90–100 million![50] Standard Oil of Indiana (Amoco) utilized the "Safe-Harbor" provisions to reduce its federal tax liability by $159 million.[51] Other large beneficiaries included IBM, Ford, Chrysler, B.F. Goodrich, CSX Corp., National Steel, and Pan American Airways.[52] Little companies, on the other hand, received no similar largesse. "Small businesses don't get anywhere near the tax benefits big companies receive from the Safe-Harbor leasing provisions," the *Wall Street Journal* reported in 1982.[53] Observed one accountant: "They left it wide open for the Occidental Petroleums and the IBMs, but they effectively knocked the little guy out of it."[54]

The capacity of the giant corporation to obtain bailouts in the form of tax favors and related dispensations is equally potent at the level of state and local government. As Carl Kaysen points out: "The large national-market firm has available to it the promise of locating in a particular area or expanding its operations there, the threat of moving or contracting its operations as potent bargaining points in its dealings with local and even state political leaders. The branch manager of the company whose plant is the largest employer in a town or the vice-president of the firm proposing to build a plant which will become the largest employer in a small state treats local government not as a citizen but as a quasi-sovereign power. Taxes, zoning laws, roads, and the like become matters of negotiation as much as matters of legislation. Even large industrial states and metropolitan cities may face similar problems."[55]

General Motors' machinations in recent years provide a case in point. For its Poletown plant in Detroit, GM obtained federal, state, and local government subsidies of approximately $220 million, which were used "to acquire the area, relocate the residents, demolish the structures, build roads and rail facilities, and for other site preparations. A twelve-year, 50 percent property-tax abatement brought a total subsidy package to General Motors of $350 million."[56]

In Missouri, GM successfully lobbied the city council of Kansas City to close a municipal airport and offer the land to GM. Thereafter, the tax breaks began to flow: GM applied for low-interest bonds; the state established an enterprise zone on the airport site, thereby exempting GM from sales, use, property, and *ad valorem* taxes; and the city agreed to issue $775 million in economic development revenue bonds for the project.

In Michigan, GM has demanded unprecedented reductions in its property taxes in localities across the state. It has demanded a 59 percent tax reduction in Genessee Township (where the firm already enjoys a twelve-year, 50 percent tax exemption on its property); a 42 percent reduction in Flint (where it already enjoys a 50 percent tax exemption on some of its assets); a 63 percent reduction in Delta Township (in addition to a 50 percent tax reduction which the firm already enjoys); a $7 million tax payment reduction in Pontiac; and a 70 percent reduction in Comstock Township. "In effect," the traditionally sympathetic Flint *Journal* observes, "GM is saying it can take its payroll elsewhere if local jurisdictions don't cry uncle."[57] Indeed, a high-ranking official of the firm has disclosed that GM intends to expand its efforts in obtaining tax privileges to states and localities across the country: "Now we are trying to go to the communities, one by one, and say to them, 'We don't intend to bring you to your knees, we can do a phase-in.'"[58]

More recently, GM capped its efforts with the lure of its "Saturn" small-car project: "Twenty-seven governors, as well as the economic development officials of nine other states, journeyed to Detroit to plead for the project. They carried promises of free land, cheap electricity, low-interest loans, tax holidays, taxpayer-financed job training."[59]

Protection From Prosecution

A sixth important bailout advantage of giantism is the capacity of bigness to immunize itself from government prosecution for illegal conduct. The benefits of bigness in this respect are substantial. They are illustrated by reviewing antitrust policy toward International Telephone and Telegraph in the early 1970s, and, more recently, by examining government prosecution of fraud and corruption in the procurement of defense weaponry.

ITT and Antitrust

ITT led the "go-go" conglomerate merger spree of the 1960s. Between 1961 and 1968, the firm acquired fifty-two domestic and fifty-five foreign corporations, with acquired domestic concerns alone representing combined assets of about $1.5 billion. During 1969, alone, ITT's board of directors approved twenty-two domestic and eleven foreign acquisitions. By purchasing large, profitable companies—including, among others, Rayonier Corp. (at the time, the world's leading producer of cellulose); Continental Baking (the world's largest baking and cake company); Avis (the world's second largest rental car system); Sheraton Hotels (at the time, the world's largest hotel and motel system); Levitt & Sons (a leading builder of single-family homes); Grinnell (the nation's largest producer of automatic fire protection systems); Canteen Corp. (operating one of the largest vending machine systems); and Hartford Fire and Insurance Co. (one of the nation's largest property and casualty insurance writers)—ITT rapidly grew in size to become the fifteenth largest of all U.S. industrial concerns by 1968.[60]

The accoutrements of ITT's giantism grew legion. The company could boast of "constantly working around the clock—in sixty-seven nations on six continents, in activities extending from the Arctic to the Antarctic and quite literally from the bottom of the sea to the moon."[61] The firm's officers and directors came to include a former secretary general of the United Nations, a former premier of Belgium, two members of the British House of Lords, a member of the French National Assembly, a former president of the World Bank, a former director of the U.S. Central Intelligence Agency, three rear admirals, two brigadier generals, and twenty-two colonels. The firm was able in one four-day period to place its corporate aircraft at the disposal of two members of President Nixon's cabinet, three senators, five representatives, and two presidential candidates.[62]

Hence, when the government attempted to challenge three large ITT acquisitions in 1969, the company mounted a vast lobbying effort reaching to the very highest levels of government. The company's complaints were personally received by the Secretary of the Treasury, the Secretary of Commerce, the president of the Council of Economic Advisors, the president of the Federal Reserve System, and the Attorney General.[63] The company argued that prosecution of a firm of the size and stature of ITT would inflict serious harm, not just on ITT, but on the nation's economy at large. In a document furnished to the White House, the firm warned that "ITT is a truly multinational corporation. It operates in 127 different countries and has facilities in seventy-seven of these countries. It employs more than 200,000 people overseas.... ITT's extensive foreign operations make it the third largest positive contributor to the U.S. balance of payments, an area of crucial national importance.... ITT has nearly a quarter of a million shareholders of record. In addition, many times that number of persons are indirectly affected by the value of ITT's stock by reason of their holdings of the shares of institutions which have an investment position in ITT, or relationship to pension funds holding ITT stock, etc. All of these people, and ITT itself, would suffer a major financial hardship," the company threatened, if the government continued to pursue its antitrust prosecution of ITT.[64] Felix G. Rohatyn, a partner in the prestigious Lazard Freres & Company investment banking firm and an ITT director, warned the Justice Department that continued prosecution "could raise fundamental issues of national policy . . . including possible U.S. balance of payments effects," and, further, that it "might unsettle our securities markets," with "possible impact on some financial organizations."[65]

These importunings—pressed by an industrial colossus, and capped by a $400,000 campaign contribution to the Republican National Convention—were not without effect. In the end, the government dropped its antitrust suit against ITT. The reason, according to Richard W. McLaren, chief of the Antitrust Division of the Justice Department at the time, "was the devastating financial consequences to the more than a quarter of a million shareholders, and to the ripple effect that might take place in the stock market and in the economy."[66] So serious were the consequences that, as the Watergate tapes subsequently showed, ITT succeeded in garnering the support of the President of the United States. A taped conversation between President Nixon and Deputy Attorney General Richard G. Kleindienst on April 19, 1971 records the following colloquy:

> President Nixon: I want something clearly understood, and, if it is not understood McLaren's ass is to be out within one hour. The IT&T thing—stay the hell out of it. Is that clear? That's an order.
> Mr. Kleindienst: Well, you mean the order is to—
> President Nixon: The order is to leave the God damned thing alone.
>
> * * * * *
>
> Mr. Kleindienst: Your order is not to file a brief?
> President Nixon: Your—my order is to drop the God damned thing. Is that clear?

Mr. Kleindienst: [Laughs] Yeah. I understand that.[67]

It was an impressive demonstration of the bailout advantages inherent in what Anthony Sampson describes as "the relentless machinery of lobbying that a giant corporation can bring to bear on government."[68]

Defense Procurement

The ability of bigness to obtain bailouts from government prosecution is also evident in the field of weapons procurement. Indeed, for bigness in defense, crime, in the form of fraud and corruption, apparently pays—and rather handsomely.

"For 1984 the Pentagon disbarred or suspended 402 contractors, a record number," according to a recent analysis. But *none of those cases involved large contractors.* During the Reagan Administration, three of the top 20 contractors, the Boeing Company, the McDonnell Douglas Corporation, and the Sperry Corporation, have entered pleas of guilty to criminal violations that could, under Pentagon regulations, lead to their disbarment or suspension. *But none were suspended.*[69]

For example, a small defense contractor recently was disbarred from all government business for a period of three years for giving a federal employee a $200 TV set and a subscription to *Playboy.*[70] For a defense giant like General Dynamics, however, the consequences of criminality are vastly different. In a front page exposé (carrying the subtitle, "Beating the Rap"), the *Wall Street Journal* reported in April 1986:

> Along with two indictments for fraud on Pentagon contracts, General Dynamics won notoriety for billing the government for dog-kennel fees incurred by one executive and country-club dues paid by another. It even got the Pentagon to bail out a corporate barbershop that had suffered financial losses.
>
> Navy Secretary John Lehman characterized the company's corporate philosophy as "catch us if you can." The Pentagon's chief spokesman called the company's actions "nauseating."[71]

The consequences? A fleeting "suspension" (during which bidding periods for major billion-dollar contracts were extended in order to allow General Dynamics to participate), followed by defense awards to the firm of "$1 billion of arms contracts, six times the $166.8 million contracts the company had won in August 1984. Another $1.4 billion came in September." As a result, "General Dynamics emerged as the year's most successful contractor."[72]

Once again, the advantage of bigness is decisive. As articulated by one military officer: "It would be swell if I could say 'you're a naughty boy and I'm going to cast you into oblivion.' But if I do, where am I going to buy the submarines and tanks and planes that I need?"[73]

Conclusion

In this article we have examined corporate size and the bailout factor. We have seen that while the efficiency and technological advantages of corporate size are disputed, the capacity of the giant firm to obtain bailouts from inefficiency, incompetence, and the discipline of the competitive market is clear and unequivocal—and substantial. We have shown that, because the giant corporation is perceived as being too big to be allowed to fail, bigness benefits from bailouts in a variety of forms: large firms are bailed out by direct government cash infusions or credit and loan guarantees. They are bailed out by restraints on foreign competition. They can demand and obtain bailouts in the form of regulatory delays and dispensations. They are bailed out through privileges in procurement. They are bailed out via government promotion, as well as through tax favors. And, as a review of antitrust and defense procurement shows, giant corporations enjoy bailouts in the form of protection from prosecution.

The most important implications of our analysis are five-fold:

First, the bailout factor casts the political economy of bigness and power in bold relief. It graphically demonstrates that "mere" size does, in fact, matter. Bigness forces society to confront an intractable dilemma: (a) to rescue corporate giants from the consequences of self-inflicted injuries, thereby subverting the fundamental discipline of a competitive market, free enterprise economy, or (b) to allow ailing giants to fail, thereby inflicting possibly catastrophic consequences upon society while, at the same time, rendering government less accountable to the concerns and fortunes of broad segments of the citizenry. In other words, corporate giantism pits the principles of a competitive market economy against those of a democratic political system.[74]

Second, the political economy of bigness thus revolutionizes an ostensibly free enterprise society in a subtle but profoundly radical way. It privatizes profit while socializing losses—provided the latter are large enough. It thereby erodes the social role (and justification) of profit as an inducement for sound decision-making in the public interest. It is thus tantamount to socialism for the big and powerful. Moreover, it is ironic as "one's mind dwells . . . on the shock troops of the revolution. Marx, in his innocent, and now obsolete, way thought it would be the workers who would force the pace of socialism. He must, from wherever he now resides, have little hope for help from Lane Kirkland or American working-class Marxists. And he must be looking with surprise at the way, in our time, it is the bankers and the big industrialists who lead the march, carry the flag."[75]

Third, bailouts of bigness pose the critical but generally neglected economic question of how a society resolves (in Walter Lippman's terms) the problem of liquidating accumulated commercial and industrial errors.[76] It is inevitable in a free enterprise economy that mistakes will be made—that some firms will miscalculate costs or product demands, that some will find themselves in uneconomic locations or product fields due to shifting economic circumstances, that efforts aimed at innovation in product and manufacturing technique will fail, that some will be unable to obtain loanable funds when they need them, and that they will suffer other unforeseen circumstances and events. So long as firms are *relatively* small in size, these private failures are prevented from becoming social disasters, and society is able to absorb mistakes.[77] But once corporations are permitted to attain Brobdignagian proportions, this is no longer the case. Then society confronts what Lippman saw as "the problems and the tragedies of semi-obsolete corporate leviathans that are unable to live and unable to die."[78] Then disproportionate size converts private mistakes into social catastrophes, the community's capacity to absorb private error is corroded, and society is rendered less stable and more vulnerable as a result.[79]

Fourth, the reality of bigness and the bailout factor obviously repudiates the currently fashionable New Economic Darwinism, and its central precepts that only efficient firms survive, that bigness is thus *ipso facto* proof of social fitness and desirability, and, therefore, that laissez faire is the optimal public policy toward corporate size and mega-mergers.[80] As we have seen, the pivotal fact of economic life in a democratic society—a fact conveniently ignored by the New Darwinists—is that giant firms are protected from failure, not by being better, but by being bigger.

Finally, if this be so, then antitrust policy is infused with heightened importance, especially in its structural orientation toward industrial organization, corporate size, and mergers and acquisitions. Structural antitrust is seen to be not just a means for maintaining competitive industry organization, or for arresting potentially anticompetitive mergers. Beyond these, it is a key *preventative* instrument for guarding society's capacity to withstand the private mistakes integral to a free enterprise economy, and thereby to vouchsafe society from bigness and the bailout dilemma. Seen in this light, recent efforts by the Reagan Administration and others to relax the nation's antitrust strictures toward mega-mergers, and to encourage corporate bigness as a matter of national policy, seem eminently unwise.

Notes

1. John Kenneth Galbraith, "Taking the Sting Out of Capitalism," *New York Times,* 26 May 1985, sec. 3, p. 1.
2. For a more detailed analysis, together with complete documentation, see Walter Adams and James W. Brock, *The Bigness Complex* (New York: Pantheon Books, 1986), Chap. 22.
3. Adams and Brock, *The Bigness Complex,* p. 298.
4. U.S. Congress, Senate, Committee on Banking, Housing and Urban Affairs, *Chrysler Corporation Loan Guarantee Act, Hearings,* part 1, 96th Cong., 1st sess., 1979, p. 179.
5. Ibid.
6. Ibid., p. 180.
7. Ibid.
8. Ibid, pp. 180–81.
9. Douglas Fraser, *Saturday Review,* 19 January 1980, p. 30.
10. William Milliken, U.S. Congress, Senate, Committee on Banking, Housing and Urban Affairs, *Chrysler Corporation Loan Guarantee Act, Hearings,* part 2, 96th Cong., 1st sess., 1979, p. 818.
11. Coleman Young, ibid., pp. 1041–42.
12. U.S. Congress, House of Representatives, Subcommittee on Economic Stabilization. The *Chrysler Corporation Financial Situation,* Hearings, part 1A, 96th Cong., 1st sess., 1979, p. 586.
13. Benjamin Hooks, U.S. Congress, Senate, Committee on Banking, Housing and Urban Affairs, *Chrysler Corporation Loan Guarantee Act, Hearings,* part 2, 96th Cong., 1st sess., 1979, p. 948.
14. Lee Iacocca, *Wall Street Journal,* 3 December 1979, p. 24.
15. U.S. Congress, House of Representatives, Subcommittee on Financial Institutions Supervision, Regulation and Insurance, *Inquiry into Continental Illinois National Bank, Hearings,* 98th Cong., 2nd sess., 1984, pp. 299–300, 458; *Wall Street Journal,* 26 July 1984, p. 2.
16. See Walter Adams and Hans Mueller, "The Steel Industry," in *The Structure of American Industry,* ed. Walter Adams, 7th ed. (New York: Macmillan, 1986), pp. 74–125; Donald F. Barnett and Louis Schorsch, *Steel: Upheaval in a Basic Industry* (Cambridge, Mass.: Ballinger, 1983); Zoltan J. Achs, *The Changing Structure of the U.S. Economy: Lessons from the Steel Industry* (New York: Praeger, 1984).
17. Adams and Mueller, "The Steel Industry," p. 94, and Gary C. Hufbauer and Howard F. Rosen, *Trade Policy for Troubled Industries* (Washington: Institute for International Economics, 1986), Table 2.2.
18. *Wall Street Journal,* 26 September 1978, p. 1.
19. Adams and Mueller, "The Steel Industry," p. 117, and Hufbauer and Rosen, *Trade Policy for Troubled Industries,* Table 2.2.
20. See *Wall Street Journal,* 7 January 1985, p. 19; Federal Trade Commission, *Aggregate Costs to the United States of Tariffs and Quotas on Imports* (Washington, D.C.: Government Printing Office), p. iv–20.
21. U.S. Congress, Senate, Subcommittee on International Trade, *Issues Relating to the Domestic Auto Industry, Hearings,* part 1, 97th Cong., 1st sess., 1981, p. 133. As in steel, the costs of the protectionist bailout of bigness in autos have not been insignificant, with U.S. new-car prices artificially inflated by possibly as much as $2,500 per car, at an aggregate cumulative

cost to American consumers of perhaps as much as $15.7 billion. See U.S. International Trade Commission, *A Review of Recent Developments in the U.S. Automobile Industry, Including an Assessment of the Japanese Voluntary Restraint Agreements* (Washington, D.C.: Government Printing Office, February 1985); *Wall Street Journal,* 3 December 1984, p. 33 and 14 February 1983, p. 3; *New York Times,* 8 April 1984, sec. 3, p. 1.

22. Robert W. Crandall, Howard K. Gruenspecht, Theodore E. Keeler, and Lester B. Lave, *Regulating the Automobile* (Washington, D.C.: Brookings Institution, 1986), pp. 29, 90.
23. U.S. Congress, Senate, Subcommittee on Energy Regulation and Conservation, *Automobile Fuel Economy Standards, Hearings,* 99th Cong., 1st sess., 1985, pp. 57, 71, 284–88; U.S. Congress, Senate, Subcommittee on Commerce, Science, and Transportation, *Rollback of CAFE Standards and Methanol Vehicle Incentives Act of 1985, Hearings,* 99th Cong., 1st sess., 1985, p. 76.
24. *New York Times,* 2 October 1985, p. 11. It merits mention that in contrast to the dire predictions and blatant threats propounded by GM before Congress on this issue, the firm informed its stockholders that "the ultimate liability under these regulations is *not expected to have a material adverse effect on the Corporation's consolidated financial position."* General Motors Corporation, *Annual Report,* 1985, p. 38 (emphasis added).
25. Department of Defense, *100 Companies Receiving the Largest Dollar Volume of Prime Contract Awards; Fiscal Year 1983,* (Washington, D.C.: Government Printing Office, 1983), p. 2.
26. For a detailed compilation of weapons systems produced by major defense contractors, see Adams and Brock, *The Bigness Complex,* Chap. 24.
27. U.S. Congress, Joint Committee on Defense Production, *Defense Industrial Base: DoD Procurement Practices, Hearings,* part 4, 95th Cong., 1st sess., 1977, pp. 76–78.
28. For a more detailed analysis of defense cost overruns, see Adams and Brock, *The Bigness Complex,* and sources cited therein.
29. *Wall Street Journal,* 12 May 1983, p. 20.
30. U.S. Congress, House of Representatives, Committee on Appropriations, *Department of Defense Appropriations for 1983, Hearings,* part 8, 97th Cong., 2nd sess., 1982, pp. 65–66.
31. Ibid., pp. 66–67.
32. U.S. Congress, Senate, Committee on Governmental Affairs, *Management of the Department of Defense, Hearing,* part 9, 98th Cong., 2nd sess., 1985, pp. 48–49; *New York Times,* 28 August 1985, p. 1.
33. See Adams and Brock, *The Bigness Complex* and the sources cited therein.
34. James Coates and Michael Kilian, *Heavy Losses* (New York: Viking, 1985), p. 242 (emphasis added).
35. Except where otherwise indicated, this section is drawn from Adams and Brock, *The Bigness Complex,* Chap. 21.
36. U.S. Congress, Joint Committee on Atomic Energy, Amending the Atomic Energy Act of 1946, *Report,* 83rd Cong., 2nd sess., 1954, p. 9.
37. Mark Hertsgaard, *Nuclear Inc.* (New York: Pantheon Books, 1983), p. 104.
38. Ibid., pp. 127–35, Appendix 4.
39. Observes *Dun's Business Month:* "Through year after year of cost overruns on nuclear power, America's electric utilities have added, by some estimates, an extra $100 billion in interest and other costs to the nation's elec-

tric power bill and placed ratepayers, shareholders, creditors and taxpayers between the proverbial rock and a hard place. . . . Worse still, a minority of users must help finance multibillion-dollar shells of nuclear reactors unlikely—at least for the next five to ten years—to generate enough power to run a toaster, let alone replace or supplement fossil fuel-based plants." *Dun's Business Month,* June 1984, p. 70.

40. Generally, see Donald L. Barlett and James B. Steel, *Forevermore: Nuclear Waste in America* (New York: W.W. Norton & Co., 1985).
41. Memorandum contained in press release dated 19 May 1986 from Public Citizen.
42. See, for example, Daniel Ford, *The Cult of the Atom* (New York: Simon and Schuster, 1982).
43. Hertsgaard, *Nuclear, Inc.,* pp. 212–20, 232–33.
44. Ibid., p. 6.
45. For a biographical sketch, see Ralph Nader and William Taylor, *The Big Boys: Power & Position in American Business* (New York: Pantheon Books, 1986), pp. 244–91.
46. Ibid., p. 269.
47. Walker's role is detailed in Thomas B. Edsall, "Three Who Sowed Tax Provision Reap Its Bonanza Benefit." *Washington Post,* 5 October 1981, pp. 1 and 20.
48. *Wall Street Journal,* 19 February 1982, p. 28.
49. U.S. Congress, Joint Committee on Taxation, *Analysis of Safe-Harbor Leasing, Staff Report,* 97th Cong., 2nd sess., 1982, p. 35.
50. U.S. Congress, Senate, Committee on Finance, *Administration's Fiscal Year 1983 Budget Proposal, Hearings,* part 4, 97th Cong., 2nd sess., 1982, p. 344.
51. Ibid.
52. U.S. Congress, House of Representatives, Subcommittee on Oversight of the Committee on Ways and Means, *Safe Harbor Leasing Provisions of the Economic Recovery Tax Act of 1981, Hearing,* 97th Cong., 1st sess., 1982, pp. 64–69.
53. *Wall Street Journal,* 8 February 1982, p. 29.
54. Ibid.
55. Carl Kaysen, "The Corporation: How Much Power? What Scope?" in *The Corporation in Modern Society,* ed. Edward S. Mason (New York: Atheneum, 1966), p. 100.
56. Nader and Taylor, *The Big Boys,* p. 122.
57. Ibid., p. 131.
58. Ibid., p. 132.
59. Ibid., pp. 114–17, 122, 129–30, 132; *Alexandria Gazette,* 13 May 1985.
60. See Willard F. Mueller, "Conglomerates: A Nonindustry," in *The Structure of American Industry,* ed. Walter Adams, 6th ed. (New York: Macmillan, 1982), pp. 432–33; and U.S. Congress, Senate, Subcommittee on Antitrust and Monopoly, *Economic Concentration, Hearings,* part 8A, 91st Cong., 1st sess., 1969, p. 260, 523–43.
61. International Telephone and Telegraph, *Annual Report,* 1968, p. 7.
62. Walter Adams, "Corporate Power and Economic Apologetics," in *Industrial Concentration: The New Learning,* ed. Harvey J. Goldschmid, H. Michael Mann, and J. Fred Weston, (Boston: Little, Brown, 1974), pp.

367–78; Anthony Sampson, *The Sovereign State of ITT* (New York: Stein & Day, 1973), pp. 205, 234.

63. U.S. Congress, Senate, Committee on the Judiciary, *Richard G. Kleindienst—Resumed, Hearings,* part 2, 92nd Cong., 2nd sess., 1972, p. 651.
64. Ibid., part 3, pp. 1409–11.
65. Ibid., part 2, p. 114.
66. Ibid., p. 123. For an account of the unsavory circumstances surrounding the ITT settlement, see Willard F. Mueller, "The ITT Settlement: A Deal with Justice," *Industrial Organization Review* 1 (1973): 67–86.
67. Quoted in Willard F. Mueller, "The Anti-Antitrust Movement," in *Industrial Organization, Antitrust, and Public Policy,* ed. John V. Craven (Boston: Kluwer-Nijhoff Publishing, 1983), pp. 23–24.
68. Sampson, *The Sovereign State of ITT,* p. 243. For a related and more recent example, see the success of large petroleum companies in quashing legislative efforts to curb mega-mergers in oil, as detailed in Kenneth M. Davidson, *Mega-Mergers* (Cambridge, Mass.: Ballinger, 1985), pp. 355–57.
69. *New York Times,* 2 May 1985, p. 36 (emphasis added).
70. *The Nation,* 15 December 1984, p. 638.
71. *Wall Street Journal,* 29 April 1986, p. 1.
72. Ibid., p. 20.
73. Quoted in *New York Times,* 15 June 1986, sec. 3, p. 4.
74. Chrysler chairman Lee Iacocca unwittingly captures this point in praising the Chrysler bailout as an example of "democracy in action." Lee Iacocca, *Iacocca* (New York: Bantam Books, 1984), p. 221.
75. Galbraith, "Taking the Sting Out of Capitalism," p. 27.
76. Walter Lippman, *The Method of Freedom* (New York: Macmillan, 1934), p. 18.
77. The key, it is important to emphasize, is *relative* firm size. As George Stigler pointed out long ago, small relative size does not imply the atomization of corporate structures: "One can be opposed to economic and in favor of technological bigness in most basic industries without inconsistency, because our economy is so large." U.S. Congress, House of Representatives, Subcommittee on the Study of Monopoly Power, *Study of Monopoly Power, Hearings,* part 4A, 81st Cong., 2nd sess., 1950, p. 996.
78. Walter Lippman, *The Good Society* (Boston: Little, Brown, 1937), p. 224.
79. It is significant to note in this regard that students of comparative economic systems report vulnerability to large-scale mistakes to be a seemingly congenital malady afflicting the centrally-planned state. Observes R.W. Davies: "When the central planners make a *wrong* technological choice, the cost (because the policy is carried out on a national scale) is proportionately heavy." Quoted in George Dalton, *Economic Systems and Society* (New York: Penguin Books, 1974), p. 134.
80. See, for example, Robert H. Bork, *The Antitrust Paradox* (New York: Basic Books, 1978), esp. p. 118.